EUROPEAN COMMUNITY LAW

AUSTRALIA
LBC Information Services
Sydney

CANADA and USA
Carswell
Toronto, Ontario

NEW ZEALAND
Brooker's
Auckland

SINGAPORE and MALAYSIA
Sweet & Maxwell Asia
Singapore and Kuala Lumpur

For John

PREFACE

European Community law continues to be a changing and dynamic area of law. Since the publication of the last edition of this book the pace of change has been as fast as ever. A great many changes have been brought about by the ratification of the Treaty of Nice and the need for the near future enlargement of the Union to 25 states. The Court of Justice and the Court of First Instance continue to play their part in this dynamic process, with an increasing number of judgments. Nevertheless, the principal aim of this edition has not changed. The aim is still to provide an introduction to the mass of legislation and case law that is the law of the European Union. To attempt to cover every area of European law would be an impossible task. With that in mind the book is selective in its approach to subject area. The book is an attempt to cover the institutional and substantive areas that make up the majority of undergraduate courses in European law. The book should also prove useful to students on professional courses coming to European Union law for the first time, and to business law students and CPE students. I hope too, that the more general reader will find the material stimulating.

This edition has kept the convention, adopted in the last edition, of citing both "old" and "new" Treaty numbers. It has been my experience that students do find some initial confusion in Treaty numbering, particularly when reading journal articles published before the changes brought about by the Treaty of Amsterdam. This new edition also anticipates some of the institutional changes to be brought into effect in May 2004, with the accession of new Member States.

My thanks are due to my students who continue to provide me with stimulating feedback on many of the issues raised in this book. I would like to thank all at Sweet & Maxwell for their encouragement. My thanks are due to my family for their continued support.

I have corrected as many errors as have been pointed out to me. I have attempted to state the law as at July 1, 2003.

James Hanlon,
Principal Lecturer in Law,
Sheffield Hallam University,
August 2003.

CONTENTS

3. The Institutions

4. The Supremacy of Community Law

5. General Principles of Community Law

6. Forms of Law

7. Administrative Control of Member States

TABLE OF CASES

CASES BEFORE THE ECJ AND CFI–NUMERICAL ORDER

Table of Cases

xxi

Table of Cases

Table of Cases xxiii

Table of Cases

xxv

CASES BEFORE THE ECJ AND CFI – ALPHABETICAL ORDER

TABLE OF CASES BEFORE NATIONAL COURTS

EUROPEAN LEGISLATION

TREATIES

REGULATIONS

DIRECTIVES

TABLE OF EQUIVALENCES

TREATY OF AMSTERDAM AMENDING THE TREATY ON EUROPEAN UNION, THE TREATIES ESTABLISHING THE EUROPEAN COMMUNITIES AND CERTAIN RELATED ACTS

ANNEXES

Tables of equivalences referred to in Article 12 of the Treaty of Amsterdam

A. Treaty on European Union

Previous numbering	New numbering
Title I Article D Article F	Title I Article 4 Article 6
Title II Article G	Title II Article 8
Title V Article J.3	Title V Article 13
Title VI Article K.7	Title VI Article 35

B. Treaty establishing the European Community

Previous numbering	New numbering
Part One	Part
Article 1	Article 1
Article 2	Article 2
Article 3	Article 3
Article 3b	Article 5
Article 4	Article 7
Article 5	Article 10
Article 6	Article 12
Article 7 (repealed)	—
Part Two	Part Two
Article 8	Article 17
Article 8b	Article 19
Part Three	Part Three
Title I	Title I
Article 9	Article 23
Chapter I	Chapter 1
Section 1 (deleted)	—
Article 12	Article 25
Article 15 (repealed)	—
Article 16 (repealed)	—
Article 18 (repealed)	—
Article 28	Article 26
Article 29	Article 27
Chapter 2	Chapter 2
Article 30	Article 28
Article 31 (repealed)	—
Article 32 (repealed)	—
Article 33 (repealed)	—
Article 34	Article 29
Article 36	Article 30
Title III	Title II
Chapter 1	Chapter 1
Article 48	Article 39
Article 49	Article 40
Article 50	Article 41
Article 51	Article 42

Chapter 2	Chapter 2
Article 52	Article 43
Article 53 (repealed)	—
Article 54	Article 44
Article 55	Article 45
Article 56	Article 46
Article 57	Article 47
Article 58	Article 48
Chapter 3	Chapter 3
Article 59	Article 49
Article 60	Article 50
Article 66	Article 55
Chapter 4	Chapter 4
Article 70 (repealed)	—
Title IV	Title V
Article 75	Article 71
Title V	Title VI
Chapter 1	Chapter 1
Section 1	Section 1
Article 85	Article 81
Article 86	Article 82
Article 89	Article 85
Article 90	Article 86
Section 3	Section 2
Article 92	Article 87
Article 93	Article 88
Article 94	Article 89
Chapter 2	Chapter 2
Article 95	Article 90
Chapter 3	Chapter 3
Article 100	Article 94
Article 100a	Article 95
Title VI	Title VII
Chapter 1	Chapter 1
Article 103	Article 99

Article 148	Article 205
Article 151	Article 207
Section 3	Section 3
Article 155	Article 211
Article 157	Article 213
Article 158	Article 214
Section 4	Section 4
Article 164	Article 220
Article 166	Article 222
Article 167	Article 223
Article 168a	Article 225
Article 169	Article 226
Article 170	Article 227
Article 171	Article 228
Article 173	Article 230
Article 174	Article 231
Article 175	Article 232
Article 176	Article 233
Article 177	Article 234
Article 182	Article 239
Article 184	Article 241
Article 186	Article 243
Article 188	Article 245
Section 5	Section 5
Article 188a	Article 246
Article 188b	Article 247
Article 188c	Article 248
Chapter 2	Chapter 2
Article 189	Article 249
Article 189a	Article 250
Article 189b	Article 251
Article 189c	Article 252
Article 190	Article 253
Article 191	Article 254
Chapter 3	Chapter 3
Article 193	Article 257

Chapter 4	Chapter 4
Article 198a	Article 263
Article 198b	Article 264
Article 198c	Article 265
Part Six	Part Six
Article 215	Article 288
Article 220	Article 293
Article 221	Article 294
Article 224	Article 297
Article 225	Article 298
Article 235	Article 308

1. INTRODUCTION

HISTORICAL BACKGROUND OF THE COMMUNITY

At the end of the Second World War mainland Europe was devastated. Many millions of lives had been lost. The misery of the six war years had induced in the people of Europe the idea that this carnage must never be allowed to happen again. The peoples of Europe were receptive to the idea that the nation-state was not the best structure for the future and that the path of integration was the path to follow.

Immediately after the war the continent of Europe was divided East-West, into two power blocs. The eastern half was given up to Soviet influence and domination. This domination was to last until the end of the 1980s. So any plans for European integration could only cover the western half of Europe. The financial support offered by the United States, under the Marshall Plan, was taken up only by western Europe. Perhaps understandably, it was refused by the states of eastern Europe, as they shared the Soviet suspicion of American dominance. Thus was born in those early days in the aftermath of the war, the east-west divide. This became known as the "cold war" and was to continue up until the late 1980s.

The United Kingdom did not share this feeling of integration with western Europe. It felt it could remain aloof. After all it had been victorious: even though it had suffered damage its territory had not been invaded and it was still a major world power. It had too, an historical legacy which involved different social and economic ties, especially the Empire and the Commonwealth. The view of the United Kingdom was that any international co-operation, however desirable should be undertaken by fully independent sovereign states. This was the initial approach of the western countries. In response to the Marshall Plan a body was set up called the Organisation for European Economic Cooperation (OEEC). (This became known as the Organisation for Economic Cooperation and Development (OECD) in 1961.) The United Kingdom played a full part in this body, as it did in the setting up of the Council of Europe in 1949. The Council of Europe, which is still in existence today, brought together governments in a forum for cooperation and negotiation. Its most valuable task was the promulgation of the European Convention on Human Rights (ECHR). The United Kingdom was one of the first states to ratify the Convention, although it never acted to incorporate it into UK law, thus allowing the national courts to ignore it. The United Kingdom also recognised the compulsory jurisdiction of the Court of Human Rights, the court established to rule on the Convention. Although, under domestic law the UK courts are not obliged to recognise the ECHR, they may have to apply the Convention as part of the general principles of Community law when they are applying that law (see Chapter 4).

After the general election on May 1997, the UK Government indicated that intended to incorporate the ECHR into UK law. The result was the Human Rights Act 1998. The Act came into force on October 1, 2000.

The Council of Europe acts by unanimity among nation states; or it does not act at all. This characteristic of intergovernmental cooperation fell short of the ambitions of the integrationists. They believed that their traditional methods were inadequate to solve the structural problems of the shattered economics of Europe. Nor did they believe that intergovernmental agreements would provide lasting political cohesion. In particular, it was seen that the division of Germany meant that the new Federal Republic of Germany had to be placed firmly in the political structure of western Europe.

The first move towards this end, and the first of the integrative measures was taken by two men, Robert Schuman, the French Foreign Minister, and Jean Monnet, an administrator in the French civil service. In May 1950 in what has become known as the "Schuman Declaration", the French Foreign Minister said:

"the French government proposes to take action immediately on one limited but decisive point. It proposes to place Franco-German production of coal and steel as a whole under a common higher authority within the framework of an organisation open to the participation of the other countries of Europe."

In 1951, six states, Germany, France, Italy, the Netherlands, Belgium and Luxembourg signed the Treaty of Paris. This established the European Coal and Steel Community (the ECSC Treaty). The United Kingdom had been invited to take part but had declined to do so, preferring to remain aloof. It did however send along officials as observers.

The essential feature of the ECSC Treaty was the creation of a new entity (the "Community") with international legal status and separate and autonomous institutions. This also made the Treaty very different from a traditional intergovernmental organisation. The vital step towards integration was the transfer of legislative and administrative powers to the institutions of the Treaty. From now on, the six signatories to the Treaty pooled their sovereignty for defined, although limited, purposes. All aspects of the production and distribution of coal and steel were brought under the control of a High Authority, which had the power to make legally binding "decisions" and "recommendations". The other institutions were the Assembly, a body representing the people of Europe, brought together in a "parliament", with some supervisory powers; a Council of Ministers representing the Member States, with some legislative and some consultative powers; and the Court of Justice whose function was to "ensure that in the interpretation and application of this Treaty . . . the law is observed".

It was no accident that coal and steel was selected as the starting point of European integration. They were the industries necessary to wage war. By placing those under common control it could be ensured that no one state possessed the capacity to prepare for war. This was particularly so for Germany. It was also seen that all states could benefit from the regeneration of Germany. But it should not be thought that the Treaty of Rome had only protective or economic inspirations. The political restructuring of Europe was also high on the agenda. The Preamble to the Treaty of Paris states that the creation of an economic community is to be seen as "the basis for a broader and deeper community among peoples long divided by bloody conflicts".

The setting up of the ECSC was followed by an attempt to establish a European Defence Community. This would consist of a unified European Army, and like the ECSC, it was designed to secure the rehabilitation of Germany within Europe. The plan had the strong support of the United States, and a treaty was signed in 1952. But it was never ratified, mainly because of French, and to a lesser extent British, suspicion and indifference. By 1954 the impetus had been lost. Although the move towards integration in the defence area had been thwarted, the determination to integrate had not been destroyed. It shifted towards the sphere of economic relations.

In 1955 an inter-governmental conference of the original six states of the ECSC met at Messina under the leadership of Paul-Henri Spack, the Belgium foreign minister. As with the ECSC Treaty, the United Kingdom had been invited, but once again had declined the invitation, merely sending observers. The conference and the report it produced on the attractions of economic integration led, in 1957, to the signing of two Treaties of Rome. These treaties established the European Atomic Energy Community (Euratom) and the European Economic Community (EEC). The immediate purpose of Euratom was to create "the conditions necessary for the speedy establishment and growth of nuclear industries". The purpose of the EEC was to establish a "common market". However, it must be remembered that the founding fathers of the treaties had longer term political aims and aspirations. The Schuman Declaration referred to "common foundations of economic development as a firm step towards a European federation"; the Preamble to the Treaty of Paris stated that the parties were "resolved to substitute for age-old rivalries the merging of their essential interests". The Preamble to the EEC Treaty resolved that Member States will "lay the foundations of an ever closer union among the peoples of Europe." Certainly, the views of the founding fathers of the Communities were that the aim of the Treaties was to achieve political ends through economic means. They thought that integration in one economic sector would "snowball" into integration in other sectors. They also believed that modern states were so closely interdependent that any element of co-operation would tend to induce further cooperation. Coal and steel were the start as they were "the basic elements of industrial production". Atomic energy, then in its infancy was seen as the principal future source of new energy. By bringing these activities, as well as economic activity generally, under common rules and common institutions, there would be economic interdependence and eventually, political integration between the Member States. This view might now seem naïve as subsequent events have shown that even economic integration has proved difficult to achieve. As the debates of the last decade have demonstrated, political integration is not even on the agenda of some Member States.

After the passing of the Treaties of Rome, there were three Communities each with a set of autonomous institutions having the power to develop new structures independently of the participating Member States. Each community had an Assembly, a Council and Court of Justice. Whereas the ECSC had a High Authority, the Treaties of Rome had established a Commission. The Commission's powers under Euratom and the EEC were more limited that the High Authority and the Commission was ranked after the Council and Assembly in order of precedence. However, the members of these institutions were the same people, albeit wearing different "caps". In order to rationalise their administration, a Merger Treaty was completed in 1967. The Merger Treaty established a single Council, a single Assembly, and the High Authority of the ECSC was merged with the EEC and Euratom Commission, to be known as the Commission. Nevertheless, although the three communities now have common institutions (although the ECSC expired in 2002) they remain legally distinct and the powers and functions of the institutions depend on the terms of the treaty under which they act. In the text of this book the "Community" will refer to the EEC (or the EC, as it is now called).

The late 1950s and early 1960s were years of low unemployment and high economic growth. It was also seen that the establishment of the EEC had created wealth, not merely pooled it. The six Member States had seen their competitiveness increased and they had taken advantage of huge economies of scale. The EEC was seen as a success. At the same time a change of attitude was occurring in the United Kingdom. The reasons for not joining the Community previously had vanished. The world power status had hardly outlasted the end of the war, the economic performance of the United Kingdom was poor by comparison with the members of the EEC and the Commonwealth countries were developing their own markets, nearer to home. The Atlantic alliance between the United Kingdom and the USA was less prominent and trade patterns were shifting towards Europe, after all, our nearest trading link. This change of attitude led, in August 1961, to the United Kingdom (under the premiership of Mr Harold Macmillan) making application to join the Community. This application was rejected by President de Gaulle of France who saw a distorting influence in the United Kingdom's membership. A further application, this time made by a Labour Government led by Harold Wilson, in 1967, was also rejected by de Gaulle.

During the 1960s France and more particularly de Gaulle became dissatisfied with the workings of the Community and in 1965 France absented herself from Council meetings thereby effectively bringing the legislative machinery of the Community to a halt. This became known as the "policy of the empty chair". The crisis was resolved by the so-called "Luxembourg Accord". Although this had no legal status, it was an agreement that allowed any member-state to veto any legislation that it thought might affect its "very important interests". The effect of this agreement was to halt any movement of importance on the political front for almost 20 years.

ENLARGEMENT OF THE COMMUNITY

It was third time lucky for the United Kingdom! In 1970, again under Mr Edward Heath, the application to join the EEC was successful. A Treaty of Agreement was signed on January 22, 1972 and the United Kingdom became a member of the EEC with effect from January 1, 1973. Also joining at the same time were Ireland and Denmark. Norway had also been accepted into membership but did not take up the opportunity because a majority of the people voted "no" in a referendum on the subject. Even after the accession of the United Kingdom there were some doubts as the wisdom of membership. The new Labour Government under Mr Wilson "renegotiated" the terms of entry and in 1975, in the only national referendum in United Kingdom history, a 2:1 majority voted in favour of continued membership.

The period between the United Kingdom accession and 1986 was a time of inactivity in the Community. There was little progress towards either economic or political union. This was caused mainly the impasse of the Luxembourg Accord. One important development to be noted during this period was the beginning of the process of political co-operation by the Member States. This took the form of a series of meetings of the heads of states and government. The "summits" or as they became known, meetings of the European Council, did not have legal status within the framework of the Community, nor did they have any power to take binding decisions. Nevertheless, the European Council increasingly assumed overall policy making authority, thereby changing the balance of power in the Community away from the supranational body (the Commission) and towards the intergovernmental body (the Council of Ministers). The meetings of the European Council are those which are most widely reported in the media. It is a separate body from, and should not be confused with, the Council of Ministers or the Council of Europe. The existence of the European Council was officially recognised in the Single European Act 1986 and subsequently reaffirmed by the Treaty on European Union 1992 (Maastricht).

Although the voice of the peoples of Europe was called the

Assembly, it was increasingly referred to as the "European Parliament". At first it consisted of nominees of the parliaments of the Member States. However, in 1979 the first direct elections to the European Parliament were held. In 1981 Greece became the tenth member of the Community, joined in 1986 by Spain and Portugal.

The stagnation in the decision making process following the Luxembourg Accord, (or Agreement) brought about considerable dissatisfaction at the slow pace at which Community goals were being achieved. Naturally, attempting to obtain the unanimous agreement of all Member States was almost impossible; and those agreements which were reached were at the "lowest common denominator" level. Thus, it was recognised that some change had to be brought about. The original Treaty of Rome had survived without major amendment for almost thirty years. There had been many and various attempts to improve the Treaty all of them failing, probably because they were too ambitious. Nevertheless, they helped to establish the climate for the eventual changes that were to be brought about by the Single European Act (SEA) 1986.

In 1985 the Dooge Committee proposed an intergovernmental conference "to negotiate a draft European Union Treaty". The conference was to discuss the decision making of the Council of Ministers, the legislative powers of the parliament, the executive powers of the Commission, and new policy areas of Community competence. The outcome of the conference was a summit meeting in Milan which brought into being the above mentioned Single European Act, which came into force on July 1, 1987. The Preamble of the Act says that it is "a step towards European union". The Act amended the EEC Treaty in a number of important ways. A major change was the different method to be adopted in the legislative process affecting ten Treaty articles. The SEA replaced the requirement for unanimity in the Council by qualified majority voting (see Chapter 3). This meant that one single state did not have the ability to block legislation. This was an important change because it applied to the legislation concerning the new date for completion of the internal market, *i.e.* the end of 1992. The need to complete the internal market (which should have been completed by January 1, 1970) was identified in a White Paper published by Lord Cockfield, the Commissioner with responsibility for the internal Community market, encouraged by the new President of the Commission, Jacques Delors. The SEA incorporated these recommendations and set "1992" as the date by which the internal market was to be achieved. The Commission had identified almost three hundred areas in which directives, or other measures, were considered necessary to complete the internal market. Measures concerning the internal market were now subject to qualified majority voting, and it says much for the efficiency of this process that by the end of 1992, all but 18 of the three hundred measures had been adopted by the Council. To all intents and purposes the internal market was completed on time.

The SEA officially recognised the Assembly as the European Parliament. In addition it introduced some changes to the legislative process which enhanced to a small extent the powers of the Parliament. Prior to the SEA, Parliament had only the right to be "consulted" on various legislative measures passed by the Council. The SEA introduced the "co-operation procedure", whereby if the procedure applies, Parliament had a "second reading" of proposed legislation. If Parliament rejected the legislation at this point, it could only be taken forward by the Council if that body was unanimous in its view. Parliament did not yet have positive powers and it could not assert its own views, and a unanimous Council could still pass legislation. However, the influence of Parliament had been increased. It can form an alliance with the Commission and one, even small, Member State. Thus the Council will often have to accommodate Parliament's view and introduce a compromise solution.

The SEA also introduced new Community competencies. One such competence was in the area of economic and social cooperation. This is not to say that the EEC had not previously introduced initiatives in this area, but rather the Act placed them on a formal footing. In this area it was provided that the Community should develop and pursue actions leading to the strengthening of its economic and social cohesion. It would attempt this by reducing disparities between the regions of the Community by setting up various funds, such as the European Regional Development Fund and the Social Fund and the European Investment Bank, all of which would provide money for projects which had the support of the Community.

Other new areas of Community competence were in research and technology, and in environmental protection. This latter competence is particularly apt for the Community, as environmental problems, (especially pollution) of a particular Member State do not stop at national borders, but impact on neighbouring states.

The achievement of the internal market was an economic success. Yet the Commission was aware that the social repercussions had not been sufficiently addressed by the SEA. To address this problem it published a Community Charter of Fundamental Social Rights of Workers, which became known as the Social

Charter. This more or less self-explanatory Charter was adopted by 11 of the 12 Member States in December 1989. The United Kingdom refused to sign it. Although it had no legal force it was intended to be the blue-print for social legislation in the Community. Following on from the Charter the Commission adopted an Action Programme containing draft proposals for legislation (see Chapter 12).

The signing of the SEA and the accompanying package of the "1992" programme quickened the pace of Community action. It was soon realised that even further action was needed to bring about further institutional change, and the adoption of common monetary and fiscal policies. To this end an intergovernmental conference (IGC) was held in 1991 that resulted in the signing on February 2, 1992 of the Treaty on European Union (TEU) (or the "Maastricht Treaty"). Following some difficulties in ratification in some Member States, notably the United Kingdom, Denmark and Germany, the Treaty came into force on November 1, 1993.

At first sight the TEU seems too complicated to fully comprehend. It consists of two main elements. The first element is a comprehensive amendment of the Treaty of Rome, with some of the numbered Articles of that Treaty being re-numbered. The second element is separate from the existing legal framework: it sets out a series of political intentions, and is delineated as Articles 1–53 [ex by the letters A–S].

The TEU created the "European Union". It consists of three "pillars". In the middle are three existing Communities (*i.e.* the ECSC, Euratom and the EC). These three Communities will be known collectively as the European Communities. It will be noted here that the TEU officially changed the name to EC, dropping the "Economic" from the title. On either side of this central "pillar" is the Common Foreign and Security Policy (CFSP) and Cooperation in Justice and Home Affairs (JHA). These three "pillars" support the over-arching constitutional order of the Union. However, only the central pillar, the EC, is governed by Community law. The CFSP pillar and the JHA pillar are governed by intergovernmental cooperation. This means they are outside the jurisdiction of the Community institutions, particularly the Court of Justice. Neither will any of the Articles of the outside pillars be enforceable, or challengeable, in national courts. Thus, although the Union is wider than the European Community it has its roots in the Community.

The objectives of the Union are set out in Article 2 of the TEU. This Article reflects the activities to be pursued under the three pillars. In addition the Union is to maintain and build on the *"acquis communautaire"*. This expression means the body of EC law as found in the founding treaties and the case law of the Court of Justice. The main changes are set out as objectives in Articles 1–45 [ex A–K] of the TEU. These represent an increase in, and further development, of policy areas. The most important, and controversial, developments are set out in Article 8 [ex G] which adds to Article 3 of the EC Treaty the following:

". . . in accordance with the timetable set out . . . these activities shall include the irrevocable fixing of exchange rates leading to the introduction of a single currency . . ."

The single currency (now known as the "Euro") was to be achieved in three stages by 1999. The United Kingdom, Sweden and Denmark have to date opted out of the third and final stage. The other 12 Member States continued with their arrangements for the single currency and on January 1, 2002 the new banknotes and coins were introduced. National currencies ceased to be legal tender by the end of March 2002, at the latest.

During the negotiations leading up the TEU, the United Kingdom, in particular, made much importance of the principal of subsidiarity. Put simply, this means that decisions should be made at the lowest level were possible. If an adequate solution can be obtained by a Member State there is no reason why that decision should be taken by a Community institution. It is about the allocation of responsibility between different levels of administration in the Community. This principle was made explicit in two places in the TEU. In the Preamble it declares that the Member States are:

"resolved to continue the process of creating an ever closer union among the peoples of Europe, in which decisions are taken as closely as possible to the citizen in accordance with the principle of subsidiarity".

Subsidiarity is also set out as a Union principle in Article 1 TEU [ex A] and as a Community principle in Article 5 EC [ex 36]. One of the interesting future developments of Community law will be to see how far this principle is justiciable. Will Member States be able to challenge a Community measure on the basis that the issue could be dealt with more efficiently at national level?

If the United Kingdom supported the idea of subsidiarity, they were definitely opposed to any extension to provisions in the social sphere. In the draft TEU there were such proposals and such was the obduracy of the United Kingdom that the Treaty would not have been finalised with the provisions as part of the

Treaty. So the "offending" provisions were removed from the body of the Treaty and "added back" as a Protocol on Social Policy. This Protocol was signed by all twelve Member States but allowed the United Kingdom to "opt-out" of its provisions. Thus eleven Member States could pursue a social policy and use the Community institutions and procedures to adopt legislation, but the measures adopted under the Protocol would not apply to the United Kingdom. This Protocol was known colloquially as the "Social Chapter". It was thought that this "two-tier" arrangement might bring with it legal problems, given that there could be difficulties in differentiating between existing social policy measures in the EC Treaty and those in the Social Chapter. However, these fears were unfounded. This was for two reasons. First, only two measures were passed under the Social Chapter provisions: these were Directives concerning parental leave and European works councils. Second, the new incoming Labour Government (in 1997) indicated its willingness to "sign up" for the Social Chapter. This was achieved through the Treaty of Amsterdam 1997 and the United Kingdom is now fully covered by the Social provisions set out in Articles 136–145 EC [ex 118–122].

In an attempt to placate the demands of the European Parliament for an increasing say in the legislative process, the TEU introduced another procedure whereby Community legislation may be implemented. This is known as the "co-decision procedure" (see Chapter 2). As with the cooperation procedure introduced by the SEA, co-decision does not give the Parliament direct legislative powers. The new procedure involves greater attempts to achieve consensus between the Parliament and the Council, but the ultimate power of the Parliament is a negative one, the exercise of a veto.

There is an increasing realisation that the different procedures available in the Treaty are extremely complicated. It has been calculated that there are 44 different procedures whereby Community legislation may be adopted, involving different combinations of institutional involvement, and different voting procedures in the Council.

Finally in respect of the TEU, the Treaty of Rome was amended so as to introduce in Articles 17–22 the notion of Union citizenship. Every person holding the nationality of a Member State shall be a citizen of the Union. The full ramifications of these rights have yet to be worked out, and at the moment citizenship of the Union in any meaningful way is largely symbolic. However, the Court of Justice has used this concept of citizenship as a fundamental right to establish residence rights in a host Member State. The concept of citizenship is discussed in Chapter 10.

There was the realisation at Maastricht that the Community was dynamic and still evolving. For some Member States it was going too fast, and in the wrong direction; for others it was not moving fast enough. The debate was a continuing one. What sort of Community did these new citizens of Europe want? Was it a common market club of co-operating sovereign states, or was it an emerging political federation?

Also, in 1993, Austria, Finland, Norway and Sweden applied to become members of the Community. The negotiations for entry were completed relatively quickly and the treaty of Accession was signed in June 1994. However, as in 1972, the Norwegian people decided in a referendum against joining. Therefore, on January 1, 1995, Austria, Finland and Sweden became members of the European Union. The Union now had fifteen Member States.

THE AMSTERDAM TREATY

It was decided at Maastricht to review the TEU. This review was to take place at the sixth Intergovernmental Conference (IGC) to be held in the history of the Community. The remit for the IGC was far reaching, and was agreed at the Brussels European Council meeting of the December 10–11, 1993. The major subjects to be discussed at the IGC were as follows:

- to examine the legislative role of the European Parliament and other matters outlined in the Maastricht Treaty;

- to review the number of commissioners;

- to review the weighting of Member States votes in the Council of Ministers; and

- to consider measures needed to facilitate the work and smooth running of the EU institutions.

The aim of the IGC was to supply answers to some important questions. How can the Union be made more efficient, democratic and transparent? How can the Union contribute to the stability of the continent in the present international context? How can a dilution of the Community be avoided when it is expected to include more than 20 members after the year 2003?

The need for reform was largely driven by the enlargement process. The current unwieldy processes would become unworkable with the expected influx of new members. Enlargement itself was not on the agenda (neither was EMU), but issues that needed to be discussed were institutional reform, decision making, flexibility, employment provisions, the abolition of border controls, the common foreign and security policy, subsidiarity, transparency and the western European Union.

To prepare the way for the IGC the European Council established a Reflection Group consisting of Representatives of the Ministers of Foreign Affairs of the 15 Member States, and representatives from the European Parliament and the Commission. The mandate of the Reflection Group was to "examine and elaborate ideas relating to the provisions of the TEU . . . and other possible improvements . . . It will also elaborate options in the perspective of the future enlargement of the Union on the institutional questions". The task of the Group was not to negotiate but to present a range of options to Heads of Government to assist them in determining the scope of the IGC itself.

The outcome of the IGC and subsequent negotiations was the Treaty of Amsterdam. This was agreed by the Heads of State and Government on June 19, 1997 and concluded on October 2, 1997. The Treaty was to be ratified by the Member States, according to their constitutional traditions. Three Member States, Denmark, Ireland and Portugal each held a referendum, which confirmed their people's support for the new Treaty. The Treaty came into force on May 1, 1999. This was a few months behind the third stage of Economic and Monetary Union, which took place on January 1, 1999.

As already stated, the Treaty of Amsterdam came into force on May 1, 1999. It amended the Treaty of Rome in many different ways. One of the most obvious and important changes was the wholesale renumbering of the Articles of the Treaty of Rome and the TEU. This accounts for the proliferation of numbers in brackets throughout this book. Both experienced teachers and novice students will encounter some difficulties. The experienced teacher will have to relearn Article numbers that have grown familiar over a lifetime of work. The student will find the different numbers confusing, especially when reading judgments of the Court of Justice or academic articles written before 1999. They, of course, will refer to the old numbering. Readers are referred back to the preface for the system adopted in this book.

The first thing to be said about the Treaty is that it has added to the complexity, and confusion, that inevitably faces a reader attempting to make sense of the documents. The Treaty of Amsterdam consists of amendments of the Treaty establishing the European Community, amendments to the Treaty on European Union, 13 Protocols, 51 Declarations, eight Declarations of which the Conference of Amsterdam took notice, and a

Declaration on the amended Article 35 [ex K7] containing provisions in the field of justice and home affairs. There are numerous cross-references which add to the confusion. One of the stated aims of the IGC was to bring about greater openness and transparency but it is difficult now even for practitioners to find their way around the legislation. For an interested lay person, or a student, it must be almost an impossibility.

To cope with the expected influx of new Member States it was considered necessary to reform the institutional structure of the Community. Three areas in particular were said to be in need of reform. First it would be necessary to simplify the complex procedures for passing legislation. Secondly it was thought that qualified majority voting would become too ponderous with twenty or more Member States, and third, it was held that the number of commissioners would need to be controlled. The outcome in the Treaty was mere tinkering! Despite a proposal to give the larger Member States more power in terms of the votes they had for Qualified majority voting (QMV), the eventual Treaty left matters as they were. There was very little change to the process of legislation, and it was agreed to limit the number of commissioners to the current Treaty. A Protocol was added to the Treaty of Amsterdam providing that on the next enlargement of the Community the Commission will be made up of one national of each Member State. But even this small rearrangement is dependent on an agreement between the Member States to an acceptable weighting of votes within the Council. The Protocol also provides that a Member State that has to give up a second Commissioner will need to be compensated, presumably by some increase in its votes in the Council.

There were also some small changes to the complex range of legislative procedures (44 different procedures were mentioned above). The "co-operation" procedure of Article 252 [ex 189c] has been abolished, except for monetary policy provisions. The vast majority of Articles are now subject to the "co-decision" procedure (Article 251 [ex 189b]). This will help to increase the power and influence of the European Parliament. This is a real, if modest, reform.

It was mentioned earlier that the TEU had created a three "pillar" European Union. One of the pillars was called Co-operation and Justice in Home Affairs (JHA). It will be remembered that this pillar (and the other pillar, Common Foreign and Security Policy (CFSP)) are outside the jurisdiction of the European Community, in particular the Court of Justice. However, the Treaty of Amsterdam introduced changed in respect of the JHA. It has now been renamed Police and Judicial Co-operation in Criminal Matters

(Title VI TEU). But, more importantly, the provisions on visas, asylum, immigration and other policies relating to the free movement of persons are brought into the EC in Articles 61–69 [ex 73i–73q]. This means that these provisions are now justiciable before the Court of Justice.

Other changes in this area have not helped clarity! There are a number of protocols attached to the Treaty of Amsterdam, which allow for special arrangements for individual Member States. The United Kingdom and Ireland are allowed to have different border controls that the rest of the Union. The United Kingdom and Denmark are allowed to develop more slowly in this area than the rest of the Union. There are other protocols in this area that only help to "muddy the waters". What acts can be challenged before the Court of Justice and which acts are merely inter-governmental and outside the central pillar of the EC, will be a matter of complex legal debate.

The restructuring of the Common and Security Policy pillar was on a much more modest scale; and it is still outside the E.C. Of interest is the recognition that some Member States "see their common defence realised in NATO" (Article 17 [ex J.7]). Article 17 also extends the CFSP to include humanitarian and rescue tasks and peacekeeping.

It has been recognised that the text of the Treaty is a compromise. One of the Declarations emphasised that the reform of the institutions which the Amsterdam Treaty failed to achieve was "an indefensible condition for the conclusion of the first accession negotiations". To this end, the Commission, clearly disappointed with the lack of progress, called for political agreement before 2000 on the weighting of Member States' votes in Council and in reducing the number of commissioners. It also called for another IGC as soon as possible to discuss the much needed far-reaching institutional reforms.

There is also a concern that with the number of Protocols and Declarations, the Community is now becoming a Europe of "bits and pieces". The main purpose of these additions to the Treaty is to allow various Member States to opt out some of the provisions of the Treaty. For example, Protocol X allows the United Kingdom and Ireland to keep border controls. Protocol Z allows Denmark to have different visa requirements from the other Member States. When the Protocols and Declaration of the Amsterdam Treaty are added to those annexed to previous Treaties (especially the TEU), there is concern that the law of the European Community is no longer uniform.

If the overall impression of the Treaty of Amsterdam was one of disappointment at the lack of political will to bring about change, there were nevertheless, some positive aspects. It was recognised that the most urgent socio-economic problem facing the Community was unemployment. To Article 3 EC has been added ". . . the promotion of co-ordination between employment policies of the Member States with a view to enhancing their effectiveness by developing a co-ordinated strategy for employment". This is to be developed through measures taken by the Council. The Social Agreement, which the United Kingdom refused to be part of at the TEU, has now been incorporated into the Treaty, and a redrafted Article 119 on the right of equal pay for equal work promises further legislation.

An important improvement was the shifting of some of the provisions for Justice and Home Affairs, from the non-justiciable part of the TEU, to the EC Treaty, where they will be subject to judicial protection by the European Court of Justice. This covers the free movement of persons, asylum and immigration and measures to combat crime. Although these principles are now in the EC Treaty they have to be translated into workable rules.

There are other provisions, often not more than statements of intent, in the fields of the environment, public health, culture and consumer protection.

THE TREATY OF NICE

The Treaty of Amsterdam left a certain number of "left-over" issues. These issues concerned the balance of power between the European Union and the Member States and between the Member States themselves. It was fairly obvious that these issues would become more problematical with the proposed enlargement of the Union.

It was therefore agreed by the Member States that the year 2000 should see yet another IGC, the primary task of which was to ensure institutional reform in order that the Union can work efficiently with a membership comprising twenty-five states. The Union's institutions had been created with just six Member States in mind. It was obvious that these institutions were experiencing difficulties with 15 Member States. The need for reform was pressing.

It was decided that the new IGC would consider the following issues:

- the size and composition of the Commission;
- the weighting of votes in the Council;
- the extension of qualified majority voting in the Council.

The IGC was convened on February 14, 2000. Negotiations were concluded in time for the meeting of the Council in Nice (France) on December 11, 2000. The result was the Treaty of Nice. The treaty had to be ratified by all the Member States. This did not prove too difficult, apart from Ireland. Like Denmark in 1992, Ireland voted against ratification in the first referendum held in June 2001. The main reason given for this anti-European Union vote was that the Irish Government had failed to properly explain the Treaty to Irish citizens. After the Irish Government had conducted a much more vigorous campaign to persuade the people of Ireland that the Treaty was necessary, a second referendum, in July 2002, gave a small majority in favour of ratification. The Treaty came into force on February 1, 2003.

The Treaty, as passed, indicates that reaching agreement on many of the issues was difficult and there is an element of postponing changes and decisions to a later date.

The Treaty of Nice limits the Commission to one member per Member State with effect from 2005. A ceiling on the number of Commissioners will be imposed once the Union has 27 Member States. At that point the Council will have to take a unanimous decision on the exact number of Commissioners, which must be less than 27. The nationality of the Commissioners will then be determined by a system of rotation. There is no requirement for the Council to consult either the Commission or the European Parliament. The rotation system has yet to be devised but it will be "based on the principle of equality" and will reflect demography and geography.

The Treaty also increased the power of the president of the Commission. Under the revised Article 217 EC the president will decide on the allocation of portfolios and may reassign responsibilities in the course of a Commissioner's term of office, albeit with the approval of the other members of the Commission.

It was recognised that it would be very difficult to obtain unanimous agreement in a Union that will have 25 or more Member States. To avoid paralysis, with the Union being unable to act, the reforms at Nice had to reduce the number of cases in which Member States can impose their veto. It was agreed to extend qualified majority voting (QMV) in the Council to a small number of new areas. In only six of those areas was the extension of QMV matched by a commensurate extension of co-decision with the European Parliament. The new Treaty provides for a change in the weighting of votes from January 1, 2005. The number of votes assigned to each Member State has been altered and the number to be assigned to the candidate countries when they enter the Union has also been set (see Chapter 3 for full details).

The powers of the European Parliament have been added to, in addition to the six new areas where the co-decision procedure will now apply. Article 7(1) of the Treaty on European Union now provides that the European Parliament may take the initiative in charging a Member State with a breach of fundamental rights. It can do this by a vote with a two-thirds majority. By a revised Article 230 EC, Parliament is given equal status with the Council and the Commission and the Member States to challenge the validity of an act of the Union before the Court of Justice (see Chapter 7). And, by virtue of Article 300(6) the European Parliament has equal status with the Council and the Commission in seeking an opinion from the ECJ about the validity of international agreements.

It was recognised that the Court of Justice is already overloaded with cases. As a result there are long delays in obtaining judgments, which is detrimental to the working of the Community and unsatisfactory for the parties concerned. This problem will be exacerbated by the accession of new Member States. The reforms to the judicial system are discussed in full in Chapter 3.

The Treaty of Nice has added only three competences to the powers of the Union. Article 31 TEU provides for the establishment of Eurojust, a unit of public prosecutors to co-ordinate the fight against crime. Article 135a EC has been added to provide a provision to combat fraud on the public finances and Article 137 adds social exclusion and modernisation of social security systems to the objectives of social policy. It should be noted, however, that the harmonisation of national social welfare systems is explicitly excluded.

The Verdict on Nice

Before the details of the Treaty were finalised, there was a meeting of the heads of government of the 15 Member States and the 13 candidate countries (including Turkey). This meeting was an attempt to concentrate minds on the challenge of enlargement. This challenge was certainly addressed in the Treaty and so, in a technical sense, it has to be said that the Treaty of Nice prepared the way for enlargement. The "left-overs" from the Treaty of Amsterdam were dealt with, even if imperfectly. However, it is difficult to be satisfied with Nice. Few will dare to suggest that the overall outcome of Nice contributed to the quality of European integration or to the efficiency or effectiveness of the Union. The reforms to the voting structures of the Council and the European Parliament are marked by a lack of generosity towards the candidate countries. There was a lack of long term vision. Much remains to be done.

The Future of the EU

The Treaty of Nice was intended to prepare the way for a new wave of countries joining the Union. Indeed, the biggest enlargement of the Union is due to take place in May 2004. For over 10 years, since the fall of the Berlin Wall and the collapse of communism in 1989, the former communist countries have struggled to transform themselves into fully fledged market economies and democracies in order to meet the Union's rigorous standards for membership. The ex-communist countries are Poland, Hungary, the Czech Republic, Slovenia, Slovakia and the three Baltic states of Lithuania, Latvia and Estonia. They are being joined by two former British colonies, Cyprus and Malta. It is planned that Bulgaria and Romania will also join the Union in 2007. Turkey would also like to become a member. In fact, it made an application to join many years ago, but because of doubts over the adherence to the rule of law in Turkey, no date has yet been set for Turkey's accession. The Commission has also approved the opening of initial talks with countries in south-east Europe, leading eventually to them becoming Member States. The countries are Albania, Bosnia and Herzegovina, Croatia, Macedonia and Serbia-Montenegro.

The accession treaty for the 10 new Member States was signed in Athens in April 2003. The accession of the ten, to bring the total number of Member States to 25, will add 75 million people to the population of the Union. Politically, the new enlargement will make it difficult to maintain the dominance of the Franco-German alliance. Poland, for example, will become one of the top six Member States in terms of size. And for the first time, small countries will outnumber big ones.

Each of the 10 candidate countries needs to hold a referendum to ratify their membership. It is not expected that any of the countries will vote against joining. The European Union may be unpopular, particularly in the United Kingdom, but the signing of the accession treaty was a reminder of how much of a magnet the Union still is to those aspiring to join.

The Convention

Reference has already been made to the European Council meeting held in Laeken in December 2001. When it was decided to establish a Convention, Valéry Giscard d'Estaing, a former French President was appointed as its Chairperson. The Convention has 113 representatives: one from each of the heads of state or government of the 15 Member States and one each from the heads of state or government of the thirteen candidate countries. There are two representatives from each of the 15 national parliaments and two each from the parliaments of the candidate countries. The European Parliament has sixteen representatives and the Commission has two.

The purpose of the Convention has already been mentioned. For ease of reference it can be repeated that the main aim is to debate the future of the Union. Among the more important tasks are the following:

(1) Simplification of the treaties. This will involve reorganising the basic provisions of the four treaties into a single treaty, which should be presented in a clearer and more readable form. (This is an admirable aim, but the inevitable renumbering of Treaty Articles will involve more pain and confusion for student and tutor alike).

(2) Demarcation of responsibilities. This is basically a question of who does what in the EU, what powers have to be exercised at EU level and what at Member State level (this is the subsidiarity argument). Another point for discussion in this area is how to rationalise the Union's legislative instruments to ensure that the different levels of legislative and administrative actions complement each other more effectively.

(3) The status of the Charter of Fundamental Rights of the European Union. This is discussed in Chapter 5.

(4) The Role of National Parliaments in the institutional architecture of the European Union.

The Convention meets on a regular basis and is expected to complete its deliberations by June 2003. Interested students can follow the progress of the Convention at *http://european-convention.eu.int*

The Community has progressed mightily since its foundation in 1957. It has grown to become the largest trading block in the world. Yet there is a growing feeling that integration is now haphazard and that there is no clear vision for the future. There is grave doubt as to which way the Community should go next. Should it retreat into a wider but inter-governmental system, or should progress be made towards a deeper "federal" union? The situation will become clearer over the early years of the twenty-first century.

2. LEGISLATION

THE LEGISLATIVE PROCESS

Introduction

Every sovereign state has a prescribed method of decision making that is part of the legislative process. Even though the Community is not a sovereign state it does make legislation. Yet it does not have one system of decision making, in fact it has many. The exact number of procedures is a matter of some debate. At the top end, some commentators have suggested that there are 48 different procedures! Other estimates put the figure between twenty and thirty. The Commission itself considers that there were 29 "main decision making procedures provided for in the Treaty". Obviously, such a plethora of procedures will be very difficult, even for an expert, to follow. For a student the difficulties will seem immense! One of the original aims of the Treaty of Amsterdam was to "tidy-up" the number of procedures, preferably by reducing them. Apart from the already mentioned move towards the use of the co-decision procedure, little progress was made.

A reasonable question to ask is why are there so many different procedures? The answer is that the procedures were arrived at after negotiations between different Member States. Each Member State had their own agenda and their own view as to when qualified majority voting (QMV) should be used in the Council of

Ministers. They would also have opinions on the influence to be granted to the European Parliament. As a result of the negotiations between different Member States, at different times, a whole series of procedures have developed, each reflecting the perceived needs of Member States at one particular time.

However, it is possible to say that the various procedures are a variation of one of four possible procedures. These are the consultation procedure, the co-operation procedure, the co-decision procedure and the assent procedure. These will now be looked at separately.

The Consultation Procedure

The original Treaty of Rome provided that in a limited number of instances, the Council was required to consult the European Parliament before coming to a decision on Community secondary legislation. For example, Article 44 [ex 54] on the freedom of establishment (although this article is now covered by the cooperation procedure—see below).

If the Council fails to obtain the opinion of the Parliament before the Council adopts the measure, then the Court of Justice (if requested by the Parliament) can annul the measure. This happened in *Roquette Frères v Council* (*Case* 138/79). Thus the need to obtain the opinion of Parliament is an essential procedural requirement. But this is as far as it goes! Having obtained the opinion from Parliament, the Council is free to ignore it.

This lack of power in Parliament has been seen as part of the "democratic deficit" whereby the unelected Council adopts legislation without the control of the (now) democratically elected Parliament. The consultation procedure reflects the early days of the Community when the Parliament was an Assembly of political appointees, and it could not be expected that they should wield power at the expense of sovereign Member States.

The passing of the Single European Act and the Treaty on European Union (Maastricht) has increased the power of the European Parliament (see below) but there are still a few Treaty Articles that stipulate a mere consultation with that body. A couple of examples are: Article 8b, concerning rights to vote and stand in municipal elections; and Article 94 on the provision of state aids.

The Co-Operation Procedure—Article 252 [ex 189c]

The original consultation procedure was in place for nearly thirty years. As has been suggested above, this was because at that time, the Parliament was not directly elected. Whatever the merits of this argument, it was no longer valid after the introduction of direct elections in 1979. Nevertheless, it took until 1986 for Parliament to acquire some increase in its powers *vis-à-vis* the Council in the legislative process. The co-operation procedure, as it is not worry about the various previous Article numbers that were attached to current provisions. An up to date book or journal article will show the current correct provision, although for pre-Maastricht writings, students may have to plot the movement of Articles through various parts of the amended Treaty].

The co-operation procedure was introduced to provide a mechanism for the adoption of the internal market, although most of these provisions have now been moved to Article 251 [ex 189b]. (see below).

When the co-operation procedure applies the Council will adopt a "common position", either by adopting the proposal by qualified majority voting (62 votes) or drafting an amended proposal (on a unanimous vote). The Council does not then proceed immediately to decide on the matter as it would under the consultation procedure. Rather, this common position is sent to the Parliament which has three months in which to act. It can approve the proposal by a majority of votes cast. If this is the case the Council will adopt the legislation in accordance with the common position.

Alternatively, Parliament can reject the proposal. If this happens the Council can consider amendments and resubmit the proposals, or if it can act unanimously it can nevertheless adopt the proposals, but only if it does so within three months. The ability of the European Parliament to reject the Council's common position is a significant increase in the powers of the Parliament.

The European Parliament can also make amendments to the proposed legislation. If this happens, the proposal is sent back to the Commission, who have one month to re-examine the proposal and resubmit it to the Council. The Council then has three months to act. It can either accept the amended proposal (by qualified majority), or adopt a different version (by unanimous vote).

It can be seen that the co-operation procedure gave the European Parliament a more important role in the legislative process than hitherto. In the evolution of the European Parliament as a legislative body, (an evolution that has still some way to go), it was a significant event. It increased the power of the European Parliament. That power was further increased by the TEU, with the introduction of the co-decision procedure (see below). However, the new co-decision procedure added to the number of legislative procedures discussed above. A small opportunity was taken in the Treaty of Amsterdam to reduce these procedures. The result was the virtual removal of the co-operation procedure from the Treaty. The co-operation procedure is now confined to some aspects of EMU (*e.g.* Article 107 [ex106] and Article 111 [ex 109]). All the areas previously covered by the co-operation procedure were transferred to the co-decision procedure. The description of the co-operation procedure has been retained because of its recent relevance.

The Co-Decision Procedure: Article 251 [ex 189b]

Further power in the legislative process was given to the European Parliament by the TEU. This was by the introduction of what is known as the co-decision procedure under the new Article 251 [ex 189b]. The purpose of this mechanism is to give greater recognition to the joint involvement of the Council and the Parliament. It should be noted though, that it does not give direct legislative power to the Parliament alone. The ultimate power of the Parliament under this procedure is that it can veto legislation; so its power is a negative one.

The co-decision procedure can be a one, two or three stage procedure. Normally, the procedure will cover one or two stages, but if the Council and the European Parliament cannot agree at either of the first two stages, the proposed legislation will pass on to be considered during a third stage.

The first stage is that the Commission's proposal is sent to both the Council and the European Parliament. The Council, acting by a qualified majority, after taking the opinion of the European Parliament, can adopt the measure if it approves any amendment made by the European Parliament, or if the European Parliament does not propose any amendments. The Treaty of Amsterdam introduced this first stage in an attempt to streamline the many difficult procedures.

However, if agreement cannot be reached at this stage, the Council adopts a common position. This is the second stage. The Council must "inform the European Parliament fully of the reasons which led it to adopt its common position". The Commission is also obliged to inform the European Parliament fully of its opinion and intentions. The European Parliament then has three months to respond to the common position. It may either approve, or amend, or reject outright, or take no action at all. If it approves or takes no action within the three months, then the Council can adopt its common position as a legislative act.

If however, the European Parliament rejects the common position by an absolute majority of its members, the proposed act cannot be adopted. Neither can a proposal be adopted if the

European Parliament amends the proposal in a manner, which the Council cannot accept. In both these cases the procedure moves on to a third stage. This is when the Council must refer the matter to a Conciliation Committee. This Committee has an equal number of representatives from the Council and the European Parliament. Its task is to reach agreement on a joint text and it is assisted in this task by the Commission, who takes part in the Committee's work. The starting point for the discussions is the common position reached by the Council, together with the proposed amendments made by the European Parliament. The Conciliation Committee has six weeks to produce a joint text. If it fails to do so the act will not be adopted. If it does produce a joint text within the six-week period then there is a further period of six weeks in which the European Parliament, by absolute majority, and the Council, by qualified majority, can adopt the act in accordance with the joint text. If either of the institutions fails to do so then the act will not be adopted.

Although the power of the European Parliament is essentially a negative power of veto, the co-decision procedure does encourage the European Parliament, the Council and the Commission to engage in inter-institutional discussion and negotiation. Most importantly, the Council, if it wishes to pass a piece of legislation, is obliged to take seriously the role of the European Parliament. In practice, the co-decision procedure has worked well, especially when the Conciliation Committee is used. There have only been about three outright failures to reach a decision under this procedure.

The Treaty of Amsterdam increased the number of Treaty articles subject to the co-decision procedure. As explained above, this was mainly done by abolishing the co-operation procedure and substituting the co-decision procedure. It now means that most Community legislation is subject to the co-decision procedure.

The co-decision procedure applies, *inter alia*, to the following provisions; free movement of workers (Article 42 [ex 49]); freedom of establishment (Article 43 [ex 57]); mutual recognition of qualifications (Article 47 [ex 57]); the internal market (Article 95 [ex 100a]), and certain aspect of environmental policy (Article 175 [ex 130s]).

The Assent Procedure

This is the simplest of the procedures. Essentially, it is a single step procedure whereby the Council can act after obtaining the assent of the European Parliament. There is no provision for the European Parliament to amend the Commission proposal and both the Council and the European Parliament have to agree. It has been said that this procedure grants the European Parliament "an infinite power of delay and an absolute power of rejection". The assent procedure is reserved for special and important circumstances. One of the most important areas is that concerning applications from states to join the Union (Article 49TEU [ex O TEU]). Because of the need for the agreement of the European Parliament, that body will have the final say in which country can, or cannot, join the Union. The assent procedure is also used for Article 107(5) [ex 106], concerning the functioning of the European Central Bank, and Article 7 TEU [ex F.1 TEU], which provides for sanctions in the event of a serious and persistent breach of fundamental rights by a Member State.

THE LEGAL BASE FOR LEGISLATIVE PROPOSALS

Each of the Articles of the Treaty which allow for secondary legislation to be passed stipulates the type of measures and the procedure for its adoption. So, for example, Article 308 [ex 235] requires measures to be passed with only the consultation procedure involving the European Parliament. Importantly, the Council must act by unanimity. On the other hand, Article 40 [ex 49] stipulates that either Regulations or Directives may be passed, but the co-decision procedure will be applied, and the Council will reach a decision by qualified majority vote. It can be seen that the legal base chosen for a particular measure can have an important effect on the institutional balance. The Council would seek to use a legal base that required a unanimous vote. Thus, they would be able to protect their national interests by their use of a veto. The Commission however, would prefer a legal base that required only qualified majority voting. There would be a much better chance of their proposals being accepted by a majority of the Member States than by them all. Naturally, the European Parliament would prefer a legal base which would give it a high level of participation (*i.e.* the co-decision procedure) rather than a legal base that requires only that Parliament be consulted.

Because the subject matter of a particular measure can straddle different areas of Treaty, it is possible to argue as to the correct base to be used. As stated above, measures for the attainment of the single market required qualified majority voting in the Council. Therefore the Commission attempted to introduce as much legislation as possible under Article 100a. The Council on the other hand, argued that proposals should have as their legal base other articles requiring unanimity. An example of this is *Commission v Council (Titanium Dioxide)* (Case C-300/89). The Council adopted a directive under Article 130s (now 175, requiring QMV), which required unanimity. The European Parliament protested, and the Commission agreed, that it should have been adopted under Article 100a (now 95) as a single market measure. The Court of Justice held that it was possible to adopt the directive under either Article, but the use of Article 130s (now 175) deprived the Parliament of its greater role in the legislative process.

The Pregnancy Directive (Dir 92/85) was introduced under Article 118 (now 137) on the health and safety at work of workers. Under Article 118a the legislation could be adopted by qualified majority in the Council. The United Kingdom was vociferous in its argument that this Directive should not have been issued under Article 118 (now 137). In the view of the United Kingdom such matters as leave, pay and other employment rights do not fall under health and safety. Even with qualified majority voting it was only after long negotiation, and a watered-down directive, that agreement could be reached.

In the cases that come before the Court of Justice, the view of the Court is that if there is a choice of legal base, then the one which allows the European Parliament the greater role must be used. This gives more democracy to the legislative process. Thus the decision in the *Titanium Oxide* case, discussed above.

3. THE INSTITUTIONS

There are five Community institutions. They are the European Parliament (originally known as the Assembly), the Council, the Commission, the Court of Justice and the Court of Auditors. In the original Treaty of Rome, Article 4 (now 7) established the first four mentioned bodies as institutions, and by the Treaty on European Union the Court of Auditors was "promoted" to the status of an institution of the Community. There are a number of other bodies established by the EC Treaty, but these have not been accorded the status of institutions. They are the Economic and Social Committee, the European Investment Bank and the Committee of the Regions. There are also a number of other bodies created by Community legislation which develops and supervises aspects of Community work. This chapter will look in turn at the three main political institutions, the Parliament the Council and the Commission. It will then look at the interaction between these bodies in the process of legislation and will then look at the European Court of Justice and Court of First Instance. Finally it will end with a brief look at the other institutions.

However, before turning to these institutions it is necessary to consider a body which may be regarded as the supreme political authority of the Community—the European Council.

THE EUROPEAN COUNCIL

In 1974, in Paris, it was agreed at a meeting of Community leaders to hold regular meetings at the highest political level within what became known as a "European Council". This European Council met regularly on an informal basis, until it was given a legal basis by Article 2 of the Single European Act. Article 2 has now been replaced by Article 4 of the Treaty on European Union (TEU) which provides:

"The European Council shall bring together the heads of state of government of the Member States and the President of the Commission. They shall be assisted by the minister of foreign affairs of the Member States and by a member of the Commission. The European Council shall meet at least twice a year, under the leadership of the head of state or of government of the member state which holds the presidency of the Council."

It is these twice yearly meetings or summits which are most widely reported by the media. Article 4 of the TEU further provides that the task of the European Council is to "provide the Union with the necessary impetus for its development". Article 4 continues with the statement that the European Council "shall define the general political guidelines thereof". The European Council also has responsibility for defining the principles of, and general guidelines for, the common foreign and security policy under Title "V" of the TEU, and it has a supervisory role in Community progress towards economic and monetary union. The European Council plays no part in the formal legislative machinery of the Community, but its role, which has become increasingly significant over the years, is an important one. It is essentially a political role. The importance of the European Council, in the progress of the Community, cannot be over estimated. It was out of the meetings and deliberations of the European Council that grew the foundations of the European monetary system and the move towards monetary union.

It might be thought that the existence of the European Council has a distorting effect on the institutional balance of the Community. After all it was not considered by the original Treaty, and it might have been thought that the task of leading the Community belonged to the Commission. This has not been the case, and to this extent, the existence of the European Council represents a triumph of the individual Member States over the collegiality of the Commission. But it can also be said that cooperation between the European Council and the Commission has achieved some real objectives. The most obvious example is the implementation of the 1992 programme on completing the internal market, which required close political support from successive European Councils.

THE EUROPEAN PARLIAMENT

Article 189 [ex 137] EC provides that the Parliament:

"shall consist of representatives of the people of the states brought together in the Community, (and) shall exercise the powers conferred upon it by this Treaty."

The original body set up by the Treaty of Rome was called the Assembly and consisted of members nominated by the governments of Member States. Even now it cannot be considered a parliament in the sense that one understands most European parliaments. It consists of only one chamber and the head of state is not a member of the parliament. Nevertheless, from its early days the assembly was termed the Parliament and this name was legitimised in the Single European Act.

As long ago as 1960 proposals were made for direct elections, but it was not until the 1979 election that Members of the European Parliament (MEP) were elected by direct universal suffrage.

The MEPs are now elected for a fixed five year term and elections take place in years ending with a four and nine (example 1999 and 2004). Article 190(4) [ex 138(3)] of the EC Treaty called for a uniform voting procedure, but this has not yet been achieved. Initially, this was because of the United Kingdom's reluctance to abandon its "first past the post" system. Up to the 1994 election the other Member States used varieties of proportional representation and the United Kingdom adopted its domestic system (which included proportional representation for Northern Ireland). However, for the 1999 elections, the UK Government introduced a system of proportional representation called the closed list system. The country was divided up into 12 large constituencies, with multiple seats, returning a total of 87 MEPs. For mainland United Kingdom the voting was purely on the basis of a prescribed list. In Northern Ireland voters had a single transferable vote, which could be given to a named candidate of their choice. So, in the 1999 election, for the first time, all the Member States used a form of proportional representation.

One of the much-discussed aspects of the European elections has been the voter turnout. Traditionally, it has always been much lower than for national elections. This is probably not surprising given that a national election will decide the "colour" of the next government, it will provide an opportunity for the opposition to make a real challenge to the sitting government and it will receive massive publicity in all the media. There will also be many issues that will be important to individual voters. Most of these elements are missing from the EU system. The media shows little interest and no group or individual is brought to power as a result of the European elections.

This lack of immediacy may explain the low voter turnout. In 1979 (the first direct election) the voter turnout was 62 per cent of those eligible to vote. This is the highest turnout in any election for the European Parliament. In 1999 the turnout was 50 per cent. In Belgium and Luxembourg, where voting is obligatory, the turnout was about 90 per cent. The United Kingdom had, and has the lowest turnout, declining from 33 per cent in 1979 to less than 25 per cent in 1999.

Before 1994 there were 518 seats in Parliament and the four largest Member States (Germany, France, Italy and the United Kingdom) had 81 each. The basic idea is that the number of seats for each Member State is broadly representative of national populations. But it is easy to see that the smaller Member States are over-represented. For example, the population of the United Kingdom is over 150 times that of Luxembourg, but the United Kingdom has only 15 times the number of seats. This is an example of the primacy of national interests over normal democratic principles.

The reunification of Germany in 1991 meant that the increase in the German electorate could no longer justify the existing allocation of seats. Germany was given an increase in seats to 99. At the same time it was decided to increase the allocation of seats for the other "big three", France, Italy and the United Kingdom, to 87 seats each.

Treaty of Nice Reforms

Looking ahead to the enlargement of the Union, the Treaty of Nice extended the number of MEPs to a maximum of 732 and reallocated seats between Member States and candidate countries, with effect from the next elections in 2004. This means that the limit of 700 agreed in the Treaty of Amsterdam has been exceeded even before it was put into practice. It also means that both recently built parliament buildings in Brussels and Strasbourg will be too small for the total number of MEPs. The candidate countries will not, of course, be represented in the European Parliament until they become members. The allocation of seats at present and from 2004 (as set out in revised Article 190(2)) is as follows:

Country	Current Seats	From 2004
Austria	21	17
Belgium	25	22
Denmark	16	13
Finland	16	13
France	87	72
Germany	99	99
Greece	25	22
Ireland	15	12
Italy	87	72
Luxembourg	6	6
Netherlands	31	25
Portugal	25	22
Spain	64	50
Sweden	22	18
UK	87	72
Cyprus		6
Czech Republic		20
Estonia		6
Hungary		8
Lithuania		12
Malta		5
Poland		50
Slovakia		13
Slovenia		7
Bulgaria		17
Rumania		33
TOTAL	626	723

It should be remembered that Bulgaria and Romania are not expected to join the Union until 2007 at the earliest. All the other candidate countries will need to have signed their accession treaties by January 1, 2004 in order to participate in the elections. Even if all candidate countries do not manage to complete their accession, the European Parliament of 2004–2009 will still have 732 MEPs. If a candidate country (such as Bulgaria or Romania does not manage to complete their accession negotiations on time, their seats will be divided up between the actual Member States.

These figures look like a good result for Germany and Luxembourg, who have an unchanged number of MEPs. But the new allocation breaks the convention that representation in the Parliament should be broadly proportionate to the size of population. For example, the Czech Republic, which has a larger population than Portugal or Belgium, will have fewer seats than those two countries. The population of Hungary is greater than that of Portugal yet Hungary will have fewer MEPs than Portugal.

MEPs can be a member of their own national parliament. Although this has not happened in the United Kingdom since the introduction of direct elections, it is not uncommon amongst continental Member States. An MEP is paid the same as a member of the national parliament and is subject to the same taxes as a national of that Member State. There are therefore big differences in the salaries of MEPs, with German MEPs at the top of the pay scale and (until their large and controversial increase in 1996) UK MEPs at the bottom. In addition to their salaries the MEPs are allowed what can amount to large expenses, and these are not subject to tax.

Members sit in cross-national political groupings and not as national deputies. This is because the Rules of Procedure provide for the official recognition of political groups. Thus the appointment to parliamentary committees, speaking time and the dispersement of funding is on a political basis. Up until the 1999 election, the largest of the political groups was the European Socialist Group, to which the UK Labour MEPs belonged. Conservative MEPs had joined the European People's Party, which despite its unlikely title was made up mainly of Christian Democrats from Germany.

However, the 1999 election swept the left wing parties out of the ascendancy and returned many candidates of right of centre parties. The European People's Party (201 MEPs) and other groups of similar political persuasion ensured a right of centre majority. This shift from left to right might not be as important as a similar shift in a national parliament. It might be that concerns for domestic interests cut across any European ideology. Another reason is that much of the legislation that comes before the European Parliament is highly technical, thus ideology is not required. There is also the important reason that under the co-decision procedure an absolute majority of votes in the European Parliament is required. As all MEPs do not always vote, it is often necessary for the two major groups to combine to ensure that legislation is passed.

By Article 190 [ex 142] EC the Parliament adopts its own rules of procedure and through these rules it elects its own President, in a secret ballot by an absolute majority of the votes cast. The

President is elected for two-and-a-half years and like the Speaker in the UK House of Commons chairs proceedings in plenary session. The President also represents Parliament at ceremonial occasions. The President is assisted by 14 vice-presidents and these (together with five non-voting MEPs called Quaestors) form The Bureau. This Bureau has a number of administrative and financial functions including the composition of the secretariat, and the selection of membership of committees. There is also an enlarged Bureau made up of the President, vice-presidents and chairs of the 20 parliamentary committees. It is this enlarged Bureau that is consulted by the Council on the appointment of the President of the Commission, and which sets the agenda for plenary sessions.

A major feature of the Parliament is the work of committees. The use of the committee structure has helped Parliament maximise its effectiveness, because a range of political views are represented in each committee and individual committees are responsible for preparing amendments to legislative proposals. In this matter it is also helped by the agreement between the Parliament and the Commission that the latter will publish each year a legislative programme. Parliament can also take the initiative itself by making suggestions to the Commission for proposed legislation. It was a parliamentary committee that prepared the original draft of what became the Treaty on European Union.

A major problem and one which must hinder the work of the Parliament is the question of its geographical location. Because of an agreement between the Member States the plenary sessions of Parliament, of which there are eleven a year and which last a week, are held in Strasbourg. The secretariat and most of the staff are in Luxembourg and committee meetings are held in Brussels. It cannot be efficient to have MEPs, officials and lorry-loads of documents travelling up and down the airways and roads of Europe, but the three Member States involved are unwilling to agree to single seat for the Parliament. The Parliament itself would pref to be based in Brussels, and has even commissioned the buildi of a new assembly there. The new Parliament building opened Brussels in February 1998. It has offices for 700 MEPs. It will used for six one-day meetings a year. A similar building Strasbourg opened in July 1999. The current Parliament buildin Strasbourg was built as long ago as 1979!

However, in *France v European Parliament* (Cases 358/85 51/86) and in *Luxembourg v European Parliament* (Case 230/8 and more lately in *Luxembourg v European Parliament* (Cas C-213/88 & C-39/98) the European Court of Justice, althou accepting that the European Parliament did not act outside i discretion when it commissioned its new building, neverthele upheld the rights of the Member States to retain some function of the Parliament in the home country.

Powers of the Parliament

The powers of Parliament fit broadly into three categories:

(a) a degree of political control over the Commission. (see further discussion under "Commission")

(b) an increasingly important role in the adoption of Community legislation. (see "Legislation")

(c) budgetary powers.

In this important area of budgets the Parliament shares power with the Commission and the Council. However the Parliament has ultimate power to reject the budget which it has done on two occasions, in 1979 and 1984 causing a temporary financial paralysis.

In its initial form as the Assembly, Parliament had few powers and those few it did have were mainly advisory and consultative (see Article 137 of the EEC Treaty). The original Treaty of Rome specified only 17 instances when Parliament needed to be consulted. For legislation passed under the authority of some Treaty Articles, *e.g.* Articles 54 and 235 it was a requirement that the Parliament be consulted before a decision could be adopted by the Council.

In recognition of the more democratic nature of the Parliament, following the direct election in 1979, Parliament was granted increased powers in the Single European Act 1986. Articles 6 and 7 of the SEA provided for a "cooperation procedure" applicable in certain instances. This procedure is now governed by Article 252 [ex 189c]. Although this new procedure increased to some extent the power of the Parliament, its legislative role was still limited. This has given rise to the term "a democratic deficit". Partly to address this deficit, and partly to address the demands of an increasingly confident Parliament, the Treaty on European Union introduced the "co-decision procedure" in Article 251 [ex 189b] (these various procedures are discussed in the chapter on legislation. See Chapter 2).

THE COUNCIL

The Treaty of Rome and the TEU refer to "The Council". As soon as the TEU entered into force it renamed itself "The Council of the European Union", but it is more commonly known as the

"Council of Ministers". The Council is the main legislative organ of the Communities and it is within that body that the interests of the Member States find direct expression. The composition of the Council is outlined in Article 203 [ex 146] EC, as amended. Article 203 [ex 146] says that:

"The Council shall consist of a representative of each Member State at ministerial level, authorised to commit the government of that Member State."

Therefore the composition of the Council is not static but is made up of the representative minister of the Member State, depending on the subject matter under discussion. For General Council meetings the Member State representative is generally the foreign minister, while, for example, agricultural or finance meetings, the representative would be the agriculture or finance minister.

By Article 202 [ex 145] the Council of Ministers has a duty to ensure the co-ordination of the general economic policies of the Member States, and it has the power to take decisions and to delegate tasks to the Commission. As mentioned above, the Council has the final power of decision making for the adoption of legislation proposed by the Commission. However, depending upon the authority of the Treaty Article, it may have to consult with the Parliament and the Economic and Social Committee, or may have to adopt the co-operation or the co-decision procedures. (See discussion under "legislation").

The Council is based in Brussels where meetings are held in private and no record of the proceedings is published. The Commission is always represented at a Council meeting, although without a vote. The presidency of the Council rotates among the Member States at six-monthly intervals, commencing in January and July. The function of the President is to call meetings, to preside at them and to chair the meetings. In recent years the presidency has become increasingly important, particularly as the President sets the agenda for his six-month term. Member States are seen to be in "competition" with each other in order to achieve both maximum progress and maximum publicity for their President during his term of office.

Decisions in the Council are made by voting. The voting procedure is governed by Article 205 [ex 148], which states in para.1 that unless specified otherwise decisions are taken by simple majority. In a few very important areas the Treaty requires unanimity. Both these methods of voting are now relatively rare and the majority of votes are taken under what is called the "qualified majority voting" procedure. Qualified majority voting (QMV) gives a "weight" to the vote of each Member State.

Treaty of Nice Reforms

As previously discussed (see Chapter 1) the Treaty provides that the Council; shall extend QMV to a small number of areas. Although this extension is to be welcomed, it is disappointing that in only six areas was the extension of QMV matched by the commensurate extension of co-decision with the European Parliament.

Article 205(2) has been revised to show the new voting weightings that will take effect after enlargement. The current allocation of votes and the revised figures is shown below:

	Current voting "weight"	After 01/01/2005
Austria	4	10
Belgium	5	12
Denmark	3	7
Finland	3	7
France	10	29
Germany	10	29
Greece	5	12
Ireland	3	7
Italy	10	29
Luxembourg	2	4
Netherlands	5	13
Portugal	5	12
Spain	8	27
Sweden	4	10
UK	10	29
Cyprus		10
Czech Republic		12
Estonia		4
Hungary		12
Latvia		4
Lithuania		7
Malta		3
Poland		27
Slovakia		7
Slovenia		4
Bulgaria		10
Romania		14

Since January 1995 the number of votes needed for a qualified majority was 62, with a "blocking minority" vote of 26. The UK Government did not agree with the raising of this blocking minority and wished to keep it at 23, the figure it had been at prior to 1995. Eventually a compromise was worked out whereby if members of the Council representing a total of 23 to 25 votes indicated that they intended to oppose the adoption of an act by qualified majority, then a reasonable time should lapse in order to see if an agreement could be found before the new blocking minority (*i.e.* 26) was actually used. There is no evidence yet as to how this compromise has worked.

The new threshold for a qualified majority on a Commission proposal will be 169 votes out of a total of 237. In the enlarged Union, the threshold for a qualified majority in the Council on a Commission proposal will be 258 votes out of a total of 345. This moves the long-standing threshold from 71.3 per cent to a threshold of 74.8 per cent. In addition, there is an important change made to the Council's voting system, the effect of which is to weigh the balance of power very heavily in favour of the bigger Member States. In addition to the "raw" votes, as set out above, any Member State will be able to demand verification that the qualified majority represents at least 62 per cent of the total population of the EU. If this is found not to be the case, the decision will not be adopted. This compares with the current informal figure where only 58 per cent is required.

Although qualified majority voting is now almost the norm, this was not always so. When qualified majority voting was introduced in 1965, it gave rise to the political crisis known as the Luxembourg compromise (see discussion earlier). It will be recalled that the crisis was precipitated by the absence of the French from the Council meetings and the compromise provided that when majority voting applied to a topic which concerned important interests of state, then Member States should attempt to reach a unanimous solution, and that discussion should continue until such unanimity had been achieved. This led to a period of stagnation in the development of the Community which was eventually addressed by the Single European Act. The Act introduced a new Article 100a (now 95) which provided for qualified majority on any proposal which had as its object the establishment and functioning of the internal market. Whether the Luxembourg agreement has been abolished is not clear since it never formally existed in legal terms but it would seem that the present climate, particularly after the passing of the TEU would render it less likely that Member States would attempt to use any explicit veto power.

As we have seen, the Council is made up of ministers from the various Member States. These ministers also change depending on the discussions in the Council meetings. Therefore, the Council is not static. In the event of serious conflict between Member States the Council can ask for assistance from the European Council. However, as the Council is not a permanent body, and in order to assist it in its work, the Committee of Permanent Representatives was established, consisting of representatives of the Member States who are usually part of the ambassadorial delegation, or civil servants on secondment. This body is usually known by its French acronym of COREPER. The legal basis for this body is set out in Article 207 [ex 151]. To assist it in carrying out its tasks COREPER has set up numerous working parties and committees. COREPER is divided into two bodies, one which discusses technical matters (COREPER 1 composed of deputy permanent representatives) and one which deals with more political issues (COREPER 2 composed of the permanent representatives themselves). It is COREPER which provides the element of continuity to the activities of the Council. It reviews all the Commissions proposals before these proposals reach Council meetings. Naturally, to do this properly it is engaged in a process of liaison with the Commission. COREPER decides whether agenda items will be placed on either agenda A or agenda B. Items under agenda A will have already be agreed by the various members of COREPER and the formal Council meeting will merely "rubber stamp" these proposals. Items on agenda B will be those where there is still some disagreement amongst COREPER and which will need to be decided in the formal Council meeting. Nevertheless the work of the Council is speeded up by this process. The existence and increasing importance, of COREPER can be seen as a sign of the predominant power of the Council which was not intended by the original treaties.

As a result of the changes in the TEU, the competence of the Council has been extended to foreign policy, political co-operation, and to the areas of justice, home affairs and immigration. It is too soon to see what effect this will have on the Community.

THE COMMISSION

Introduction

The Commission is often described as the civil service, or bureaucracy, of the EU. This is not entirely correct. One of its functions is to act as an executive of the Community, but it does much more. It does carry out Community policies and decisions, but this is only one of its roles. It is the Community body that proposes legislation, and it plays a major role in the shaping of that legislation. In some areas, (*e.g.* Article 86 [ex 90] on state aid and Article 81 [ex 85] on competition law), it has its own delegated processes to enact binding measures. The Commission is also the body that acts as "guardian of the treaties". By Article 226 [ex 169] it is empowered to act against Member States, undertaking and individuals who, the Commission believe, is not carrying out duties under the treaties, or secondary legislation. It also acts against Member States and other bodies who it believes is acting contrary to Community law.

In reality the Commission has no analogy in national government systems. It is part government, part executive and possesses some of the characteristics of a parliament. In the power balance within the Community, the Commission represents the supranational counter-weight to the inter-governmental tendencies of the Council. The Commission lies at the very heart of the Community.

The Commission has not had a good press! It is seen as greedy for power, remote from the people and unaccountable and corrupt. In the United Kingdom in particular, it is blamed for the proliferation of unnecessary rules: the banning of paper boys, rules on straight bananas and a prohibition of electric lawnmowers. These are so-called Euro "myths". So far as corruption is concerned, it would seem that the sceptics are correct. The Commission reached its lowest ebb in March 1999 when it resigned *en masse* in the face of charges of mismanagement and corruption. Even then the resignation was seen to be reluctant and, indeed, the Commission decided that in spite of its resignation, it could remain in power until the expiry of its natural term in September 1999. The new Commission has promised to reform itself and has given the task specifically to Neil Kinnock, the Vice-President of the Commission. It remains to be seen whether the Commission can regain the influential position it attained under the leadership of the charismatic Jacques Delors.

Composition and Structure

Composition

At the head of the Commission stands the President. He (to date all the Presidents have been male) has a special position. The personality of the President counts for much. The President of the Commission, the "first among equals", sets the tone for the term of the Commission. The role of the President was first thrust into the limelight by Jacques Delors, who was President from 1985–1995, an unprecedented "reign". There were two contradictory views of Delors; some saw him as manipulative and arrogant, while others saw him as a powerful leader who achieved enormous prestige for the Community and for the Commission. Whatever one's view, it is undeniable that Delors had a profound effect on the office of President and on the position of the Commission in general. Delors built upon the right won by a previous president, Roy Jenkins (1977–1981) for the President to attend meeting of the European Council. Delors, with a firm grasp of economics and as a powerful orator, was able to assert the influence of the Commission on the European Council. He, for the same reasons, was also responsible for uplifting the Commission's influence on the wider European stage. His greatest triumph was as the architect of the single market. Delors and the Commission played a major role in the White Paper which led to the Single European Act 1986, which set out the programme for the journey to 1992, the date by which the single market would be achieved. It is to Delors credit that, to all intents and purposes, that goal was achieved.

The President of the Commission is nominated by the common accord of the Member States (Article 214(2) [ex 158(2)]. That nomination is then subject to the approval of the European Parliament. For the Commission that will be in place for the period January 1, 2000 to December 31, 2004 (the "Millennium Commission"), the Member States selected Romano Prodi, an ex-prime-minister of Italy. Prodi was seen as a powerful politician and a person untainted with corruption or nepotism. He has stated that one of his prime tasks will be a reform of the Commission, so that it is seen as a well managed organisation free of corruption.

For the remainder of the Commission, Article 214(2) sets out that the Member States, in consultation with the nominee for President, nominate the other persons who they intend to appoint as Commissioners. The total number of Commissioners is 20 (including the President) and, as is required by Article 214 they "shall be chosen on the grounds of their general competence and whose independence is beyond doubt". The term "general competence" has not been defined. However, in most cases Commissioners have been national politicians. There has also been the practice, particularly in the United Kingdom, of using the Commission as a "dustbin", either as a "thank you" to a politician who needs to make way for a promoted colleague, or as a "retiring place" for a failed domestic politician. In the United Kingdom there has also developed the convention that ensures that the two

"British Commissioners" are shared between the major political parties. The two Commissioners nominated by the United Kingdom for the period 1995–1999 illustrate both points. Sir Leon Brittain was a member of the Conservative Government of Mrs Thatcher. In 1993 he resigned over his alleged part in the Westland helicopter affair. He was appointed to the Commission in Brussels to neutralise any nuisance he might become to the UK Government. Neil Kinnock was the leader of the Labour Party until 1997. Despite initiating many reforms in the party he was unable to lead the Party to success in a general election and resigned from the leadership of the Labour Party after the election defeat in 1997. His "failure" was soon rewarded with his appointment as a Commissioner. In the event both these appointments were relatively successful.

There are signs that Member States are now allowing greater consideration to the person or persons they nominate. This may be because of the changes in the appointment procedures. When Jacques Santer was proposed as President of the Commission in June 1994 he addressed the European Parliament and answered questions put to him by the Parliament. The Parliament approved his nomination by a small majority. There was no legal force behind this vote. If Mr Santer had not been endorsed by the Parliament it is not certain what would have happened next. Probably, Mr Santer would have taken a negative vote as a sign of no confidence, but equally the Member States could have insisted on his appointment. These procedures were introduced by the Treaty on European Union and the Treaty of Amsterdam; they are now set out in Article 214 EC. The most important change in the nomination procedure is that the nominees for the Commission are subject as a body to a vote of approval by the European Parliament. The European Parliament takes this new power very seriously.

Likewise, when it came to the appointment of Commissioners, the European Parliament insisted on a role. All the nominated Commissioners appeared before the Parliament. All were questioned. It was clear that Parliament did not like, in particular, five of the nominations. However, under the Treaty, the power of Parliament is to reject the Commission as a whole; it has no power over individual Commissioners. To reject the whole Commission would have been a political act too far, and so, perhaps reluctantly, all the nominations were approved.

Structure

At present there are 20 Commissioners (Art 213 [ex 157(1)]). Although not laid down in the Treaty, it has become the accepted custom for the large Member States (Germany, France, Italy, Spain and the United Kingdom) to supply two Commissioners, while the remaining Member States supply one each. It is recognised that this number is the maximum that can work effectively. Prior to the Amsterdam Treaty, proposals were made to change the systems. It was particularly thought that large Member States should have only one Commissioner and the smaller Member States should nominate a lower number of Commissioners by rotation. One of the reasons for these proposals was the envisaged enlargement of the Community. A Commission with more than twenty Commissioners would become unwieldy and would not have enough "jobs" to go around. At the negotiations leading up to the Amsterdam Treaty there was no agreement on the subject and a decision was deferred. What was agreed was that, before enlargement, the Commission should be restricted to one national of each of the Member States and that the number of Commissioners should be capped at 20. This proposal (set out in a protocol attached to the Treaty of Amsterdam) is linked to a change in the weighting of qualified majority voting in the Council (see above). The changes were agreed at the Treaty of Nice.

The Treaty of Nice limits the Commission to one member per Member State with effect from 2005. A ceiling on the number of Commissioners will be imposed once the Union has 27 Member States. At that point the Council will have to take a unanimous decision on the exact number of Commissioners, which must be less than 27. The nationality of the Commissioners will then be determined by a system of rotation. There is no requirement for the Council to consult either the Commission or the European Parliament. The rotation system has yet to be devised but it will be "based on the principle of equality" and will reflect demography and geography.

After the governments of the Member States have nominated the Commission President, and the Parliament has approved the nomination, the Member States then go on to nominate, with the Commission President, the other proposed Commissioners. Once this body has been approved by the Parliament the Commission is appointed the joint agreement between the governments of the Member States [Article 158(2)]. As has been seen above, one of the qualifications required for nomination is "independence". The Commissioner who is appointed is no longer a "British" or a "French" Commissioner, but a "European" Commissioner. The Commissioner does not take instructions from their national government, but acts in a collegiate manner for what is best for Europe. This is the theory of how the Commission will operate but it is not possible in practice. Most of the Commissioners appointed in the last ten years have been, at one time or another, senior politicians in their own country. It would be to expect too much to suggest that as soon as they are appointed they should "throw off" the experience of national political service. Nor would this really be desirable. The Commissioners do bring with them a vast experience of the political system and the culture of their Member States. Thus they are in a position to know what is acceptable to "their" Member States and they will also have a bank of contacts "at home" who they can call on to help oil the wheels of negotiation. A Commissioner who does "forget" his or her nationality stands the risk of not being renominated by their government. A classic example is the British Commissioner, Lord Cockfield, who was appointed by Mrs Thatcher in 1985. Mrs Thatcher made little secret that Lord Cockfield had been appointed to safeguard British interests in the Community. In the event, Mrs Thatcher was disappointed and she refused to renominate Lord Cockfield on the grounds that he had "gone native".

Commissioners are appointed for a term of five years [Article 158(1)]. The term of office was recently (1995) increased from four –five years to fit in with the terms of appointment of the Member of the European Parliament. Once appointed, only death, resignation or compulsory retirement can remove a Commissioner before the end of the five-year term. The Commission can only be removed *en bloc*. This would happen if the European Parliament passed a motion of censure by a two-thirds majority of the votes cast. The European Parliament has never passed such a motion, although it might have done in March 1999, had not the Commission resigned *en bloc* in the face of the corruption scandal. In normal circumstances it is unlikely that the European Parliament would have the will to vote a motion of censure on the Commission. To do so would be an act of political challenge to the Member States who appoint the Commissioners. What the European Parliament would like is the power to challenge and vote a motion of censure on the Commission. If it had had this power in March 1999 it would almost certainly have used it against those Commissioners most deeply implicated in the scandals.

The Commission is divided into 24 administrative services. These are called Directorates General (DGs), which are themselves divided into Directorates, which are in turn subdivided into divisions. Each DG is responsible for an aspect of EU policy. For example, DG IV is responsible for competition policy, DG VII for transport policy and DG XXII for education, training and youth.

The size of each Directorate-General varies widely. Perhaps not surprisingly the largest is Directorate-General VI, dealing with agriculture. Each Directorate-General is headed by a Director General who is responsible to the Commissioner who has been appointed to the same portfolio by the President of the Commissioners. It is possible and it does happen in practice, for a Commissioner to have more than one portfolio, or for the responsibilities of a Directorate-General to be spread over the portfolio of more than one Commissioner. In some cases a Commissioner will not have a portfolio at all. In the Commission appointed for 2000–2005, Neil Kinnock, (who was Commissioner for Directorate-General VII, Transport in the previous administration) was made Vice-President and given the special role of reforming internal Commission practices.

The Commission employs a total of approximately 19,000 people. These employees staff the Directorate-General and the auxiliary services, such as the Secretariat-General, Legal Service and the Statistical and Publications Office. About 4,000 of the employees are interpreters, working in one of the 11 official languages. A total work force of 19,000 might seem a huge bureaucracy. Yet this number represents 0.9 per 10,000 of population which is considerably better than the figures for corresponding individual UK government departments.

The Amsterdam Treaty gives the President of the Commission the right to allocate portfolios to individual Commissioners. Nevertheless this does not stop national governments fighting for important portfolios for "their" Commissioners. This leads to the suspicion that Commissioners may not be "completely independent in the performance of their duties". Various committees and reports over the years have suggested ways to avoid the spectacle of too many Commissioners chasing the important portfolios. Most of the recommendations have been to reduce the number of Commissioners, to at least one per Member State. But as noted above, none of the recommendations have been acted on. What can be said is that national sensitivities have ensured that a rough "quota system" applies, at least for the important portfolios. The Treaty of Nice also increased the power of the president of the Commission. Under the revised Article 217 EC the President will decide on the allocation of portfolios and may reassign responsibilities in the course of a Commissioner's term of office, albeit with the approval of the other members of the Commission.

Each Commissioner has a personal staff, the *cabinet*. A *cabinet* consists of staff personally appointed by the Commissioner. These are political and administrative advisers whose job it is to brief the Commissioner about their individual portfolio and about the activities of the Commission as a whole. They also speak on behalf of their Commissioners in meetings. As many of the Directorate-General portfolios overlap, an important aspect of the *cabinet's* job is to co-ordinate and liase between the two or more Directorate-General's, other EC institutions and the home Member States. The appointment of personal to *cabinets* has been the subject of some controversy, particularly the practice of "parachuting-in" national civil servants and advisors into senior positions, often over career members of the Commission. Although this might appear unfair, it is a reflection on practical reality. As in national politics, a person appointed to an important governmental position will want to bring with them advisers on whose advice they can trust and rely. The role of the *Chef de Cabinet* has grown in importance. It has become institutionalised to the extent that a meeting of *Chef de Cabinet* takes place before every meeting of Commissioners.

The Commissioners meet every Wednesday. The meetings are in Brussels except for the one week each month when the European Parliament is in plenary session, when the meeting is in Strasbourg. At the weekly meetings of the College of Commissioners, decisions are taken on important matters. These will include initiatives and proposals to go before the Council of Ministers. As is the collegiate nature of the Commission, an attempt will be made at unanimity. But if this is not possible a resolution will be passed by a majority vote. The proposals that are discussed at the weekly meeting have passed through a hierarchical structure of some complexity.

An initial proposal will have been drawn up at middle ranking level, often with the help of outside assistance. The proposal will pass upwards through the Directorate-General, to the *cabinet* and to the weekly meeting of the *chef de cabinet*. Along the way, the initial proposal may be changed many times. There may also be the necessity to consult with other Directorates-General. For example, a draft proposal on the environment, made by Directorate-General XI may have implications for Directorate-General III, Industry or Directorate-General VI, Agriculture. At each stage of the process, if all individual interests reach agreement, the College of Commissioners will have delegated their authority to take decision on their behalf. On this basis, only the most important and controversial matters come up for discussion and decision at the meeting of Commissioners.

Functions and Powers

The functions and powers of the Commissioner are set out in Article 211 [ex155]. However, as will be shown, the Commission has taken on a number of other functions and powers. This has arisen out of political necessity. Most of the newspapers in the United Kingdom present the Commission as the bureaucracy of Europe, or at best, the Community Executive. Certainly, if has some of the powers of an Executive, but it does not possess other powers normally associated with an Executive. A reading of Article 211[155] reveals most of, but not all, its powers:

In order to ensure the proper functioning and development of the Common Market, the Commission shall:

- ensure that the provisions of this Treaty and the measures taken by the institutions pursuant thereto are applied;
- formulate recommendations or deliver opinions on matters dealt with in this Treaty, if it expressly so provides or if the Commission considers it necessary;
- have its own powers of decision and participate in the shaping of measures taken by the Council and the European Parliament in the manner provided for in this Treaty;
- exercise the powers conferred on it by the Council for the implementation of the rules laid down by the latter.

In addition to these powers the Commissioner exercised a judicial function in competition law matters. It also acts as a representative of the Community in international agreements, it has responsibility for the Community budget and has taken on many administrative duties. In practical terms the Commission's role can be split into three different areas.

Initiator of Community Policies and Legislation

It is a well-rehearsed saying that "the Commission proposes and the Council disposes". Article 211 [ex 155] states that the Commission "shall formulate recommendations or deliver opinions on matters dealt with in this Treaty, if it expressly so provides or the Commission considers it necessary". Thus, the Commission is given the task of advancing the development of the Community. It is the exclusive right of the Commission to propose legislation: a right it guards jealously. This right may now be the subject of a challenge from the European Parliament but the Commission can still claim to be the only initiator of legislation. The Commission has also gained a joint role with the European Parliament in the Common Foreign and Security policy pillar of the TEU. This may be surprising given that the CFSP pillar is intergovernmental in nature rather than supranational.

Normally, the Council or the Parliament will ask the Commission to initiate a piece of legislation. However, the initiative can, and often does, come from the Commission itself. Suggestions can also come from the Committee of the Regions or the Economic and Social Committee. It would be wrong to think that the Commission acts in isolation. Since the SEA the Commission has 'joined forces' with the EP and each year a joint legislative programme is announced. Arising out of this co-operation is an increased dialogue between the two institutions. And since the early 1990s the Council has participated in the negotiations. The intention of this tripartite planning is to programme legislation so that the Community will operate more effectively.

The proposed legislation starts somewhere in the Commission bureaucracy. There will often be an internal committee, made up of officials of two or more DGs, to ensure co-ordination between the departments. There will be much informal co-ordination and co-operation by officials of all levels and between commissioners and members of their *cabinets*.

Once the Commission's proposal has been agreed "in house" it is sent to the Council, to follow the legislation route as set out in the Treaty (see Chapter 2). But this is by no means the end of the matter for the Commission. The Commission will have a representative at all of the various decision-making stages. This will start with one of the Council's working groups, go on to COREPER until it finally ends with a meeting of the Council itself. Thus, in effect there is a system of negotiation at each stage. The Commission will know the views of individual Member States and will know what will not be acceptable to them and what could be the subject of compromise. The trump card for the Commission is that they can threaten to withdraw the proposal. During the legislation stage the Commission will be talking to the officials of individual Member States in the Council, in an attempt to put that Member State with another to ensure that there will be enough states in favour to form the necessary qualified majority. Obviously, the task of the Commission is much harder where a proposal requires unanimity. The Commission has a strong hand in that the Council can only request the Commission to change its proposal if it (the Council) acts unanimously. The Commission has rejected suggestions made by the Council that the Council should be able to change Commission proposals by qualified majority.

For an efficient legislative programme it is important that there is a good working relationship between the Commission and the Council. To this end, at the start of each Council presidency (every six months), the College of Commissioners and the President's team meet for a day for a full discussion. The purpose of the discussions is to complement, as far as is possible, the legislative aims of the two bodies. Throughout the presidency, Commission officials will be in contact with the Council in order to anticipate and prevent problems in policy making.

Executive Agency of EC

The Commission has a large role to play in the management and implementation of Community policies. In some areas it has a heavy involvement. For example, in competition law it will be involved in watching developments between undertakings, it will carry out investigations, and will be able to rule on agreements made between undertakings. As a last resort, it is able to levy fines on recalcitrant undertakings and bring them before the CFI.

One of the Commission's most important functions as the executive agency of the Community is its rule making powers. It is not possible for the Treaty, or legislation flowing from the Treaty, to cover all conceivable areas and every eventuality. To "fill in the gaps" the Commission is given delegated law making powers. This power of delegated rule making is essential for areas of administrative and technical law. It is especially necessary in order to regulate the changing needs of the Common Agricultural Policy.

In recent years there has been a reduction in the number of legislative measures issued by the Commission. In 1998 it issued 773 regulations, 44 directives and 537 decisions. These numbers can be compared with the 4,000 measures that were the norm in the eighties and early nineties. Generally speaking the role of the Commission is that of filling in the details. Most of the regulations and decisions of 1998, and of earlier years, deal with price regulations and market support measures under the Common Agricultural Policy.

Another major task for the Commission is the management of the Community budget. The Council and the EP decide on the limits of the budget and they take the basic framework decisions. The task of the Commissions is the day to day running of the budget. On the income side it is the duty of the Commission to see that the correct rates of duty are applied within the various categories. Then it has to ensure that the correct payment is made to the Community by the appropriate national authorities. When it comes to dispensing funds, the Commission has the task of operating within the approved budget. By far the largest slice of the Community budget (about 45 per cent) is taken up by agricultural prize support for the CAP. The next largest part of the budget is given up to the structural funds. These are the European Regional Development Fund (ERDF) and the European Social Fund (ESF). The amounts of these funds have increased dramatically since the SEA and by 1993 they accounted for 25 per cent of the budget. One of rules for the operation of the funds is additionality. That is that any money granted by the Community is to be in addition to monies granted by national authorities. Thus a programme or project will be cofinanced. This means that the Commission has to manage a project in conjunction with the relevant national authority. Usually the Commission delegates its decision making in this area to one of the management committees.

This has led to complaints about the system. On the one hand there are those who see decision by committee as being one of the weaknesses of the system of monitoring and controlling spending. This was one of the factors that led to the resignation of the Santer Commission. On the other hand, critics argue that the power of the Commission to control the committees means that the Commission can ignore unfavourable decisions. Yet another criticism is that the committees are under the real control of the Council.

"Comitology"

In many areas of Community policy, legislation passed by the Council will need to be implemented. The Treaty provides that the Council can delegate powers of implementation to the Commission. This is set out in Article 202 [ex 145] which provides that the Council shall "confer on the Commission . . . powers for the implementation of the rules which the Council lays down". The corresponding duty on the Commission to exercise these powers is set out in Article 211 [ex 155].

At this stage, some explanation needs to be given to role of committees and the system known as "comitology". The comitology procedure is a complicated process of various types of committee. It is a method of implementing legislation whereby committees, chaired by an official of the Commission but consisting of representatives of Member States assist the Commission in implementing legislation. The system of comitology was evolved to limit the executive powers of the Commission. Far from having a free hand in the implementation of legislation and in the exercise of its executive powers, the Commission must take account of various management and regulatory committees. It has been said that comitology is "possibly one of the most significant organic developments in the EU's institutional structure".

By the middle of the 1980s the role of committees in the implementation process had become so complicated that reform was essential. Before 1986 comitology had no legal basis. The Single European Act gave it a legal base in Article 201 [ex 145]. The Single European Act 1986 provided for a reform of the committee system and this reform was implemented by a Council Decision, known as the "Comitology Decision" of July 13, 1987 (87/373 [1987] O.J. L197/33). Although no new procedures were introduced, the existing procedures were (comparatively) clarified. Also, some new guidelines were set out indicating which procedures should apply in individual circumstances.

There are three types of committee; advisory, management and regulatory. Each of the committees is chaired by a Commission official but is composed of national civil servants or experts, appointed by national governments. The type of committee to be used is specified in the enabling legislation.

The advisory committee can only advise. The procedure is that the Commission submits a draft of the measures to be taken to the committee. The committee then delivers an opinion on the proposal. If it cannot reach agreement, the committee can submit a report that has the approval of a simple majority. All that is required of the Commission is that it takes the "utmost account" of the committee's opinion.

In the main, there are two types of advisory committee; an expert committee and a consultative committee. An expert committee will be made up of experts and specialists, nominated by national government, and some national civil servants. As might be expected they provide helpful technical advice on proposals for legislation. These committees are especially useful in that some of the national civil servants may also sit on Council working groups. They will be able to provide the Council with the rationale for many of the proposals.

On the other hand, a consultative committee is made up of representatives of interest groups, trade or professional associations (of which there are many in Brussels), nominated by the commission. The purpose of a consultative committee is to keep the Commission up to date with the 'real' work of commerce and business. Both the expert committee and the consultative committee will be keen to exert influence on the shape and context of the proposed legislation. So will many "lobbyists" of which it is estimated there are about 10,000 in Brussels.

It may be that the implementing legislation requires the engagement of a management committee. This type of committee can block a Commission proposal. The Commission must submit its proposal to the management committee. If the committee approves the proposal the proposal can proceed. However, if the proposal is opposed by a qualified majority in the committee, the matter is effectively blocked for either one month or three months. During these times the Council may take a different decision by qualified majority vote.

The most important type of committee is the regulatory committee. If the engagement of such a committee is required, the Commission will, once again, submit its proposal. The Regulatory committee can approve the proposal by qualified majority. If it cannot reach such an agreement, or it fails to deliver an opinion, the matter is referred to the Council. The Council then has three months to take a decision on the Commission's proposal. Such a decision is by qualified majority. If the Council does not act within the three months period, there are two possibilities, depending on the implementing legislation. Either the Commission can adapt the proposal or the Commission can adapt the proposal provided that the Council does not, by a simple majority, oppose it.

In addition to the use of the three types of committees, the Council also introduced in 1987 a "safeguard clause". If the safeguard clause is invoked, no committee is formed but the Commission must notify the Member States of the proposal. If the Member State does not like the proposal it can refer it to the Council, who can, in a number of variations, reject the proposal or take a different decision.

If comitology is difficult to follow, the system in practice is even more complicated. In some cases, in the same meeting, a group of experts will be sitting on one question as an advisory committee and on another question as a regulatory committee. It has been estimated that there have been over 1,400 different committees and at present there are about two hundred. The number of comitology committees gives rise to one of the most frequent complaints about the system. It is far too difficult to understand. The system is also criticised by the European Parliament on the grounds that there is a lack of transparency as a result of the number of committees and the number of procedures. The European Parliament also believes that the use of comitology gives the Council the ability to scrutinise the powers of the executive, a task, which the European Parliament believes, is their prerogative.

Despite the complicated nature of comitology, it has been said that disputes between the Commission and the Council over the appropriate procedure are more ritualistic than real. Nevertheless, even theoretical discussions about the procedure to use do slow down the legislative process.

The European Parliament has taken a keen interest in comitology. After the 1987 Council Decision, the European Parliament challenged the validity of the Decision before the ECJ. In *European Parliament v Council (Comitology)* (302/87) the ECJ dismissed the challenge on the procedural point that the Parliament did not have standing to bring the case (although it later reversed this ruling in *European Parliament v Council (Chernobyl)* (C-70/88). After the TEU this interest became even stronger. This was because the TEU gave the European Parliament the power of co-decision (see Chapter 2 with the Council (Article 251 [ex 189b]). The European Parliament now saw comitology as a device to be used by the Council to limit the co-decision rights of the European Parliament. The basic argument of the European Parliament was that comitology disturbs the equality between the Council and itself on matters decided by the co-decision procedure. Because of this disagreement there was much discussion between the European Parliament, the Council and the Commission. Eventually, the comitology procedures were further refined by a Council Decision of June 1999 (1999/468 [1999] O.J. L184/23). This new Decision simplified the various comitology procedures and, recognising the concerns of the European Parliament, it provided for more information to be made available to the Parliament. It was also intended that the system should become more transparent, but given the complicated and complex system in operation, even after simplification, this desire is some way from fulfilment.

"Guardian of the Treaty"

This is the grandiloquent name often given to the Commission. As "guardian" the Commission has two functions. The first is that the Commission may use its powers to compel Member States to make those states meet their Treaty obligations. It also has the power to ensure that other Community institutions, as well as natural and legal persons, comply with Treaty obligations. The procedure by which the Commission enforces Community law in Member States, other institutions and on natural and legal persons is set out in Article 226 [ex169]. It will be noted that the final procedural act in Article 226 [ex169] is to bring the matter before the ECJ. Thus the Commission is joined with the Court of Justice in ensuring that the Treaty is enforced. The procedure under Article 226 is discussed in full in Chapter 7.

Conclusion

One of the former Commissioners has written that the rule of the Commission is 'to represent the general interest in the welter of national ones and to point the way ahead, but also drawing the attention of Member States to new and more daring possibilities". If this represents the ideal of the Commission role, it is interesting to judge how successful, or otherwise the Commission has been.

On the negative side is the often-asserted observation that the power of the Council has declined since the 1960s. There was some merit in this claim, at least until the mid 1980s. The original aim of the Treaty of Rome that the Commission should be the most powerful institution has not materialised. The political interests of the Member States have ensured that politics have outweighed the legal structure of the Community. The emergence and growth of the European Council upset the delicate power balance between the institutions. The scales of power are now set firmly on the side of inter-governmentalism. The European Council to a large extent now sets the agenda for Community development. The ability of the European Council to shape the future of the Community has removed much of the power of initiative from the Commission.

Those in the Commission who see power in the EU as a zero-sum game will also regard the influence and growth of power of the European Parliament as a negative factor. Since the SEA 1986, the legislative power of the European Parliament has been incrementally increased (mainly by an extension of the co-decision procedure). This has given the European Parliament more influence with the Council of Ministers. There has also been a growth in the accountability off the Commission towards the European Parliament. Since the Treaty of Rome it has been possible for the European Parliament to sack the entire Commission (by a two-third's majority). Although this has never happened, it has been threatened on a number of occasions. The last threat to sack the Commission was in January 1999. The threat arose out of parliamentary criticisms of mismanagement on the part of some individual commissioners. There were also accusations of corruption and nepotism. Although it was unlikely that the European Parliament could have secured the full two-third's majority needed to vote out the Commission, the Commission, in March 1999, felt pressurised to resign, nine months before the end of its scheduled term of office.

The revisions made to the Treaty during the negotiations at Maastricht that led to the Treaty on European Union also formalised the degree of control enjoyed by the European Parliament over the Commission. Since 1985 the practice had developed of each new Commission presenting itself to the European Parliament for the latter's approval. This practice was formalised by Article 214 of the Treaty, which stipulated that each new Commission "shall be subject as a body to a vote of approval" by the European Parliament. In 1995, before voting their approval for the Commission, the European Parliament insisted on interviewing all the prospective commissioners. The European Parliament indicated its disapproval of at least five of the prospective candidates. Although it could only dismiss the Commission as a whole, and therefore the five "unsuitable" commissioners were appointed, nevertheless, the European Parliament had placed a strong marker that it was flexing its muscles over its control of the Commission.

Nevertheless, and on the positive side, one should not over-estimate the negative aspects of the changing place of the Commission in the institutional balance. There is no doubt that the Commission still takes a central role in Community affairs. All the major initiatives since 1980 have come from the Commission. One can point to the Single Market Programme of 1992, the Social Charter, EMU and the 1993 White Paper on Growth, Competitiveness and Employment. There have been other initiatives too; institutional reform, enlargement, reform of the Common Agricultural Policy and reform of the Commission itself. Another, more up to date example, is the Commission's Communication entitled *Agenda 2000: For a Stronger and Wider Europe*. In 1995, the Commission was requested by the European Council to prepare comprehensive proposals concerning how the EU should move into the next millennium in terms of its finances and policies. *Agenda 2000* was the Commission's response, issued in July 1997. It set out an ambitious framework for the development of Community policies up to 2006. It proposed changes to, and reform of, the CAP and the structural funds. It also gave the Commission's opinion on the 10 applications to join the Union. The 10 candidate countries will take their place in the Union in 2004.

The last word on the Commission (and its main problem) is that it lacks a legitimate democratic base. Unlike the European Parliament it is not elected. The Commission would like to see itself as an executive, directly answerable to the elected European Parliament. However, such a change would require a change in the Treaty. There is little likelihood that the Council would agree to such a change, given the shift in power to the Commission that this would entail.

OTHER INSTITUTIONS AND COMMUNITY BODIES

The Court of Auditors

The Court of Auditors was established in 1977 and since the enactment of the TEU (Article 4) now has the status of the fifth Community institution. Its composition and functions are now governed by Articles 188a–188c EC. The court consists of 15 members—one for each Member State—who are persons qualified to serve on a body which has the task of carrying out the Community audit, and whose independence is beyond doubt. The European Parliament is consulted on the appointments which are for six year terms. The qualification for membership for the Court of Auditors is that the person must belong to, or have belonged in their country to an external audit body, or they must be "specially qualified for this office". A member of the Court of Auditors may not engage in any other occupation, whether paid or unpaid, and even after leaving office they must "behave with integrity and discretion as regards the acceptance . . . of certain appointments or benefits". They have the same protected legal status during their term of office as the members of the Court of Justice.

The task of the Court of Auditors extends to the revenue and expenditure of the Community, but in addition it includes all bodies set up by the Community. The Court of Auditors has to provide both the Parliament and the Council with a statement of assurance as to the reliability of the accounts and the legality of transactions. At the end of each financial year the Court of Auditors issues an annual report which is sent to the other Community institutions. This report is published in the Official Journal and has been characterised in recent years by the stinging criticism of the management and control of Community finances.

The Treaty of Nice states that the Court of Auditors will consist of a national of each Member State. The Court will be able to set up chambers to adopt certain types of report or opinion. The Treaty also exhorts the Court to improve cooperation with national audit institutions.

The Economic and Social Committee (ECOSOC)

ECOSOC was established by Article 257 [ex 193] of the EC Treaty which provides that it shall consist of representatives of various economic and social interests. Worthy of note is that the Committee shall include representatives of the general public. However, there seems to be little evidence of membership by the general public and the main components are workers, principally represented by trade unions, employers' groups, consumer groups and the professions. The number of members is 222. Each country has a specified number of members, the largest being 24 and the smallest 6. As with membership of the Commission and the Court of Auditors, members of the ECOSOC must be "completely independent in their performance of their duties, in the general interests of the Community". The ECOSOC is organised into specialist sections, for example, agriculture and transport, and these sections prepare draft reports on legislation for consideration by the whole body in plenary session. In certain instances the Treaty stipulates that ECOSOC must be consulted; and the Council or Commission may consult it on other matters. The Committee will normally be required to express an opinion in matters concerning agriculture, competition, environment, health and safety, and the free movement provisions.

The Treaty of Nice has increased the number of members to a maximum of 350, with a new number of 344 as soon as the candidate countries become members.

The Committee of the Regions

This body was established by the TEU, in Articles 263–265 [ex 198a–198c], the purpose of which is to provide opinions on issues which might have a particular affect on regions of the Community. The composition of the body largely parallels those governing the ECOSOC. The Committee of the Regions functions in a similar way to ECOSOC except that it is not empowered to set up specialised sections or sub committees. It has the right to be informed when the ECOSOC is consulted and, if it considers that significant regional interests are at stake, it may issue its own opinion. The Treaty of Amsterdam now provides that the Committee of the Regions must be consulted on education, vocational training and youth, culture, public health, trans-European networks and economic social cohesion. The Treaty of Nice has introduced similar changes to those in the Economic and Social Committee.

THE EUROPEAN COURT OF JUSTICE AND THE COURT OF FIRST INSTANCE

To give it its full name, the Court of Justice of the European Communities has the status of a Community institution. This is so even though its functions are purely judicial. Nevertheless, as will be seen throughout this book, its activities have had a profound effect upon the development of Community law, particularly with regard to the foundation of a "constitution" of the Community. There is little doubt that the Court of Justice saw the Treaties as expressions of purpose, and further saw their role as adding substance to those "dry bones". The Court has been concerned to ensure that Community law is effective, both in respect of a new legal system in its own right, and in terms of its integration with the legal systems of the Member States. It could, and has, been argued that the Court has gone far beyond what was intended by the Treaty; nevertheless, the Court has developed a package of fundamental rights which have become an entrenched part of the Community system.

It has developed the doctrine of direct effect, by which means individuals have been able to use Community law in their own domestic courts, and which has been a major step in preventing Member States from neglecting their duties of implementation of Community legislation. It should be remembered, that the decisions made by the Court, particularly in the early days of the Community, have not always met with favour from the domestic courts of Member States. Also, at various times there has been tension between the approach taken by the Court and the approach taken by other institutions. The result of this is that the Court's approach to integration has not been a gradual one but can be characterised by periods of fertile law making, and at other times by an almost reactionary progress. Some contemporary opinion is that the Court has too much power and there were some signs that the inter-governmental conference in 1996, would seek to constrain this power. The United Kingdom in particular, put forward such proposals. However, as the IGC progressed the various proposals were "talked-out" or dropped.

The function and jurisdiction of the Court of Justice is to be found in Articles 220–245 [ex 164–188] of the EC Treaty. There is a protocol on the Statute of the Court of Justice which is attached to the Treaty which deals with the organisation and procedure of the Court. Further to this Statute, by the authority of Article 245 [ex 188], the Rules of Procedure have also been adopted by the Court of Justice. Article 220 [ex 164] states that the function of the Court of Justice is to "ensure that in the interpretation and application of this Treaty the law is observed".

The Court of Justice now consists of 15 judges assisted by nine Advocates General. Article 223 [ex 167] provides that:

"The judges and Advocates General shall be chosen from persons whose independence is beyond doubt and who possess the qualifications required for appointment to the highest judicial offices in their respective countries or who are jurisconsults of recognised competence; they shall be appointed by common accord of the governments of the Member States for a term of six years."

In practice, each Member State nominates one judge, although in the past when there has been an even number of Member States an additional judge, nominated by one of the five larger Member States has been appointed to ensure an uneven number of judges. Five of the Advocates General are nominated by the larger Member States, and four by the smaller Member States in rotation. The term of office is six years and the appointment of new judges or reappointment of the existing judges is staggered so that there will be a partial replacement of judges every three years. Except for the Advocates General from the smaller Member States, appointment is renewable, and in practice, most members of the court have had their appointments renewed. The court elects a president from amongst the judges, whose term of office is three years. The president is responsible for the business and administration of the court and allocates cases to colleagues and appoints the Advocate General for each case. Except in some rare occasions where the president can act alone, the court always sits as a college, sitting in either plenary session (*i.e.* the whole court) for which the quorum is nine judges, or in chambers. These chambers consist of three or five or seven judges and this ability to sit in chambers has proved to be an important method of addressing its ever increasing case load. If so requested by a Member State, or a Community institution, a case before the court must be heard by the court in plenary session.

The Advocate General

An Advocate General is assigned to each case which comes before the Court of Justice. The function of the Advocate General, which is set out in Article 222 [ex 166] of the EC Treaty is:

"acting with complete impartiality and independence, to make, in open court, reasoned submissions on cases brought before the Court of Justice, in order to assist the court in the performance of the task assigned to it."

Although the Advocate General participates at the oral stage of the judicial hearing the most important task for this official is the production of a written opinion for the Court. This written opinion will set out the Advocate General's understanding of the law applicable to the case, and will recommend to the Court how the case ought to be decided. Although this opinion is generally very influential it is not binding on the Court, although the opinion is followed in the majority of cases. It has been said that the opinion delivered by the Advocate General can be likened to the judgment of a single judge at first instance, to be followed by a compulsory and definitive appeal—the judgment of the Court. In practice the opinion tends to be a thoroughly reasoned account of the law governing each case. Often the Court will give a judgment as recommended by the Advocate General in his opinion but without going into any of the detailed argument. In these cases it is assumed that the Court agrees with the reasoning of the Advocate General and this makes the opinion worthwhile reading.

Both written and oral pleadings may be in any of the 11 official languages of the Community, or in Irish (although no case has yet been conducted in Irish). The use of a particular language is at the option of the applicant. However, where the defendant is a Member State or a natural or legal person having a nationality of a Member State, the language of the proceedings will be the official language of that Member State. In preliminary rulings the language of the referring court is used. If a state intervenes in a case (see later) it may use its own language irrespective of the language of the case. The working language of the Court is French, including the deliberations of the judges. Advocates General may use their own language for opinions. Judgments are formally delivered in the language of the case and that text constitutes the only authentic version of the judgment.

The Court of First Instance (CFI)

It became increasingly apparent during the 1980s that the Court of Justice was being over-burdened with its case load. The length of time taken between the arrival of a case at the Court and when judgment was handed down was lengthening. By the middle of the 1980s, on average, a case took 23 months to come to judgment. The Single European Act added Article 168a (now 225) to the Treaty which gave the Council the power to create the Court of First Instance, attached to the Court of Justice. The Court of First Instance was ultimately established on the October 24, 1988. This court now consists of 15 judges, appointed on the same criteria as judges of the Court of Justice, but it did not have its own Advocates General. The CFI which has its own rules of procedure may sit in chambers with three or five judges or in plenary session. An Advocate General is not always assigned to each case and is only done so when the case before it presents legal or factual complexities. An Advocate General is always appointed when the court sits in plenary session. It is usual that one of the judges of the Court of First Instance acts as an Advocate General when one is required. The jurisdiction originally conferred on the CFI covered only staff cases, matters arising out of the ECSC Treaty, and actions raised by natural or legal persons in the area of competition law. In 1993 and 1994 this jurisdiction was extended to include any action brought by any natural or legal persons against an act of a Community institution. Therefore, the only cases which now go immediately to the European Court of Justice are those cases brought by Member States or Community institutions. Even here there is nothing in the Treaty to prevent these cases from being transferred to the Court of First Instance with the agreement of the parties concerned. The only express provision is in Article 225 [ex 168a] which expressly provides that the Court of First Instance has no jurisdiction to hear preliminary rulings.

It should be noted that since the formation of the CFI the case number is now accompanied by a prefix "C" or "T". Thus the prefix "C" indicates a case before the ECJ and the prefix "T" a case before the CFI.

Procedure before the Court

The procedure before either of the courts is governed by their respective rules of procedure. The procedure before the Court of Justice takes place in two stages, the written and the oral stage. What will be surprising to the UK lawyer brought up on the adversarial common law background, is that the written stage is the most important part of the proceedings. It is at this stage that all applications, statement of case, defence and any other written submissions or relevant documents are communicated to the parties, and to the institutions whose decisions are being contested. The Court itself may also request any further information which it considers desirable at this point in the case. The President of the Court will assign the case to one of the chambers and designate a judge from that chamber as judge rapporteur. The task of the judge rapporteur is to prepare a preliminary report dealing with the issues of fact arising in the case. This is presented to the court as a "Report for the Hearing". This report is distributed to the parties a few days before the oral hearing so that they can comment on it at the hearing.

The oral stage of the hearing is short and limited. The judge rapporteur presents the Report for the Hearing to the Court and then the legal representatives of the party may make oral submissions to the court. It is not unknown for the Court to indicate quite short time limits for these speeches. It has now become the practice for the Advocate General and the judges to ask questions of the parties. The Court then normally adjourns and the Advocate General prepares his opinion which is presented to the hearing resumed at a later date. The presentation of his Opinion by the Advocate General marks the end of the hearing and the Court must now consider its judgment. All judgments of the Court of Justice are reserved judgments. The judges meet in secret to deliberate over their judgment and no other person other than the judges are present. The procedure is that each judge gives his opinion in turn, starting with the most junior. Only one judgment is given which means that if there is dissent amongst the judges a vote will be taken. There are no dissenting or separately concurring judgments. The main reason for the secret deliberation of the judges is, of course, that their complete independence is protected, and their opinion in a case will not have to be judged against national interests. However, the need for one consenting judgment does lead to rulings which are obscure or which are ambiguous. This is exacerbated by the need for the judgments to be translated into all the official languages of the Community. One can understand that not all judges will be equally efficient in French, the working language in which the secret deliberations take place.

Students of the UK common law system of judgments will be familiar with the three "rules" of statutory interpretation. They will also be aware of the doctrine of binding precedent. Judgments of the Court of Justice will therefore come as a surprise to such students. Although the Court shows a tendency to follow its previous decisions, and often cites earlier cases in its judgment, it does not consider itself bound by a system of precedent. This is not altogether surprising given that the Court of Justice is the highest court in the Community. In the United Kingdom, the House of Lords, since 1966, has not considered itself bound by its own previous judgments. Two examples of the Court of Justice's judgments will illustrate this. In *European Parliament v Council (Comitology)* (30/87) the Court held that the European Parliament did not having standing to bring an action for the annulment of a Council regulation. Nevertheless, less than two years later in *European Parliament v Commission (Chernobyl)* (C-70/88) the Court felt confident enough to reverse the original decision. In a more recent case, *Keck and Mithouard* (Cases C-267 & 8/91) the Court expressly said it was departing from some of its past case law although it failed to state which previous cases it considered overruled. Even more recently, in *Brown v Rentokil Ltd* (C-394/96) the Court expressly overruled its previous decision in *Larsson* (C-400/95).

In terms of interpretation, it can be said that the Court adopts a contextual and purposive interpretation. This has also been called a teleological method of interpretation. The main reason for adopting this course of interpretation is that the Treaty articles are basically statements of intent and need to be "fleshed out". The Court sees it as its role to develop these Articles. Naturally the Court does this in the context of the Treaty itself and will construe its interpretation in the light of the objectives set out in the pre-amble and Articles 2 and 3 of the Treaty. In other words, the Court interprets the various provisions of the Treaty in order to achieve the desired objective. A very early example of this purposive or teleological approach is shown in *Van Gend En Loos* (26/62). The Court was called upon to interpret Article 12 (now 25) of the Treaty and said "it is necessary to consider the spirit, the general scheme and the wording of these provisions". Another example can be seen in the Court's broad interpretation of the phrase "any charges having equivalent effect" in Article 12 (now 25) (see Chapter 11). This method of interpretation has been criticised on some occasions on the grounds that the Court often enters the realms of policy making. This cannot be denied given the wide discretion that the Treaty wording gives to judges, nor where the Treaty is silent on important points of law. In these cases the Court of Justice has an important gap-filling duty. The Court has also issued judgments where it appeared to have exercised a policy choice. Some examples of this might be the development of the doctrine of direct effect and the doctrine of the supremacy of Community law.

The Jurisdiction of the Court of Justice

The jurisdiction of the Court of Justice is set out in the Treaty, and by the Treaty its jurisdiction is limited to the area of the Community, but nevertheless, its judgments can and do have consequences outside the Community area. Its first area of juris-diction is that of direct judicial control, what has been called "the contentious jurisdiction of the Court". This involves the hearing of actions against Member States brought either by the Commis-sion under Article 226 [ex 169], or by another Member State under Article 227 [ex 170]. It has also jurisdiction to hear actions against any of the institutions of the Community. Under Article 230 [ex 173] it will hear actions for the annulment of Community acts, and under Article 232 [ex 175] it will hear actions brought by one institution against another, for the latter's failure to act. Under

Article 241 [ex 184] it also has jurisdiction for the judicial review of legally binding acts. It also has jurisdiction for indirect judicial control, what is known as the preliminary ruling procedure. This is the ability under Article 234 [ex 177] for national courts to ask the Court of Justice for ruling on the interpretation and validity of the Treaty and other legislation. The development of this jurisdiction is considered in the relevant chapters.

Treaty of Nice Reforms

A major reform of the judicial system has been provided for in the Treaty. The revision of Articles 220–224, 255, 255a, 229a, 245 and a revised Protocol on the Statute of the Court of Justice is intended to improve the working methods and performance as well as the autonomy of the judiciary of the Union. The revisions to the Treaty include the setting up of separate panels for the CFI and of special; judicial panels for specific class actions. The Treaty provides that there will always be one judge for each Member State and eight Advocates General appointed for six year renewable terms, with partial replacements every three years. The ECJ will be able to meet as a plenary body, or as a grand chamber of 13 judges or in chambers of fewer judges.

By an amendment to the Statute of the Court of Justice it has now been decided that a case may be determined without a submission from an Advocate General. The Court can come to this decision if it considers that the case raises no new point of law.

Although it was stated above that the ECJ had the sole jurisdiction to hear cases referred to it under Article 234, the Treaty of Nice has introduced what may become an important shift in competence. A revised Article 225(3) provides that the CFI shall have jurisdiction to hear and determine questions referred for a preliminary ruling under Article 234, in specified areas laid down in the Court's statute. At present, there have been no changes made in the statute.

4. THE SUPREMACY OF COMMUNITY LAW

INTRODUCTION

In the 30 years since the United Kingdom joined the European Economic Community we have become used to newspapers bemoaning the fact that the Community (through the Commission) was against our crisps, sausages, bathing water, noise levels and newspaper boys. All these actions we were told by the newspapers were attacks on our "sovereignty". Sovereignty in this sense is taken to mean the supremacy of Parliament. That is that Parliament has the unfettered right to make or repeal any domestic law. Parliament has jurisdiction over the territory in its hands and presides over a system of laws and procedures which is free from outside interference. Even when the United Kingdom entered into international treaties and has enacted statutes to implement treaty provisions, these statutes are regarded as in no way different from ordinary Acts of Parliament.

Although the issues of sovereignty and the supremacy of Parliament have been recurring features since our accession to the Community in 1973, *R v Secretary of State for Transport Ex p. Factortame* brought them to the forefront of attention again.

If we say that sovereignty means the ability to legislate independently of any other state, if it means that our domestic laws will prevail over all other external laws, then the United Kingdom long ago gave up some of its sovereignty. Even before our membership of the Community we accepted limitations on our right to act or legislate in certain areas. One has only to think of the Hague and Geneva Conventions, GATT, the United Nations, NATO and other international treaties.

Even before the United Kingdom joined the Community it was well established that Community law was supreme when in conflict with national domestic law and that Member States had abrogated a part of their sovereignty to the Community. This was first established in *Van Gend en Loos* (26/62) where the Court of Justice said that Member States "have limited their sovereign rights, albeit within limited fields".

In *Costa v ENEL* (6/64) the Court was asked if it could give a ruling in a situation where a national law seemed applicable in the particular case as against a Community law. While the Court would not rule on the compatibility of national law with Community law, it did say that:

". . . transfer by the States from their domestic legal system to the Community legal system of the rights and obligations arising under the Treaty carries with it a permanent limitation of their sovereign rights, against which a subsequent unilateral act incompatible with the concept of the Community cannot prevail."

This concept of the supremacy of Community law was given further impetus in *Internationale Handelsgesellschaft* (11/70) where the Court of Justice said:

". . . the validity of a Community Measure or its effect within a Member State cannot be affected by allegations that it runs counter to . . . the principles of a national constitutional measure."

In *Simmenthal* (106/77) the ECJ went even further and said:

". . . any national court must . . . apply Community law in its entirety . . . and must accordingly set aside any provision of national law which may conflict with it, whether prior or subsequent to the Community rule."

SUPREMACY IN THE UNITED KINGDOM

In 1973 when the United Kingdom joined the Community, the Treaty of Rome, which it signed, was incorporated into United Kingdom law by the European Communities Act 1972. Section 2(1) of the Act states that the principles established by the Treaty "are without further enactment to be given legal effect". Section 2(4) provides that "any enactment passed or to be passed" must be construed subject to the foregoing. This gives rise to a few problems as to whether this section does give priority to Community law thereby limiting the sovereign rights of the United Kingdom. The traditional view has been to treat s.2(4) as a rule of construction. It would seem so long as s.2(4) is applied as a rule of construction our courts would remain free to apply an English statute which was contrary to Community law and it is clear that Parliament wished to breach its Community obligations.

This rule of construction was useful in so far as it enabled the United Kingdom courts to avoid any outright statement of the supremacy of Community law. But it did lead to some initial confusion in the courts. In a number of cases the courts were prepared to give precedence to Community law over United Kingdom law if there was a conflict but in other cases they construed inconsistencies between Community law and United Kingdom law in favour of the latter.

The first of these approaches can be seen as early as 1979 in *Macarthys Ltd. v Smith* (129/79). This case broke new ground in that it was the first case to be given the "European view." Cummings-Bruce and Lawton L.J.J. citing *Costa* and in particular the *Simmenthal* case were prepared to give priority to European law. Lord Denning M.R. preferred to see the case as one of interpretation or construction of s.2(4) and he interpreted the Equal Pay Act 1970 to conform to the principles of equal pay for equal work as set out in Article 119 EC. He said

". . . we are entitled to look to the Treaty as an aid to its construction: and even more, not only as an aid but as an overriding force."

He was also prepared to say that if domestic legislation was inconsistent with Community legislation then "it is our bounden duty to give priority to Community law".

The House of Lords continued with the rule of construction approach in *Garland v British Rail Engineering Ltd.* Once again, the case involved a conflict between the Equal Pay Act 1970 and Article 119 (now 141) EC. In the earlier hearing of the case the courts had been prepared to construe s.6(4) of the Act as allowing derogation from the principle of equal pay if the discriminatory provisions related to death or retirement. The plaintiff sought to rely on Article 119 EC. The House of Lords said that s.6(4) must be construed with Article 119. Lord Diplock said that national courts must construe domestic law to conform, "no matter how wide a departure from the prima facie meaning may be needed to achieve consistency".

In both the above cases there was no real difficulty in construing domestic law to conform to Community law. In these cases it appeared that the House of Lords had managed to adopt a "rule of construction" approach to accommodate the idea of the supremacy of Community law with Parliamentary sovereignty. But a quartet of cases that came before the House of Lords threw doubt on this consensual approach. The first of these cases was *Duke v GEC Reliance* [1988]. In the *Macarthys* and *Garland* cases there had been no great difficulty in construing domestic law in line with Community law. However, in *Duke,* the issue in question, s.6(4) of the Sex Discrimination Act 1975 had been passed before the provision relied on by Ms Duke namely the Equal Treatment Directive of 1976. It was also clear that the Act was not passed to give effect to the Directive. In those circumstances Lord Templeman refused to construe s.6(4) of the domestic Act to give effect to the Directive. In a trenchant passage, he said:

"Section 2(4) of the European Communities Act does not in my opinion enable or constrain a British court to distort the meaning of a British statute in order to enforce against an individual a Community Directive which has no direct effect between individuals."

The House therefore rejected Ms Duke's claims. Thus there has arisen a distinction between domestic legislation passed to implement a directive and legislation that pre-dated the directive. In the former the House of Lords was prepared by use of the "rule of construction" under s.2(4) of the European Communities Act to give priority to Community law. In the latter it considered that to give priority to Community law would require a distortion of a British statute which it was not prepared to do.

In *Finnegan v Clowney Youth Training Programme Ltd,* the House was given an opportunity to reconsider its position. The issue was similar to that in *Duke,* except that the relevant legislation was Article 8(4) of the Sex Discrimination (Northern Ireland) Order 1976. This was a parallel provision to s.6(4) of the Sex Discrimination Act 1975 except that it had been passed after the Equal Treatment Directive. Also, in the case of *Johnston v Chief Constable of the Royal Ulster Constabulary,* the Court of Justice had ruled that the Order should be interpreted in the light of the Equal Treatment Directive. Despite these distinctions the House of Lords held there was no material distinction between the Northern Ireland Order and the Sex Discrimination Act. It said that the accident of timing of the Order was irrelevant and in also ignoring the distinction in *Johnston* it refused to give a purposive construction to the Order. Once again it said that national law not passed to implement Community law would take priority over subsequent Community legislation.

However, in two cases the House was prepared to allow priority to Community law passed before a piece of domestic legislation. The two cases also illustrate a striking departure from the normal approach of the British judiciary. The first of the cases was *Pickstone v Freemans plc*. The Equal Pay Act 1970 had been amended by statutory instrument in 1983 to comply with the Equal Pay Directive. The 1983 amendments were less than clear and led Lord Oliver to observe that "the strict and literal construction of the section does indeed involve the conclusion that the Regulations although purporting to give full effect to the United Kingdom's obligations under Article 119 (now 141), were in fact in breach of those obligations". The House examined the Directive, and the Court of Justice decision which had led to the 1983 amendments and in an unprecedented step had consulted Hansard to determine the motive for the national legislation. Based on these examinations Lord Oliver was able to depart from the literal wording of the legislation. He said:

". . . a construction which permits the section to operate as a proper fulfilment of the United Kingdom's obligations under the Treaty involves not so much doing violence to the language of a section as filling a gap by implication which arises, not from the words used, but from the manifest purpose of the Act and the mischief it was intended to remedy."

Lords Keith, Brandon and Jauncey expressly concurred with Lord Oliver. Remarkably, Lord Templeman, who had given the leading judgment in *Duke* a year earlier, now said:

". . . I can see no difficulty in construing the Regulations of 1983 in a way which gives effect to the declared intentions of the Government . . . and is consistent with the objectives of the EC Treaty . . ."

This willingness to overrule a piece of domestic legislation was extended again in the case of *Litster v Forth Dry Dock*. The Transfer of Undertakings (Protection of Employment) Regulations 1987 had been passed to implement the Acquired Rights Directive. When, as in this case, there was a conflict between the words of the Regulations and those of the Directive, the House of Lords was prepared to treat the words of the Directive as overriding the words of the domestic Regulations. Lord Keith said:

". . . the precedent established in *Pickstone* . . . indicates that this is to be done by implying the words necessary to achieve that result."

Lord Oliver was prepared to add words to the regulations to enable the legislation to "fulfil the purpose for which they were made of giving effect to the provisions of the Directive", and Lord Templeman was again also prepared to imply words into the Regulations to enable them to comply with Community obligations.

The *Duke* and *Finnegan* cases have been criticised but any unfairness that was felt to be in these decisions has been addressed by a decision of the Court of Justice in *Marleasing SA v La Commercial Internacional de Alimentacion SA* (C-106/89). The case arose out of a conflict between the Spanish Civil Code and an EC Company Law Directive which was unimplemented in Spain. In its decision the Court broke new ground by holding:

"It follows that in applying national law, whether the provisions pre-date or post-date the Directive, the national court asked to interpret national law is bound to do so in every way possible in the light of the text and the aim of the Directive to achieve the result envisaged by it and thus to comply with Article 189(3) of the Treaty."

The effects of this case have ramifications for the concept of sovereignty. Although the Court of Justice did concede that Directives should be followed only "so far as possible" bearing in mind the principles of legal certainty and non-retroactivity, it does now appear that the "rule of construction" approach has been severely circumscribed.

THE "FACTORTAME" SAGA

Although questions of sovereignty and the supremacy of Parliament have been a recurring feature since our accession in 1973 the *Factortame* case brought them to the forefront of attention again. The facts of the case are well known. In an attempt to prevent "quota-hopping" by Spanish fishermen operating behind nominally British companies, the UK Government passed the Merchant Shipping Act 1988 and a series of delegated regulations. The legislation set out residence and domicile conditions for fishing companies, the effect of which was to disqualify 95 Spanish fishing boats from fishing from British ports. The companies sought interim relief by means of judicial review in the Divisional Court. The grounds on which they sought interim relief were that the Act and regulations were contrary to Articles 7, 52, 58 and 221 (now 14, 43, 48 and 294) of the Treaty and that interim relief was needed because of the irreparable damage that would be caused if the companies had to wait for the full trial to come before the court.

In the Divisional Court, a brave Neil L.J. granted provisional relief. Relying on *Simmenthal* he said:

"The High Court now has a duty to take account of and give effect to Community law and where there is a conflict, to prefer Community law to national law."

On appeal by the UK Government to the Court of Appeal the interim relief was set aside on the grounds that under the British Constitution the courts have neither the power to suspend the application of an Act of Parliament nor to grant an injunction against the Crown (*i.e.* the Government).

When the case was further appealed to the House of Lords, Lord Bridge held that there is a presumption that an Act of Parliament was compatible with Community law unless and until it was decided otherwise, but that nevertheless, by s.21 of the Crown Proceedings Act 1947 there was no jurisdiction to grant interim relief. However, the House made an Article 177 (now 234) reference to the Court of Justice which asked, *inter alia*, whether Community law empowers or imposes an obligation on a national court to grant interim relief in a situation where a preliminary reference has been made to the Court of Justice.

The reply from the Court of Justice should not have come as a total surprise. The Court replied in the affirmative basing its judgment on the twin pillars of Article 5 and its previous and recent decision in *Simmenthal*. The Court stressed the importance of ensuring that direct effect was a matter of substance, not form and further held:

". . . the full effectiveness of Community law would be . . . impaired if a rule of national law could prevent a national court . . . from granting provisional relief . . . It follows that a court which . . . would grant interim relief, if it were not for a rule of national law, is obliged to set aside that rule."

The *Factortame* decisions have obvious and perhaps damaging ramifications for the British fishing industry, but the major area of interest is the effect on British constitutional law. Prior to *Factortame* it could be argued that UK courts had not unequivocally accepted the supremacy of Community law. We have seen that the twin conflicting claims of this supremacy and the British constitutional principle of parliamentary sovereignty have been accommodated by the device of the "rule of construction". But now, *Factortame* makes it clear that a national court is under a Community law obligation to give effective protection to directly effective rights, and this will be so even in the face of conflicting domestic legislation.

The source of this obligation is Article 5 (now 10) of the EC Treaty. This reflects a growing reliance by the Court of Justice on the "gap filling" properties of this Article. Article 5 (now 10) has become the "tool" by which the Court of Justice has developed general principles of Community law to ensure the effective judicial protection of individual rights.

The Court of Justice went on to say that the duty upon national courts "cannot fail to include the provision of interim relief". But the Court did not go on to say on what basis such interim relief was to be awarded. This is still to be a matter for applying national criteria as set out in *American Cyanamid v Ethicon Ltd*. The crucial point is that interim relief should be available and if necessary the national courts would have to invent a system of reliefs.

CONCLUSIONS

What lessons does the *Factortame* decision hold for UK law? It can certainly be concluded that any lingering doubts about the supremacy of Community law over domestic law have been laid to rest. Lord Bridge in *Factortame* expressed it thus:

"Under the terms of the European Communities Act 1972 it has always been clear that it was the duty of a United Kingdom court when delivering final judgment, to override any rule of national law found to be in conflict with any directly enforceable rule of Community law . . . Thus . . . to insist that national courts must not be inhibited by rules of national law from granting interim relief . . . is no more than a logical recognition of that supremacy."

The only uncertainty left in this area is the question of what the position would be if an Act expressly said it was to take effect notwithstanding the European Communities Act. It may well be that the English courts would have to follow the domestic legislation. But the supremacy of EC law was well established in the jurisdiction of the Court of Justice long before the United Kingdom joined the Community. So, whatever limitations to its sovereignty Parliament accepted when it enacted the European Communities Act 1972 were entirely voluntary. For Parliament to change its stance to such an extent would require a renegotiation of the Treaty of Rome. This is an unlikely scenario.

Factortame is important on a wider basis. It, together with *Emmott* (C-208/90), *Francovich* (C-6 & 9/90) and *Zuckerfabrik* (C-143/88 & C-92/89) cases represent a new development in Community law. Up until recently, priority had been given to the establishment of a Community legal order, separate from national law and giving rights which individuals could plead in their national courts. It was this concept of the direct effect of Community law that the Court fought to establish. This battle appears to be won! All the national courts have accepted the supremacy of the Community legal order. What *Factortame* and the other cases illustrate is a move by the Court of Justice towards the provision of effective judicial remedies. It is now the application of Community law that has become the focus of attention. The decisions can also be seen as representing a major shift towards a partnership of Community law and national legal systems. This can only strengthen the remedies available to individuals and will lead to the availability of these remedies within a Community context. Certainly, the House of Lords appear to have accepted that a purposive approach, even overruling national legislation, is an essential and integral part of the development of Community law.

5. GENERAL PRINCIPLES OF COMMUNITY LAW

INTRODUCTION

The development of a set of principles of Community law, along with the doctrines of the supremacy of Community law, and direct effect, has been the major contribution of the Court of Justice to the development of the Community. The body of principles of law now established in the Community can be referred to as "the unwritten" law of the Community.

Fundamental Human Rights

It may at first be surprising that these seemingly important principles were not addressed by the Treaty itself. However it had been seen in the ECSC Treaty that the wording therein could not cover all the cases that were coming before the Court of Justice. Indeed it must be understood that no Treaty can cover all possible eventualities. In cases such as this we look to the courts to "fill in the gaps." In the United Kingdom, of course, we are accustomed to the common law tradition that is designed to deal with the need for flexibility and creativity in law.

It may also be that the founding fathers of the Treaty felt a certain diffidence in proposing more than an economic relationship. They would have had in mind the failure of the European Defence Treaty, which had incorporated (in Article 3) the entrenchment of the fundamental rights of individuals. This had led to disagreements among the proposed participants of the Treaty because they felt it would be impossible to take into account the constitutions of all the Member States. For that reason the Treaty of Rome was a Treaty for economic integration only. It is only in the preamble of the Treaty that any references to a broader ideology are to be found. Here it states that it is:

"Resolved to ensure the economic and social progress of their countries by common action to eliminate the barriers which divide Europe, . . . Resolved by thus pooling their resources to preserve and strengthen peace and liberty, and calling upon the other peoples of Europe who share their idea to join in their efforts."

It was not until the expansion of Community law had affected individuals, an affect originally not foreseen, that the need for fundamental rights was understood by the Court. These rights were initially enunciated, and then protected, by the Court of Justice. Initially these rights grew out of the challenge to the supremacy of Community law over national law. Various Member States, particularly Germany and France, felt that Community legislation was imposing on important rights and interests which were protected by national law. The need for fundamental rights and general principles of law followed the evolution of the Community from an economic one into a broader social and political community. Here, the Court of Justice was to play an important role in the integration of the legal systems of the Member States. If the Court of Justice was to keep its authority and status it had to be shown to exercise a "rights" jurisprudence.

The question has to be asked why these general principles of Community law have become so important. There are three probable reasons:

(1) These general principles of law can act as an aid to interpretation. In other words, if a Community legislative act is in conflict with the general principles of Community law, the Court of Justice can interpret the legislation in such a way as to accord to the general principles.

(2) The general principles can be invoked to annul or invalidate acts of the institutions.

(3) The general principles of Community law permeate into domestic law. In the case of UK law this can be seen by s.2(1) of the European Communities Act, 1974 which states that "all such rights, powers, liabilities, obligations

and restrictions . . . are without further enactment to be given legal effect . . . in the United Kingdom".

It should also be mentioned that the Treaty itself does provide some justification for recourse to general principles as a source of law. In all, three bases can be found, mainly Articles 230 [ex 173], 288 [ex 215], and 220 [ex 164]. Article 230 [ex 173] states the grounds on which a Community act may be annulled by the Court. One of those grounds is "infringement of this Treaty, or of any rule of law relating to its application". Article 288 [ex 215] which governs Community liability in tort, provides that liability is to be determined "in accordance with the general principles common to the laws of the Member States". And perhaps the most important of the legal basis in the Treaty is Article 220 [ex 164] which states:

"the Court of Justice shall ensure that in the interpretation and application of this Treaty the law is observed."

There is also much to be said for the theory that the specific doctrine of human rights endorsed by the Court of Justice has been as much a matter of expediency as conviction. Indeed, in the early years of the Community, the European Court was unsympathetic in cases where Community law clashed with fundamental rights guaranteed by domestic law. In the early days the Court of Justice was keen to ensure that the doctrine of the supremacy of Community law led to its effectiveness. Initially, this tension was felt particularly between the Court of Justice and the German Constitutional Court (Grundgesetz). Most of the initial cases were brought under the ECSC Treaty, and in *Stork v High Authority* (1/58) the European Court of Justice said that, "the High Authority [now the Commission] is not empowered to examine a ground of complaint which maintains that, when it adopted its decision, it infringed principles of German constitutional law".

The Court of Justice insisted in further cases, such as *Geitling v High Authority* (36, 37, 38 and 40/59) and *Sgarlat v Commission* (40/64) that Community law, "does not contain any general principle, express or otherwise, guaranteeing the maintenance of vested rights". These decisions were, naturally, disliked intensely by the German constitutional court and it was quite probable that there would have been a "rebellion" by the German courts. No doubt aware of this the Court of Justice, in 1969 adopted a new approach whereby from now on, the European Court would define a Community concept of human rights and would itself protect those human rights.

The first opportunity the Court had to announce this new doctrine was in *Stauder v City of Ulm* (29/69). This case concerned a Commission decision to allow Member States to distribute cheaper butter to citizens who were receiving state assistance and who would not be able to afford butter at normal prices. To obtain this butter the citizen had to obtain a coupon from the relevant welfare benefits office, and in Germany the coupon had space for the applicant's name and address. The plaintive in this case was entitled to butter coupons, but felt that it was humiliating to have to reveal his name and address to retailers, and argued that this was a violation of his fundamental rights under the *Grundgesetz*. The action was originally brought before the German courts and ultimately a reference was made to the Court of Justice. The crux of the matter revolved around the various translations of the Commission decision, with the result that the Court of Justice said the coupon did not need to be personalised. However, the Court went even further and said that ". . . the provision at issue contains nothing capable of prejudicing the fundamental human rights enshrined in the general principles of Community law and protected by the Court".

This was the first recognition that fundamental human rights are a general principle of Community law. *Stauder* was a relatively easy case for the Court of Justice to decide, but a case concerning an alleged infringement of basic principles of German constitutional law would be of more concern. In the next case the applicant was in effect asking the German constitutional court to disapply a Community provision. This case was the famous *Internationale Handelsgesellschaft GmbH* (11/70). The case concerned the common agricultural policy, and a system to control the cereal market. The applicants in this case claimed that the whole system was invalid as being contrary to fundamental human rights as guaranteed by the German Grundgesetz. The case was referred to the European Court of Justice under Article 234 [ex 177]. The Court of Justice first stated that the validity of Community measures cannot be judged according to the rules of national law. This was because the law that stemmed from the Treaty was an independent source of law that would be deprived of its character of Community law if it was so judged. However, the Court went on to say that:

"a respect for fundamental rights forms an integral part of the general principle of law protected by the Court of Justice. The protection of such rights, whilst inspired by the constitutional traditions common to the Member States, must be ensured within the framework of the structure and objectives of the Community."

It will be noted here that the Court of Justice, in order to reassure national courts, stressed that Community human rights are "inspired" by the constitutional traditions common to the Member States.

In *Nold v Commission* (4/73), the Court of Justice went a step further. This was a case arising under the ECSC Treaty that provided that coal sellers must purchase a minimum quantity of coal from the mine. The applicant, who was not in a position to meet this requirement, claimed that the decision was a violation of his fundamental human rights, as the right to pursue his trade had been infringed. When the case arrived at the Court of Justice, that Court reiterated its view that fundamental rights form an integral part of the general principles of Community law. It again recognised that the Court of Justice drew inspiration from the constitutional traditions common to the Member States, but it went on to say that:

". . . similarly, international treaties for the protection of human rights on which the Member States have collaborated or of which they are signatories, can supply guidelines which should be followed within the framework of Community law."

It can be seen here that the Court is gathering to itself a wide range of sources from which to develop a system of human rights. It can also be seen from the above quotation that the Court spoke about treaties on which Member States have "collaborated", or of which they were signatories. This could be seen to suggest that it is not necessary that the Member State is actually a party to the treaty, thus giving the Court a wide range of guidelines.

The treaty which has been most important in this respect is the European Convention for the Protection of Human Rights and Fundamental Freedoms (ECHR). Not surprisingly, this has been the source of most of the Court's judgments in human rights cases, particularly in recent years. All the Member States are signatories to the ECHR. Indeed, the ECHR is a common standard for all Member States of the Community. It has now been incorporated into the Treaty on European Union: Article 6 states the Union shall respect fundamental rights, as guaranteed by the European Convention for the Protection for Human Rights and Fundamental Freedoms signed in Rome on November 4, 1950. Thus this respect for human rights arises from the constitutional traditions common to the Member States, as general principles of Community law. Even before this there have been numerous occasions on which the Court has made express references to the Convention. In *Johnston v The Chief Constable of the RUC* (222/84), the Court of Justice said that the principles on which the ECHR is based must be taken into consideration in Community law. The Court of Justice again referred to the ECHR in *Rutili* (36/75) which case involved an attempt by the French authorities to prevent a Community worker from living in a particular part of that country. Even though the applicant did not argue that his rights were protected under the ECHR, the Court nevertheless said that the principles governed by the Convention were general fundamental principles of Community law. The Court said:

"taken as a whole, these limitations placed on the general powers of Member States in respect of control of aliens are a specific manifestation of the more general principle, enshrined in Articles 8, 9, 10 and 11 of the Convention on Human Rights . . . which provide. . . that no restrictions in the interest of national security or public safety shall be placed on the rights secured by the above quoted Articles other than such as are necessary for the protection of those interests 'in a democratic society'".

There has been a lot of discussion, and much disagreement, as to whether the ECHR formed part of Community law which the Court of Justice therefore has a duty to protect. Some have regarded it as a mere source of principles, common to the Member States, while others have considered that it has already been incorporated into Community law. Since the ECHR was recognised in the preamble to the Single European Act, the Court of Justice has accorded a special significance to the Convention. In *ERT* (C-260/89) the Court of Justice confirmed this. In addition, the number of cases in which particular fundamental rights were evoked gradually increased and the Court's approach was followed, and given official legitimacy, by a declaration of the three political institutions of the Community. Over the years the Court of Justice has established a number of fundamental rights. They include the right to a fair hearing in *Pecastaing v Belgium* (98/79); freedom of expression (Article 10 ECHR) in *ERT* (260/89); and the right to privacy (Article 8 ECHR) in *Watson and Belmann* (118/75).

The Court of Justice continued its development of fundamental rights by "cherry picking" specific constitutional provisions from different Member States. One of the most detailed discussions on human rights is to be found in *Hauer v Rhineland Pfalz* (44/79). In this case the Court went into some detail in its analysis of the relevant provisions of the European Convention of Human Rights and also referred to particular provisions in the constitutions of Germany, Italy and Ireland in order to establish that the right to property is subject to restrictions particularly where these restrictions were to promote the public interest.

However, not all the decisions of the Court of Justice in this area of fundamental rights are derived from the ECHR or similar instruments. One such case was *AM and S Europe Ltd v Commission* (155/79) which concerned the principle of lawyer/client confidentiality, of which there is no mention in the Convention of Human Rights. In this case the Court said that Community law which derives from the legal interpenetration of the Member States must take into account the principles and concepts common to the laws of those states concerning lawyer/client confidentiality. The Court did admit that although the principle of such protection is generally recognised, its scope and the criteria for applying it did vary from Member State to Member State. Nevertheless, the Court was able to hold that communications which emanated from independent lawyers (lawyers who are not bound to the client by a relationship of employment) are able to rely on this confidentiality as a principle of Community law. It should be noted that this principle of confidentiality between lawyer and client was not readily accepted by all Member States. Indeed, the French Government went so far as to suggest that the case represented an attempt to foist on the Community what was no more than a domestic rule of English law.

This case highlights a number of difficulties that are inherent in the piecemeal methods adopted by the Court of Justice in furthering a system of fundamental rights. It is difficult for an individual to be able to ascertain exactly what his fundamental rights are at any particular time. But the difficulty goes deeper. The rights acknowledged to be fundamental by the Court of Justice have been, generally speaking, accepted throughout the Community and did not therefore prejudice fundamental Community aims. There may well be some difficulties where a fundamental right in one Member State was not recognised, or was controversial, in another Member State.

Such a controversy arose in *SPUC v Grogan* (C-159/90). This case concerned the action brought by the Society for the Protection of Unborn Children (SPUC) before the Irish courts to prevent student unions in Ireland from publicising the addresses of British abortion clinics. They based their complaint on the fact that the right to life of the unborn is constitutionally protected by Article 40.3.3 of the Constitution of Ireland; as a result of which abortion is prohibited there. In their defence the students argued that abortion was a service within the terms of Article 49 [ex 59] and that Community law therefore prohibited Ireland from placing restrictions on the right of Irish residents to have abortions in other Member States. The matter was referred to the Court of Justice by the Irish Supreme Court. The Court of Justice accepted that abortion was a service for the purposes of Article 49 [ex 59], because it was a service which was generally performed for remuneration. The activity of abortion was also legal in the other Member State concerned, *i.e.* the United Kingdom. However, the Court went on to hold that the defendants could not benefit from this right because they were not acting on behalf of the abortion clinics: there was no economic nexus between the two. They were simply trying to help their fellow students. It is a pity that the decision should have been reached on such a small technicality. After all, all that was needed was for the students union to have charged a nominal price for the advertisement, and the "economic nexus" would have been established.

This case illustrates the difficulties that can arise when the fundamental rights enshrined in a Member State's constitution (Ireland), clash with economic interests. It would seem that the promotion of trade takes precedence over the fundamental rights.

THE CHARTER OF FUNDAMENTAL RIGHTS OF THE EUROPEAN UNION (CFREU)

The European Council, meeting in June 1999, decided to "establish a Charter of Fundamental Rights of the European Union in order to make their overriding importance and relevance more visible to the Union's citizens". A body, which later decided to call itself the Convention, was set up to draft the Charter. The Convention was comprised of representatives of Member State governments and parliaments, the Commission and the European Parliament. The Charter was agreed by the Convention on October 2, 2000 and was jointly and solemnly "proclaimed" at Nice by the Council, Commission and the European Parliament.

The CFREU sets out the civil, political, economic and social rights of European citizens (see Chapter 10) under six headings: dignity, freedom, equality, solidarity, citizens' rights and justice. These rights are based on the fundamental rights and freedoms recognised by the European Convention for the Protection of Human Rights and Fundamental Freedoms and on the constitutional traditions of the countries of the European Union.

However, at the insistence of the United Kingdom, there is no reference to the CFREU in the Treaty of Nice. This omission will inevitably result in legal uncertainty and political controversy when the Charter begins to be used in the courts. The CFREU is not legally binding although this may change. A Declaration (No.23) on the Future of the Union was attached to the Treaty of

Nice. The Declaration states that the status of the Charter will be considered in time for the next Intergovernmental Conference in 2004. At the European Council held in Laeken, Belgium in December 2001, this Council established (another) Convention, charged with considering the future of the European Union prior to the IGC in 2004. The task of the Convention is to consider the key issues for the future development of the Union. Several issues have been identified by the Convention. Among them is that some thought "would also have to be given to whether the Charter of Fundamental Rights should be included in the basic treaty". This would mean, of course, that the Charter would have legal force.

There are those who wish to see the CFREU take on a binding nature and those who do not. The Commission, which is among the former has stated that it believes the Charter "is destined to be incorporated sooner or later into the treaties". The UK government, on the other hand, regards the Charter as "simply a statement of policy".

Despite the controversy and the uncertainty, the CFREU has begun to have some legal impact. In *PZ v European Parliament* (C-270/99), Advocate General Jacobs said that the Charter "while itself not legally binding, proclaims a generally recognised principle". In *Council v Hantala* (C-353/99P), Advocate General Leger said that one of the rights in the CFREU (the right to information) was evidence of its status as a fundamental right. So even though, at present, the Charter is not legally binding, it may have some legal consequences. As previously stated, the status of the CFREU is to be decided by the European Council in 2004.

Procedural Rights

There are a number of principles that are closely associated with administrative law principles. In the United Kingdom, they would be called natural law principles. They can be found in differing forms in the legal systems of Member States, *e.g.* as part of the written constitution in Germany and France, and as part of the common law in the United Kingdom.

The Right to a Hearing

This general principle of European law is of interest because it is an example of the Court of Justice drawing on English law systems for the development of Community law. The right to a hearing basically reflects the natural law principle of *audi alterem partem, i.e.* the right for both parties to present their cases. The case in which this arose was *Transocean Marine Paint Association v The Commission* (17/74). In this case it was the Advocate General who proposed that the right to a hearing was a general principle of Community law. In developing his argument, he pointed out the important role that natural justice plays in the United Kingdom, and by conducting a survey of the legal system of other Member States he was able to show that it had some application in those states also. The Court agreed with its Advocate General and declared "a person whose interests are perceptibly affected by a decision taken by a public authority must be given the opportunity to make his point of view known".

There was initially some confusion as to when the right to a hearing would arise. This situation was clarified in *Hoffman La-Roche v The Commission* (86/76). In that case, which involved competition policy, the Court said that the right to a hearing arose "in all proceedings in which sanctions, in particular fines or penalty payments, may be imposed".

Confidentiality or Legal Privilege

A corollary to the right to a fair hearing includes a right of access for one party to the documentation on which the case against it is based. However, that right must be limited by the opposite right to preserve confidential information, particularly that information which is passed between a client and their lawyer. This issue mainly arises in competition law, where the Commission will often amass a wealth of information, much of it confidential. The Commission must always be careful not to betray the source of information about an alleged breach of competition rules. This issue came before the Court of Justice in *AM & S v The Commission* (155/79) in which a company refused to hand over certain documents to the Commission, when it had been subjected to a raid by that body in connection with some alleged infringement of the competition law rules. Their refusal to hand over the documents was based on the principle of legal privilege. The Court held that the Commission had no right of access to documents relating to a defendant's right of defence that had been submitted by independent lawyers. In an earlier case, *Gutmann v The Commission* (35/65) the Court had held that it was acceptable for the Commission to have access to the advice of "in house" lawyers. The *Gutmann* case was later confirmed by the Court in *Luxembourg v Court of Auditors* (69/83).

Certainty: Legitimate Expectation

The principle of certainty is that the application of the law to a specific situation must be predictable. The Court of Justice first invoked the principle in *Defrenne v Sabena (No.2)* (43/75). The Court noted that the concept of legal certainty was to be found in all the legal systems of the Member States, although the precise legal content might vary from one Member State to another. The principle, which is one of the widest principles of Community law, has been applied in two specific senses. The first sense is the principle of legitimate expectation, which is derived from German law. The principle arises because it is recognised that the boundaries between legality and illegality should be clearly marked in advance. Also the type and scope of any punishment for infringement of the law should be reasonable ascertainable in advance.

The principle of legitimate expectation states that in the absence of an overriding matter of public interest, Community measures must not violate the legitimate expectation of the parties concerned. A legitimate expectation is one held by a reasonable person as to matters likely to occur in the normal course of affairs. For the principle to be activated it requires that a defendant has been encouraged by a reasonable expectation that they have relied on that expectation, and that as a result of that reliance they have suffered some loss. It will be seen that this principle is similar to the principle of estoppel in UK law. The principle is well illustrated in the case of *Topfer & Co v Commission* (122/77). This concerned a sugar exporter who had been granted a number of export licences. These licences contained rules concerning certain refunds which were payable, the amount of the refunds being fixed in advance. This scheme was suddenly altered by a Community Regulation and the changed rules operated to Topfer's disadvantage. Topfer sought to have the Regulation annulled for breach of the principle of legitimate expectation. The case did not succeed on its merits, but the Court of Justice upheld the principle of legitimate expectation as a principle of Community law. Many challenges are made on the basis of a breach of legitimate expectation, but they rarely succeed. In *Delacre v The Commission* (C-350/88) the Court held that it was a long established principle that "traders cannot have a legitimate expectation that an existing situation which is capable of being altered by the Community institutions in the exercise of their discretionary power will be maintained". A case in which it was successfully argued that the principle of legitimate expectation had been breached was *Mulder* (120/86). In this case the Court of

Justice found a Community Regulation relating to milk marketing to be invalid on the grounds that the regulations breached the principle of protection of legitimate expectations. The case involved the Community milk "lake". In order to reduce this excess it paid producers to cease milk production for a certain period, in exchange for a premium for non-marketing of the milk. The arrangement started in 1979 and was for a period of five years. Mulder was such a milk producer, and in 1994 he began to plan a resumption of his production and he applied to the relevant Dutch authorities for an indication of the quantity of milk which he would be allowed to produce without incurring the payment of a levy. He was refused on the grounds that he had not produced milk during the relevant year, which was 1993. Mr Mulder argued, of course, that he had not produced any milk in 1983 because of the bargain struck in 1979. When he challenged the Dutch authorities' denial of his quota, the Court of Justice found in his favour saying:

"it must be conceded . . . that a producer who has voluntarily ceased production for a certain period cannot legitimately expect to be able to resume production under the same conditions as those which previously applied and not to be subject to any rules of market or structural policy adopted in the meantime."

However, the Court went on to say that:

"where such a producer, as in the present case, has been encouraged by a Community measure to suspend marketing for a limited period in the general interest . . . he may legitimately expect not to be subject, upon the expiry of his undertaking, to restrictions which specifically affect him precisely because he availed himself of the possibilities offered by the Community provisions."

Certainty: Non-Retroactivity

The second of the senses arising under the heading of certainty is the principle of non- retroactivity. This principle, which is applied to Community secondary legislation, precludes a measure from taking effect before its publication. This might seem obvious, and indeed one of the basic principles of the rule of law is that people ought to be able to plan their lives, secure in the knowledge of the legal consequences of their actions. This would be particularly so in relation to the criminal law, where the effect of a retrospective measure may be to criminalise activity which was lawful when it was undertaken. The application of retrospective rules could also be extremely damaging to commercial transactions where a retrospective measure might upset the assumptions on which important transactions had been based.

For criminal measures, a case that gives a good illustration is *R v Kirk* (63/83). Captain Kirk was a Danish fisherman who was arrested while fishing within the United Kingdom's 12-mile coastal zone on January 6, 1983. The captain argued that he had a right as a Community national to fish anywhere in Community waters and the case was referred to the European Court by the Crown Court for a preliminary ruling. When the United Kingdom had become a member of the Community in 1973, they had been allowed to derogate from some provisions of Community law, including the right to exclude fishing boats from other Member States from the United Kingdom's 12-mile zone up to the December 31, 1982. The United Kingdom had applied for a further derogation for another 10 years, but the Council did not grant this until January 25, 1983 backdating their decision to January 1, 1983. It will be noted that Captain Kirk was therefore fishing after the derogation under the original application had expired, and before the new Council regulation had been adopted. The Court of Justice held in favour of Captain Kirk and said that "the principle that penal provisions may not have retro-active effect is one that is common to all the legal orders of the Member States and is enshrined in Article 7 of the ECHR as a fundamental right; it takes its place among the general principles of law whose observance is ensured by the Court of Justice".

So far as non-criminal activity is concerned, the court has held that in exceptional circumstances its rulings will be non-retroactive. In *Defrenne No.2* (43/75), the Court said that "important considerations of legal certainty" meant that Article 119EC could only apply prospectively. In this case, the Court would not allow Article 119 (now 141) to be relied on to support claims concerning pay periods prior to the date of the judgment. The Court stressed that *Defrenne* was an exceptional case. Normally, rulings from the Court of Justice are retroactive: the Court merely declared the law as it always was. That the Court's rulings would only by non-retroactive in important cases was confirmed in *Barber v GRE* (262/88). This case concerned the provision of equal pensions for male and females and the Court of Justice, in response to submissions made by the UK Government concerning the serious financial consequences the ruling would have, decided, as it had done in the *Defrenne* case to limit the retroactive nature of its rulings. The Court said:

". . . in those circumstances, overriding considerations of legal certainty preclude legal situations which have exhausted all their effects in the past from being called into question where that might retroactively upset the financial balance of many contracted-out pension schemes."

Although this judgment was remarkably ambiguous it was later held in *Ten Oever* (C-109/91) that no claim for equal treatment could be made prior to the judgment of the *Barber* case (May 19, 1990).

Proportionality

This principle of Community law can be described in the phrase, "the punishment must fit the crime". In other words, the means used to achieve a given end must be no more than that which is appropriate and necessary to achieve that end. It has now been written into the EC treaty by the Treaty on European Union as a formal principle of Community law. Article 5 [ex 3b] states: "any action by the Community shall not go beyond what is necessary to achieve the objectives of this Treaty". It may be lawful to limit economic activity, but only where the measures taken are appropriate and necessary in order to achieve legitimate objectives. In *FEDESA* (331/88) the Court held that if there is a choice between several appropriate measures, then the measure selected must be the least burdensome. In *R v Bouchereau* (30/77), the Court held that a penalty must be proportionate to the gravity of the offence, and a heavy burden should not be imposed upon some people in order to achieve something that is only of small importance to others.

The test of what is proportionate is placed on the authority relying on a particular measure. That authority is required to justify its actions and must take into account, or at least consider, possible alternatives. To a student of English law, the principle of proportionality is most likened to the English concept of "reasonableness". However, it must be stressed that proportionality is a much more rigorous test than one based on reasonableness. The principle of proportionality was invoked in *Internationale* (11/70). There have also been a number of cases in which the essence of the proportionality argument is that a penalty which has been imposed is excessive in relation to the aim of the measure in question. The Court has not been afraid to find in favour of individuals. This is perfectly illustrated in *Man (Sugar) v IBAP* (181/84). In this case, Man (Sugar) was required to give a security deposit when seeking a licence to export sugar outside the Community.

Man (Sugar) was late applying for the licence, but only by four hours. However, in line with a Community Regulation, they lost their entire deposit of £1,670,317. The company was not happy! The Court of Justice found a violation of the principle of proportionality. The Court held that the automatic forfeit of the entire deposit, in the given circumstances, was too drastic.

In another case, *Atlanta* (240/78), an Article of a Commission Regulation provided that "the security shall be wholly forfeit if the obligations imposed by the contract are not fulfilled". The Court of Justice struck out this Article because it did not "permit the penalty for which it provides to be made commensurate with the degree of fairness to implement the contractual obligations or with the seriousness of the breach of those obligations".

In both cases the Court suggested that the absolute rule of total loss of security should be replaced with a discretionary rule making the level of forfeiture proportionate to the gravity of the breach of contract.

Another illustration of the proportionality rule can be seen in *Bela-Muhle* (114/76). This involved a scheme whereby producers of animal feed were forced to use skimmed milk in their product. Normally, they would use soya, but a regulation had been introduced to force the use of skimmed milk because of a surplus in that product. The Court of Justice held that this regulation was unlawful because skimmed milk was three times more expensive than soya. Therefore the obligation to purchase the milk imposed a disproportionate burden on the animal-feed producers. The principle of proportionality has been used by the Court in a number of other areas apart from agriculture. The case of *Rutili* (36/75) concerned the rights of free movement of persons. Mr Rutili was an Italian national, who had been married to a French woman, and had been resident in France since his birth. While he was working as a trade union official deportation and restriction orders were made against him. These restrictions forbade him to live in certain parts of France. In this case, the Court held that any derogation from the fundamental principle of the right to free movement could only be sanctioned in a case which posed a genuine and serious threat to public policy. The Court went further and said that even then the measure must be the least restrictive possible in all the circumstances.

The principle of proportionality can also be seen in cases concerned with the free movement of goods. In the famous *Cassis de Dijon* case (120/78) the Court considered whether a German rule which prescribed the minimum alcohol content for Cassis could constitute an impediment to the principle of the free movement of goods under Article 30 EC. The Court decided that the rule could constitute such an impediment, and then had to decide whether the rule was necessary in order to protect German consumers from being misled. The Court said that although German consumers had a right not to be misled their interests could be safeguarded in other, less restrictive, ways. The Court suggested that perhaps a label displaying the alcoholic content of the Cassis would be a more proportionate way of achieving the same end. The Court came to a similar conclusion in the *German Beer Purity* case (178/84).

Equality

The principle of equality is specifically enshrined in the EC Treaty. Article 6 EC (formally Article 7 EEC) is concerned with general non-discrimination on the grounds of nationality. Article 119 EC is a general probation against discrimination on the grounds of sex in the context of the equal pay, and Article 48(2) concerns non-discrimination with regard to the free movement of workers. In addition to provisions in the Treaty it is also a general principle recognised by the Court of Justice. Indeed, the Court of Justice has said that these provisions are merely specific annunciations of:

"the general principle of equality which is one of the fundamental principles of community law. That principle requires that similar situations shall not be treated differently unless the differentiation is objectively justified".

In *Sotgiu* (152/73) the Court extended the prohibition on discrimination by reason of nationality to "all covert forms of discrimination which, by the application of criteria of differentiation, lead in fact to the same result". Another example of how the Court has used the equality of treatment principle to extend the scope of the prohibition of discrimination on the grounds on sex is in the context of pension rights. For example, in *Razzouk and Beydoun v Commission* (75 & 117/82) the Court has held that the Community institutions are bound by the principle of equal treatment of the sexes, and that this is not restricted to equal pay, or to what is specifically provided for in Article 119 EC, and in the relevant secondary legislation. A good example of the principle of equality in practice is seen in the first isoglucose case, *Royal Scholten-Honig Holdings Ltd* (103 & 145/82). In this case the plaintiffs were glucose producers and they sought to challenge the legality of a system of production subsidies whereby sugar producers were receiving subsidies financed in part by levies on the production of glucose. The plaintiffs argued that since glucose and sugar producers were in competition with each other the regulations implementing the system were discriminatory, *i.e.* they were in breach of the general principle of equality, and therefore invalid. The Court of Justice agreed.

It should be noted that this principle is not absolute. Sometimes a difference in treatment can be objectively justified. So, in terms of Community law, the principle of equality will only apply when discrimination is practised without adequate justification. This may seem an easy situation to judge and a straightforward example of discrimination on the grounds of sex would be where a woman was paid a lower wage than a man for doing exactly the same job. A simple example of discrimination on the grounds of nationality would be where a UK employer refused to hire any employee who was not British.

More difficult situations however, arise where the discrimination is not clear and direct but is either indirect and/or disguised; or indeed is entirely unintentional, but which nevertheless has a discriminatory impact. For example, a form of unintentional and indirect sex discrimination has occurred when an employer has paid part-time workers less per hour than full-time workers. The discrimination has arisen because the overwhelming majority of part-time workers are women. This type of indirect or unintentional discrimination may be justified on objective grounds. So, in *Jenkins v Kingsgate* (96/80), the Court said that the payment of a higher hourly wage to full-time workers, even though it indirectly discriminates against women, must be "objectively justified" on the grounds relating to the needs of the employer. This is issue is treated in more detail in Chapter 13.

CONCLUSIONS

The discussion above illustrates the importance of general principles of law in the judicial protection of individual rights. That the European Court of Justice has been successful in establishing these general principles of law can be illustrated by the German case of *Re Wunsche* in which the German constitutional court accepted that Community law gave as much protection for fundamental rights as German law. This can be compared to that Court's position in the earlier case of *Internationale Handelsgesellschaft* (11/70).

However, a point to remember is that these fundamental rights are not absolute rights. They are subject to limitations in the public interest. In *Nold* (4/73), the Court said that fundamental rights are always subject to limitations laid down in the public interest and that sometimes individual rights must yield to the common good.

SUBSIDIARITY

It is not clear whether subsidiarity is yet established as a general principle of Community law. Its origins are in Roman Catholic philosophy, as expressed by Pope Pius XI. Article 30 of the German basic law (*Grundgesetz*) states that "except as otherwise provided or permitted by this basic law the exercise of governmental powers and the discharge of governmental functions shall be incumbent on the *Länder*". It was later invoked in the Community context in Article 130r concerning environmental measures in the Single European Act. It is now incorporated as a formal principle into the EC Treaty by Article 5 [ex 3b] as follows:

"In areas which do not fall within its exclusive competence, the Community shall take action, in accordance with the principle of subsidiarity, only if and in so far as the objectives of the proposed action cannot be sufficiently achieved by the Member States and can, therefore, by reason of the scale or effects of the proposed action, be better achieved by the Community."

Put simply, it means that decisions must be taken as closely as possible to the citizens affected by them. First there is a two-tier test—

Community action will be justified only if it serves an end which both:

(a) cannot be achieved satisfactorily at the national level and;

(b) can be better achieved at Community level.

What has not yet been determined is how far the principle of subsidiarity will be subject to judgments of the Court of Justice. One can foresee a political minefield in which the Court is required to review a Commission assertion that Community action is required in a particular area. If the Court becomes too involved it may be accused of a political decision, in that it concerns the most effective level of government for different regulatory tasks. If the Court of Justice decides to take a less intensive view it may be open to criticism from Member States that it is abrogating its responsibilities under Article 5 [ex 3b] in this respect.

REMEDIES

The doctrine of direct effect gives important rights to individuals which they can enforce in their national courts. However it would be a spurious right if an individual could not obtain an effective remedy for a breach of their Community law rights. Neither the Treaty nor any of the secondary legislation lays down a system or procedure for the enforcement of Community law, nor is there a general scheme of Community-specific remedies. What will be seen in the discussion that follows is that, in the early years in the life of the Community, the Court of Justice left the issue of remedies as a matter for national law to be decided by domestic courts. In those early days the Court was concerned with establishing a Community legal order of substantive law. Once the Court of Justice was convinced that all Member States had accepted the substantive supremacy of Community law, (perhaps by the 1990s), it could increasingly turn its attention to the establishment of a system of Community procedural law. There is some evidence that the Court is in this process at present.

The main tool used by the Court of Justice to build up a system for providing remedies for breach of Community law has been Article 10 [ex 5] of the EC Treaty. This provides:

"Member States shall take all appropriate measures, whether general or particular, to ensure fulfilment of the obligations arising out of this Treaty or resulting from action taken by the institutions of the Community. They shall facilitate the Community's tasks.

They shall abstain from any measure which could jeopardise the attainment of the objectives of this Treaty."

In some of the earliest cases before it, *e.g. Humblet* (6/60) and *Salgoil* (13/68), the Court of Justice held that it was for the national legal system to determine the remedy available to a person who had suffered as the result of a breach of Community law. However, in terms of an individual seeking a remedy by pleading the direct effect of Community law, the first case was *Rewe-Zentralfinanz* (33/76). Applying the principle of co-operation laid down in Article 10 [ex 5], the Court of Justice held that it was the national courts which were entrusted with ensuring the legal protection which citizens derive from the direct effect of the provisions of Community law. Accordingly, *in the absence of Community rules on this subject*, it was for the domestic legal system of each Member State to determine the procedural conditions governing actions at law, provided that such conditions were not less favourable than those relating to similar actions of a domestic nature. Thus the situation is one of co-operation in which Community law and national law operate in combination, the latter taking over where the former leaves off, and working out its consequences.

In cases following on from *Rewe-Zentralfinanz,* the Court of Justice reiterated this theme. It is possible to identify three conditions for the application of national remedies:

(i) Community remedies must be no less favourable than remedies available for similar breaches of domestic law.

(ii) that national rules must not render the exercise of a Community right impossible in practice, and

(iii) that any penalties imposed for breaches of Community law must be proportionate.

The next case in which the Court of Justice elaborated in great detail on the obligation of national courts to provide remedies to ensure the enforcement of Community law, and to penalise breaches of that law, was *Von Colson and Kamann* (14/83). In this case, the plaintiffs, (both women) had applied for jobs in the German prison service. Two male candidates were appointed and the two female plaintiffs successfully argued before the German courts that they had been the victims of sex discrimination. At issue in the case was the amount of damages for compensation they could receive. By German law they could only claim for "reliance loss", that is, reimbursement of their travelling expenses. In addition to the three conditions previously imposed, and after citing Article 10 [ex 5], the Court of Justice held:

"Although . . . full implementation of the Directive does not require any specific form of sanction for unlawful discrimination, it does entail that the sanction be such as to guarantee real and effective judicial p.rotection.

. . . If a Member State chooses to penalise breaches . . . by an award of compensation in order to ensure . . . it has a deterrent effect, that compensation must in any event be adequate in relation to the damage sustained and must therefore amount to more than purely nominal compensation . . ."

What is seen in *Von Colson* is an extension by the Court of Justice of the issue of the adequacy and effectiveness of Community rights. But the question was bound to arise as to the situation where a Member States did not have a legal remedy that would give individuals an adequate or effective compensation for a breach of Community law. In such circumstances was there an obligation on a national court to create a new remedy?

The issue was addressed, and partly resolved, in the dramatic case, *Factortame* (C-213/89). (The complicated series of cases is explained in Chapter 4). In *Factortame No.2*, the Court of Justice emphasised the importance of effective remedies and placed this principle above national rules of procedure. In *Factortame No.2*, the issue was whether a national court was bound to grant a particular remedy, when according to the House of Lords, English law did not recognise this particular remedy in the given circumstances of the case. The remedy sought in this particular case was an interim injunction against the Crown, so as to suspend an Act of Parliament until a decision on its compatibility with Community law has been given. The Court of Justice was forthright in its judgment. First it repeated the importance of Article 10 [ex 5] in order to ensure the effectiveness of Community law. Then it held:

". . . the full effectiveness of Community law would be just as much impaired if a rule of national law could prevent a court seized of a dispute governed by Community law from granting interim relief in order to ensure its full effectiveness of the judgment to be given on the existence of the rights claimed under Community law. It follows that a Court who in those circumstances would grant interim belief, if it were not for a rule of national law, is obliged to set aside that rule".

Although the Court of Justice was so forceful in its judgment it again left to the national court to decide the conditions under which a national remedy (such as interim relief) should be granted in a particular case. However, in *Zuckerfabrik Süderdithmarschen* (C-143/88 & C-92/89) the Court of Justice did lay out the precise conditions under which interim relief could be granted (see below). Then, in *Marshall No.2*, (C-271/91), the Court extended the effectiveness principle even further. The challenge in this case was based, as in *Von Colson* on Article 6 of Directive 76/207. In *Marshall No.2*, the damages awarded to Mrs Marshall had been calculated subject to a fixed statutory limit under the Sex Discrimination Act 1975. The Court of Justice ruled that Article 6 required that the remedy must be "sufficiently effective to achieve the objectives of the Directive". In order to comply with the principle of non-discrimination, and its obligation under Article 6 of the Directive, the state must provide *full* compensation for those damaged as a result of a breach of the principle. Therefore, a limit on compensation would mean, in some cases, that full compensation could not be awarded. The domestic legislation was incompatible with Community law.

It can be seen that the judgments of the Court of Justice represent a shift away from the principles of national procedural and autonomy in remedies towards a system, however putative at this stage, of Community remedies. This is the only meaningful interpretation that can be given to the requirements to modify national laws, or the "invention" by national courts of new remedies and sanctions. The Court of Justice has seen that national laws are not always effective to protect the Community rights of individuals, no national laws always deter breaches of Community law. The Court has urged the "competent institutions" to issue general rules of substance and procedure to bring about harmonisation in national rules and time limits. The Commission however has had little success in this area, and so it has been left to the Court of Justice to decide, on a case-by-case basis, whether particular national rules provide effective protection for individuals' Community rights. This the Court has done in increasingly specific terms. It will be worthwhile to look at their actions in three specific areas, interim relief, damages and limitation periods.

Interim Relief

As was noted above this issue was brought before the Court of Justice in *Factortame No.2*. In this case, a group of Spanish fishermen were seeking an interim injunction to prevent the application of the Merchant Shipping Act 1988, which they claimed was in breach of Community law. As it had not yet been shown that the statute was in breach of Community law, the rights claimed by the fishermen were putative. The Divisional Court had referred the question to the Court of Justice but the matter was not yet decided. In the meantime the application for interim relief had come before the House of Lords, who had found that it had no jurisdiction under English law to grant an interim injunction against the Crown. The House of Lords referred this point to the Court of Justice, and as was seen above, the Court was unequivocal in its reply. But apart from saying that, if interim relief was the remedy that would provide full and effective protection of Community rights then such interim relief must be provided for, it did not set out any conditions for the granting of such relief. The Court of Justice held that such conditions were a matter for national law.

However, in *Zuckerfabrik Süderdithmarschen,* the Court was prepared to go further. The facts of the case are not important in an understanding of the judgment, but simply, the applicants were attempting to resist further demands from a national authority for the payment of a levy. Their argument was that the Community regulation, on which the levy was based, was invalid. The national court asked the Court of Justice if a national court was obliged to grant interim relief when the invalidity of the Regulation had not yet been established. The Court of Justice confirmed that there was such an obligation. The Court repeated its ruling in *Factortame* and held further:

". . . (individual) rights would be compromised if, pending delivery of a judgment by the Court, which alone has jurisdiction to decide EEC Regulations invalid, individuals were not in a position to obtain a decision granting suspension of enforcement which would make it possible for the effects of the disposal Regulation to be rendered for the time being inoperative against them".

The Court of Justice further held:

"The interim legal protection which Community law ensures for individuals before national courts must remain the same, irrespective of whether they contest the compatibility of national legal provisions with Community law or the validity of secondary Community law, in view of the fact that the dispute in both cases is based on Community law itself".

This paragraph of the judgment is important because it implies that the rules for interim relief which the Court set out in *Zückerfabrik* would also apply in *Factortame*-type cases, were an individual is challenging the compatibility of a national law with Community law. The Court of Justice suggested that national courts should grant interim relief:

(a) if the facts and legal circumstances are such as to persuade the court that serious doubt exist as to the validity of the contested Community measure. The national court must set out the reasons for which it believes that the provision is invalid;

(b) in cases of extreme urgency; and

(c) to avoid serious and irreparable damage to the party seeking them.

In addition the Court noted that purely financial damages would not be irreparable.

Zükerfabrik is significant because it is the first attempt by the Court of Justice to set out Community rules for the application of a particular remedy for actions based on Community law. In *Atlanta* (C-465/93) and *Atlantic Container* (C-149/95), the Court of Justice confirmed the conditions necessary for the granting of interim relief, as set out in (a)–(c) above. The Court also added two further conditions. First, the matter in dispute must be referred to the Court of Justice under Article 234 [ex 177]. Second, the national court should take due account of any Community interest and respected any decision from the Court of Justice (or CFI) already given on the substance of the disputed matter.

Damages

All of the Member States of the Community recognise damages as a remedy under national law. In Community law terms it has long been recognised that damages could be claimed, on the basis of direct or indirect effect, for a breach of a substantive provision of Community law. In *Von Colson* the Court of Justice found that a Member State was "free to choose between different solutions for achieving its objective". This was because the Directive in dispute (76/207) was not sufficiently clear and precise to give rise to a specific Community sanction. It will be recalled (see above) that the Court said that, in accordance with their obligation to provide "real and effective" remedies, states must provide compensation which is more than nominal; it must be "adequate in relation to the damage sustained".

As has also been discussed above, the Court of Justice, in *Marshall No.2* (C-271/91) held that damages had to be "full". This would also include entitlement to interest on the award running from the date of discrimination to the date when compensation was paid.

The landmark judgment in *Francovich* (C-6 & 9/90) established another basis or a claim for damages, this time against the state. (For a full discussion of this case, see Chapter 4). *Francovich* has introduced a new Community principle of state liability. This principle was laid down in specific terms, but the Court of Justice also held that "a state is liable to make good damage to individuals caused by a breach of Community law for which it is responsible". *Francovich* can be regarded as an innovative price of law-making by the Court of Justice, in that in the fulfilment of the fundamental requirement of effectiveness, the Court has ruled that state liability in damages is a principle of Community law, and not merely the adoption of a national remedy to Community circumstances.

Limitation Periods

Although limitation periods are a feature of the legal system of all Member States, these periods differ between Member States both as to period of time and to circumstances of claim. Thus, it has been pointed out, limitation periods in respect of the same claim can range from 2 months–10 years. This obviously gives unequal protection for individuals across the Community. In contrast to the progressive development in the areas of interim relief and damages, the Court of Justice has not been consistent in its judgments on limitation periods. This lack of consistency on limitation rules has limited the effectiveness of individual rights because it has caused uncertainty. Individuals may have lost the protection of Community law because they failed to act on time.

Initially, in *Rewe-Zentralfinanz v Landwirstschaftskammer Saarland* (33/76), the Court of Justice was content to leave the issue to be resolved by national jurisdiction, subject only to the caveat that a "reasonable period of limitation" would not make it impossible in practice for national courts to protect an individuals Community rights. There was a slight hint of exasperation in *Express Dairy Foods* (130/79) when the Court of Justice "regretted" the absence of a Community system of limitation periods: but the Court itself was not prepared to set down general rules.

The Court of Justice achieved a *volte face* in *Emmott v Minister for Social Welfare* (C-209/90). This Irish case is complicated because it involves two other non-connected cases before the Court of Justice. Ms Emmott's claim for disability benefit was refused. She claimed the refusal was discriminatory in breach of Directive 79/7. Ms Emmott initially did not know that the Directive was directly effective, but when she became aware of this (after the decision of the Court of Justice in *McDermott v Minister for Social Welfare* (286/85)), she asked the Minister to review her case. The authorities deferred her application while they waited for a decision in another case before the Court of Justice, *Cotter and McDermott* (C-377/89). When her application eventually came up for consideration the Minister argued that her application was out of time. The Court of Justice was asked whether it was contrary to Community law to rely on a national time limit so as to defeat a claim for compensation. The Court repeated its assertion that, in the absence of Community rules, it was for the individual domestic legal systems to set the limits, provided only that such conditions are no less favourable than those of a domestic nature, and do not render it "virtually impossible" to exercise Community rights.

In addition to this, the Court said that account must be taken of the particular nature of directives:

"So long as a directive has not been properly transposed into national law, individuals are unable to ascertain the full extent of their rights . . . It follows that, until such time as a directive has been properly transformed, a defaulting Member State may not rely on an individual's delay in initiating proceedings against it in order to protect rights conferred upon him by the provisions of the directive and that a period laid down by national law within which proceedings must be initiated cannot begin to run before that time".

The Court of Justice in *Emmott* is relying on the concept of estoppel. That is, that a Member State cannot rely, or profit from, its own default. So, in *Emmott*, the state could not benefit from a national time limit as a bar to an action until such time as a directive had been properly implemented. It was only at this moment that an individual would have clear knowledge of their rights.

Emmott left a number of questions unanswered. Particularly, the Court did not say what "properly transposed" meant. This could give rise to a number of ambiguities. What if a Member State implemented a directive in good faith, or had done nothing to change domestic law, believing it to be consistent with the requirements of a directive? Or what if a judgment by the Court of Justice had placed a contradictory interpretation on the reasonable belief of a Member State?

It might have been because of these problems that the Court of Justice was notably more cautious in *Steenhorst-Neerings* (C-338/91). The facts of the case were very similar to *Emmott*, and the applicant invoked *Emmott* in their pleading. Nevertheless, the Court distinguished *Emmott*. That case, the Court said concerned national rules fixing time limits for bringing an action, which prevented individuals from asserting their rights under the directive. The challenge in *Steenhorst-Neerings* was not against a rule affecting an individual's right to rely on a directive, but was against the limitation of the retroactive affect of a claim. The argument used by the Court is almost sophistry. It is certainly not convincing. The rules challenged in *Emmott* and *Steenhorst-Neerings* did serve different purposes, but the *effect* of both rules was to prevent both applicants from relying on the Directive. Even though *Steenhorst-Neerings* fits badly with previous Court of Justice decisions, and even undermines the principle of the effectiveness of Community law, it was followed by the judgments in *Johnson No.2* (C-410/92). This case also involved Directive 79/7, and the Court held that a rule restricting to one year the retroactive effect of a claim for a non-contributory incapacity benefit was compatible with Community law. If *Steenhorst-Neerings* and *Johnson* can be seen as a reining in of *Emmott* and a movement to a more restrictive interpretation, then the case of *Fantask* (C-185/95) was the climax of that movement. Denmark had levied charges on the registration of companies. These charges were found to be contrary to Directive 69/335. Danish law set a limitation period of five years for the recovery of such charges. The claimants argued, on the *Emmott* principle, that a Member States could not rely on the limitation period so long as the Directive (69/335) had not been properly transposed into national law. The Court of Justice said that the judgment in *Emmott* was justified by the particular circumstances of that case. In *Emmott*, the Court said, the time limit had "the result of depriving the applicant of any opportunity whatever" to rely on her rights arising from the directive at issue. However, the Court confirmed *Steenhorst-Neerings* and *Johnson* and held that the Danish five-year limitation period was reasonable. The time limit was also applied, without distinction, to domestic claims and those based on Community law and was therefore compatible with Community law.

Fantask appears to confirm that *Emmott* now only applies to directives and to the given circumstances of that case. Apart from those narrow circumstances *Emmott* has been distinguished out of existence.

Conclusion

The development of a system of Community remedies will not be without its problems. This is because any development will rely on national courts to enforce Community law based on "similar actions of a domestic nature". There could be a difficulty on deciding what such an equivalent action was and in different Member States the notion of equivalence would be different. Another difficulty is establishing whether a particular rule of national law makes it "impossible in practice" for an individual to exercise Community rights. What are the exact meanings of "effective", "sufficiently effective" or "adequate", expressions used by the Court of Justice on numerous occasions? The only way to resolve these issues is by bringing cases before the Court of Justice. But this is often difficult. It may not be easy to persuade the Commission to bring an action under Article 226 [ex 169], nor may it be possible to persuade a national court that an Article 234 [ex 177] reference should be made. In any event, as has been seen frequently, the judgment in an Article 234 [ex 177] case often raises more questions than answers, and these questions in turn need to be resolved by the Court of Justice in further cases. The question of a coherent and effective system of individual rights is best achieved through legislation, proposed by the Commission and agreed by the Member States.

6. FORMS OF LAW

This chapter concerns all forms of law employed in the Community, from the treaties and secondary legislation, to the doctrines and principles of law developed or used by the Court of Justice. The chapter will attempt to answer two key questions.

(1) Where does Community law come from?

(2) What rights can individuals enforce?

The order in which the material is covered does not correspond exactly with the "hierarchy" of EC legislation, but the reasons for this will be explained in the text.

Community law can be split into primary and secondary sources. The primary source of Community law consists of the three original constitutional treaties, as amended by a number of subsequent treaties. It also consists of the Merger Treaty, the Budgetary Treaty, the Single European Act and the Treaty on European Union. And, following the completion of the IGCs in 1996/97 and 2000, it now includes the Treaty of Amsterdam and the Treaty of Nice.

The treaties, particularly the EC Treaty, give powers for the institutions (generally the Council), to pass secondary legislation. These measures are the secondary sources of European law. The main types of secondary legislation are regulations, Directives and decisions. The forms of these measures are set out in Article 249 [ex 189]. Each of the Treaty bases that allows for secondary legislation also stipulates which type of measure is to be used. For example, Article 137 [ex 118] requires further implementing legislation to be undertaken by means of Directives. An additional source of law arises from the international agreements entered into by the Community on behalf of the Member States. There are also those agreements where the Community has taken over the competence of the Member States. The most notable of these agreements are the GATT and the Lomé conventions between the Member States and many third world nations.

Finally, and in some cases most importantly, there are the judicial developments of the Court of Justice. In this chapter we will be examining the establishment of the doctrines of direct applicability and direct effect.

THE TREATIES

When a Member State joins the Community, all of the provisions of the treaties automatically become part of the generally binding law of that Member State and are applicable, not only to the Member States, but also to the peoples of that country. This might seem surprising, given that the Treaty is an international agreement. The domestic effect of international agreements has traditionally been a matter to be determined in accordance with the constitutional law of each of the states which is a party to that Treaty. In countries such as the United Kingdom which adopt a dualist approach to international law, international treaties do not of themselves give rise to rights or interests which individuals of the state can plead and enforce before their national courts. Even such international agreements as the European Convention on Human Rights, which was designed for the protection of individuals cannot, because it has not been implemented in the United Kingdom, be domestically invoked by the citizens of the United Kingdom. The texts of the treaties make no reference to the affect which their provisions are to have for individuals. It is also apparent that the original members of the Community did not envisage that the treaties would be any different in terms of their domestic affect from other international treaties and agreements. However, the leading case of *Van Gend En Loos* (26/62) confirmed that Community law is also the legal concern of individuals, and not only the Member States.

THE LEGISLATIVE ACTS OF COMMUNITY INSTITUTIONS

The legislative acts of the Community are provided for by Article 249 [ex 189] of the EC Treaty which empowers the institutions to create legislation. Article 249 [ex 189] envisages five different measures, *i.e.* regulations, Directives, decisions, recommendations and opinions. However, only the first three forms are legally binding. Article 249 [ex189] provides

"In order to carry out their tasks . . . the European Parliament acting jointly with the Council, the Council and the Commission shall make regulations and issue Directives, take decisions, make recommendations or deliver opinions."

Regulations

Article 249 [ex 189] declares regulations to be directly applicable. This means that they are self-executing in that they take effect in all Member States on the date specified in them, or if no date is specified, on the 20th day following the publication in the Official Journal. Regulations are the most powerful law making tools available to the Community. It will be seen from a perusal of Article 249 [ex 189] that regulations have three qualities. They are of general application; they are binding in their entirety; and they are directly applicable. First, it will be seen that regulations are applicable to all, rather than specific individuals or groups. A regulation is a detailed form of law that attempts to ensure that the law in all Member States is exactly the same.

It was noted above that a regulation was directly applicable i.e. it becomes legally valid in the Member States without any need for further implementation. In fact, it was held in *Leonesio* (93/71) that Member States cannot subject the regulation to any implementing measures other than those required by the regulation itself. In some circumstances, however, the regulation may require a Member State to introduce implementing measures to ensure the effectiveness of the regulation.

In order to constitute a regulation the act of the Community organ must comply with certain conditions:

    (a)   it must be based on the authority of the Treaty, which means that regulations can only be made where they are provided for in the Treaty. So, for example, Article 40 [ex 49] of the EC Treaty on free movement of workers allows the institutions a choice between regulations and Directives.

b) under the terms of Article 253 [ex 190] a regulation has to be "reasoned". This was not defined by Article 253 [Ex 190] but the Court of Justice defined "reasoned" in *Barge v High Authority* (18/62). The Court said that regulations should indicate in general terms the aims pursued by the regulation; they shall give the reasons that justify the regulation, and the outlines of the systems adopted.

It is important to note that there is not a clear-cut distinction between the various measures allowed for by Article 249 [ex 189]. In order to determine whether a measure is a regulation it is necessary to consider its contents rather than its form. In *Confederation Nationale* (16 & 17/62) the Court of Justice interpreted what had been called a regulation as a series of decisions.

Directives

A Directive is binding "as to the results to be achieved". It sets out the aims which must be achieved but leaves the choice of the form and method of implementation to each Member State. It therefore does not automatically become part of the national legal system and is therefore not directly applicable, or self-executing. It has to be implemented by national Parliaments. Whereas a regulation is aimed at uniformity, a Directive is a method in which national laws can be harmonised in line with Community law. Each Member State has discretion as to how to implement the requirements of a directive. In some cases, a Member State may have nothing to do at all, as it considers that the existing national law is already in conformity with the requirements of a new directive. It would merely need to notify the Commission as to how the directive has been implemented, as this is now generally one requirement of directives. The directive will also set out a period for implementation by a Member State. This can range from one year to five or more. The time scale will depend on the complexity of the subject matter and the urgency of the legislation, and it is common for the newer Member States of the Community to be given a longer period before which they are required to implement the directive.

Some directives may have what is called direct effect (see below). This will give rights to individuals to enforce the provisions of the directive before their own national courts. Even if a

Member State fails to implement the directive within the time scale, or fails to implement it correctly, this may still lead to the right for individuals and legal persons to be able to persuade their national courts to interpret domestic law in the light of the purpose of the directive. They might even be able to sue the State for its failure to implement the directive. (see below).

Decisions

Decisions are binding and enforceable acts of law which are usually addressed to Member States, or sometimes to specific individuals. A decision is binding in its entirety upon those to whom it is addressed. The Treaty provides for the exclusive use of decisions in many different contexts. For example, Article 85(2) [ex 89(2)] allows the Commission to pass decisions that competition policy has been breached. This is also one example of where the Council can delegate power to the Commission to take decisions on matters within the competence of the Council.

Recommendations and Opinions

It has been noted that these are not legally binding. They have not been questioned in the Court of Justice as to their validity but they are often considered to be of persuasive quality. It should be obvious that recommendations and opinions are not directly applicable.

It was stated earlier that Article 253 [ex 190] requires that regulations shall state the reasons on which they are based. Indeed, Article 253 applies to all binding acts of the institutions. It is also a requirement that the Treaty base must be cited when legislation is passed. Failure by the institutions to comply with these requirements will give rise to grounds for judicial review of the measure under Article 230 [ex 173]. The choice of legal base can be of major significance to the legislative procedure to be followed. It may mean the difference between the European Parliament being consulted or being involved in the "co-operation procedure" or the "co-decision procedure". It could also mean the difference between the Council acting by unanimity or by some form of majority voting. For example, in *European Parliament v Council (Chernobyl)* (C-70/88) the Council sought to have a regulation adopted under Article 31 of the Euratom Treaty which required that Parliament be consulted. Parliament argued that the measure should have been adopted under Article 100a (now 95) which meant that the co-operation procedure would have been applicable. The Court of Justice decided that the prerogatives of

Parliament include participation in the drafting of legislative measures, in particular participation in the co-operation procedure laid down in the EC Treaty.

As the treaties are largely framework constitutional treaties they require substantial supplementation. Much of this is covered by the promulgation of regulations, etc, but these measures need to be interpreted. There is thus much scope for activity on the part of the Court of Justice. The Court of Justice has determined that the Treaty and secondary legislation which flows from the Treaty must be interpreted and applied according to the scheme of the Treaty as a whole, and in the light of the broad principles of the preamble to the Treaty and Articles 2, 3, 5 [ex 3b] and 7 [ex 4], to achieve the result required for the Community. The Court of Justice has adopted a purposive or teleological approach, which has resulted in jurisprudence that encompasses a wide variety of law. Unlike a UK court which often restricts itself to the interpretation of words or phrases from legislative provisions, the Court of Justice has led the development of some of the most fundamental doctrines and principles of Community law. This includes the supremacy of Community law, (see Chapter 4), the development of general principles of law (see Chapter 4) and direct effect, to which we now turn our attention.

DIRECT EFFECT

Direct effect is one of the most remarkable features of Community law and has probably attracted more attention than any other concept. This is because of the impact it has had on the legal and political integration of the Member States. It has been described as the "infant disease" of Community law, but has now become to be recognised as part of the "new legal order" that confers rights on individuals. The doctrine of direct effect is a judicial development of the Court of Justice and is very closely connected to the notion of direct applicability: it is also very often confused with this concept. However, there are fundamental differences between them. Unfortunately, for the student, the terminology of the Court of Justice and of many of the national courts has not been consistent. Particularly in the early years of the Community the two terms tended to be used interchangeably. Most often, the Court of Justice has used the term direct applicability when the sense of the expression meant that the provision gave rise to rights enforceable by individuals before their national courts. The remainder of this chapter will look at direct effect of the different types of Community law. It will start with the treaties, followed by regulations and decisions. The direct effect of directives will be left until last because this is a particularly complicated (and interesting) area of the concept.

Treaties

It was as early as 1963 that the Court of Justice established the concept of direct effect in the Community legal order. In *Van Gend en Loos* (26/62) the Court stated that:

"the objectives of the EEC Treaty . . . implies that this Treaty is more than an agreement which merely creates mutual obligations between the contracting states. . .the Community constitutes a new legal order of international law for the benefit of which the states have limited their sovereign rights, albeit within limited fields, and the subjects of which comprise not only Member States but also their nationals. Independently of the legislation of the Member States, Community law therefore not only imposes obligation on individuals but is also intended to confer on them rights which become part of their legal heritage".

The rationale of direct effect is to place the enforcement of Community law on two levels. This has been called the notion of dual vigilance. On the one hand, the Commission, acting in its role as "guardian of the Treaty" may invoke an Article 226 [ex 169] action against a recalcitrant Member State. On the other hand it also gives individuals, at a domestic level, the ability to rely on the principle of direct effect. There is also the issue of public policy in that the provisions of a directive will be more effective within national legal systems if they can be invoked by individuals before their national courts. A further rationale for direct effect is what has become known as the "estoppel" argument. In other words, by giving rights to individuals, which they can enforce against the state, a Member State is estopped from relying on its own failure to properly implement a directive.

The *Van Gend en Loos* case was a seminal judgment for the Community. A reading of the submissions of the governments in that case indicates that direct effect was not one of the original assumptions when these countries became members of the Community.

However, not every Treaty Article has been held to be directly effective. In the *Van Gend en Loos* case, the Court of Justice set out the criteria for the direct effect of Treaty provisions. The Court said:

"the wording of Article 12 (now 25) contains a clear and unconditional prohibition which is not a positive but a negative obligation. This obligation, moreover, is not qualified by any reservation on the part of the states which would make its implementation conditional upon a positive legislative measure enacted under national law. The very nature of this prohibition makes it ideally adapted to produce direct effects in the legal relationship between Member States and their subjects . . . It follows from the forgoing consideration that, according to the spirit, the general scheme and wording of the Treaty, Article 12 (now 25) must be interpreted as producing direct effects and creating individual rights which national courts must protect."

Then the Court set out three criteria for direct effect. The measure must be clear and unambiguous, it must be unconditional and it must take effect without any further action being required by the Community or a Member State. In a series of cases the Court of Justice has held that many of the Treaty Articles have this quality of direct effect. These include Articles 39–42 [ex 48 –52] on the free movement of persons; Articles 28–31 [ex 30–34] on the free movement of goods; Article 141 [ex 119] on equal pay; and Articles 85 and 86 [ex 85 and 86] on competition law. The relevant cases are discussed in the chapters concerning these topics. Based on the dual vigilance notion of enforcement and the estoppel principle it can be seen that direct effect gives rights to individuals against the Member State. The individual and the state can be seen to be in a hierarchical relationship, the state being at the apex and the individual beneath it. This is a vertical relationship, and thus it has been said that Treaty Articles have "vertical" direct effect. But the judgment in *Van Gend en Loos* talked about individual rights and these rights may sometimes need to be exercised against other individuals or legal persons. Because this relationship is between equals it has been termed a horizontal relationship and has given rise to the term "horizontal" direct effect. The first case to confirm this was that of *Defrenne v SABENA* (43/75). This case concerned the rights of Miss Defrenne, an air hostess with SABENA airlines for equal pay with a male employee doing the same work. She argued that her right to equal pay was guaranteed under Article 141 [ex 119] EC. The Court of Justice held that SABENA, a private company, was in breach of their obligations under Article 141 [ex 119]. The Court said:

". . . the fact that certain provisions of the Treaty are formerly addressed to the Member States does not prevent rights from being conferred at the same time on any individual who has an interest in the performance of the duties first laid down . . ."

So, if a Treaty Article satisfies the three criteria, set out above, it will have direct effect. This is not to say however that a student will find it easy to determine whether a Treaty Article, or any other measure, will satisfy these criteria. Indeed there are many cases where it can be shown that a measure seems to exhibit none of three requirements, yet the Court of Justice has held that the Article, or measure, has direct effect. For example, Article 141 [ex 119] of the EC Treaty, which seeks to establish the principle of equal pay for equal work, seems neither to be sufficiently clear and precise, nor unconditional. In fact it could be said that such requirements as specified by the Court of Justice are merely a "code" by which the Court decides whether a particular measure is capable of being sufficiently operational in itself to be applied by the Court. In *Banks v British Coal* (C-28/92), the Advocate General expressed it thus:

"the clarity, precision, unconditional nature, completion or perfectness of the rule and its lack of dependence on discretionary implementing measures are . . . merely aspects of one and the same characteristic feature which that rule must exhibit, namely it must be capable of being applied by a court to a specific case."

This has been termed the requirement of "justiciability". This concept has been defined as meaning "a rule can have direct effect whenever its characteristics are such that it is capable of judicial adjudication, account being taken both of its legal characteristics and of the ascertainment of the facts on which the application of each particular rule has to rely".

Regulations

Regulations are clearly directly applicable by reason of Article 249 [ex 189]. However, they are not necessarily directly effective. The question of whether they can also give rise to direct effect depends on whether they satisfy the same criteria as that set out in *Van Gend en Loos* for Treaty Articles. A case in which a regulation was held to be directly effective was *Leonesio v Ministry of Agriculture* (93/71).

Decisions

Article 249 [ex 189] EC also lists a decision as being "binding in its entirety upon those to whom it is addressed". Unlike a regulation, a decision will not be a general measure, but an individual one that is directed to a specific addressee. Nevertheless the Court had little hesitation in holding that decisions could be directly effective. In *Grad* (9/70), the plaintiff sought to rely directly on a Council decision on VAT in order to have a German law on transport tax declared incompatible with them. The Court of Justice said:

"where . . . the Community authority by means of a decision have imposed an obligation on a Member State . . . to act in a certain way, the effectiveness (*l'effet utile*) a measure would be weakened if the nationals of that state could not invoke it in the courts and the national courts could not take it into consideration as part of Community law".

In that case the Court held that the obligation imposed in the decision in question satisfied the criteria for direct effect.

Directives

Directives have caused particular problems for the Court of Justice. The concept of the direct effect of Treaty provisions can be argued on the basis that the fundamental aims of the Treaty would be seriously hampered if those it affected could not enforce its clear provisions before domestic courts. In respect of regulations it could be cited that Article 249 [ex 189] specifically provided for their direct applicability, which the Court treated as being the same as directly effective. In the case of decisions it could be argued that since they were intended to be binding upon the person to whom they were addressed, then if the terms of the measure were sufficiently clear there should be no reason why that decision should not be directly replied upon and enforced before a national court. Directives, though, at least in the early stages were regarded as not being precise enough to give rise to direct effect. First, because they were not directly applicable and secondly because they obligated Member States to achieve an end result, thus giving rise to a wide margin of discretion. The implementation of a directive need not be uniform in every Member State and each Member State has a number of discretionary options open to it. In terms of Article 249 [ex 189] it will always require further implementing measures.

Nevertheless, these arguments have not dissuaded the Court of Justice from considering the direct effect of directives. The Court has declared that arguments of legal integration and effectiveness as equally strong in this area. The Court has considered that if the

Treaty is to be properly realised it needs the proper implementation of directives. If Member States renege on their obligations, for any reasons, to implement such measures then the Community will suffer and the overall progress of the Community will be seriously undermined. Thus, the Court decided that it was a requirement that individuals, who became aware that a directive may give them some rights which were incompatible with national law, would be able to enforce those Community rights in their own domestic court.

The *Grad* case (90/70) discussed above in connection with decisions, also by implication covered directives. But the Court formally supported the concept of direct effect for directives in *Van Duyn* (41/74). In this case Miss Van Duyn, a Dutch national, had come to the UK to take up a job with the Church of Scientology. She was refused permission to enter, as the United Kingdom government believed that the church was socially harmful, although it was not illegal. She challenged this refusal on the basis of, *inter alia*, Directive 64/221 which regulates the freedom of movement of workers within the Community. The High Court referred several questions to the Court of Justice, one of them being whether Directive 64/221 was directly effective. Article 3 of this Directive states that "measures taken on the grounds of public policy or public security [as grounds for exclusion] shall be based exclusively on the personal conduct of the individual concerned". This does not seem to be "clear and precise", which is one of the criteria for direct effect. Nor did the Directive define the permissible range of public policy or public security concerns, leaving this for each Member State to regulate in accordance with its own cultural and legal traditions. Nevertheless, the Court of Justice in *Van Duyn* said that the Directive did exhibit the three criteria necessary for direct effect and that therefore the Directive gave rise to rights directly enforceable by Miss Van Duyn before the British courts against the state.

In *Van Duyn* the Court of Justice set out the general principle that directives could have direct effect. In a further series of cases the Court added a more specific line of reasoning. The special concern of directives and the time limits given for the implementation was considered in *Ratti* (148/78). This case concerned the prosecution by the Italian authorities of Mr Ratti for breaches of national law concerning the labelling of products. Mr Ratti had complied with Community directives regulating this area. Mr Ratti relied in his defence on the directives. However the Court of Justice held that he could rely on the directive, for which the time period had expired, provided it satisfied the other requirements. However, in the case of the directive whose implementation period had not expired the Court said:

"it is only at the end of the prescribed period and in the event of the Member States default that the directive . . . will be able to have the effects described . . . until that date the Member States remain free in that field".

The argument here seems logical. As each directive gives Member States a specific date by which implementation must be assured, until that date the Member State has a discretion as to the "choice of form and methods".

After that date, however, the state has forfeited the discretion granted to it under Article 249 [ex 189] EC and is "estopped" from relying on its own failure to implement the directive. In *Ratti*, the date for the implementation of the directive has not expired. In the case of *Verbond* (51/76), the Court was prepared to extend the situation to where a directive had been implemented, but the domestic implementation had not fulfilled the requirements of the directive. The Court held that the useful effect of the directive would be weakened if individuals could not invoke it before the national courts, and by allowing individuals to invoke the directive the Community could ensure that national authorities kept within the limits of their discretion.

The ruling in favour of the direct effect of directives was not well received by some national courts, and not all national courts were prepared to concede that directives could be directly effective. In France, the Conseil d'Etat in *Minister of the Interior v Daniel Cohn-Bendit*, ruled against the ability of an individual to rely on a directive at national level. It argued that Article 249 [ex 189] EC gave national authorities the power to decide on the form to be given to the implementation of a directive and to fix the means appropriate to cause them to produce effects in national law. In the United Kingdom, the Court of Appeal in *O'Brien v Sin-Chem Ltd* would not give direct effect to the Equal Pay Directive (75/117) on the grounds that it had been already implemented in the Equal Pay Act 1970 (as amended in 1975). In Germany, the federal tax court in *Becker* argued that the Community 6th VAT Directive was not directly effective, since it conferred a margin of discretion on the Member States with respect to the manner of implementing the tax exemptions. The national courts' reasoning in all these cases ran on the similar line that Article 249 [ex 189] expressly distinguishes regulations and directives. Only regulations are described as directly applicable; directives are intended to take effect within the national order by means of national implementing measures. However, the effectiveness argument advanced by the Court of Justice is compelling. The useful effect of directives would be weakened if Member States were free to ignore their obligations, and the enforcement of Community law was left to the Commission or other Member States under Article 226 [ex 169] or Article 227 [ex 170].

For a considerable time, the question of whether directives could be held to give rise to horizontal direct effect, and thus be enforceable against other individuals, was a question avoided by the Court of Justice. It could be argued that the Court wished to avoid aggravating the misgivings emanating from national courts in this respect and did not wish to exacerbate the situation further. The arguments for horizontal effect are that Community law should be equally actionable against states and others in order to ensure a uniform constancy throughout the Community. Horizontal direct effect would also avoid giving rise to two categories of rights. It could be argued by analogy that Treaty articles were addressed only to Member States but nevertheless created rights and obligations for individuals. The arguments against horizontal direct effect are that directives do not have to be published (and this offends against legal certainty): this was true before the Maastricht Treaty. Following the Treaty, directives are now published in the Official Journal.

Another argument against extending horizontal effect is that directives are addressed to Member States and obligate them and not individuals, and therefore the latter should not be obligated by something that is beyond their control. Over the years a number of references to the Court of Justice were made in which the issue of the horizontal effect of directives was raised and for many years the Court managed to avoid the question. However, the Court finally faced the issue in *Marshall v Southampton and South West Hampshire Area Health Authority* (152/82). In this case, Mrs Marshall, an employee of the area Health Authority was compelled to retire at the age of 62. This was in line with the Health Authorities compulsory retirement age of 65 for men and 60 for women. The difference in age was permissible under the Sex Discrimination Act 1975 which expressly excluded "provisions relating to death or retirement" from its ambit. Mrs Marshall argued that the difference in retirement ages was discriminatory as it was in breach of the Equal Treatment Directive 76/207. In this case the questions of vertical and horizontal effects were fully argued. The Court held that a compulsory different retirement age was in breach of Directive 76/207 and could be invoked against a public body such as a health authority. The Court continued:

". . . where a person involved in legal proceedings is able to rely on a directive as against the state he may do so regardless of the capacity in which the latter is acting, whether employer or public authority".

However the Court also quoted its reasoning in *Becker* (8/81) and said that since a directive is, according to Article 249 [ex 189], binding only on "each member to which it is addressed", it follows that a directive may not of itself impose obligations on an individual and that a provision of a directive may not be relied upon as against such a person. Thus it seems that the Court opted for the estoppel rationale as set out in *Ratti*, particularly when it commented that "it is necessary to prevent the state from taking advantage of its own failure to comply with Community law". The effectiveness argument seemed to be quietly forgotten. In terms of the distinction between vertical and horizontal direct effect the Court in examining whether this was an arbitrary distinction said that "such a distinction may easily be avoided if the Member State concerned has correctly implemented the directive in national law".

So, in the *Marshall* case, the issue of the horizontal effect of directives was finally determined. By denying horizontal effect on the basis of Article 249 [ex 189] the Court of Justice strengthened the case for their vertical effect. Nevertheless the issue did not end there and attempts were made to persuade the Court on subsequent occasions to extend direct effect of directives to a horizontal relationship. In 1993 and 1994, three Advocates General had delivered opinions in favour of over-ruling *Marshall* and acknowledging the horizontal direct effect of directives. In *Marshall No.2* (C-271/91) and *Vaneetveld* (C-315/93), the Court managed to avoid answering the question. However, in the third case, *Faccini Dori* (C-91/92) the Court of Justice was unable to avoid addressing the issue directly.

It is instructive to follow the arguments put forward by the Advocates General, and to compare the counter arguments raised by the Court of Justice in *Faccini Dori*. First, however, there is Advocate General Slynn's Opinion in *Marshall No.1* that to attribute horizontal effect to directives would be to blur the distinction between regulations and directives. The Court accepted this Opinion, and also added the estoppel argument (as noted above) to its reasons for refusing to extend the direct effect of directives.

In *Marshall No.2* (C-271/91), an attempt was made by A.G. Van Gerven to articulate the counter-argument. He suggested that:

". . . provisions of directives have obtained direct effect as against public institutions and undertakings but not as against private institutions or undertakings (with which the former are sometimes nevertheless in competition), even though the negligence of the state in implementing the directive can generally be attributed as little to public bodies as it can to private bodies".

This, according to Advocate General Van Gerven leads to economic inconsistencies and distortions. The Advocate General also thought that the development of state liability in *Francovich* (see below) was not of much assistance to individuals:

". . . that . . . development does not remedy the fact that individuals who are operating in a Member State which implemented the directive correctly and are therefore bound by the obligations to which they are subject under the directive, are disadvantaged in comparison with individuals (perhaps their competitors) who are operating in a Member State who has not yet correctly implemented the directive".

In the light of these perceived weaknesses, it was the opinion of the Advocate General that the coherence of the Court's case law would benefit if the Court was prepared to confer horizontal direct effect on directives which passed the test for direct effect.

The matter was raised again, by a different Advocate General in *Vaneetveld* (C-315/93). Advocate General Jacobs argued that granting horizontal direct effect to directives would not "blur the distinction" between regulations and directives (one of the main arguments put forward by AG Slynn in *Marshall No.1*). This was because regulations and directives "will remain different instruments, appropriate in different situations and achieving their aims by different means". He also argued that it was difficult to sustain the distinction of horizontal and vertical direct effect because directives are sometimes the only form of Community legislation provided for under many areas of the Treaty. Yet other binding forms of Community law, such as the Treaties and Regulations did impose obligations on individuals. Lastly, Advocate General Jacobs argued that the disparity between the horizontal and vertical relationship would cause economic distortion, which rather than benefiting certainty, would be to the detriment of all persons in the Community.

In *Marshall No.2* and *Vaneetveld*, the Court of Justice was able to avoid addressing the issue. However, in *Faccini Dori*, the Court of Justice, despite a powerful argument by yet another Advocate General (Advocate General Lenz), decided that directives could not be directly effective against individuals (*i.e.* they could not have horizontal direct effect). The Court declined to overrule *Marshall* and maintained that directives are incapable of horizontal direct effect. The ruling insisted on keeping the distinction, as set out in Article 249 [ex 189], between regulations and directives. It ruled out the possibility of a private individual relying directly on an unimplemented directive in national proceedings against another private individual.

Faccini Dori has been confirmed in a number of subsequent cases, including *Luigi Spana* (C-472/93), *El Corte Ingles* (C-192/94) and *Arcaro* (C-168/95). It might be thought that however unsatisfactory the reasoning of the Court of Justice in this matter, at least the law was certain: there was no horizontal direct effect for directives. However, some confusion has been thrown on this whole area by the judgment in *CIA Security v Signalson* (C-194/94). This case concerned the omission, by Belgium, to notify the Commission of technical regulations about alarm systems, as required by Directive 83/189. CIA brought a case against a competitor, who had made a number of allegedly libellous statements, one of which was that their alarm system was not approved for sale in Belgium. CIA argued that there was no need for them to apply for authorisation, as the Belgium system of authorisation had not been notified to the Commission.

Giving his Opinion in the case, Advocate General Elmer drew a distinction between the directive at issue in *Faccini Dori* and the directive at issue in the present case. The latter directive did not, on its wording aim to impose duties on individuals. Therefore, no question could arise as to whether the directive should have direct effect so far as individual obligations were concerned. In its judgment the Court of Justice made no mention of *Faccini Dori* or *Marshall* and held that a breach of the obligation to notify rendered the technical regulations concerned inapplicable. Although this case involved a challenge to national legislation and its compatibility with EC law, it was a case between two private parties. It must have been evident to the Court of Justice that although CIA Security was using the directive as a "shield" against the state, it was nevertheless false to assume that this use would not penalise individuals, in this case Signalson. The directive would as severely effect this firm as if it had horizontal direct effect.

The result in *CIA Security* is the exact opposite as the reasoning and judgment in *Faccini Dori*. This seems unfortunate given the decisive nature of *Faccini Dori*. The position is now unconvincing. The Court has said that the basis for the direct effect of directives is the failure of a Member State to transpose the directive. This makes the decision in *CIA Security* seem very harsh. Was the Court arguing that the effectiveness of Community law would be improved by imposing a duty on national courts to ignore conflicting national legislation? If it was, then an easier, and more open, solution would be to extend horizontal direct effect to directives. It is to be hoped that this lack of clarity will be resolved, at some stage, for once and for all.

In all the cases discussed above, the Court of Justice was insistent that individuals had other remedies they could pursue. These remedies will now be examined.

The Concept of the "State"

Having imposed the particular "horizontal" limitation on the scope of the direct effect of directives, the Court then proceeded to enhance the domestic application of these provisions in other ways. First it attempted to expand the concept of a "public body" or an "agency of the state" against whom a directive may be invoked. In *Marshall,* the court had concluded that Mrs Marshall could rely on the provisions of the directive as against the health authority, since that body could be regarded as an organ of the state. In *Marshall,* the Advocate General had said that what constitutes the "state" in a particular national legal system must be a matter for the national court to decide. However, he also said, "I consider that the 'state' must be taken broadly, as including all the organs of the state . . .". In confirmation of this the Court of Justice said,

"where a person involved in legal proceedings is able to rely on a directive as against the state he may do so regardless of the capacity in which the latter is acting, whether employer or public authority."

This is not an entirely satisfactory judgment. The justification for giving direct effect to directives is based on the estoppel argument, that is, on the notion that the state is responsible for failing properly to implement a directive, and therefore cannot rely on its failure to resist the applicability of the measure. Therefore, it would seem unfair to impose liability on a body that has no responsibility for implementing Community legislation, such as a health authority.

In a series of cases the court expanded the concept of "state" so that the provisions of a directive could relied on against tax authorities (*Becker*), local authorities (*Costanzo* (103/88)), and the police authority *Johnson v RUC* (222/84). In *Foster v British Gas* (C-188/89) the Court of Justice addressed the question of what constitutes an "organ of the state". The Court said:

"it follows . . . that a body, whatever its legal form, which has been made responsible, pursuant to a measure adopted by the state, for providing a public service under the control of the state and has for that purpose special powers beyond those which result from the normal rules applicable in relations between individuals, is included in any event among the bodies against which the provisions of a directive capable of having direct effect may be relied upon."

In this case the Court held British Gas (in its pre-privatisation stage) to be an organ or emanation of the state. Nevertheless, considerable uncertainty remains as to what other bodies or institutions will, on account of their connection with the state, similarly be held responsible for failure to comply with the provisions of non implemented directives. The *Foster* ruling is remarkably silent on the solution to the problem of categorising the extent of state involvement in commercial life.

The difficulties can be illustrated by the case of *Doughty v Rolls Royce Plc* where the Court of Appeal, applying the *Foster* ruling, found that Rolls Royce, a nationalised undertaking at the relevant time, although "under the control of the state", had not been made responsible pursuant to a measure adopted by the state for providing a public service. The public service which Rolls Royce provided was to the state and not to the public, nor did Rolls Royce possess or exercise any special powers of the type enjoyed by British Gas. A distinction will always remain and because of this distinction a different result can occur in each Member State, where national concepts of what is part of the state, or an emanation of the state, may differ.

INDIRECT EFFECT

One method of circumventing the problems encountered by the denial of horizontal direct effect is by widening the concept of the state, as discussed above. However, there comes a point at which it is impossible to stretch the definition further so that some organisations, and individuals, can never be encompassed by the definition. The Court therefore needed another method of extending the application and effectiveness of directives and it attempted this by developing a principle requiring the interpretation of national law in the light of directives. The solution, which became known as "indirect effect" was suggested in two cases decided shortly before the *Marshall* case. The cases, heard by the Court of Justice on the same day, were *Von Colson* (14/83) and *Harz* (79/83). The two cases had remarkably similar facts.

The plaintiffs had applied for jobs with the respective defendants and both had been rejected. The German court found that the rejection had been based on their sex, but under German law they were entitled only to compensation in the form of travelling expenses. Both parties claimed that this remedy did not meet the requirements of Article 6 of the Equal Treatment Directive 76/207. This Article provided that:

"Member States shall introduce into their national legal systems such measures that are necessary to enable all persons who consider themselves wronged by the failure to apply to them the principles of equal treatment to pursue their claims by judicial process after possible recourse to other competent authorities".

The interesting difference in the facts of the individual cases was that Miss Von Colson was claiming against the prison service, a public body, whereas Miss Harz was claiming against a private company. The questions of vertical and horizontal direct effect and the public/private anomaly were openly raised and argued in the proceedings before the Court of Justice, and one could see that the Court was on horns of a dilemma.

The judgment of the Court was ingenious. Rather than highlight the unfortunate results of the lack of horizontal direct effect of directives, the Court of Justice concentrated on Article 10 [ex 5] of the EC Treaty, which requires Member States to comply with Community obligations. The Court held that this requirement applies to all authorities of Member States including the courts. Therefore, a national court was obliged to interpret national law in such a way as to ensure that the obligations of the directive were obeyed, regardless of whether the national law was based on any particular directive. The effectiveness of this depends on the willingness, or the ability, of a domestic court to interpret national law, if it exists, to achieve the correct result. Thus it was for the German courts to interpret German law in such a way as to ensure an effective remedy as required by Article 6 of the Directive. The result of this approach is that Community law must be applied indirectly to domestic law by way of interpretation.

The principle of indirect effect, or the *Von Colson* principle, soon gave rise to a number of questions as to the extent of the interpretation requirement. One question was whether the obligation to interpret arose only where there was a sufficient degree of uncertainty or ambiguity in the domestic legislation, or where the language clearly lent itself to more than one meaning. A second question was whether the interpretation requirement arose only after the expiry of the date of implementation, and a third question was whether the principle of interpretation was limited to the interpretation of national implementing legislation. This third question in particular gave difficulties to UK courts and is discussed below.

In the case of *Kolpinghuis Nijmegen* (80/86) the Court of Justice suggested a limitation to the indirect effect principle which answered some of these questions. In this case Mr Kolpinghuis was prosecuted by the Dutch authorities for breach of Directive 80/77 on water purity. Although this Directive had not been implemented in the Netherlands the prosecutor was of the view that the Directive already had the force of law. However, the Court of Justice ruled that the obligation of national courts to interpret domestic law to comply with Community law was:

"limited by the general principles of law which form part of Community law and in particular the principles of legal certainty and non-retroactivity. Thus where an interpretation of domestic law would run counter to the legitimate expectation of individuals the Von Colson principle would not apply."

The Court illuminated some of the uncertainties surrounding the concept of indirect effect in *Marleasing* (C-106/89). The case concerned a directive which had not been specifically implemented in Spain. The Spanish court wished to know whether a directive could be upheld directly against an individual. The Court of Justice repeated the view it had expressed in *Marshall* that a directive cannot of itself "impose obligations on private parties". It repeated its position in *Von Colson* that national courts must *as far as possible* interpret national law in the light of the wording and purposes of the directive in order to achieve the results pursued by that directive. Significantly, it added that this obligation applied whether the national provisions in question were adopted before or after the directive. It added that national courts were "required" to interpret domestic law in such a way as to ensure that the objectives of the directive were achieved. It should be noted that in *Marleasing* the Court expressly stated that the interpretative obligation applied to national legislation enacted either before or after a directive. The Court of Justice said that this obligation flowed from two sources; firstly, the obligation set out in Article 249 [ex 189] for Member States to achieve the results provided for in directives; and secondly the Member States' obligations of loyalty under Article 10 [ex 5].

Nevertheless, despite the wording of the judgment there are still some unresolved problems. First, there is the escape clause "as far as possible". This raises the question as to how far it will be necessary for a domestic court to distort the meaning of domestic legislation to comply with the directive. It seems unlikely that national courts will readily be prepared to accept this. Where national law is clearly at odds with a Community directive and there is no evidence that the parliament intended national law to comply with the provisions of the directive they will be reluctant to abandon the traditional rules of interpretation.

This has been evident in some of the cases that have come before the domestic courts in the United Kingdom. There has been some doubt whether s.2(1) of the European Communities Act 1972 covers Community law which is not directly effective. This doubt was evident in *Duke v Reliance Systems*, where the plaintiff sought damages under the Sex Discrimination Act 1975 (SDA). She had been required to retire from her employment at age 60, whereas a male employee was not forced to retire until age 65. The employer relied on s.6(4) of the 1975 Act which allowed employers to keep discriminatory provisions relating to retirement. However the Equal Treatment Directive 76/207 (which was passed after the 1975 Act) prohibited discrimination with regard to retirement, but the United Kingdom did not amend s.6(4) of the SDA until 1986, some years after Ms Duke's retirement. Ms Duke argued that the court ought to construe the SDA as from its enactment, in accordance with the Equal Treatment Directive. The House of Lords refused to construe the SDA in terms of the requirements of the Equal Treatment Directive. Lord Templeman said:

"Where an Act is passed for the purpose of giving effect to an obligation imposed by a directive imposed by a directive . . . a British court will seldom encounter difficulty in concluding that the language of the Act is effective for the intended purpose. But the construction of a British Act of Parliament is a matter of judgment to be determined by British courts and to be derived from the language of the legislation considered in the light of the circumstances prevailing at the date of enactment . . . The Acts were not passed to give effect to the Equal Treatment Directive and were intended to preserve discriminatory retirement ages . . ."

Lord Templeman took the view that the *Von Colson* approach did not require a British court to "distort" the words of a national statute. The *Duke* case was followed in a number of cases, in particular *Finnegan v Clowney Youth Training Ltd*. However, in *Litster v Forth Dry Dock*, the House of Lords *was* prepared to construe UK legislation implementing Directive 77/187 so as to comply with the Directive. It was also prepared to do the same in *Pickstone v*

Freemans. In these two latter cases it was prepared to construe the UK legislation in conformity with the Directives, even though this involved a departure from the literal meaning of the statute. The difference between the *Duke* case and *Litster* and *Pickstone* is that in the case of the latter, the UK legislation had been enacted specifically to implement the requirements of the non-directly effective Community law. Whereas in *Duke* it could not possibly be argued that a UK law enacted before a Community directive, could be intended to give effect to that directive. These differences should now be academic following *Marleasing* (C-106/89), in which the Court of Justice held that it was a domestic court's responsibility to interpret national law in accordance with directives, whether the directive was subsequent or prior to the domestic legislation. In *Webb v EMO*, after hesitation by the inferior courts and the Court of Appeal, the House of Lords after making a reference to the Court of Justice, was prepared to read provisions of the SDA 1975 in conformity with a non directly effective directive.

Since *Marleasing* the ECJ has seemed prepared to leave it to national courts to decide whether an interpretation in conformity with a directive is possible. In *Wagner-Miret* (C-334/92) the Court accepted that it was not possible for the Spanish court to read a directive in such a way as to conform to national law.

STATE LIABILITY FOR THE NON-IMPLEMENTATION OF DIRECTIVES

The landmark decision in *Francovich* (C-6 & 9/90) added a new dimension to the lack of horizontal direct effect of directives. Indeed, it went beyond direct effect and fixed liability for damages on the state, if that state's failure to implement a directive results in loss to an individual. *Francovich* can also been seen as the commencement of a system of *Community* remedies, for it is clear that the Court of Justice sees the principle of state liability to be more than a national remedy.

The case arose out of Italy's failure to implement Directive 80/987 on the protection of employees in the event of the insolvency of the employer. Ms Francovich and a number of other persons were owed wages by their insolvent employer. As no system for payment of these outstanding wages had been set up by Italy, as required by the Directive, the applicants sued the Italian state claiming that it was liable to pay them the sums owed. The Court of Justice held that the Directive did not have direct effect. This was because it was insufficiently precise in identifying the institution which was to guarantee compensation to beneficiaries under the Directive. The Court of Justice went further and pointed to the duty of a Member State under Article 5 (now 10) to give effect to Community law. This duty includes the obligation to make good the unlawful consequences of a breach of Community law.

The Court of Justice set down three conditions before a Member State may be found liable:

(i) the directive must confer rights for the benefit of individuals.

(ii) the content of the right must be identifiable from the directive.

(iii) there must be a causal link between the breach and the damage suffered.

It is the responsibility of the Member State to determine the procedures and courts to enable individuals to pursue claims against the state. These must not make a remedy impossible and should be no less favourable than procedures necessary to pursue a similar claim under national law.

The implications of *Francovich* are enormous, and much remains to be clarified. What is certain is that *Francovich* complements, rather than replaces, the principle of direct effect. There is no doubt that if a Member State fails to implement a directive correctly, it will be open to a claim for damages. This is so even with directives that are not directly effective, as this was the situation in *Francovich* itself.

As is not unusual in ground-breaking cases, *Francovich* left a number of unanswered questions. The major areas of doubt were the issues of fault, and whether *Francovich*-type liability extended to areas concerning other breaches of Community Law of Member States (apart that is from failure to implement directives).

The answers were provided by a series of cases. *Brasserie du Pêcheur* and *Factortame III* (C-46 & 48/93); *British Telecommunications* (C-392/93); *Hedley Lomas* (C-5/94) and *Dillenkofer* (C-178/94).

The result of these cases is a slight reformulation of the conditions for liability as set out in *Francovich*. The conditions are now as follows:

(i) the rule of law must confer rights on individuals. In the case of a directive the content of the right must be discernible from the provisions of the directive; and

(ii)   the breach must be sufficiently serious; and

(iii)   there must a casual link between the breach and the damage.

These conditions may look very similar to those originally set out in *Francovich*. Indeed, in *Dillenkofer* the Court of Justice stated that "in substance, the conditions laid down in that group of judgments are the same." But there are differences. For example, the Court has now introduced a condition that the breach must be sufficiently serious. The Court of Justice explained that this condition, missing from the original *Francovich* formula was "evident from the circumstances" of that case.

This condition of a "sufficiently serious" breach would be met if there had been a "manifest and grave" disregard of the limits of discretion allowed to a Member State. In *Brasserie du Pêcheur* and *Factortame III* the Court of Justice set out some of the factors that would need to be taken into account in determining this manifest and gave disregard. They were:

(1)   clarity and precision of rule breached

(2)   measure of discretion left by rule to national authorities

(3)   whether infringement was intentional or involuntary

(4)   whether any error of law was excusable

(5)   the fact that a position taken by an EC institution may have contributed towards the omission.

The Court went on to state that "in any view" it would be sufficiently serious if the breach had persisted after an Article 226 [ex 169] judgment (as in *Francovich*), or after an Article 234 [ex 177] ruling, or in the face if settled Community Law.

It would seem that the failure by a Member State to take any action to implement a directive is an obvious and clear instance of a "manifest and grave" disregard of Community law, amounting to a sufficiently serious breach. On the other hand, a genuine, but mistaken attempt at implementation does not give rise to liability. In *British Telecommunications* (C-392/93), the directive was implemented, but because of a mistaken interpretation of that directive, certain activities were excluded from the scope of the national law. These activities should have been included. The Court of Justice held that there had not been a sufficiently serious breach of Community law. The Court based its decision on the imprecise wording of the directive. The Court said that the wording was reasonably capable of bearing its construction of the words and the construction given to them by British Telecommunications. Also, the Member State had acted in good faith when it implemented the directive, other Member States had shared the same interpretation as the United Kingdom and their interpretation was not manifestly contrary to the purposes of the directive.

In so far as the concept of "fault" was concerned, the Court of Justice held that a Member State's obligation is to make good loss caused to individuals. This obligation cannot depend on fault, going beyond that of a serious breach of Community Law. The Court was also aware that liability based on a subjective notion of fault could give rise to serious difficulties. Particularly as the concept of fault is different in the various legal systems of the Member States.

There is no doubt that liability in damages is available in respect of breaches of Community law. For each type of failure Community law will lay down the conditions under which that liability will arise. It is possible that national law will cover substantive and procedural rules for the bringing of such claims. However, this is subject to the proviso that those rules do not make it impossible in practice to enjoy the right to compensation and that liability for a breach of Community law is not treated less favourably than liability for the breach of a similar domestic law.

It has been argued that the judgment in *Francovich* signals the start of a system of European remedies (as discussed in "Remedies" in Chapter 5). The basic requirements governing what is necessary for an effective remedy are matters of Community law and not national law. Some matters, particularly of procedural law, may be left to national law, but are subject to scrutiny by the Court of Justice to ensure the effective enforcement of Community law.

In *Francovich* and *Dillenkofer*, the Court of Justice was definite that liability was automatic in the case of non-transposition of directives. It seems to have softened its stance in *Brinkmann* (C-319/96). In this case, the applicant produced a tobacco product called "Westpoint". This product was made up of tobacco rolls that needed to be wrapped in cigarette paper for them to be smoked. The product was taxed in Germany as smoking tobacco, but in Denmark the authorities classed it as a cigarette, and therefore liable to a higher rate of tax. The applicant was successful in arguing before the Court of Justice that "Westpoint" was indeed smoking tobacco, within the meaning of the relevant Directive, 79/32. The applicant also sought damages for the loss it had suffered while its product had been subject to the higher tax. The Court of Justice found that Articles of the directive, which defined smoking tobacco and cigarettes, had not been properly implemented into national law. The Court stated that failure to implement was, *per se*, a serious violation. In this case, however, the Court said that there was no causal link between the breach of Community law and the damage suffered by the applicant. The reason for this was because, even though the provisions of the directive had not been correctly implemented, the Danish authorities had acted as though they had been. This brought the Court of Justice to the conclusion that the Danish authorities had not committed a serious breach by their failure to implement. The Court came to this conclusion because of the difficulties of classifying "Westpoint", as the product did not correspond exactly to any of the definitions in the directive. The Court was persuaded by the fact that the Commission had also come to the same conclusion.

This softer stance by the Court of Justice may mean that liability for damages is no longer automatic in cases of non-implementation. A national authority may be able to argue that it has complied with the requirements of the directive, even though that directive has not been properly transposed into national law. This may allow it to argue that the breach of Community law was not "sufficiently serious".

There is not doubt that these cases will lead to further litigation to test the boundaries of state liability. But there is equally no doubt that, with the doctrine of direct effect, the concept of state liability as per *Francovich* will become a fruitful source for the enforcement of individual rights. The possibility of being brought before their national court by a dissatisfied citizen will also encourage Member States to be more vigilant in carrying out their obligations under Community Law.

7. ADMINISTRATIVE CONTROL OF MEMBER STATES

This chapter looks at the enforcement of Community law against Member States. No law could properly function if parties were allowed to infringe the law with impunity, and in contrast with many international organisations, the European Community has an effective control mechanism to ensure compliance by Member States. Thus, if a Member State refuses to implement a directive within the correct time period, or introduces a domestic measure that conflicts with a Treaty obligation, the Treaty provides for administrative and judicial procedures to ensure adherence to community obligations.

The task of ensuring the proper application of Community law is given to the Commission. Article 211 [ex 155] provides that:

In order to ensure the proper functioning and development of the common market the Commission shall:—ensure that the provisions of this Treaty and the measures taken by the institutions pursuant thereto are applied.

This general duty of the Commission is fleshed out by other specific Treaty provisions, mainly Articles 226 and 227 [ex 169 and 170], although other provisions will be examined briefly at the end of this chapter.

Article 226 [ex 169] is the Treaty basis for an action brought by the Commission against a Member State for the latter's failure to comply with its Community obligations. Article 227 [ex 170] allows one Member State to bring another Member State before the Court of Justice for an alleged failure to comply with Community obligations.

ARTICLE 226 [EX 169]

Article 226 [ex 169] provides a three-stage procedure under which the Commission may press a Member States to comply with its obligations:

"If the Commission considers that a Member State has failed to fulfil an obligation under this Treaty, it shall deliver a reasoned opinion on the matter after giving the State concerned the opportunity to submit its observations.

If the State concerned does not comply with the opinion within the period laid down by the Commission, the latter may bring the matter before the Court of Justice."

This procedure has three main functions. First it seeks to ensure that Member States comply with their obligations towards the Community. Second, it provides an informal non-contentious means of resolving disputes; and third, if the informal methods are unsuccessful, the Court of Justice can give detailed judgments on the correct application of Community law.

Article 226 [ex 169]] does not give a definition of "failed to fulfil an obligation", nor does it define what will constitute a breach of a duty. The Court of Justice has held that an act or omission can constitute a breach. Indeed, a great many proceedings under Article 226 [ex 169] are concerned with a Member State's failure to implement Community legislation, particularly directives. "Failure" is construed very widely and covers any breach of the Treaties secondary legislation or the general principles of Community law.

The first stage of the procedure is commonly known as the preliminary or administrative procedure. This is an attempt by the Commission to reach a negotiated resolution to the problem. The Commission will notify the Member State that it considers the Member State to be in breach of Community law, and will ask for comments on the matter. There will be discussions between the Commission and the Member State. This informal procedure is largely successful and the majority of Article 226 [ex 169] actions go no further than this point.

If, however, the matter cannot be resolved informally, the Commission may move the issue into the formal stage. This results in the Commission notifying the Member State by a formal letter of notice, that the Community considers the Member State to be in breach of Community law, and requesting that the Member State presents its own comments on the matter. It has been held in *Commission v Denmark* (211/81) that a Member State need not respond at this stage. So far as the Commission is concerned, the formal letter of notice is important because it defines the scope of their case. The Court of Justice will not allow them to include further issues in their case that were not originally in the formal letter of notice.

The Member State is given a reasonable period of time to reply to the Commission's formal notice. What is a "reasonable period" will vary with the circumstances of each case, but the standard period appears to be thirty days. If after this period, agreement between the Commission and the Member State has not proved possible, the Commission may then move to issue its reasoned opinion. It should be noticed that this decision is discretionary, despite the phrase "shall deliver" in Article 226 [ex 169]. This is because there is no party who could bring an action against the Commission, forcing it to act. In *Alfons Lütticke v Commission* (48/65) it was held that, as the Commission has a discretion to act under Article 226 [ex 169], there was no action available under Article 232 [ex 175] (see Chapter 6) for its failure to act. Another reason why the Commission must have discretion over whether or not to act is the sheer impracticality of policing the number of possible infringements of the Treaty. The Commission is a relatively small body and cannot give the manpower or the time to investigate all alleged infractions that come to its notice. It has to be able to choose the cases it considers to raise important points of principle, or to involve major breaches of Community obligations.

The reasoned opinion will set out the legal grounds for the Commission's belief that the Member State is in breach: it will also contain the Commission's legal arguments and what measures it feels are necessary to bring an end to the breach. It will also set out a time limit for the State to comply. As with the formal notice, the Commission may not change the legal grounds and submissions if it later decides to take the matter further to the Court of Justice. The reasoned opinion must be exactly that. In *Commission v Italy (Re Pigmeat)* (7/61) the Court of Justice declared that:

"the opinion . . . must be considered to contain a sufficient statement of reasons to satisfy the law when it contains . . . a coherent statement of the reasons which led the Commission to believe that the State in question has failed to fulfil an obligation under the Treaty".

If the Member State fails to comply with the reasoned opinion within the specified time limit, the Commission can then bring the matter before the Court of Justice. This is the final stage in the procedure and involves a full examination of the case by the Court of Justice. As stated previously the Commission can only rely on the grounds set out in its reasoned opinion. If it fails to do this the Court of Justice may strike out the case. When the case is before the Court, the Member State involved may submit its defence. Any other Member State that has an interest in the proceedings may make observations, as may any of the Community institutions. However, an individual is not allowed to make observations or submissions to the Court.

The Commission bears the burden of proof in Article 226 [ex 169] actions. If the Commission is successful before the Court of Justice, the Member State will be found to be in breach of its duties under Treaty. If this is the case, Article 228 [ex 171] declares that:

". . . the State shall be required to take the necessary measures to comply with the Court of Justice."

At this stage the judgment is declaratory only, and no sanction can be applied. However, in practice most cases involving findings against Member States result in the Member State amending its law to comply with the Community requirement. Nevertheless, there are an increasing number of instances were Member States fail to take corrective action after a Court of Justice judgment. There is nothing to be done, except for the Commission to start the Article 226 [ex 169] procedure over again, this time citing the failure of the Member State to comply with an Article 228 [ex 171] ruling. The leading example of this is the three visits by the Italian Government to the Court of Justice concerning Italian art treasures. The first judgment handed down in 1968 was not complied with, and it took until 1972 until Italy finally came to terms with its obligations.

In an attempt to give Article 228 [ex 171] some "teeth" it was amended by the Maastricht Treaty to enable the Court of Justice to fine a Member State for a breach of Community law. This can only happen though, if a Member State is taken back to the Court for a second time in relation to its failure to obey an Article 228 [ex 171] declaration. On the second occasion the Commission will specify a lump sum or penalty payment which it will ask the

Court of Justice to impose on the Member State. The Court will have discretion over the amount of the penalty, and can impose a larger or smaller sum or no penalty at all.

It was some time before the Commission made use of the procedure. In 1996 the Commission adopted a memorandum, which set out the proposed method of calculation for penalties. The Commission proposed that the penalty be calculated on a daily basis and that it should be based on three criteria; the seriousness of the infringement, its duration and the need to ensure that the penalty acted as a deterrent against further infringements. The Commission started to bring proceedings under Article 228 in 1996, but to date only one case has reached judgment at the Court of Justice. In *Commission v Greece* (C-387/97) the ECJ set out its view of the Commission's guidelines and its own view of the penalty payment. The Court said that the Commission's suggestion that account should be taken both of the gross domestic product of the Member State concerned and the number of its votes in the Council appears to be appropriate in that it enables that Member State's ability to pay to be reflected while keeping the variation between Member States within a reasonable range. The Court added that regard should be had in particular to the effects of failure to comply on private and public interests and the urgency of getting the Member State concerned to fulfil its obligations.

It should be noted that Article 228 does not provide a mechanism to ensure that any fine is actually paid. Nevertheless, the Commission has stated in its annual reports that the Article 228 procedure is a success.

INTERIM MEASURES—ARTICLE 243 [EX 186]

Article 228 [ex 171] cannot force a Member State to comply with a Community obligation. However, it may be possible to rectify the alleged breach on an interim basis until the Court of Justice has determined the matter in a full hearing. Under Article 243 [ex 186] the Court of Justice "may in any case before it prescribe any necessary interim measures". In *Commission v United Kingdom (Pigmeat Producers)* (31/77R & 53/77R), the Commission applied for interim measures to prevent the United Kingdom from continuing financial aid to United Kingdom pigmeat producers, in defiance of a Commission decision that the aid should stop immediately. The Court of Justice granted the request and declared that the United Kingdom could not decide whether or not Community law was being correctly applied; that power was reserved solely to the Court of Justice. Shortly after, in *Commission v Ireland (Irish Fisheries)* (61/77), the Court made an interim order for Ireland to suspend certain fishing laws which the Commission regarded as contrary to Community fishing rules. From a UK point of view, the most famous case of interim relief was the *Factortame* litigation (*Commission v United Kingdom* (246/89R)), where the Commission requested, and was granted, the suspension of UK laws alleged to be incompatible with Community rules.

It is usually the case that, in the event of an interim order, the Member State complies immediately. In addition to formal interim measures, a Member State may be influenced by political pressure brought to bear by another Member State, or group or individual, and so may change its original stance.

Parallel Proceedings

A Member State whose laws are alleged to be incompatible with Community law may face a challenge other than from the Commission. The principle of direct effect (see Chapter 4) may give an individual the right to challenge domestic legislation in the national courts. Or the individual may argue that the domestic courts is bound by the interpretive imperative, (or "indirect effect"), as declared in *Von Colson* (14/83) and *Marleasing* (C-106/89). Even if an individual cannot avail of these provisions they may be able to argue that a point of Community law is at issue, and persuade the national court to make an Article 234 [ex 177] reference (see Chapter 9).

A relatively new form of parallel or alternative action is to sue the state for damages caused to individuals by the state's failure to comply with its Community obligations. This was attempted in the UK courts in *Bourgoin v Ministry of Agriculture*. This case followed *Commission v Italy* (40/82), when the Commission successfully argued that a British ban on imported poultry was contrary to Community law. In *Bourgoin* the poultry importers attempted to sue the Ministry of Agriculture, who applied the ban. The importer's claim was dismissed as showing no good cause of action, because it could not be shown that the Minister has acted in bad faith (and then the proper action was that for judicial review and not a tort action for damages). However, it is instructive to note that *Bourgoin* was later settled out of court, and the UK Government paid £4 million compensation to French poultry farmers.

The more recent case of *Francovich* (C-6 & 9/90) has opened up this area, so that it now represents an important source of rights for individuals. It is discussed fully in Chapter 6. In *Francovich*, the Italian Government had to pay the claimants compensation as a result of failure to implement Community legislation. *Francovich* is similar to *Bourgoin* in that in both cases a breach of Community law had already been established under an Article 226 [ex 169] action.

DEFENCES

Many are attempted, but few succeed! Over the years Member States have raised various defences to Article 226 [ex 169] actions. However, even though many defences are recognised in international law, the Court of Justice has looked unfavourably upon them. It has been estimated that only about one in ten cases brought before the Court of Justice under Article 226 [ex 169] result in a declaration favourable to the Member State. Given the prolonged procedure of the administrative stage of Article 226 [ex 169] proceedings this is perhaps not surprising.

One of the "popular" defences put forward by Member States is *force majeure*, that is, matters beyond the control of the Member State. This was the defence in *Commission v Italy (Traffic Statistics)* (101/84) where the Italian government defended its non-implementation of a directive by reporting that the centre which was to provide the statistics required by the directive had been bombed. The Court of Justice agreed that the act of bombing could be *force majeure*, but refused to accept this as a defence, particularly as the delay of almost five years in this case was unreasonable.

Sometimes, a Member State will argue that they are unable to implement a Community measure because of constitutional, institutional or administrative difficulties. The Court of Justice will not accept this as an excuse. In *Commission v Italy* (21/81) the Italian Government argued unsuccessfully that a turbulent political period had made it impossible to pass necessary measures to comply with Community rules. In *Commission v United Kingdom (Tachographs)* (128/78), the United Kingdom was unsuccessful with its defence of political difficulties with trade unions in the attempt to introduce tachographs into UK lorries.

In international law the defence of reciprocity is often successful. That is, that if a contracting state is in breach of the agreement, the other state which is party to the agreement is absolved from its obligations under the treaty. In *Commission v Belgium and Luxembourg* (90 & 91/63), the two Governments argued that the only reason they were in breach of their Community obligations was because the Council had failed to adopt certain measures. The Court of Justice accepted that this was an acceptable defence in international law, but held that the Treaty went beyond international law and established a new legal order which required that Member States should not take the law into their own hands. Therefore the fact that the Council had failed to carry out its obligations did not relieve the defendants from carrying our their obligations. Likewise, in *Commission v France (French Lamb)* (232/78), the Court ruled that France was not justified in its breach of Community obligations because of the failure of another Member State to comply with Community law.

ACTION BY MEMBER STATE AGAINST MEMBER STATE: ARTICLE 227 [EX 170]

Article 227 [ex 170] is the basis for an action by one Member State against another, when one Member State considers another to have breached a Community law obligation. The procedure for bringing an action under Article 227 [ex 170] is similar to that for Article 226 [ex 169], in that the Commission need to be notified, after which they deliver a reasoned opinion. The Commission can also be persuaded by a Member State to take the matter up itself, and proceed on an Article 226 [ex 169] basis. The Member State prefers this, as it is less politically obvious than direct confrontation. In fact, Member States have been loath to push a complaint against another Member State to a hearing before the Court of Justice. If the Member State cannot persuade the Community to take the case they then attempt to seek a political solution. Only one case has been brought under Article 227 [ex 170]. In *France v United Kingdom (Fishing Nets)* (141/78), the United Kingdom was found to be in breach of its Treaty obligations in relation to net mesh sizes. France had brought the matter before the Court of Justice, the Commission supported the French argument and the Court of Justice upheld the Commission opinion.

In addition to Article 227 [ex 170], an alternative mechanism for the resolution of disputes is provided for by Article 239 [ex 182]. By this Article, Member States can agree to submit any dispute concerning the subject matter of the Treaty to the Court of Justice.

Special Enforcement Actions: Articles 82(2), 298 and 95(9) [ex 93(2), 225 and 100A(4)]

Although Articles 226 [ex 169] and 227 [ex 170], especially Article 226 [ex 169], are the main enforcement provisions of the Treaty, the Commission can use other provisions of the Treaty for some specific purposes.

Article 88(2) [ex 93(2)] is concerned with state aids. The concern of the Commission is to prevent such aid from distorting or threatening to distort the common market with the resultant deleterious effect on intra-Community trade. Under Article 88(2) [ex 93(2)] the Commission may issue a decision which requires the state concerned to change or abolish the unlawful aid within a set time. A Commission decision, made under Article 88(2) [ex 93(2)], unlike a reasoned opinion under Article 226 [ex 169], can be challenged before the Court of Justice under Article 230 [ex 173] (see Chapter 6).

If a Member State fails to comply with an Article 88(2) [ex 93(2)] decision, the Commission is entitled to bring the matter before the Court of Justice under Article 226 [ex 169]. In *Commission v United Kingdom* (31 & 53/77) the Commission issued a decision to United Kingdom pig producers to end a subsidy immediately. The United Kingdom did not take any action, so the Commission brought the case to the Court of Justice. In *British Aerospace and Rover Group v Commission* (C-292/90), the Commission made a decision under Article 87 [ex 92] ordering the United Kingdom to recover payments which the Commission had considered were illegally made to Rover in the takeover by British Aerospace. The Court of Justice agreed with the Commission's decision but nevertheless annulled it because of the failure to observe the rights of interested parties.

Articles 297 and 298 [ex 224 and 225]

Article 297 [ex 224] requires Member States to consult each other, with a view to protecting the functioning of the common market, if there is a threat of serious internal disturbances effecting the maintenance of law and order. Article 298 [ex 225] enables the Commission to challenge the action of a Member State under Article 297 [ex 224], if it considers that the state concerned is acting in an improper manner. The ruling of the Court of Justice is given *in camera*. Articles 269 and 297 [ex 223 and 224] allows Member States to derogate from the obligations under the Treaty in the essential interests of its security, and where those interest involve arms production or the withholding of information.

Article 95 [ex 100a(4)]

This Article allows a Member State after adoption of a harmonisation measure, to apply stricter national measures under Article 30 [ex 36] or relating to the protection of the environment or working environment. Paragraph 9 of Article 95 [ex 4 of Article 100A] enables the Commission (or other Member State) to use a similar procedure to that under Article 298 [ex 225] where it considers that a state is making improper use of its powers under Article 95 [ex 100A].

Conclusion

The enforcement procedures outlined above, provided by the Treaty, play an important part in remedial scheme of Community law. This is particularly so with Article 226 [ex 169] which is the effective means by which the Commission can "police" the Community. It should be remembered that it is not only litigation that is the weapon of the Commission, but rather the opportunity for maintenance of dialogue through the pre-litigation procedures. A few figures will illustrate the effectiveness of the Article 226 [ex 169] procedure. The Commission publishes figures each year in a report to the European Parliament. Although the figures are different for each year, of the cases taken up by the Commission, only about ten per cent proceed as far as the Court of Justice, the other ninety per cent being resolved in the pre-judicial stages.

Thus, it can be said that Article 226 [ex 169] is a valuable tool in maintaining control of the Community institutions. The fact that individuals can make a complaint to the Commission, and hope that the Commission will then act, gives individuals also a state in the remedial provisions of Community law.

8. ACTIONS TO ANNUL COMMUNITY ACTS: ARTICLES 230 [EX 173], 232 [EX 175] AND 241 [EX 184]

INTRODUCTION

The system of judicial review under Articles 230 [ex 173] and 232 [ex 175] is based on French administrative law. This chapter deals with the role and nature of judicial review by the Court of Justice in determining the legality of Community acts. Under Article 230 [ex 173] the Court of Justice may examine the activities of the institutions to determine the validity of their legislation. Article 232 [ex 175], on the other hand, the Court may consider the inactivity, or failure to act, if the institutions when they are under a legal duty to act. Article 241 [ex 184] provides a means of indirect review where the "plea if illegality" is invoked.

There are a number of important issues. While there is little doubt as to the ability of the Council and the Commission to bring actions before the Court of Justice under these Articles, there was some controversy over the position of the European Parliament under both Articles 230 [ex 173] and 232 [ex 175]. There is also the complex issue of ascertaining the standing of individuals, and other non-privileged applicants under the articles. Finally, there were some indications that the Court of Justice was changing its stance on the availability of judicial review for individuals. More recent events, however, seem to suggest that the Court is having second thoughts on this matter and that the situation is reverting to its original, difficult, position.

ARTICLE 230 [EX 173]

Article 230(1) [ex 173(1)] provides that the Court of Justice may review the validity of acts of the community. If any act is found by the Court to be invalid, the Court has the sole right to declare such acts to be void. The Article as originally set out in the Treaty provided that the Court of Justice shall review the validity of acts of the Council and the Commission other than recommendations and opinions. For this purpose the Court of Justice had jurisdiction in actions brought by a Member State, the Council or the Commission on grounds of lack of competence, infringement of an essential procedural requirement, infringement of the EC Treaty or any rule of law relating to its application, or misuse of powers. Article 230(4) [ex 173(4)] provides that in certain circumstances, any natural or legal person may challenge a decision before the Court of Justice, provided the proceedings are initiated within the time limits set out in Article 230(5) [ex 173(5)].

An important amendment was made to Article 230 [ex 173] by the TEU which incorporates some of the established case law of the Court of Justice. In *"Les Verts" v European Parliament* (294/83), the Court allowed the Parliament to be challenged in respect of an apportionment of election campaign funds. In *Luxembourg v European Parliament* (230/81 and 108/83) the Court allowed a challenge to Parliament's decision to remove its seat from Luxembourg. By the amended version of Article 230 [ex 173], post TEU, the Court is now permitted to review "the legality of acts adopted jointly by the European Parliament and the Council". This amendment recognises the extension of the powers of the European Parliament over the last decade and recognises that Parliament can be responsible for acts which create legally binding effects in respect of third parties, and these should therefore be open to review.

Reviewable Acts

As mentioned above, the jurisdiction of the Court of Justice under Article 230 [ex 173(1)] applies to legally binding acts of the Council or Commissions, but does not include recommendations or opinions. The legally binding acts set out in Article 249 [ex 189] are Regulations, Directives and Decisions. However, it is important to note, that the Court of Justice has not confined itself to a narrow interpretation of these legally binding acts. The Court of Justice is concerned with the substance of a measure rather than its form. In *Commission v Council (ERTA)* (22/70) it held that it could consider all measures taken by the institutions which are designed to have legal effect. In the *ERTA* case, "discussions" of guidelines before the signing of the European Road Traffic Agreement were held to be measures capable of review by the Court. In *Re: Noordwijk's Cement Accord* (8–11/66) a "communication" in the form of a registered letter from the Commission stating that the company was no longer immune from fines was held to be a reviewable act.

Some acts have been held not to be reviewable. Perhaps the most important is the "reasoned opinion" issued by the Commission under an Article 226 [ex 169] proceedings (see Chapter 7). This was the outcome of *Commission v Italy (Pig Meat)* (7/61). In *Lütticke v Commission* (57/65) the applicants had requested the Commission to take action against Germany regarding a breach of Community law. The Community refused and Lütticke applied under Article 230 [ex 173] to have the decision not to act annulled. The Court of Justice held that the refusal to act was not legally binding and was therefore not reviewable.

The Right to Challenge (*locus standi*)

Before the amendment of Article 230 [ex 173] by the TEU, the right to challenge was limited to the Member State, the Council and the Commission and, in certain limited circumstances, individuals. The Member State, the Council and the Commission are known as "privileged applicants", and they have the right to challenge any act. It will be noted that to right to challenge an act was not given to the European Parliament by the Treaty. However, the Court of Justice recognised that the Parliament should have some limited rights to safeguard its own prerogatives under Article 230 [ex 173]. In *European Parliament v Council (Comitology)* (303/88) the Court of Justice held that the Parliament could not challenge under Article 230 [ex 173], but could under Article 232 [ex 175]. Perhaps sensing that it had made a mistake, the Court quickly overturned its ruling. In *European Parliament v Council (Chernobyl)* (C-70/88) the Parliament challenged the legal basis of a Council regulation on the permitted level if radioactive contamination in foodstuffs. The measure had been passed under Article 3 Euratom under which Parliament need only be consulted. Parliament however, thought it should be carried out under Article 100a (now 95) of the EC which required the co-operation procedure to be carried out. The Court of Justice ruled that:

"the circumstances and the arguments . . . should . . . the evidence of those various legal remedies . . . however effective and varied they may be, were not sufficient to guarantee in all circumstances, that an act of the Council or the Commission which disregarded the Parliament's prerogatives would be censured."

Therefore, while the Court was still not prepared to grant Parliament privileged status, it was prepared to accept that there was a restricted right of action in those cases where the Parliament had a legitimate interest in the annulment of an act, such cases being where the Council or the Commission infringed upon its prerogatives.

This revised stance of the Court of Justice is evident in *European Parliament v Council (Students Residence)* (C-295/90). In this case, the United Kingdom attempted to have the Parliament's action declared inadmissible. The Court of Justice rejected these arguments and held that:

"an action for annulment brought by the Parliament is admissible providing that the action seeks only to safeguard its prerogatives and that it is founded only on submissions alleging their infringement."

The wording of Article 230 [ex 173] was amended by the TEU to reflect (in particular) the decision of the Court of Justice in *Chernobyl*. After the amendment the Article provided that the

"Court shall have jurisdiction . . . in actions brought by the European Parliament and the European Central Bank for the purposes of protecting their prerogatives . . ."

The increasing power of the Parliament has been further recognised in another amendment to Article 230 [ex 173]. The Treaty of Nice has now added the European Parliament to the list of privileged applicants.

Locus standi of individual applicants

If the issue of the standing of Parliament has been a thorny issue for the Court of Justice, the main problems has always been how to deal with those applicants who come under the heading of "natural or legal persons" in Article 230 [ex 173(4)]. These are known as non-privileged applicants and Article 230 [ex 173(4)] states that any natural or legal person may institute proceedings against a decision addressed to that person, or against a decisions which, although in the form of a regulation or a decision addressed to another person, is of direct and individual concern to that person. In this area it will be seen that the Court of Justice has proceeded with great caution, perhaps fearing a flood of cases if individuals were allowed any access to the Court. Thus, applicants are faced with a rigorous two-stage test in order to determine their standing to bring an action.

The first part of the test sets out the situations where a non-privileged applicant can bring an action for judicial review:

(a) A decision is directly addressed to the applicant. As might be expected, this head poses the least problems for the Court of Justice. If the applicant can show that the act addressed to him will affect his legal position, that act will be a decision, whatever its legal form. If however the act in dispute is not legally binding, cannot be a decision, and thus may not be challenged. Most successful challenges to decisions concerning individuals have been brought in competition law cases under Articles 81 and 82 [ex 85 and 86] (see Chapter 12).

(b) A decision is addressed to another person. In these circumstances the applicant must prove that the act in dispute is a decision. In addition they must also show that the act is of direct and individual concern to them. In terms of "another person", the Court of Justice held in *Plaumann v Commission* (25/62) that a Member State could be "another person" and not just other individuals.

(c) A regulation is really a disguised decision. As can been deduced from Article 249 [ex 189], a regulation is applicable to a wide range of people, viewed abstractly and in their entirety. It is not applicable to a limited number of people: this is the quality of a decision, it binds those to whom it is addressed, either by name or by identification. A true regulation is a normative act and is not open to individual challenge. This was confirmed in *Calpack* (789/89).

In *Confédération Nationale des Producteurs de Fruit et Legumes v Council* (16 & 17/62) the Court of Justice held that it was the nature and content of a provision that is the determining factor and the label attached to it. The structural reasons for this judgment are two-fold. First, regulations are legislative measures which are directly applicable in all Member States. To allow them to be easily challenged by individuals would lead to a disruption of the legislation process. In order to prevent such disruption the Article 230(2) [ex 173(2)] is rigidly interpreted and true regulations may not be challenged.

On the other hand, it would be advantageous for the Council to carry out all legislation as regulations: they would not be open to challenge. Hence the Court will look beyond the form or label attached to the measure, and if a "regulation" is a disguised decision, the Court will allow it to be challenged. This was the case in International *Fruit v Commission (No.1)* (41–44/70) where a group of fruit importers was held entitled to challenge a regulation prior to its adoption where the identity of the natural and legal persons affected was already known and thus was fixed and identifiable. The regulation was in effect, a "bundle" of decisions addressed to each applicant.

In *Timex v Commission* (264/82), a company exporting watches was held to have *locus standi*. This was because the Commission had in mind the behaviour of this particular company when it produced a regulation imposing anti-dumping duties. If a particular company is named in a regulation, as in *Maizena v Council* (139/79), the action will be held to be of direct end individual concern (see below). The majority of cases in this area arise out of anti-dumping measures where, as a result of an investigation of individual importers, a general regulation is issued to catch all importers. In the *Japanese Ball Bearing* cases (113–118–121/77), the Court of Justice ruled that the disputed regulations were "hybrid". That is, they were of general application but operated as a decision for identifiable individuals.

The Measures Must be of Direct and Individual Concern

If the applicant can show that, although not addressed by the contested act, it is of concern to them, or can show that a regulation is in substance a series of decisions, there is still a major hurdle to be surmounted before establishing *locus standi*. The applicant must prove that the act challenged is of direct and individual concern. This has proved a major stumbling block for individuals, because the Court of Justice has adopted a highly restrictive view of both "direct" and "individual" concern.

Despite being second in mention in Article 230(4) [ex 173(4)] the test of individual concern has proved the greatest difficulty for applicants. So it has often been used as the first test by the Court of Justice to decide whether or not a case is admissible. To establish individual concern the applicant must show that the act in question affects the applicant in the same way as if it had been addressed to him, either alone or as a member of a fixed and closed class. The test to pass was set out by the Court of Justice in *Plaumann*. The Court held:

"persons other than those to whom a decision is addressed may only claim to be individually concerned if that decision affects them by reason o certain attributes which are peculiar to them or by reason of circumstances in which they are differentiated from all other persons and by virtue of these factors distinguishes them individually just as in the case of the person addressed."

Plaumann concerned a decision addressed to the German government refusing permission to reduce the duty on clementines. The test was whether Plaumann, a fruit importer, could claim individual concern by virtue of the fact that he was a member of the abstractly defined class addressed by the measure (he was a fruit importer who imported clementines) or if it affected him because he had some attributes which made him different from all other persons. The Court of Justice held that Plaumann was merely an importer, and as anyone could set up in business as an importer, Plaumann was not, therefore, individually concerned.

As previously mentioned, applicants in anti-dumping cases are frequently successful in proving direct and individual concern. Success in other areas is rare. One of those rate successes was *Alfred Toepfer v Commission* (106 & 107/63). The applicant was an importer of cereals who requested a licence from the German government to enable him to import cereals from France into Germany. The Germany government refused to grant the licence. The decision issued by the Commission was a confirmation of the government's refusal. As the decision affected only the existing applicants it was thus if individual concern to the applicant. Here the action of the Commission was retroactive in nature and it was clearly possible to differentiate the applicants from all others. This line of reasoning was followed in *Bock v Commission (Chinese Mushrooms)* (62/70). Here the Court held that the company was individually concerned because the application made to import Chinese mushrooms was made on September 11, and refused by Germany on the same date, but was upheld by the Commission on September 15. The decision of the Commission was in direct response to the application from Bock.

The case of *Spijker Kwasten v Commission* (231/82) concerned a Commission decision to the Dutch Government, allowing the Dutch government to ban the import of Chinese brushes. Despite the fact that the applicants had previously applied for an export licence for these objects, the Court of Justice held that the decision was not of individual concern to the applicants. By way of contrast, in *AE Piraiki-Patriki v Commission* (11/82), the applicants who manufactured and exported cotton yarn sought to challenge a decision addressed to the French government authorising the imposition of a quota on Green cotton yarn. The decision was applicable generally. The Court of Justice held that the applicant was of individual concern because they have entered into a contract to supply cotton yarn prior to the decision from the Commission. In *Sofrimport v Commission* (C-152/88), the Court of Justice held that importers whose goods were in transit at the time a Commission regulation was adopted were individually concerned. This was because "goods in transit" was a fact that the Commission was specifically required to take into account.

An attempt to describe the reasoning of the Court of Justice in the areas of individual concern is fraught with difficulties. There have not been many successful applications (outside the areas of anti-dumping, and it may be better to regard this as a special issue), and what case law there is often conflicting, or decided on the particular merits of an individual case. However, if an applicant can show that he and a defined group of others were affected by an act, he would be individually concerned. The cases seem to point out that it is only in retrospective measures, so that the result is the creation of a closed and fixed group, that individual concern can be show. The act cannot be regulatory in nature because it has no effect on future behaviour. The act is therefore a decision which would individually (and directly) concern the known members of the fixed group.

Direct Concern

The Court of Justice has been more concerned with the issue of individual concern. In cases where the applicant has managed to prove individual concern the Court of Justice has appeared to automatically assume direct concern. Nevertheless, the general rule for direct concern is that if a Member State is granted any discretion to act under the disputed provisions, then the provision by its nature cannot give rise to direct concern. This approach can be seen in the *International Fruit Company* cases (41–44/70), discussed above in relation to regulations disguised as decisions. In deciding that the matter was of direct concern for the applicant, the Court of Justice held that the disputed provision made it "clear that the national authorities do not enjoy any discretion in the matter of the issue of licences" and that the "measures whereby the Commission decides on the issue of the import licence thus directly effects the legal position of the parties concerned". In *Alcan* (C-69/69), the Court held that the applicant was not directly concerned, because Belgium, the Member State to whom the decision was addressed, was free to choose how to implement the distribution of aluminium allocations. In *Bock*, the

Chinese mushroom case, the German Government had a choice of whether or not to use the authorisation granted by the Commission. Despite this discretion, the Court of Justice held that the fact that the government had indicated to the applicant that they intended to use the authorisation to reject his application was sufficient for their discretion not to be an issue. Therefore, the matter was of direct concern to the applicant.

The difficulties for an individual in bringing an action under Article 230 [ex 173] have been ameliorated by the possibility that in many instances the applicant would be in a position to bring an action in their national courts and persuade the national court to make an Article 234 [ex 177] reference. However, in 1994 there appeared to be evidence that the Court of Justice had changed its stance. The case of *Codornui* (C-309/89) indicated a number of relaxations to enable individuals more easily to mount an Article 230 [ex 173] action. This "new" approach was also coupled with a tightening of the rules for an Article 234 [ex 177] reference in *TWD Textilwerke* (C-188/92). This putative new approach and the disappointing eventual outcome is discussed below. Meanwhile, it is difficult to disagree with the commentator who suggests that in Article 230 [ex 173] actions it is hard to avoid the feeling that the Court of Justice first decides whether it wants the application to be admissible, and then applies whichever test will provide the desired result.

Time Limits

Article 230(5) [ex 173(5)] provides that the applicant has two months from the publication of the measure, or from the date of notification to the applicant, or from the date on which it came to the knowledge of the applicant. As Article 254 [ex 191] requires that regulations, directives and decisions are published, time will run from the date of publication. (Directives and Decisions were added to the requirement to be published under Article 254 [ex 191] by virtue of amendment in the TEU).

After the expiry of the two-month period, the measure may not be challenged by other means, such as Article 241 [ex 184], or Article 232 [ex 175].

GROUNDS FOR ANNULMENT

The first hurdle to be established is that the case is admissible. Once this has been successfully crossed the grounds or substantive merits of the claim must be provided. Article 230(2) [ex 173(2)] sets out for grounds for annulment. It should be noted that the four grounds will often overlap in individual cases, so that it is possible to plead more than one ground. The grounds were originally based on French administrative law but are now influenced by the administrative law of other Member States including that of the United Kingdom. The four grounds for annulment are:

(a) a lack of competence;

(b) infringement of an essential procedural requirement;

(c) infringement of the EC Treaty or of any rule relating to its application; and

(d) a misuse of power.

Lack of Competence

This ground is the equivalent of the English doctrine of *ultra vires* in substantive law. The institutions may adopt measures only where they are empowered to act by the EC Treaty or by secondary legislation. Article 7 [ex 4] of the EC Treaty requires each institution to act within the limits of the power conferred on it. An early example is *Meroni v High Authority* (9/56) which concerned the successful challenge to decisions taken by a subordinate authority when there were no powers to delegate decision making to that body. A more recent example is *France v Commission* (C-303/90), where France successfully challenged a Commission measure under a requirement for the application of structural funds under Article 157 [ex 130].

Infringement of an Essential Procedural Requirement

This ground is the equivalent of the English doctrine of *ultra vires* in procedural law. It is based on the principle that institutions adopting legislation must follow the correct procedure. The procedure to be followed is laid down either in the Treaty or in secondary legislation. A number of cases have invoked Article 253 [ex 190] which provides that all Community secondary legislation must give reasons and refer to any proposals and opinions made in respect of those provisions. Nor will the Court of Justice accept reasons that are not fully explained. *Germany v Commission (Tariff Quotas on Wine)* (24/62) concerned an application by Germany to the Commission to import wine for blending. The application was partly unsuccessful, the Commission giving as its reason that there was sufficient wine of that type within the Community. The

Court of Justice annulled the decision on the grounds of vagueness. The Court held that reasons must not be too vague or inconsistent. They must set out in a clear and relevant manner the main issues of law and fact on which they are based. This will enable the parties to defend their rights and the Court of Justice will be better able to exercise its supervisory functions, and Member States and interest nationals will be kept informed.

In two cases, *Roquette Frères* (138/79) and *Maizena v Council* (139/79) it was held that the failure to consult the European Parliament where this is required by the Treaty, was an infringement of an essential procedural requirement. The case of *Commission v Council (Titanium Dioxide)* (C-300/89) was more complex. In this case the Council based a measure to harmonise the regime for titanium dioxide waste on Article 157 [ex 130]. This provides for the use of the consultation procedure and for unanimous voting in the council. The Commission argued that the measure should be based on Article 95 [ex 100a], which provided for the co-operation procedure and for qualified majority voting in the Council. The Court of Justice held that a single legal base, Article 95 [ex 100a], should have been used, particularly as this would enable the Parliament to influence decision-making in environmental issues. The choice of legal base is likely to become increasingly important as the result of new competencies and procedures added by the TEU and the Treaty of Nice.

Infringement of the Treaty or of any Rule to its Application

This is a widely-drafted ground and covers the provisions of all relevant Treaties, secondary legislation, and the general principles common to the laws of the Member States (see Chapter 5). This ground is argued in almost all the annulment actions. In *KSH v Intervention Board* (103 & 145/77) the Court of Justice considered the principle of equality. From a UK point of view, a case worth noting is *Transocean Marine Paint Association* (17/74). In this case, the Court recognised that the bedrock of British justice, the principle of natural justice including the right to be heard, was also one of the general principles of Community law.

Misuse of Powers

The basis of the ground is the use of power for the wrong purpose, or, if lawful was not the purpose for which the power was originally intended. In English law the equivalent ground would be abuse of power or bad faith. Not many cases are successful under this head, probably because of the difficulty in establishing a case.

The Effects of Annulment

Article 231 [ex174] provides that if the action is well founded, the Court of Justice shall declare the act concerned to be void. This declaration means in effect that the act never existed. Under Article 231(2) [ex 174(2)] the Court can declare part of a regulation to be invalid, and part to be definitive. Thus the Court can sever parts where possible. This is what it did in *Consten and Grundig v Commission* (56 & 58/64). In *Commission v Council (Staff Salaries)* (81/71) the Court ordered that staff salaries should still be paid even though it had annulled the regulation authorising payment. In *European Parliament v Council (Student Residence)* (C-295/90), the Court of Justice granted the annulment of Directive 90/366 which provided for the right of residence for students, on the grounds that the measure had been passed under an incorrect legal base. Nevertheless, the Court ordered that the provisions of the directive should remain in force until correctly based legislation was adopted. (This was achieved by Directive 93/96). Article 233 [ex 176] provides that where an act has been declared void, the institutions are obliged to take the necessary measures to comply with a judgment of the Court of Justice.

Review for Inactivity—Article 232 [ex 175]

Article 232 [ex 175] concerns actions against the Council, or the Commission, or the European Parliament for a failure to act. If they fail to act when they have a legal obligation to do so, action may be brought against them by a Member State or any of the institutions of the Community. The European Parliament was added to the list of possible defendants by amendment to Article 232 [ex 175] in the TEU. Prior to the TEU there was no specific provision made for the European Parliament. As with their inclusion in Article 230 [ex 173], this recognised the increasing influence of the Parliament in the legislation process.

Article 232 [ex 175] complements Article 230 [ex 173], and both can, and often are, pleaded in the same action. Inconsistency between the provisions of Article 230 [ex 173] and Article 232 [ex 175] can be resolved by applying what is called the "unity principle". In *Chevalley v Commission* (15/70), the Court of Justice held that the Court would adopt the same approach to both Articles, and that it was not necessary to state which action was the subject of the application. However, it should be noted that under Article 232 [ex 175] the European Parliament is a privileged applicant, being included in the term "any of the institutions".

Standing

Like Article 230 [ex 173] Article 232 [ex 175] draws a distinction between privileged and non-privileged applicants. As noted above, all of the institutions are privileged applicants under Article 232 [ex 175]. Individuals on the other hand, have a restricted right of *locus standi* under Article 232 [ex 175]. Article 232 [ex 175(3)] gives natural and legal persons the right to complain to the Court of Justice then an institution has failed to address to that person any act other than a recommendation or opinion. It should be noted here that there is no requirement for direct and individual concern. Some difficulties arise where a decision should be addressed to a third party. By analogy with Article 230 [ex 173] it would be consistent if an applicant could challenge an omission in relation to a third party where the applicant is directly and individually concerned. In *ENU v Commission* (C-107/91) the Court of Justice ruled that *locus standi* would be available to an applicant provided they were directly and individually concerned. It was not necessary for the applicant to be the actual addressee of the decision. This case might overrule *Lord Bethel v Commission* (246/81). In this case Lord Bethel, a frequent air traveller, complained of a failure to act on price fixing by airlines. The Court of Justice rejected Lord Bethel's standing, holding that any potential measure would be addressed to the airlines and not to Lord Bethel, who was only one of many air travellers.

Procedure

Article 232 [ex 175(2)] sets out a preliminary procedural step, which must be taken before any court action can ensue. First, the institution in question must be called upon to act. The institution then has a two-month period to define its position, or to comply with the request. If the institution fails to comply by the end of the two months' period, the matter may be brought before the Court of Justice within a further two months.

Where the institution has defined its position, but has not adopted a measure, the applicant may not invoke Article 230 [ex 173], nor is there any further actions they can take under Article 232 [ex 175]. In *Lutticke v Commission* (48/65) the applicants had requested that the Commission take action against Germany regarding a breach of Community law. The Commission was of the opinion that there was no breach and that therefore no action was necessary. They notified the applicant of this. The Court of Justice held that a definition of position by the institution ends its failure to act, and thus the refusal to act was not actionable. In

GEMA v Commission (125/78), a complaint was made to the Commission about a "pirate" radio station of youthful memory, Radio Luxembourg. The Commission refused to act and wrote to GEMA notifying them of its decision. The Court of Justice held that this was a sufficient definition of position to defeat GEMA's action.

This situation, where an institution can overcome an Article 232 [ex 175] action by defining its position can create a situation where the institution is immune from judicial review on that issue. Any other action, or inaction, it takes is subject to challenge under Article 230 [ex 173] or Article 232 [ex 175]. But if an institution defines its position it cannot be challenged. This may be the reason the Court of Justice mitigated the circumstances of defining a position in *European Parliament v Council (Transport Policy)* (13/83). In this case the Court stated that:

"in the absence of taking a formal act, the institution called upon to define its position must do more than reply stating its current position which in effect neither denies or admits the alleged failure nor reveals the attitude of the defendant institution to the demanded measures."

Effects of Successful Action

Article 233 [ex 176] lays down the effects of a successful action under that Article. The institution concerned is required to take the necessary measures to remedy its failure in accordance with a judgment of the Court of Justice.

Indirect Review under Article 241 [ex 184]

Article 241 [ex 184] provides that, notwithstanding the expiry of the time limit laid down in Article 230(5) [ex 173(5)], any party may, in proceedings in which a regulation adopted jointly by the European Parliament and the Council, or a regulation of the Council, of the Commission, or of the European Central Bank is at issue, plead the grounds specified plead the grounds specified in Article 230(2) [ex 173(2)], in order to invoke before the Court of Justice, the inapplicability of that regulation. This provision is known as the plea of illegality. Under this Article, an applicant may challenge the legality of a general act on which a subsequent act or omission is based. There are no time limits for bringing an Article 241 [ex 184] action.

However, the plea of illegality does not give rise to an independent cause of action. It can only be used indirectly in the context of proceedings already before the Court of Justice. For example, in an action for a challenge to a decision the applicant may wish to raise the legality of a more general measure on which the challenged decision is based.

It will be noted that Article 241 [ex 184] is stated to apply only to regulations. However, in line with the approach adopted for Article 230 [ex 173], the Court of Justice has held that it is the substance of a measure rather than its form which will determine the remedy. In *Simmenthal* (92/78) the Court of Justice held that Article 241 [ex 184] was applicable to other acts of the institutions, which although not in the form of a regulation, produced similar effects. In *Simmenthal* the applicant was challenging a decision by the Italian government not to award a contract. In the course of the proceedings the applicant challenged the invitation to tender on which the government's decision was reached. As a result the decision was annulled.

Article 241 [ex 184] gives the right to bring an action to "any party". There have been some doubts as to whether this entitlement is extended to the institutions or to Member State and, as yet, the Court of Justice has not issued a definitive judgment. The grounds for review are the same as those for annulment under Article 230 [ex 173].

A successful action under Article 241 [ex 184] will not mean that the regulation will be annulled (as in Article 230 [ex 173]). Instead, the Court of Justice will declare the regulation in question to be inapplicable, and any decisions based on the inapplicable regulation will be void.

Conclusions

It seems clear the Treaty itself is inadequate in its provisions for judicial review. It also seems clear that the Court of Justice has not developed a consistent case law in its attempts to fill in the gaps. There appears to be diverse strands of law so that, for example, in anti-dumping cases it is far easier to establish direct and individual concern than in the more general policy areas. The Court of Justice should either draw the stands of law together to form a seamless whole, or acknowledge that there are different tests for different areas of case law. The present situation is unclear, and therefore unsatisfactory.

Codorniu—a Lost Opportunity?

The case of *Codorniu SA v Council* (C-309/89) was thought to herald a new, more open approach by the Court of Justice to a challenge by an individual under Article 230 [ex 173]. In *Codorniu*, the applicant challenged a regulation which stipulated that the term *crémant* should be reserved for sparkling wines of a particular quality coming from France or Luxembourg. The applicant made sparkling wine in Spain, as did other producers, and had held a trademark containing the word *crémant* since 1924. The Council argued along the traditional lines that the measure was a regulation to identify the number or identity of wine producers affected by it. The Court of Justice agreed with this argument, and it also agreed that the contested measure was "by nature and by virtue of its sphere of application, of a legislative nature". In other words, that the measure was a true regulation, in substance as well as form. Nevertheless, the Court held, that did "not prevent it from being of individual concern to some of them". The Court then found, on not altogether clear reasoning, that the applicant was individually concerned in the matter.

Thus, the Court of Justice in this case eased the burden on individual applicants attempting to bring a challenge under Article 230 [ex 173]. First, the Court held that a true regulation could be challenged. It was not necessary in *Codorniu* to demonstrate that a regulation was in fact a series, or bundle, of decisions. And secondly, in the instant case it dispensed with the complicated and difficult test to establish direct and individual concern.

Codorniu has been followed in a number of subsequent cases. One example is the case of *Antillean Rice* (T-480 & 483/93). The Commission had fixed a minimum price for certain goods and the applicant challenged this decision. The Court of First Instance held that the measure under challenge was in reality a legislative measure. Nevertheless, it held that the applicant was individually concerned. On slightly different grounds, the Court of Justice allowed the applicant in *Extramet* (C-358/89) to challenge anti-dumping regulations. The Court held that the applicant was individually concerned because it was the largest importer of the product concerned (calcium), and its whole business depended on the easy availability of the product.

The judgment in *Codorniu* and subsequent cases should be looked at in conjunction with the Court of Justice judgment in *TWD Textilwerke Daggendorf v Germany* (C-188/92). In the latter case, TWD failed to challenge under Article 230 [ex 173] a Commission decision to refuse state aid. This was despite a notification in writing by the German Government of the decision and the right to challenge it. The notification also stated that TWD would almost certainly have standing to bring an action. When an action was brought by TWD in the German domestic court, they persuaded the German court to make an Article 234 [ex 177] reference to the Court of Justice. The Court of Justice refused to accept the reference, holding that TWD should have brought an action under Article 230 [ex 173]. They should not be able to evade the two-month time limit of Article 230 [ex 173] by bringing domestic proceedings and attempting to resurrect the matter by way of an Article 234 [ex 177] reference.

It may be that Article 234 [ex 177] is used, in practice, as an indirect means of challenge to a contested measure. Article 234 [ex 177] allows national courts to refer to the Court of Justice questions concerning the "validity and interpretation of acts of the institutions of the Community". There are a number of reasons why a private applicant may attempt to use Article 234 [ex 177] as a mechanism to challenge a Community measure. First, any action under the usual channel of Articles 230 [ex 173] and 232 [ex 175] is subject, as explained above, to the strict time limit of two months. It may well be beyond this point in time before the applicant becomes aware of the need to challenge the alleged illegal act. Then, second, there is the difficulty of establishing *locus standi*. The applicant will have the very difficult task of showing that the contested act is of direct and individual concern. It may well be, that by the time the applicant is in a position to bring an action under Articles 230 [ex 173] or 232 [ex 175], the time limit has passed. The applicant might then turn to Article 234 [ex 177]. This was the position in *TWD Textilwerke Daggendorf v Germany* (C-188/92). There were special circumstances in *TWD*. The company was notified immediately by the German government of the right to challenge the decision. The company was told that it would have standing to bring an action. Yet the company failed to act, waiting instead for the chance to bring an indirect action under Article 234 [ex 177]. In *R v Intervention Board Ex p. Accrington Beef* (C-241/95), it was not clear or obvious that the applicant would have standing to bring an action under Article 230 [ex 173]. In this case, because of the uncertainty, the failure to mount a challenge under Article 230 [ex 173] was not a bar to an indirect action under Article 234 [ex 177].

Even though *Codorniu* was thought of as ground breaking, the anticipated development did not take place until 2002. When the breakthrough did take place, it came from the Court of First Instance (CFI). The euphoria, however, was short-lived!

The case that appeared to herald the breakthrough was *Jégo-Quéré v Commission* (T-177/01). The decision of the CFI in this case did mark a dramatic, if short-lived, reappraisal and relaxation of the procedural rules facing private parties under Article 230. *Jégo-Quéré* concerned an action for annulment by a private applicant against a Commission Regulation. The Regulation

(1162/2001) concerned the size of mesh in fishing nets and Jégo-Quéré was a French fishing company that was affected by the Regulation. The chances of success for Jégo-Quéré were not very high, given the admissibility criteria laid down in the established case law. The Commission, in its submission to the CFI, argued that Jégo-Quéré was not individually concerned because the Regulation at issue was a measure of general application applying equally to all operators fishing in the same area.

In giving judgment (on May 3, 2002), the CFI did agree that the Regulation was of general application. Nevertheless, the CFI, relying on the Court of Justice decisions in *Extramet* and *Codorniu*, held that such provisions may be of direct and individual concern to a private applicant. The CFI went on to say that one of the essential elements of Community law was the right of access to a court. This right is derived from Articles 6 and 13 of the ECHR and can now be found in Article 47 of the Charter of Fundamental Rights of the European Union. The CFI came to the conclusion that to dismiss the application of Jégo-Quéré would deprive them of this right.

The CFI then decided that the only satisfactory solution was a reconsideration of the existing case law. The CFI proposed a new test:

". . . a natural or legal person is to be regarded as individually concerned by a Community measure of general application that concerns him directly if the measure in question affects his legal position, in a manner which is both definite and immediate, by restricting his rights or by imposing obligations on him."

According to the CFI, the fact that there may be an indeterminate number of others who were likewise affected was not of relevance. The CFI therefore dismissed the Commission's objection of inadmissibility.

In its judgment, the CFI had undoubtedly been influenced by the Opinion of Advocate General Jacobs in another case before the ECJ. (It will be remembered that the CFI does not always have an Advocate General. This was the situation in *Jégo-Quéré*). The case that had come before the ECJ was *Unión de Pequeños Agricultores v Council (UPA)* (C-50/01). In this case, UPA, a Spanish trade association lodged an application seeking partial annulment of a Regulation (1638/98) on the organisation of the market in oils and fats. This case had already been dismissed by the CFI on the grounds of admissibility and now UPA had appealed to the ECJ. In his Opinion (given on March 21, 2002), Advocate General Jacobs said that the time was now ripe for an evolution in the interpretation of the notion of individual concern. In his view, the preliminary ruling procedure under Article 234 [ex 177] did not provide full and effective protection against Community measures. In the Opinion of the Advocate General, the only solution that would provide effective judicial protection is one which constitutes a new, more liberal interpretation of the notion of individual concern. The Advocate General therefore proposed the following new criteria:

"an individual should be regarded as individually concerned within the meaning of (Article 230(4)) by a Community measure where, by reason of his particular circumstances, the measure has, or is liable to have, a substantial adverse effect on his interests."

The Advocate General therefore advised the Court to annul the CFI's Order on the ground that it was based on the "old" restrictive interpretation of the notion of individual concern.

To settle the matter, the ECJ interrupted its summer break to issue its judgment in *UPA* (on July 25, 2002). It rejected the path taken by both the CFI in *Jégo-Quéré* and the Advocate General in *UPA*. The ECJ reaffirmed the traditional position on individual concern. The ECJ stated that it would have to step beyond the boundaries of its jurisdiction under the Treaty if it wanted to change the system of judicial review. The Treaty had already provided adequate judicial protection via a combination of both domestic and Community courts. It was not within the remit of the ECJ to examine whether national courts offered sufficient protection. It was only Member States, in accordance with the procedures for amending the Treaty, who have the power to reform the system of judicial review. In *UPA*, the Court of Justice overruled the CFI's new approach in *Jégo-Quéré*. In future it will not be possible for the CFI to continue to apply *Jégo-Quéré*.

The judgment in *UPA* seems to be a missed opportunity. An action under Article 234 [ex 177] is not always satisfactory. If, as in *UPA*, there were no national implementing-measures, the only option available to the applicant was to knowingly break the rules as set out in the Regulation and then wait for the authorities to bring infringement proceedings. Only then could the applicant challenge the legality of the Regulation. Even then, the applicant can only attempt to persuade the court that a reference under Article 234 [ex 177] is necessary. This hardly constitutes an adequate means of judicial protection. Also, the comment of the ECJ that only an amendment to the Treaty could fill the gap, if any, of judicial protection in the Community is not convincing. The many cases handed down by the Court of Justice, the Court has stressed its "gap-filling" role in the interpretation of the treaties.

At the time of *Codorniu* and *TWD*, it was suggested that the Court of Justice was attempting to limit the ever increasing number of Article 234 [ex 177] references that came before it. But at the same time it was making it easier for individuals to challenge under Article 230 [ex 173]. In the light of the subsequent judgments, discussed above, both *Codorniu* and *TWD* can be explained as "one-off" cases, each dependent on the particular fact of each case.

9. PRELIMINARY RULINGS: ARTICLE 234 [EX 177]

INTRODUCTION

Article 234 [ex 177] of the EC Treaty is the mechanism whereby a national court can ascertain from the Court of Justice its views on the correct interpretation and status of Community Law. Thus the use of this mechanism ensures a uniform, consistent and harmonious application of Community law throughout the national legal systems of all the Member States. The request for a ruling must be made at some stage in the proceedings before the national court and the national court must apply the ruling from the Court of Justice to the facts of the case. This is what is meant by the term "preliminary".

It is designed to work in co-operation with the national courts but at the same time is an attempt to prevent those courts from giving their own interpretation on the validity of Community law. It would be inimical to the concept of the supremacy of Community law if each Member State was able to apply its own interpretation to that law. This expression of supremacy has also been instrumental in developing a consistent body of fundamental principles of Community law (see Chapter 5). These fundamental principles are in fact a recognition by the Court of Justice that Community law has to protect human rights at least to the same level as that provided by the legal systems of the Member States. But it is also an instrument whereby the Court of Justice can impose those principles on an unwilling court. An early example of this can be seen in the case of *Internationale Handelsgesellschaft mbH* (11/70) where the Court of Justice said that ". . . the law born from the Treaty [cannot] have the courts opposing to it rules of national law of any nature whatever . . .". More recently the overriding strength of Community law was recognised by the House of Lords in *Factortame* (C-221/89) where their lordships were prepared to, in effect, disapply the Merchant Shipping Act 1988.

It is important to remember that Article 234 [ex 177] is not an appeal system. In an appeal system the initiative is with the parties to the action whether to appeal or not. In the appeal it is the appellate court which decides the case. In other words, the court hearing the appeal can substitute its own decision for that of the lower court. Whether it does this or not it is the decision of the appellate court that is important, having more authority than the decision of the lower court. By contrast, an Article 234 [ex 177] reference is made by the national court and not by the parties to the action before that national court. The national court may take into consideration the wishes of the parties but is under no obligation to proceed on the basis of those wishes. For example, in *Duke v Reliance* [1988] the House of Lords refused to make a reference to the Court of Justice, arguing that the issue before it did not involve any EC law issues.

When a reference is made to the Court of Justice it is on specific issues where there is need for clarification or interpretation on EC law, which cannot be resolved by the national court. Although the factual background of the case must be given to the Court of Justice that Court will not give its ruling on the particular facts of the case before it. Indeed the Court of Justice will often reformulate the questions referred to it by the national court in order that it is not seen to be deciding the substantive issues. The Court of Justice will answer the questions put to it by the national court but the Court of Justice will remit the case back to the national court so that that court can make its final decision. Of course, this decision will be based on the answers given by the Court of Justice to the reference made to it.

Because Article 234 [ex 177] is a "reference" procedure and not an "appeal" procedure its success is based on the willingness of national courts to co-operate by making references and by loyally accepting the subsequent judgment of the Court of Justice. This relationship between the Court of Justice and national courts is a recognition of the separate functions of these bodies. The idea of mutual co-operation was recognised in the very first case to reach the Court of Justice by way of an Article 234 [ex 177] reference. In *De Geus en Uitdenbogerd v Robert Bosch GmbH* (13/61) the Advocate General said:

". . . the provisions of Article 177 (now 234) must lead to a real and fruitful collaboration between the municipal courts and the Court of Justice of the Communities with mutual regard for their respective jurisdiction."

This suggestion of co-operation rather than hierarchy is typical of the hybrid character of EC Law.

SCOPE

Article 234 [ex 177] provides that:

"The Court of Justice shall have jurisdiction to give preliminary rulings concerning:

(a) the interpretation of this Treaty,

(b) the validity and interpretation of acts of the institutions of the Community and of the European Central Bank,

(c) the interpretation of the statutes of bodies established by an act of the Council, where those statutes so provide."

The name of the European Central Bank was added by the TEU and paragraph (c) has not had any practical importance.

It can be seen that the EC Treaty confers jurisdiction on the Court of Justice to give preliminary ruling decisions on a wide range of Community laws, and acts of the institutions. This fairly obviously, covers the legally binding provisions of Article 249 [ex 189], namely regulations, directives and decisions. The Court of Justice has also held, in *Grimaldi* (C-322/88) that its jurisdiction also extends to non-binding recommendations and opinions. The "interpretation of this Treaty" also includes all Treaties amending or supplementing it and the Court of Justice has also ruled that international treaties entered into by the Community are "acts of the institutions" (*Haegeman v Belgium* (181/73). However, the Court said in *Hurd v Jones* (44/84) that it had no jurisdiction to rule on treaties entered into between Member States, where those treaties had not been negotiated on the basis of the EC Treaty or secondary legislation.

Although the Court of Justice can be asked to rule on validity or interpretation, it is the latter which is most common. Because of this the Article 234 [ex 177] procedure has been an important factor in the development of the substantive law of the EC. Many of the major principles of law established by the Court of Justice in cases heard by it came to that Court by means of the Article 234 [ex 177] procedure. Thus, in *Van Gend en Loos* (26/62) the Court of Justice was able to establish the concept of the supremacy of EC Law and in *Costa v ENEL* (6/64) the important concept of direct effect was recognised.

As important as this development of substantive law has been, another equally valuable development has taken place. This has been the availability of a means of access to the Court of Justice for individuals. So, when more direct avenues have been closed, the individual has been able to persuade the national court or tribunal that there was a matter of Community Law at issue. The individual had no right to insist on a reference to the Court of Justice: that discretion lies wholly with the national courts, but national courts have shown an increasing willingness to use their discretion. Also important from the individual party's point of view has been the development of the doctrine of direct effect (see Chapter 6). This has meant that an individual can plead a point of Community Law before a national court and that court will apply the Community provision to the case. As national courts are now required to apply Treaty Articles and other provisions, including directives, this means that national courts have a major role to play in the enforcement of EC Law.

JURISDICTION OF NATIONAL COURTS: WHO MAY MAKE A REFERENCE

Article 234 [ex 177] states that the Court of Justice may accept a reference from "any court or tribunal of a Member State". The Court of Justice has interpreted this in the widest sense and has insisted that the decision of whether or not a body qualifies for the purposes of Article 234 [ex 177] is a matter of Community Law and not national law. The case law shows that the only requirement is that the body performs a judicial function: the name of the body is irrelevant. In *Broekmeulen* (246/80), the Dutch Government stated that the Royal Netherlands Society for the Promotion of Medicine was not a court or tribunal. The Society had refused to register Mr Brockmeulen as a GP. On an Article 234 [ex 177] reference to it, the Court of Justice held that the Society's Appeals Committee was a "court or tribunal" because there was no appeal against a decision of the Appeal Committee and

". . . in a matter concerning the application of Community Law, the appeal committee, which performs its duties with the approval of the public authorities and operates with their assistance, and whose decisions are accepted following contentions proceedings . . . must be deemed a court of a Member State for the purposes of Article 177 [now 234]."

Not to have held that the Society's Appeal Committee was a "court or tribunal" might have had serious repercussions on a doctor's right of establishment in the Netherlands.

The Court of Justice has accepted references from many bodies. As early as *Van Gend en Loos* it was clear that an administrative tribunal was acceptable for the purposes of Article 234 [ex 177]. In *Vaassen* (61/65), the Court of Justice decided that a Dutch arbitration tribunal was capable of making a reference because it was a body instituted under the law, with its members appointed by a Minister. It operated under rules of procedure and applied the law in its decisions.

It does not seem to make any difference at what stage in the proceedings the reference is made. In *Pretore di Salo v X* (14/86) the *pretore* (magistrate) had not reached the stage of identifying the perpetrators of a criminal act. Nevertheless, the Court of Justice accepted a reference from that Court on the basis that it was acting within the general duty to act, "independently and in accordance with the law".

Although, as stated earlier a wide interpretation has been given to "court or tribunal", the Court of Justice has refused jurisdiction in some cases. The Court of Justice will give a ruling only where the national court or tribunal is called upon to give judgment in proceedings intended to lead to a judicial decision. So, in *Borker* (130/80), a reference from the Paris Bar Association Council on the right of a French lawyer to appear before a German Court, was refused because the Council did not have before it a case that it was under a duty to try but was merely making a declaration relating to a dispute between one of its members and a tribunal of another Member State.

In *Nordsee v Reederei Mond* (102/81), a reference from an arbitrator, appointed by the parties under a contract, was refused on the grounds that there was no involvement of national authorities in the process, nor were they called upon to intervene automatically before the arbitrator. This was so even though the decision of the arbitrator had the force of law between the parties.

What seems to be the deciding factor for the Court of Justice in deciding whether or not to accept a reference is not that the body is public or private or that there is no appeal against its decision. Rather it is the element of public control or involvement of national authorities which bring a body within the definitions of "court or tribunal" for the purposes of Article 234 [ex 177].

JURISDICTION OF THE NATIONAL COURTS: THE DECISION TO REFER

Normally, the Court of Justice will not question the reason for the reference. A national court or tribunal can make a reference "if it considers that a decision on the question is necessary to enable it to give judgment". In *Costa v ENEL* (6/64) it was stated that Article 234 [ex 177] "cannot empower (the Court of Justice) either to investigate the facts of the case or to criticise the grounds and purpose of the request for information".

Even though a body wishing to make an Article 234 [ex 177] reference is clearly a "court or tribunal" the Court of Justice may nevertheless refuse to accept a reference in the manner put by the national court or indeed, may refuse to accept a reference at all.

We have seen earlier that the Court of Justice will give a ruling only in proceedings intended to lead to a decision of a judicial nature. An example of this was the *Borker* case. In *Simmenthal* (106/77) it refused to review the facts of the case and it has also steadfastly refused to rule on the validity of national law. If the Court of Justice feels that the questions are inappropriately phrased it will merely reformulate the question or questions, so that it answers what it sees are the relevant Community issues. In *SPUC v Grogan* (C-159/90) the Court of Justice refused to answer questions put to it by an Irish court on the grounds that as the case had been terminated at the national level there was no question left to be resolved.

A special area where the Court of Justice will not answer questions is when it considers that the questions asked by the national court are contrived or hypothetical. The important cases in this area are *Foglia v Novello (No.1)* and *(No.2)* (104/79 & 244/80). The first case concerned a contract for wine between a French buyer, Novello and an Italian supplier, Foglia. In the contract there was a clause that Mrs Novello was not to be liable for any duties on the wine that were levied by either the French or Italian authorities contrary to the provisions relating to the free movement of goods. The carrier engaged for the task of transporting the goods was charged tax by the French authorities. It paid the tax and included the amount of tax in the total invoice it presented to Mr Foglia. He then attempted to recover this tax from Mrs Novello who declined to pay. Mr Foglia brought proceedings in the Italian courts against Mrs Novello to recover the amount. The Italian court made a reference to the Court of Justice asking whether the French tax was compatible with the free movement of goods provisions. The Court of Justice refused to accept the reference on the grounds that there was no genuine dispute between the parties and that the action was simply one to challenge the French authorities. Consequently the reference was not "genuine" the Court of Justice explained that:

"the parties to the main action are concerned to obtain a ruling that the French tax system is invalid for liquor wines by the expedient of proceedings before an Italian court between two private individuals who are in agreement as to the result to be attained and who have inserted a clause in their contract in order to induce the Italian court to give a ruling on this point . . ."

The Court went on to say that if it was obliged to give rulings on such arrangements it would jeopardise the whole system of legal remedies available to private individuals.

This ruling that the Article 234 [ex 177] procedure had been abused did not satisfy the Italian judge and in *Foglia v Novello (No.2)* he made a further reference. Included in the reference was a series of questions on the place of Article 234 [ex 177]. In particular, the Italian judge asked about the powers and functions of the referring court. The Court of Justice reiterated its reasoning in the first case and reinforced the point that its duty was in assisting the administration of justice in Member States and not that of delivering advisory opinions on general or hypothetical questions.

The judgments in *Foglia* have been criticised. If a judge in a national court feels in his discretion, that a reference is necessary, a refusal by the Court of Justice to accept that reference is a denial of the right to have a point of Community law decided by the forum established for that very purpose. It would also lead to an uneven development of the law between the Member States. It can also be said that friendly litigation is practised in many countries and that in any event, it is not the role of the judiciary to judge whether litigation is appropriate. On the other hand, the Court of Justice is in a position of "special vigilance" when a question is referred to it in which the national court of one Member State asks the Court of Justice to rule on the compatibility of Community law with the law of another Member State. The Court of Justice must avoid decisions that seem to bring into conflict the courts (and governments) of different Member States.

What can be said is that, until fairly recently, *Foglia* appeared to be an isolated case, turning on its own particular facts. In other cases, the Court of Justice has rejected arguments that there was no genuine dispute. In *Parfumerie Fabrik v Provide* (150/88) it accepted a reference regarding a challenge to an Italian law in the German courts. The Court of Justice said that there was a genuine dispute and it was under a duty to answer questions of interpretation, which a national court needed to settle a dispute. The Court of Justice also found that there was a genuine dispute in *Vinal* (46/80) and in *Van Eycke* (267/86).

However, more recently, the Court has departed from the liberal approach which it had hitherto adopted, by which the Court of Justice would not question the discretion of the national court to refer and would attempt to extract from the file the information it needed to come to a decision. The first of a series of cases was *Meilicke v ADV/ORGA.FA Meyer* (C-83/91) which was decided on the same day (July 16, 1992) as *Lourenço Dias* (349/90). In *Meilicke*, the Court of Justice held that it would exceed its jurisdiction under Article 234 [ex 177] if it was to rule on a problem which was of a hypothetical nature in the absence of those elements of fact or national law necessary to enable it to give a useful answer to the questions asked. There were unusual circumstances in this case: the proceedings seem to have been undertaken to test the compatibility of an academic economic theory with a Community directive (Second Company Law Directive 77/91). So it still could be argued that *Foglia* and *Meilicke* were not of general application but were confined to their own particular facts.

However, a trend can now be discerned, starting with *Meilicke* that suggests that the Court of Justice may be taking a stricter approach to references made by national courts. The cases that illustrate this trend are *Telemarsicabruzzo SpA v Circostel* (C-320/92), *Pretore di Genova v Banchero* (C-157/92] and *Monin* (C-386/92). In all of these cases the information given to the Court of Justice was inadequate. The Court of Justice said that the need to give a useful ruling for the purposes of Article 234 [ex 177] made it essential for the national judge to define the factual and legislative background to the case. This was particularly so in cases such as these which involved competition law issues which were complex in both their facts and legal issues. Therefore, the Court of Justice held that because the information before it was fragmentary, it could not interpret the competition rules in the light of those facts. It therefore declined to give a ruling on the questions submitted to it by the Italian court.

The judgment in *Telemarsicabruzzo* was given in plenary session (*i.e.* with all of the (then) 13 judges sitting) and can be seen as a clear message to national courts that the background to the case must be clearly set out. Certainly, in the *Banchero* and *Monin* cases, *Telemarsicabruzzo* was used as authority by the Court of Justice to enable it to dismiss references on the grounds that they were inadequately explained. The *Telemarsicabruzzo* decision has been used to decline references because they were inadequately explained. Three such cases are *Testa* and *Modesti* (C-128/97 C-137/97) and *Nour* (C-361/97). The Court of Justice went even further in *Zabala Erasun* (C-422/93). In this case, the Court admitted that the reference was valid at the time it was made, but held that the reference should have been withdrawn in the light of further developments. The Court declined to accept the reference.

Despite all the cases discussed above, which indicate that the Court is adopting a stricter stance to Article 234 [ex 177] references, there are still some cases to show that the Court has not yet worked out a coherent plan in this area. It could still be argued that the Court adopts a case-by-case approach. In *Baumbast* (C-413/99) the Court accepted an Article 234 [ex 177] reference despite the fact that the case had been completed at a national level. In effect, there was nothing left for the Court of Justice to decide.

The cases discussed above could be used to support a move to a more formalist approach by the Court of Justice. This would seem to go against the spirit of Article 234 [ex 177], which is to foster co-operation between national courts and the Court of Justice. The introduction of this new formalism threatens this co-operation. National courts may be discouraged from making references to the Court of Justice.

One reason for this new approach may be the desire of the Court to control its increasingly heavy workload. It must be very time consuming for the Court to deal with cases which lack detail, or in which the background has not been clearly set out. However, not all the members of the Court of Justice are happy with a restrictive approach. In *Vaneetveld* (C-316/93), Advocate General Jacobs delivered a forceful Opinion as to why the Court should answer the questions posed by the national court. This was in spite of the fact that the reference contained no information about the facts of the case. The Advocate General distinguished *Monin* and *Banchero* on the grounds that they were concerned with competition policy and therefore it was important to have sufficient legal and factual information. In *Vaneetveld* the Advocate General said that the issue was a straightforward one. He also said that an answer to the questions would be very helpful to the national court. The Court of Justice held:

"It is true that the Court has held that the need to arrive at an interpretation of Community law . . . requires the [national] court to define the factual and legislative context of the question . . . None the less, that requirement is less pressing where the questions relate to specific technical points and enable the Court to give a useful reply even where the national court has not given an exhaustive description of the legal and factual position."

In *Leclerc-Siplec* (C-412/93), the Commission urged the Court of Justice to find the reference inadmissible, on the grounds that the parties were not in a real dispute. The Court did not agree with the Commission and, although it declined to answer some of the questions that did not relate to the dispute between the parties, it did accept the reference.

In an attempt to make co-operation between national courts and the Court of Justice more effective and to enable the Court of Justice better to meet the requirements of national courts by providing helpful answers, the Court issued a Note for Guidance in December 1996. Although the Note for Guidance stressed that it had no binding or interpretative effect, it did contain practical information on which, in the light of experience in applying the preliminary ruling procedure, would help to prevent the kind of difficulties which the Court had sometimes encountered.

Even though the establishment of the Court of First Instance, relieved the Court of Justice of some categories of direct action, Article 234 [ex 177] references remained the exclusion preserve of the higher court. Recent statistical evidence provided by the Information Service of the Court of Justice shows that in 1998 the average time taken for a reference to reach judgment was 22 months. This compares with 17.5 months in 1988. As has been previously mentioned, references represent a substantial part of the workload of the Court of Justice and certainly that Court needed to examine methods of reducing the amount of time spent on them. What should be remembered is that in the cases where a reference is refused there is nothing to prevent the national court resubmitting the questions with more information about their factual or legal background. It must be hoped that this stricter approach will not discourage judges of national courts from making references to the Court of Justice. This might lead to uneven development in the application of EC law in the Member States. It might also change what has been, up to now, a notable success story.

ARTICLE 234(2) [EX 177(2)]: THE DISCRETION TO REFER

So long as it does not fall within Article 234(3) [ex 177(3)] (see below) a court or tribunal at any time during the proceedings is free, if it considers it necessary to make a reference. All that is needed is that a national judge considers it *necessary* to enable judgment to be made. It should be noted however, that the jurisdiction under Article 234(2) [ex 177(2)] is permissive. It is entirely up to the national court to come to a decision whether to refer or not, even though the national court may take the wishes of the parties to the case into account. In *Rheinmuhlen* (166/73) the Court of Justice declared that the power to make a reference arises "as soon as the judge perceives either of his own motion or at the request of the parties that the litigation depends on a point referred to in the first paragraph of Article 234 [ex 177]". In *De Geus* (13/61) the Court of Justice held that national courts could make a reference whether or not an appeal is pending. This ruling was confirmed in *Da Costa en Schaake* (28–30/62). This case also confirmed that a reference could be made even though the Court of Justice had given a prior ruling on similar questions.

Although national courts can apply for a reference at any time the Court of Justice in *Irish Creamery Milk Suppliers v Ireland* (36 & 71/80) advised that the proper time for a reference was when the facts had been established and any questions involving national law exclusively had been settled. This would enable the Court of Justice to give due weight to all matters of fact and law that may have a bearing on the point of Community Law that it is called upon to decide.

A question arises as to whether there are any circumstances when it is not necessary to make a reference to the Court of Justice. (see "Avoiding the Obligation to Refer" below)

ARTICLE 234(3) [EX 177(3)]: THE OBLIGATION TO REFER

Article 234(3) [ex 177(3)] states that courts or tribunals against whose decision there is no judicial remedy under national law *shall* bring a question of Community law before the Court of Justice. There has been some discussion on the exact meaning of what exactly is meant by the expression "court or tribunal . . . against whose decisions there is no judicial remedy under national law". This has lead to the development of two theories, which for convenience have been labelled the "concrete" theory and the "abstract" theory.

The "abstract" theory (it has also been called the organic theory) suggests that the relevant court or tribunal is the highest court in the Member State. This means that Article 234(3) [ex 177(3)] applies to those courts or tribunals whose decisions are never subject to appeal. This would include the House of Lords in the United Kingdom, the Irish Supreme Court and the *Conseil d'Etat* in France.

The "concrete" theory (it has also been called the specific case theory) on the other hand, suggests that the relevant court of tribunal is the court or tribunal whose decisions *in the case in question* are not subject to appeal. This would cover in certain circumstances the English Court of Appeal when leave of appeal to the House of Lords has been refused. There are also certain circumstances when an appeal from an interior court is restricted. Such a case would be when the High Court refuses leave for judicial review from a tribunal decision. An example of an inferior court refusing to make a reference under Article 234(3) [ex 177(3)] is *Re A Holiday in Italy* [1975]. The case arose out of a National Insurance Commissioner's decision which was not subject to appeal. This would seem to be a perfect example of the application of Article 234(3) [ex 177(3)] and the "concrete" theory but the Commissioner refused to make a reference on the grounds that there was a possibility of an order of certiorari. In his view this was not a tribunal against whose decisions there was no judicial remedy.

However, it is probably the better view that the "abstract" theory is the way that the Court of Justice views the application of Article 234(3) [ex 177(3)]. This can be illustrated by *Costa v ENEL* (60/64), where there was no right of appeal from an Italian magistrate's court because the sum of money involved was too small. The Court of Justice held that national courts or tribunals against whose decisions there is no national judicial remedy (as in this case), must refer a question of Community law to the Court of Justice. This would seem to cover most cases and Article 234(3) [ex 177(3)] should apply to any proceedings which deny an appeal or judicial review.

There is still a situation that may not be so easy to determine and this is when a United Kingdom court refuses leave to appeal: this will be particularly relevant to the Court of Appeal or the House of Lords' Appeal Committee. This has the result that this lower court then becomes a court of last instance and the applicant may be denied a consideration of a point of Community law. In *R v Henn & Darby* [1980], a case concerning the importation into the United Kingdom of pornographic material, the Court of Appeal looked at the case purely on a English law basis and refused to make an Article 234 [ex 177] reference to the Court of Justice. They also refused leave to appeal. Fortunately the House of Lords granted leave to appeal and subsequently were persuaded that a reference was necessary.

In *Hagen v Fratelli & Moretti* (1980), another case when leave to appeal was refused by the Court of Appeal, Buckley L.J. stated that the ultimate court of appeal in the United Kingdom is either the Court of Appeal, if leave to appeal to the House of Lords is not obtainable, or the House of Lords. It is likely that the judge had in mind that the decision meant one obtainable in any one particular case, rather than as a general rule that a decision would be ever attainable. This argument is supported by *Magnavision v General Optical Council (No.2)*(1987) in which a point of Community law was raised in the first case of this name. In the first case, which was a criminal prosecution, the issue of Community law was not considered, an Article 234 [ex 177] reference was not made and leave to appeal to the House of Lords was refused. The applicant then appealed to the High Court (in Case *No.2*) on a point of law of general public importance, that the previous refusal meant that the High Court was a court of last instance for the purposes of Article 234(3) [ex 177(3)]. This appeal was also rejected. In judgment Watkins L.J. admitted that in such a case as this the High Court was a court of final appeal and that a reference should have been made. However, in this instant case the court had already given its decision. The matter had been terminated by judgment of the court and in effect, there was nothing left on which to base an appeal. As the case had been completed there was nothing on which a preliminary reference could be sought. According to Watkins L.J. the same situation would apply if the House of Lords refused leave to appeal. This approach is to be regretted for two reasons. First, it deprived the applicant of having a point of Community law considered which might have been in his favour. Second a reference to the Court of Justice on the matter of courts or tribunals of first instance, such as in this case, might have led to an authoritative ruling by the Court of Justice. A great chance had been missed!

Avoiding the Obligation to Refer

Although the wording of Article 234(3) [ex 177(3)] is imperative, the Court of Justice has recognised that there may be occasions when it is not necessary to make a reference. Consequently, the Court of Justice has limited the mandatory nature of Article 234(3) [ex 177(3)]. The first situation in which it will not be necessary to make a reference is when the Court of Justice has previously answered an identical question. In *Da Costa* (28 & 30/62), the Court of Justice was faced with the identical questions as had come before it in an earlier case, *Van Gend en Loos*. In the *Da Costa* case the Court of Justice referred to its previous judgment in *Van Gend en Loos* as the basis for its decision and advised that such a situation might, if the national court wished, excuse the obligation to refer. The Court of Justice said:

"the authority of an interpretation under Article 177 (now 234) already given by the Court may deprive the obligation of its purpose and thus empty it of its substance. Such is the case especially when the question raised is materially identical with a question which has already been the subject of a preliminary ruling in a similar case."

This decision is important because it showed that the Court of Justice was willing to allow national courts to rely on the authority of earlier rulings. It is also an example of the co-operative nature of Article 234 [ex 177] proceedings.

This relaxation of the strict mandatory nature of Article 234(3) [ex 177(3)] was further evidenced in the case of *CILFIT v Ministry of Health* (283/81). The Court of Justice referred to its judgment in *Da Costa* and in response to the Italian Supreme Court, set out in what circumstances it was not necessary to refer. The Court of Justice outlined three reasons:

(a) where a question of Community law is irrelevant to the case at issue;

(b) the point has already been decided by a previous decision of the Court of Justice. This re-affirms the decision in *Danfos* (109/88), but even here, the national court was free to make a reference if it wished;

(c) if the correct application of Community law is so obvious as to leave no doubt as to the manner in which the matter is to resolved. However, mindful that this might lead to an uneven interpretation between the Member States, the Court of Justice went on to say that before a national court comes to this conclusion it must be satisfied the matter would be equally obvious to a court in another Member State.

The Court of Justice then set out some guidance as to how a court would reach such a conclusion. Community law will be applied with regard to the objectives of the Community. The national court must be sure that any language difficulties will not result in a decision inconsistent with decisions in other Member States. Here the national court would take into account the different interpretation often given by different Member States to the same legal terminology: the fact that certain terminology is exclusive to one particular Member State and has no exact equivalent in any of the other states and many terms have different meanings as between national and Community law. The Court of Justice did not set out how it thought a national court would be capable of such a thorough analysis and it is likely that the *CILFIT* "formula" will be used only rarely.

In *Magnavision*, for example, the High Court thought that the matter was one of domestic law only. Although points of Community law were argued the court held that they had no application to the present case. In the highly technical case of *R v London Borough Transport Committee Ex p. Freight Transport Association* (1992), a case involving a conflict between Community Directives and domestic law on sound levels from vehicle exhausts, both the Court of Appeal and the House of Lords failed to make a reference to the Court of Justice. Yet they came to different decisions, the House of Lords overturning the decision in the Court of Appeal. This refusal can be regarded as an example of the first *CILFIT* principle, *i.e.* the House of Lords thought that the issue of Community Law was irrelevant to the case. But it also illustrates the difficulties inherent in the approach taken by the national courts.

Failure to make a reference can often leave an individual in the unhappy position of having no authoritative interpretation on the point of Community Law being argued before the national court. There is no individual redress against a failure to make a reference. All that a dissatisfied applicant can do is appeal against the decision and hope that the next court will be persuaded that a reference is necessary. This assumes, of course, that the applicant has the means and the stamina to continue to the higher courts.

ARTICLE 234 [EX 177] AND UNITED KINGDOM COURTS

The ability of national courts to ask the Court of Justice for a preliminary ruling has been the cause of some controversy in the United Kingdom. The difficulties have arisen out of the different conditions necessary to comply with Article 234(2) [ex 177(2)] and Article 234(3) [ex 177(3)]. It will be recalled that Article 234(2) [ex 177(2)] confers a discretion on courts who *may* refer a question to the Court of Justice and that Article 234(3) [ex 177(3)] places a court, whose decision is final, under an obligation to make such a reference. Two problems have surfaced in UK courts. The first problem area can best be summed up by the question, "when is English court, a court 'against whose decision there is not judicial remedy' for the purposes of Article 234(3) [ex 177(3)]?". The second is the extent to which courts from which there is no appeal should make references under Article 234(2) [ex 177](2).

The major source of controversy in the first problem area relates to the identification of the court of last resort. In England there are a number of occasions when a decision by a court cannot be appealed against. The problem is that this refusal to allow an appeal will only be made after the decision in the case has been handed down (as in *Magnavision*). For example, a case may be decided upon, that revolves around a point of Community law, without a preliminary reference to the Court of Justice. Providing the losing party can take advantage of an appeal to the Court of Appeal and, if necessary, to the House of Lords, there is no problem. The House of Lord is obviously the final court of appeal for the purposes of Article 234(3) [ex 177(3)].

However, if in our example, either the Court of Appeal refused leave to appeal to the House of Lords, or the House of Lords' Appeal Committee also refused permission to appeal, the position is more difficult. The House of Lords cannot make a reference because it does not have a case before it and the Court of Appeal cannot make a reference because it has already disposed of the case. This was the crux of the issue in *Magnavision* except that the courts concerned were the Divisional Court and the House of Lords.

In England it was probably correct to say that the relevant court for the purposes of Article 234(3) [ex 177(3)] was the highest court in the land (*i.e.* the House of Lords), rather than the highest court in the case. This was certainly the view of Lord Denning M.R. in *Bulmer v Bollinger* (1974) and his view has been authoritative until very recently. This leads to the second problem identified above, that is, the position of lower courts that may wish to make a reference.

In *Bulmer v Bollinger*, Lord Denning laid down guidelines for English courts as to when they should refer cases to the Court of Justice for a preliminary ruling. He set out four guidelines as to whether a decision from the Court of Justice was "necessary". These were:

(a) the decision on the question of Community law must be conclusive of the case;

(b) the national court could follow a previous ruling of the Court of Justice on the same point of Community law;

(c) the national court may consider the matter *"acte clair"* and decide the case itself. This would depend on how difficult and important the case was;

(d) before determining whether to refer, "in general it is best to decide the facts first". This point anticipated the Court of Justice decision in *Irish Creamery Milk Suppliers*

Association v Ireland where the court suggested that the facts and questions of national law should be settled before a reference is made.

Lord Denning continued by listing several factors that a national court should take into account before deciding to make a reference:

(a) bear in mind the length of time it takes to obtain a reference from the Court of Justice;

(b) bear in mind the expense involved; the Court of Justice holds that a reference is incidental to the main matter and therefore leaves the question of expenses to the national courts;

(c) the wishes of the parties should be taken into account; a national court should hesitate to refer where one of the parties did not wish it.

The guidelines set out by Lord Denning were not accepted without some criticisms by the judiciary. Even in *Bulmer v Bollinger*, the majority of the Court of Appeal did not fully support his guidelines. Stephenson L J said that the guidelines should be few and firmly related to the basic requirement that the decision on the questions must be necessary at the time. A judge should exercise his right to refer sparingly, and only in case of serious doubt or difficulty.

To Lord Denning's guidelines could be added those of Bingham J. in *Commissioners of Customs and Excise v Samex* [1983] 3 C.M.L.R. 194. He was of the opinion that a case should be referred to the Court of Justice as soon as it was realised that the Court of Justice was in a better position to determine questions of Community law than a national court. It was also better able to make comparisons between Community texts in difference languages, all of them equally authoritative, it could take representation from any of the Community institutions and any of the other Member States and was better equipped to undertake the purposive interpretation of Community legislation.

These guidelines, as to when to refer a question to the Court of Justice have been persuasive in English courts until fairly recently. However, the decision in *R v International Stock Exchanges of the United Kingdom and the Republic of Ireland Ex p. Else (the Stock Exchange case)* [1993], may signify a change of approach. In the Court of Appeal, Sir Thomas Bingham M.R. set out a significant reformulation of Lord Denning's principles covering the making by lower courts of an Article 234 [ex 177] reference. Bingham M.R. does not mention Lord Denning's two stage approach with its multiple factors to be taken into account. Rather he said:

". . . the correct approach in principle of a national court (other than a final court of appeal) (is) quite clear. The appropriate course is ordinarily to refer the issue to the Court of Justice unless the national court can with complete confidence resolve the issue itself. In considering whether it can with complete confidence resolve the national issue itself the national court must be mindful of the differences between national and Community legislation, of the pitfalls which face a national court venturing into what may be an unfamiliar field, of the need for uniform interpretation throughout the Community and of the great advantages enjoyed by the Court of Justice in construing Community instruments. If the court has any real doubt, it should ordinarily refer."

So, three factors should be present before a referral is made. First, the national court must determine the facts. Second, it must consider that the Community law issue is critical to the final determination, and third, it must consider whether it can with complete confidence resolve the issue itself. As a point of interest, in the *Stock Exchange* case, the Court of Appeal overturned the decision of the High Court to make a reference. This is the first example of such an occurrence.

In addition to these three factors, Bingham M.R. suggests four further guidelines: the need to be mindful of legislation, of the pitfalls awaiting a national court venturing into an unfamiliar field, of the need for uniform interpretation throughout the Community, and the great advantage enjoyed by the Court of Justice in construing Community legislation. He went on to say that if the national court had any real doubt, it should ordinarily refer. It would seem that this new formulation stresses the arguments in favour of a referral, thus rejecting Lord Denning's approach. In the latter approach the majority of the factors put forward tend to highlight the negative aspect of a referral. This suggests that a referral will be made only in exceptional cases. Whereas, in the *Stock Exchange* case, the factors are positive, and would indicate a presumption to make a referral.

It might be noted that the decisions in the *Samex* case and in the *Stock Exchange* case were decided by the same judge (Bingham J., being elevated to Bingham M.R. in the Court of Appeal), and that in *Samex* the judge's readiness to make referrals was already apparent. This "new" approach acknowledges the close working relationship between the national courts and the Court of Justice and enhances the possibilities of a uniform interpretation of Community law. It also reduces the risk of an English court "getting it wrong".

The use of the guidelines set out in the *Stock Exchange* case can be seen in *R v Secretary of State for National Heritage Ex p. Continental TV* (1993). Here, the High Court's decision to follow the Master of the Rolls was approved by the Court of Appeal.

Reform of the Preliminary Ruling Procedure

There is no doubt that the Court of Justice is stretched to breaking point in its workload. One has only to look at the increase in thickness of the European Court Reports to realise that the number of cases coming before the Court is increasing every year. In 2004, the Community will be enlarged by a further 10 Member States, and although the number of judges at the Court of Justice will increase, the number of cases coming to the Court will increase out of proportion to the number of new judges. This is because many of the cases will be Article 234 [ex 177] references made by national courts still unsure of the relationship between their domestic law and Community law. Already, Article 234 [ex 177] references make up over half the cases coming to the ECJ. Concern for the heavy workload has been officially recognised and reforms were proposed in the Treaty of Nice.

Some of the options that were discussed prior to agreement will be of interest. It was suggested that Article 234(2) should be abolished, leaving only Article 234(3). This would have the effect that only a national court or tribunal against whose decision there is no judicial remedy in national law would be able to make a reference. (In the United Kingdom, this court would usually be the House of Lords). The Court of Justice was very much against this proposed change, arguing that the ability of any court or tribunal to raise a reference was part of the co-operative relationship between domestic courts and the Court of Justice. In the event, this proposal was not acted upon.

Another suggestion to control the number of cases was to set up some form of "filtering system" to allow only "difficult" or important cases to come before the Court of Justice. It was suggested that courts of final resort should refer only questions that were sufficiently important from the point of view of the development of Community law. This difficulty with this proposal is that the ECJ and national courts might have a differing view about what was "important". If the ECJ refused to answer a reference the national court would be left having to decide the matter of Community law for itself. This suggestion was not proceeded with.

A radical suggestion was that the Article 234 [ex 177] system should change, from a reference system to an appellate system. This suggestion would, however, change the whole basis of the regime envisaged in Article 234. The system of co-operation between national courts and the ECJ, built up over many years would be irrevocably altered, with all the attendant difficulties. There may well be an argument for a move to an appellate system because such a system is characteristic of a mature legal system such as the Community, but it is not easy to see how such a system would bring about a reduction in the number of cases. This suggestion was not followed.

The Treaty of Nice has provided that the CFI will have an increased jurisdiction. Article 225 has been modified to provide that the CFI can hear actions covered by Articles 230, 232, 235, 236 and 238 except those cases reserved in the Court's Statute for the ECJ itself. An important change has been made to Article 225 which now provides that the CFI has the power to hear preliminary rulings in specific areas laid down by the Statute of the Court of Justice. It remains to be seen what type of cases will be allocated to the CFI, but in any event, the practical operation of the changes are to be evaluated after three years.

10. FREE MOVEMENT OF PERSONS

The principle of free movement, either to seek and take up employment, to work on a self-employed basis, or to provide services in another Member State is one of the fundamental freedoms guaranteed by the Treaty. Along with the other free movement policies, it is broadly outlined in the Preamble to the Treaty, and Article 3(c) [ex 3c] requires "the abolition, as between Member States, of obstacles to freedom of movement of persons". Article 12 [ex 6] is also an important element in this area of Community competence. It declares:

"Within the scope of application of this Treaty, and without prejudice to any special provisions contained therein, any discrimination on ground of nationality shall be prohibited."

In addition Article 18(1) [ex 8(a)] gives to every citizen the right to move and reside freely within the territory of the Member States. However, this right remains subject to the limitations and conditions laid down by the Treaty and by measures adopted to give it effect (see discussion on Citizenship, below).

The Treaty deals with persons and services in Title III of Part Three. Articles 39–42 [ex 48–51] deal with "workers": this is the right of persons to take up employment in another Member State, the right to earn a wage or salary. Articles 43–48 [ex 52–58] address the "Right of Establishment": that is the right of self-employed individuals and companies or firms to establish a permanent base in another Member State, and there pursue economic activities in their own name. Articles 49–55 [ex 59–66] deal with "Freedom to provide Services"; this is the right to move from one Member State to another to provide and receive services without establishing a permanent base in that Member State.

It was probable that the free movement provisions were inserted in the Treaty for economic reasons. The original aim of the common market was the increase in wealth of the participating Member States. One way of assisting this process was to create a flexible and mobile labour force which could contribute to the overall economic improvement of the market. In the early days of the common market it was also considered easier to move people to seek jobs than it was to move capital in order to set up production forces in places where there was a surplus of labour. If this original purpose has not lost its relevant it has certainly been modified so that a social purpose is also now important. It could be argued that this social purpose reached its highest place with the concept of citizenship introduced by the TEU, whereby every person holding the nationality of a Member State becomes a citizen of the Union.

One must also consider, whether in overall terms, the guarantees to free movement have been a success in practical terms. Certainly, there have been many successes on an individual level. But there have been no large scale movements from areas of high unemployment to areas of low unemployment. Of course, cultural and linguistic differences are a large disincentive. So if the Treaty, in this area, has had only a limited impact, that impact has nevertheless been a symbolic significance. Taken together with other objectives of social policy, particularly those not based on economic activities, the rights to free movement now represent a valuable package of rights for citizens of the Union.

The role of the Court of Justice must also be borne in mind. As with all areas of fundamental Community rights, the Court has declared that fee movement rights are to be interpreted very widely. On the other hand, any exceptions or derogations from the rights allowed to Member States are to be interpreted very strictly.

FREE MOVEMENT OF WORKERS

The basic Treaty provisions set out in Article 39 [ex 48], which provided that freedom of movement of workers should be secured by the end of the transitional period. The Article has been held to be directly effective in *Commission v France (Ref. French Merchant Seamen)* (167/73) and in *Van Duyn*. In the former case proceedings were brought against France by the Commission on grounds that the French Maritime Code was discriminatory in that it required a certain proportion of a ship's crew to be French nationals. The Court upheld the Commission's complaint and said that Article 39 [ex 48] was "directly applicable in the legal system of every Member State" and would render inapplicable all contrary national laws.

Article 39(2) [ex 48(2)] requires the addition of any discrimination based on nationality between workers of the Member States. This is to apply in respect of employment, remuneration and other conditions of work and employment.

It should be obvious that no person has totally unrestricted rights to move to another Member State. The ability of a Member State to restrict entry is set out in Article 39(3) [ex 48(3)]. It states that Member States may impose restrictions on the grounds of public policy, public security and public health (see later). But Article 39(3) [ex 48(3)] also sets out general rights for workers. These rights are:

(a) to accept offer of employment actually made;

(b) to move freely within Member States for this purpose;

(c) to remain in the Member State while working; and

(d) to remain in the Member State after working, subject to conditions laid down by secondary legislation.

There is a further derogation allowed to Member States in that Article 39(4) [ex 48(4)] states that the provisions of Article 39 [ex 48] do not apply to employment in the public service.

Article 40 [ex 49] provides that Article 48 will be supplemented by secondary legislation. The main measures are:

(a) Directive 64/221 which expands on the rights of Member States to derogate from free movement provisions on the grounds of public policy, public security or public health;

(b) Directive 68/360 which provides details of rights of entry and residence for workers;

(c) Regulation 1612/68 which sets out the detailed rights of access to employment, and rights once employed;

(d) Regulation 1251/70 which concerns the right to remain in a Member State when employment has ended there.

THE SCOPE OF THE LEGISLATION

The scope of Article 39 [ex 48], and the implementing secondary legislation is wide. To come within the scope of the provisions it is only necessary to be a national of a Member State and to be a worker. However, the expressions "national" and "workers" need to be defined. The term "national" is a concept that can be achieved by each individual Member State. In the United Kingdom, the definition of a British national is set out in the British Nationality Act. As a point of interest, Commonwealth citizens are not nationals for Community law purposes.

Another example is that Germany gave German nationality to the citizens of the former German Democratic Republic (East Germany). This is now academic since the reunification of Germany in 1989, but Germany still gives nationality to certain people of German descent living in Poland. Third country nationals have no rights to free movement within the Community, unless these rights are "parasitic", by virtue of Treaty rights conferred on their spouses and families. In *Rush Portuguesa* (C-113/89) the Court of Justice gave free movement rights to non-national employees of a Community firm providing services in another Member State.

One will look in vain in the Treaty for a definition of the term "workers". Neither is it defined in any of the secondary legislation. Therefore one will need to look to the Court of Justice for an explanation; and one will find a progressive definition of the term, giving it a very wide meaning. As Article 39 [ex 48] is about workers it is clear that some economic activity is involved. It is also clear that it is necessary to establish some economic status. If individual Member States could establish what constituted a "worker" within their national territory, the expression would evolve in a piecemeal fashion, so that there was no uniform application across the Community. Member States could also interpret the status of worker restrictively, therefore denying Community rights to many individuals.

Very early on in the life of the Community the Court of Justice took the opportunity to address this problem. In *Hoekstra/nee Unger* (75/63) it said that "Articles 48–51 (now 39–43) of the Treaty . . . have given Community scope to this term". In other words, the expression "worker" was to be defined as a Community concept. The Court also said it recognised the temptation, if left to individual Member States, for them to define the term restrictively, and indicated that the Court would interpret the term generously. These two features, that the Court of Justice will reserve to itself the authority to define the key concepts of free movement provisions and that rights will be widely construed, are key factors recurrent in the case law of the Court of Justice.

In *Hoekstra*, the Court did not go further in defining a worker. The first clear indication of the Court's intention came in *Levin* (53/81). This case concerned a British woman working in Holland on a part-time basis. She was married to a non-EC national and had not worked for over a year when she was refused a residence permit. Her argument was that she had sufficient funds to maintain herself and her husband. The Dutch authorities argued that her income from her work was inadequate. The Court, in its judgment, took the opportunity to reiterate the judgment in *Hoekstra*, that "worker" was a Community concept. It then went further and declared that the amount of the wage was irrelevant to the status of the worker. All that was required was that the work was an activity of an economic nature. The Dutch authorities have also argued that Ms Levin had only taken employment in order to obtain a residence permit. The Court held that the motive of the person in taking up employment was irrelevant; all that was required was that the person was pursuing a genuine and effective economic activity.

The point about the motives of the person taking up employment is interesting because it contradicts the judgment of the UK court in *R v Secchi*. This case concerned a young person of 20 years who was financing a travelling holiday by taking "odd-jobs". The UK court said that a determining factor was the reason for the work, and held that Secchi was not a worker.

In the subsequent case of *Kempf* (139/85), the Court took the issue a step further. Mr Kempf was a German national living in the Netherlands. He worked for about 12 hours a week giving music lessons, but as his earnings were so low he had to rely on state supplementary benefits to top his earnings up to subsistence level. The Dutch authorities, in refusing to grant him a residence permit, argued that work at a level which meant that it was necessary to claim from social security funds could not be regarded as genuine and effective work. As in *Levin*, the Court disagreed. They said that when genuine part-time work needed to be supplemented it was:

"irrelevant whether those supplementary means of subsistence are derived . . . from financial assistance drawn from the public funds of the Member State in which he resides."

One can perhaps understand the concerns of Member States that their social security schemes will become overburdened by migrants moving from Member State with less generous provisions, particularly if those migrants do not really intend to engage in effective employment. Nevertheless, the exclusion of a great number of part-time workers from the rights afforded by Article 39 [ex 48] would be difficult to justify. This is particularly so given that a large proportion of the part-time work force is made up of women, the elderly and the disabled. There is also an increasingly growing body of workers who wish to work full-time but are obliged to accept part-time work because that is all there is on offer.

The Court of Justice went even further in *Lawrie Blum* (66/85), setting out three essential characteristics to establish an employment relationship. They are:

(a)   the provision of some type of service;

(b)   under the direction of another person; and

(c)   in return for remuneration.

This concept of remuneration was expanded in *Steymaan* (196/87). This is an interesting case in that Mr Steymaan, a German national living in the Netherlands had previously been a plumber. However, at the material time he was a member of a religious community. He took part in the religious life of the community and performed plumbing jobs and other general duties. In return the community provided for his material needs (as it did for all its members), and gave him a small amount of pocket money. He applied for a residence permit to pursue an activity as an employed person. The Netherlands (again) refused. The Court of Justice held that the work done by Mr Steymaan played "a relatively important role in the . . . Community". The Court then said that:

"In so far as the work, which aims to ensure a measure of self sufficiency . . . constituted an essential part of participation in that community the services which that latter provides to its members should be regarded as being an indirect quid pro quo for their work".

This case can be contrasted with *Bettray* (344/87), another Dutch case which came before the Court of Justice a short time after *Steymaan*. In *Bettray*, the Court held that paid activities carried out as part of a state-run drug rehabilitation scheme did not amount to a real and genuine economic activity. It may be that the distinction between the two cases is that in *Steymaan* the work was carried out to serve the economic purpose, whereas in *Bettray*, although the work undertaken did have some commercial value, it primary purpose was social. It can also be said that *Bettray* is one of the few cases where the Court has adopted a restrictive approach to its definition of "worker".

However, it may be that as a result of Member States' concerns, the Court of Justice is developing a "multi-tier" status of worker. That is, that those workers in employment are afforded a wider range of rights and benefits than those workers who are currently unemployed, or those workers who are seeking to re-train by undertaking further education.

In *Lebon* (316/85) the Court held that those in search of work were not entitled to the same benefits as those in work. Ms Lebon was the daughter of an EC worker, but she no longer lived with her parents, and therefore did not qualify for benefits as a dependant of a worker. She argued that she should qualify for workers benefits as she was seeking or intended to seek for work. The Court of Justice dismissed this argument. They held that the benefits provided by legislation on free movement were available only for those in actual employment. Although she could be temporarily classed as a worker, this right did not extend to the payment of benefits. Nor was she entitled to the same social and tax advantages guaranteed to workers in actual employment. In *Raulin* (C-357/89), a French waitress in the Netherlands had worked under contract, but for only 60 hours in an 8-month period. The Court held that, in considering whether the works is genuine and effective, the national court shall take account of all the services actually performed, and the duration of the activities.

A combination of the judgments in *Lebon* and *Raulin* could be read to indicate that it is now left to national courts to determine the most difficult and unclear cares. This seems to be an abrogation of responsibility by the Court of Justice. It is precisely in this type of situation that their guidance is most needed.

There is also developing a difference in treatment between those workers seeking vocational training and those seeking "pure" education. The former is part of the worker training programme of the Community and the latter part of education policy; this policy is still exclusive to Member States and not part of Community competence. In this area too, the judgment of the court can be said to reflect concern of some Member States that their generous provisions for further and higher education will be overburdened by a rush of migrants wishing to take advantage of them. The first limitation on the absolute rights of workers to take advantage of educational opportunities was in *Lair v Universität Hannover* (39/86). In his case Mr Lair, a French national was refused a grant by a German university for the payment of maintenance and course fees. Ms Lair had worked on and off for five years in Germany, and although she had been involuntarily unemployed on some occasions, she claimed the status of a worker. She also claimed that her period at university would lead to a professional qualification and would only be a break in her employment. The Court held that certain rights had been granted to workers who had finished employment. Such rights included the rights to remain in that Member State and the right to social security benefits. This could also be extended to university training. But, and this is the restriction, there had to be a link between the work previously done and the university course to be undertaken. The Court did allow one exception, and that was in cases where a worker involuntarily became unemployed and was "obliged by conditions on the job market to undertake occupational retraining in another field of activity". In the present case, because Ms Lair had come to Germany with the intention of working, and the course was intended to add to her qualifications, she fulfilled the criteria.

A case in contrast is *Brown v Secretary of State for Scotland* (case 197/86). In this case Mr Brown, who had dual French/English nationality had lived in France for many years. He was refused a grant by the Scottish education department. This was despite the fact that Mr Brown had worked for eight months in the United Kingdom prior to taking up his place at university. However, this work was a precondition of taking up the place at university: it was not considered possible to undertake the technical demands of the course without the period of work experience. The Court of Justice ruled that he was a worker but that he was not entitled to a maintenance grant because his employment was merely "ancillary" to the course of study he wished to undertake. As well as being a restrictive approach to the concept of worker, the Court also seems to be contradicting its earlier judgment in *Levin* that the purpose of motive for work was irrelevant.

In *Bernini* (C-3/90) the Court of Justice emphasised that the link to work and vocational training was crucial for the determination of the status of the worker and the consequent rights and benefits. Ms Bernini was an Italian national, who had hired in the Netherlands since she was two. She started a training course in the Netherlands which involved ten weeks work as a trainee in a factory. She then went to Italy to take up a course in architecture. At this point she was refused a grant by the Netherlands. The Court held that her work in the Netherlands (*i.e.* the ten weeks in the factory as part of her course) was sufficient for her to gain the status of worker. The Court further held that if the worker voluntarily left employment in order to take up a course of full-time study, the status of worker would be retained so long as there was a link between the previous studies and the course undertaken.

The question of how long may a migrant worker remain in a Member State in order to seek work was raised in *Antonissen* (C-292/89). He was a Belgium national who had come to the United Kingdom to seek work. After three years he was still unsuccessful, and was then convicted of an imprisoned for drug offences. The Secretary of State decided to deport him, and Mr Antonissen applied for judicial review of the dismissal of his appeal. The case was referred to the Court of Justice and it was given in evidence that United Kingdom legislation gives EC nationals six months in which to find employment. The Court of Justice gave a purposive interpretation to Article 39 [ex 48] (and to Regulation 1612/68—see below). As was seen earlier Article 39(3)(a) [ex 48(3)(a)] gives rights to Community nationals to move freely for the purposes of accepting offers of employment actually made. But if nationals could only move between Member States when they already had an offer of employment, the number of people who could move would be very small indeed. Therefore, the Court held that Article 39(3) [ex 48(3)] EC entailed not only the freedom to enter and move freely in the host state, but also the rights to stay there for the purposes of seeking employment. But this right was not unlimited. A Member State may deport a migrant worker if he has not found employment after a reasonable time, unless there is some evidence that there is a genuine chance of employment being found. Nor did a Community national seeking work have the same status as an EC national actually working in the Member State.

RIGHTS OF ENTRY AND RESIDENCE

It has been seen that Article 39(3) [ex 48(3)] is concerned with the rights to enter, to move freely within, and to seek and take up employment in another Member State. As has also been seen, the rights under this Article have been expanded on by secondary legislation.

Directive 68/360 mainly specifies what documents a Community worker will require to enter another Member State and it provides for the issuing of residence permits to workers and their families.

Article 1 is straightforward, and abolishes restrictions on the movement and residence of nationals and their families. The "family" is defined in Regulation 1612/68 (see below). Article 2 provides that a Member State must grant such persons the right to leave and to grant passports. No visa requirements may be imposed. Article 3 states all that is required to enter another

Member State is a valid identity card or passport. However, a visa may be required of a member of a family who is not a national of the Community. Article 4 provides for the issuing of renewable residence permits for the worker and members of the worker's family. Article 5 makes it clear that rights to reside or work are not conditional on correct application of the formalities. Nor can the Member States impose disproportionate penalties on workers who fail to comply with national legal requirements. For example, in *Re Pieck* (159/79), Mr Pieck who was a Dutch national re-entered the United Kingdom after his original permit had expired, and he had failed to renew it. The United Kingdom sought to deport him. The Court of Justice held that Article 4 means that a failure to obtain a permit could carry only sanctions of a minor offence. The residence permit is not a pre-condition of residence, it is merely evidence of the right to enter and reside.

This had been decided in the earlier case of *Procureur du Roi v Royer* (48/75). The issue in this case was whether a worker's rights were conditional upon the issue of a residence permit, or whether the rights were granted directly by the Treaty (*i.e.* by Article 39 [ex 48]). The Court of Justice was unequivocal in its reply. It confirmed that the rights of an EC national to enter and reside in another Member State was conferred directly by the Treaty, and that Article 4 of Directive 68/360 entails an obligation for the Member State to issue a residence permit to anyone who could supply the proof required by the Directive. It added that the failure to comply with the entry requirements was not behaviour threatening to public policy, and by itself could not justify imprisonment or deportation.

Article 6 provides that permits must be valid for the whole of the territory of the Member State. This issue arose in *Rutili* (36/75) who was an Italian trade union activist living in France. He had been involved in the student riots in Paris 1968 but had not been convicted of any offence. When he had cause to apply for a residence permit, it was granted with the condition that he did not live in a certain part of France. The French authorities argued that this was on the grounds of public policy and that convicted French nationals can be banned from certain parts of the country. The Court of Justice rejected this argument and declared that the right of entry "is defined in the Treaty by reference to the whole territory of those States".

Member States should not make it administratively difficult for workers to comply with regulations; nor should there be excessive penalties for non-compliance. In *Watson and Belmann* (118/75) a British national in Italy was subject to a possible fine of 80,000 lire, or deportation for failure to register with the police within three days of his arrival in Italy. The Court of Justice agreed that Member States were entitled to keep records of population movements with their territory, so it was acceptable to require newcomers to report to the police. However, the Court went on to say that the period of three days was unreasonable and that Italy was "not justified in imposing a penalty so disproportionate that it becomes an obstacle to the free movement of persons".

Other rights of entry and residence are set out in Regulation 1612/68. Articles 1–5 of the Regulation concern the principle of non-discrimination in the seeking of and the taking up of employment. An interesting case arose out of Article 3(1) which states that the principle of non-discrimination shall not apply where linguistic ability is necessary. The case was *Groener v Minister for Education* (379/87). Ms Groener was a Dutch national who applied for a post as a lecturer in an Irish art college. One of the requirements of the post, (and this applied to nationals and non-nationals) was a level of proficiency in the Irish language. This was necessary even though all the lessons would be given in English. Ms Groener was unable to pass the oral exam in Irish and she complained that the requirements were contrary to Article 39 [ex 48] and to Article 3 of Regulation 1612/68.

The Court of Justice was influenced by the arguments of the Irish Government that it was a long standing policy to maintain and promote the use of Irish as a means of expressing national identity and culture. The Court thought that the role of teachers was important in the implementation of such a policy, and so long as the language requirement was not disproportionate it could fall within the exceptions under Article 3(1). This judgment is probably best viewed as being decided on the particular facts of the case. After all, Ireland is the only Member State whose official language is understood by few, and used by even less, of its population.

RIGHTS OF WORKERS AND THEIR FAMILIES

The rights that we have already seen under Article 39 (2) [ex 48(2)] of the EC Treaty are expanded on in Regulation 1612/68, in particular Article 7, which has been the subject of much judicial determination. In general the Regulation requires that Member States will grant to workers the same benefits granted to nationals. There would be little point in allowing the free movement of a worker, if those rights were prejudiced by the inability of the worker to move his family with him. To this end the Regulation ensures "the workers right to be joined by his family and the conditions for the integration of that family into the host country".

The Regulation is split into three parts. Title One of Part 1 (Articles 1–6) expands on the workers eligibility for employment; Title Two (Articles 7–9) on equality of treatment; and Title Three (Articles 10–12) with workers' families. However, as previously mentioned it is Article 7, and in particular Article 7(2), which has excited most judicial (and academic) comment.

Article 7(2) stipulates that the migrant workers "shall enjoy the same social and tax advantages of national workers". Article 10 of the Regulation extends this right to the spouse and descendants and ascendants of the worker. The descendants can be any nationality and includes those under 21 and adult children over that age if they are dependent on the worker. The Court of Justice has afforded an extremely wide scope to Article 7(2), as can be seen in the case of *Fiorini v SNCF* (32/75). Here, the Italian widow of an Italian working in France was refused reduced rail fares on the grounds of her nationality. The widow of a French rail worker would have been entitled to reduced cost rail travel. The SNCF (the French nationalised railway) argued that entitlements of this sort arose out of the employment contract and as there was no express mention in the contract the widow was not entitled to it. The Court of Justice rejected this argument and said that Article 7(2) must be broadly interpreted. Therefore, the area of application must include all tax and social advantages, whether or not attached to the contract of employment.

In the previously discussed case of *Bernini*, the Court of Justice held that an educational grant paid by a Member State to the children of workers was a "social advantage" covered by Article 7(2) of the Regulation. Provided the child was dependent on the worker it could rely on Article 7(2) to obtain a grant on the same condition as those which applied to children of nationals.

Thus, Article 7(2) was held to cover social and tax advantages not linked to employment. In *Deak* (case 94/84) the Court of Justice held that Article 7(2) could cover even indirect benefits. Mr Deak was a Hungarian son of an Italian national who was working in Belgium. He was refused an unemployment benefit on the grounds that there was no reciprocal agreement between Belgium and Hungary. The Court held that unemployment benefit was a social advantage within the meaning of Article 7(2) and that Mr Deak derived his rights to this benefit as the defendant of a worker. This was regardless of his nationality. In *Even* (207/78) the Court said that:

". . . the advantages which this regulation extends to workers who are nationals of other Member States are all those which, whether or not linked to a contract of employment, are generally granted to national workers primarily because of their objective status as workers or by virtue of the mere fact of their residence on the national territory . . ."

This "formula" can be illustrated in the subsequent case of *Reina* (65/81) in which a "childbirth loan" granted by Germany to German nationals was held to be a social advantage within Article 7(2). Therefore, an Italian worker in Germany was also entitled to the grant. This was so despite the argument that the loan had nothing to do with the free movement of workers, but was a political motivated issue of demographic policy. The Court held that the main aim of the loan was to assist low income families and was therefore a social advantage.

It has already been seen, that in *Lebon* (316/85) the Court of Justice pointed out that the right to equal treatment with regard to social and tax advantage applied only to workers and families of workers. It has already been indicated that the rights of those seeking work are not as extensive as those who are in work. The definition of who is part of the family is set out in Article 10(1) of the Regulation. The Article gives rights to a "spouse" as part of the workers family.

Two cases illustrate the traditionally defined family linkage adopted by the Court. In *Diatta v Land Berlin* (267/83) a non-EC national had married an EC national. They had separated and divorce proceedings had been initiated. The German authorities refused to renew her residence permit on the grounds that she was no longer a member of the workers family for the purposes of Regulation 1612/68. The Court of Justice ruled that the Regulation did not require that the members of the family must live permanently with the worker. It was the right of family members to take up employment throughout the territory of a Member State and that activity could take place some distance from the place where the worked resided. The Court also said that marriage cannot be regarded as dissolved so long as it has not been terminated by a competent authority. Living separately did not amount to dissolution. Mrs Diatta was therefore entitled to remain in Germany. The Court resisted the temptation to state what the position would be after a divorce.

The second case concerns the question whether the term "spouse" includes cohabitants. This was considered by the Court of Justice in *Reed* (59/85). Mrs Reed had wanted to go to the Netherlands with her long term partner who was a British national working there. She was refused a residence permit. The Court acknowledged that the term "spouse" referred only to a marital relationship. The Court could not go further given the lack of "general social development" amongst Member States towards treating non-married couples as spouses. However, the Court still found that Article 7(2) could be of assistance to Mrs Reed. This was because the Netherlands would have allowed a person who had a stable relationship with a Dutch national to remain on the territory. Therefore a member of another Member State who was a worker in the Netherlands was entitled to the same advantages as a Dutch national, and this included the right to have a cohabiting partner remain.

Purely Internal Situations

It has to be stressed that these family rights apply only to the families of "workers". They have no relevance to those who have never exercised the right to freedom of movement within the Community. This would be an internal domestic situation covered by domestic law. This is rather tragically illustrated by the case of *Morson and Jhanjan* (35 & 36/82) . The Court of Justice held that two Dutch nationals working in the Netherlands had no right under EC law to bring their Surinamese parents into that country to reside with them. This shows the anomalous position that had the Dutch nationals been working in another Member State they would have had the right under Article 10 of Regulation 1612/68 to bring their parents with them.

There are generally considered to be three "classic" cases in which the Court of Justice established the core of its approach to the purely internal situation, or what is also known as reverse discrimination. For Article 39 [ex 48] purposes the case is *R v Saunders* (175/78). [The other two cases of *Knoors* (115/78) and *Auer* (136/78) relate to the freedom of establishment]. In *Saunders*, the ECJ held:

". . . the provisions of the Treaty on freedom of movement for workers cannot therefore be applied to situations which are wholly internal to a Member State, in other words, where there is no factor connecting them to any of the situations envisaged by Community law."

Again, in *Criminal Proceedings against Morais* (C-60/91) the Court held:

". . . the Treaty provisions on free movement of persons and services cannot be applied to activities which are confined in all respects within a single Member State . . ."

The purely internal rule was highlighted by the Advocate General in *R v Secretary of State for the Home Department Ex p. Kaur* (C-192/99). The Advocate General said:

". . . the Court's position in regard to internal situations is justified by the need to confine application of the Treaty . . . to situations involving certain extraneous factors . . . characterised by the existence of cross-border elements."

However, there is one case that stands in contrast to the cases discussed above. In *Singh* (C-370/90) the complainant was luckier. Mr Singh (a non-EU national) had married a British national and had gone with her to the Netherlands where they had both worked. On his return to the United Kingdom he was refused entry and the UK authorities argued that the case came under national law and not Community law. The Court of Justice said that Mr Singh's spouse had acquired the status of "worker" by virtue of her employment in Germany, and that Mr Singh could now claim rights as the spouse of a Community worker. As an interesting aside, the *Singh* case became known as the avenue for "backdoor entry" for people otherwise denied entry to the United Kingdom. Following *Singh*, if an application to stay in the United Kingdom on the basis of marriage was refused, the couple could go to another Member State. The United Kingdom national could there establish himself or herself as a worker and after a brief period, could return to the United Kingdom. Their non-national spouse could enter with them on the basis of Community law rights. The Court of Justice held:

"This case is concerned not with a right under national law but with the rights of movement . . . granted by Articles [39 and 43] of the Treaty. These rights cannot be fully effective if such a person may be deterred from exercising them by obstacles raised in . . . their own country of origin to the entry and residence of her spouse. Accordingly, when a Community national who has availed . . . herself of those rights returns to . . . her country of origin . . . her spouse must enjoy the same rights of entry and residence as would be granted to him . . . under Community law if . . . his spouse chose to enter and reside in another Member State.'

The problem with *Singh* is that a UK national, with a non-EU spouse, living in the United Kingdom but never having moved to another Member State, is in a worse position in the United Kingdom than (say) a French national with a non-EU spouse, who has moved to work in the United Kingdom. This is because the former case is governed by domestic law (the purely internal situation) and the latter case by Community law (because there has been some cross-border movement).

The possible potential for abuse by means of marriages of convenience and very short stays in other Member States was highlighted by both the UK Government and the Commission in their submissions to the Court in *Singh*. Although the Court accorded legitimacy to the argument, it was held to be not sufficiently grave to justify a more restrictive approach.

However, this loophole of *Singh* appeared to be closed by the Court of Appeal in *Sahota v Secretary of State for the Home Department* (1997). With similar facts to *Singh*, the Court of Appeal held that no authority in Community or national law had been cited in support of the proposition that the two separate legal systems, created independently from each other by the Community and the United Kingdom should, as a matter of Community law, be treated as a single system. There was no basis under Community law for concluding that rights under Community law should be amalgamated with those arising under domestic law. Therefore, in *Sahota*, a UK national returning to the United Kingdom by virtue of UK rights must accept that the position of a non-national spouse is governed by UK law.

Some recent cases have shown that the Court of Justice may be drawing back from its earlier "hard" position. There is also some evidence that the Court of Justice is willing to revisit and confirm its judgment in *Singh*. In these cases, having the nationality of one of the Member States remains crucial, but all that is required to give rise to Community law rights is evidence of some cross-border element. In *Scholz* (C-419/92), Mr Scholz was German but had acquired Italian nationality by marriage. Now living in Italy, he was deemed to come within the scope of Article 39 [ex 48] in respect of an employment competition at an Italian university. The Court of Justice held:

". . . any Community national who, irrespective of residence and nationality, has exercised the right to freedom of movement for workers and who has been employed in another Member State falls within the scope of Article 39 and Regulation 1612/68."

In *Boukhalfa* (C-214/94), Ms Boukhalfa was a Belgium national residing in Algiers. She was employed by Germany in its embassy in Algiers and, although her contract of employment was governed by German law, she had never resided in Germany. Nevertheless, the ECJ held that Article 39 applied to her position.

A case with even more tenuous links to movement across borders was *Kulzer* (C-194/96). In this case, Mr Kulzer, a German national, lived and worked in Germany. Even so, the Court of Justice decided that for the purposes of social security benefit, the requisite cross-border requirements were fulfilled by the fact that his daughter lived in France. This case was confirmed with approval by the ECJ in *Humer* (C-255/99). In *Humer* the Court held that the "cross-border nexus" may be established by residence of a dependent family in another Member State. It was not necessary that it was established by the worker himself.

In relation to the "problem" in *Singh*, it was surprising that the open-ended nature of the judgment was not tested for 10 years. However, the test was made in *Mary Carpenter* (C-60/00). In this case, a non-EU national (Philippine) claimed a right of residence in the United Kingdom with her spouse (a UK national) on the ground that he provided services from time to time in other Member States. Mr Carpenter had always lived and worked in the United Kingdom. His work involved selling advertising space in scientific journals and some of his clients lived in France and Italy. Once or twice a year he travelled to those countries to visit his clients. Mrs Carpenter looked after the children of Mr Carpenter, which he had from a previous marriage. Mrs Carpenter argued that her situation was analogous with *Singh*. The reverse discrimination aspect was referred to when it was argued that the "spouse must have the same rights in the United Kingdom as in other Member States".

In her Opinion, the Advocate General stressed that the differences between *Mary Carpenter* and *Singh* were "not legally significant". The main consideration in the Opinion of the Advocate General is the right to respect for family life. On the point of the possibility of the risk of abuse the Advocate General merely noted that no such concern was expressed by the United Kingdom. The Court held that Article 49 had to be read in the light of the fundamental right to respect for family life. Although the Court did confine its judgment to Article 49 (the freedom to provide services), there can be little doubt that the judgment would also cover Article 39. It may be that *Mary Carpenter* is the end for the purely internal situation.

The UK Immigration Appeal Tribunal has referred some direct questions on the *Singh* points to the Court of Justice. The case is *Secretary of State for the Home Department v Hacene Akrich* (C-109/01). Mr Akrich is a Moroccan national. He was originally refused leave to enter the United Kingdom, but in 1989 he was then allowed to enter for one month as a tourist. He remained in the United Kingdom longer than one month, and eventually, in

1990 he was deported after being convicted of a criminal offence. Mr Akrich returned to the United Kingdom again in 1992, but was again deported. In 1996, he came to the United Kingdom again and this time he married a UK national. In 1997, both Mr Akrich and his spouse went to Ireland, where Mrs Akrich established herself as a worker in terms of Community law. They had no intention in remaining in Ireland beyond six months, because in their view this short period would give them residence rights. They regarded the *Singh* judgment as forming the basis of their re-entry into the United Kingdom.

These circumstances give rise to a legal anomaly. A citizen of the Union who wishes to marry and thereafter live together with a national of a non-Member State has no automatic right to entry by her spouse into the Member State concerned. The spouse is granted entry only after an individual assessment by the national immigration authorities on the basis of strict rules. The assessment includes amongst other matters the nature and duration of the relationship and the spouse's past. However, if the citizen of the Union instals herself in any other Member State of the European Union those rules do not apply. The spouse is then exempt from national immigration law and under Community law gains automatic entry. It is only otherwise if that spouse constitutes a serious threat to public policy.

In a wide-ranging Opinion the Advocate General said that it was the right of a worker under Regulation 1612/68 to establish herself and her spouse in a Member State. According to the preamble of the Regulation that right must now be regarded as a fundamental right, for both the worker and her family. Neither the nature nor duration of the work was reviewed by the Advocate General. The Advocate General also said that, in accordance with the *Levin* case, the intentions of the person making use of Community law were not relevant. In the end of his Opinion the Advocate General said that a national of a Member State who has pursued an occupational activity in another Member State as a worker within the meaning of Article 39 EC continues after returning to his own country to enjoy rights under Community law, in particular Article 39 EC. Those rights include the right in favour of the worker's spouse to installation with the worker in the worker's country, irrespective of the nationality of the spouse. In such a case the worker's spouse has an autonomous right under Article 10 of Regulation 1612/68 on freedom of movement for workers within the Community to remain in the Member State of which the worker is a national.

Nonetheless, the Member State of which the worker is a national may, relying on an overriding national interest, refuse entry to the worker's spouse, following a prior individual assessment, on the basis of criteria laid down in national immigration law in a case where a spouse who is a national of a non-Member State has not been admitted to the European Union in accordance with the immigration laws of a Member State.

This case may have important ramifications for the wholly internal rule and students should watch out for the judgment from the Court of Justice.

In conclusion, it can be stated that a worker and his or her spouse must be treated no differently than a national. But workers cannot expect to be treated more favourably than nationals, so they must fulfil any requirements demanded of nationals. Also, they must be aware that the laws of Member States will differ and that which is permissible in one Member State cannot be made permissible in another, unless its prohibition is contrary to Community law.

THE RIGHT TO REMAIN IN THE HOST STATE

The principle is set out in Article 39(3)(d) [ex 48(3)(d)] of the EC Treaty and is given effect by Regulation 1251/70. As in Regulation 1612/68, this regulation affords rights to the worker and to members of the worker's family. The right for the family to remain in a Member State will remain even in the event of the worker's death. Article 2(1) states that workers who have worked for one year prior to retirement, or have lived there for two years while incapacitated, qualify for the right to remain permanently. Article 3 extends this right to the family.

Restriction on Entry and Residence

The right to freedom of movement to take up employment, to establish a business, or to offer or receive services, cannot be absolute. A Member State must have some scope to be able to refuse entry to EC nationals wishing to cross its borders. The derogations allowed to Member States are set out in Article 39(3) [ex 48(3)] for free movement of workers, in Article 46(1) [ex 56(1)] for the right of establishment, and Article 55 [ex 66] makes Article 46 [ex 56] applicable to the freedom of services. These restrictions are similar in all three areas and allow for derogation on the grounds of public policy, public security or public health. There are also restrictions, allowed by Article 39(4) [ex 48(4)] on employment in the public services, and on exceptions for official authority by Article 45 [ex 55]. Directive 64/221 was issued to implement these exceptions and to set out the general principles governing the circumstances in which restrictive measures may be taken to refuse entry or residence to non-nationals. The Directive has been held to be directly effective and has given rise to a large number of challenges before the courts.

The Directive relates to all measures that concern entry into the territory of a Member State including the issue and renewal of residence permits, or expulsion from the Member State on any of the grounds mentioned above. The term "measure" was defined in *R v Bouchereau* (30/77) as any action which would affect the rights of a person who qualifies under Article 39 [ex 48] to enter and reside freely in a Member State on the same conditions as nationals of the host state. It also applies to the self-employed, the recipients of services and the families of each.

The first qualification is set out in Article 2(1). This states that measure must not be taken on economic grounds. So it would not be permissible to refuse entry because of high unemployment in a particular Member State.

Public Health

Of the three grounds for derogation, that for public health has caused the least problems. This is because Article 4 of the Directive refers to a list of diseases in an annex to the Directive. Entry may only be refused if the person is suffering from one of the diseases on that list. Most of the diseases are highly infectious or contagious illnesses such as syphilis or tuberculosis, or those diseases which may threaten public policy or public security such as drug addiction or profound mental disturbances. Aids is not on the list. There is also the proviso that development of one of the diseases after obtaining a first residence permit will not justify the refusal to renew the permit, or expulsion.

Public Security and Public Policy

Public Security has not been defined by the Court of Justice but in many cases it is pleaded in justification as an alternative to public policy. Clearly, there are occasions when some activities, for example terrorism, pose a threat to both public security and public policy. "Public policy" has proved to be the most difficult concept for the Court of Justice to define and interpret, and has given rise to the most litigation. As in all areas of fundamental rights, the Court of Justice has sought to interpret derogations from the right as strictly and narrowly as possible.

The Court made its initial venture into the area of public policy in *Van Duyn* (41/74). It first of all declared that, while the concept of public policy would vary from state to state, its scope could not be decided unilaterally by each Member State. There had to some control by the Community institutions. The case itself concerned an attempt by a Dutch woman to enter the United Kingdom to take up employment in the Church of Scientology, which while not unlawful, was considered to be socially undesirable and harmful by the UK authorities. Mrs Van Duyn was refused entry on the ground of public policy. The provision at issue was Article 3(1) of Directive 64/221 which states that:

"Measures taken on the grounds of public policy or public security shall be based exclusively on the personal conduct of the individual concerned."

Ms Van Duyn claimed that the refusal was based not on her personal conduct but on the conduct of the group. The Court of Justice held that personal conduct must be an act or omission to act on the part of the person concerned and must be voluntary. It need not be however, illegal or criminal in order to offend public policy. It was further held that present association which reflected participation in the activities and identification with the aims of the group, may be considered a voluntary act and could therefore, come within the definition of personal conduct. The Court recognised that concepts of public policy vary from Member State to Member State and indeed within one Member State from time to time.

This case has been criticised in that it seemed to allow a difference of treatment between nationals and non-national, and therefore discriminated again non-nationals. It can be contrasted with *Adoni and Cornuaille* (115 &116/81) where two French nationals had been working in Belgium as prostitutes. They had been refused residence permits. The Court of Justice held that, as prostitution was not illegal in Belgium, a Member State was not entitled to refuse residence to non-nationals on account of conduct which was not unlawful when undertaken by nationals of the host state.

The definition of "personal conduct" was again at issue in *Bonsignore* (67/74). In this case an Italian national resident in Germany shot his brother by accident with a pistol for which he did not have a permit. The German authorities wished to deport him in order to deter other foreign nationals and because they considered the unlawful possession of firearms by aliens to be a danger to the peaceful coexistence of Germans and foreigners. The Court of Justice was clear in its ruling that any departure from the freedom of movement rules must be interpreted strictly.

Therefore, a Member State could not use deportation as a deterrent and any decision to depart had to be based on the behaviour of the individual concerned. The possibility of future behaviour was only relevant in so far as there were clear indications that the individual would commit further offences. As the German court had not sought to punish Bonsignore (probably in view of the circumstances), it was not now acceptable to deport him.

Previous Criminal Convictions

In addition to the personal conduct proviso, Article 3(2) of Directive 64/221 states that previous criminal convictions shall not of themselves constitute grounds for exclusion or expulsion. This means that a criminal conviction can be only one of a number of factors that a Member State has to take into account when considering the exclusion or expulsion of an EC national. How far the previous conviction can be taken into account was one of the issues in *Rutili* (36/75), where Mr Rutili was an Italian national living in France. Some years previously (in 1968), he had been involved in the student riots in Paris but had not been convicted of any offence. He left France for a time and on his return he was granted a residence permit which limited his movements to certain parts of the country. This issue has been discussed earlier, but in terms of the exclusion the Court of Justice was forceful in its judgment that exclusion, or limits on travel within the national boundary, can only be justified if a person's "presence or conduct constitutes a genuine and serious threat to public policy".

The Court of Justice went even further in *R v Bouchereau* (30/77). This case concerned a French national living in England who was twice convicted in England of unlawful possession of drugs. After the second conviction, the sentencing court recommended that he be deported. A reference was made to the Court of Justice, asking among other things, in what way a criminal conviction might be taken into account in deciding to recommend deportation. The Court said that Article 3(2) must be understood as requiring the national authorities to carry out a specific appraisal from the point of view of the interest inherent in protecting the requirements of public policy. These interests would not necessarily coincide with the appraisals which formed the basis of the criminal convictions. Then, reiterating its judgment in *Rutili*, the Court stated that in addition to the "genuine and serious threat to public policy", the person's presence must also threaten "one of the fundamental interests of society".

The judgments in *Rutili* and *Bouchereau* demonstrate now how restrictively the Court of Justice interprets the restrictions on the free movement of persons. They also send a clear message to national courts that the exception is not to be lightly invoked.

Another case of interest is *Santillo* (131/79). Here, Santillo was sentenced to prison for sexual offences and when the judge passed sentence he also recommended that when the sentence was completed, Mr Santillo be deported. When he was released from prison Mr Santillo argued that the deportation order was unfair as it had been made some years ago and did not take into account his present conduct. The Court of Justice agreed with him and ruled that the social danger resulting from a foreigner's presence should be assessed at the time when the decision to expel him is made. This was because those factors, particularly the person's conduct could change in the course of time.

The whole issue of previous criminal convictions was reviewed by the Court of Justice in *Donatella Calfa* (C-348/96). In this case, Ms Calfa, an Italian national, was charged with possession and use of prohibited drugs while staying as a tourist in Crete. The Greek court found her guilty of the offence and sentenced her to three months' imprisonment. In addition, and in accordance with Greek legislation, the judge ordered her to be expelled for life from Greek territory. Ms Calfa appealed against the decision to expel her for life on the grounds that the Treaty did not allow a Member State to adopt a measure expelling a national of another Member State for life if a comparable measure could not be taken against a Greek citizen. The Court of Justice held that criminal legislation was a matter of national law, but nevertheless, the Community had set certain limits to the power of national legislation in that such legislation may not restrict the fundamental freedoms guaranteed by Community law. The decision to exclude Ms Calfa for life might be justified by the public policy exception. The Court examined most of its previous judgments in this area and came to the conclusion that any restrictions had to be very narrowly defined. Because the expulsion from Greece was automatic following such a criminal conviction, no account could be taken of the personal conduct of the offender or the danger which that person represents for the requirements of public policy. The Court found that the conditions for the public policy exception had not been fulfilled and that the Greek legislation was not compatible with Community law.

Following *Calfa*, in 1999, the Commission issued a Communication to the Council and the European Parliament on the Special measures Concerning the Movement and Residence of Citizens of the Union which are Justified on Grounds of Public Policy, Public Security or Public Health. The Communication was an attempt by the Commission to draw attention to some of the main difficulties in the implementation of Directive 64/221, and to offer guidance as to how these might be resolved. By offering information the Commission hoped that the Communication would serve to reduce the number of future infringement cases.

Procedural Safeguards

In addition to setting out the grounds on which Member State may derogate from the free movement provisions, Directive 64/221 in Articles 5–9) also sets out specific and detailed rights by which persons can challenge the derogation. These include to right of appeal, the rights to be given reasons for deportation, and the availability of judicial review of decisions.

Article 5 provides that a decision to grant or refuse a residence permit should be taken as soon as possible but in any event no later than six months after application. Article 5(2) allows inquiries to be made about police records in the home Member State, but the applicant must be allowed to remain in the host Member State until a decision has been made. Article 6 provides that the grounds for deportation must be precisely and comprehensively stated. Unless security is involved, the person concerned has the right to be informed of the grounds of refusal or deportation. In *Rutili* (36/75) it was held that the grounds must be indicated in a clear and comprehensive statement, such as would enable a person to prepare a defence.

Article 8 requires that the same legal remedies shall be available as are available to nationals; and Article 9 provides that if there is no right of appeal to a court of law then the decision to expel can only be taken if the host state has obtained the opinion of a competent authority before which the person concerned could defend themselves in person. In order to protect the right to natural justice, Article 9 provides that the appeal body must be independent of the body that refused entry in the first place. In *Pecastaing v Belgium* (98/79), a French prostitute was threatened with deportation on personal conduct grounds. She claimed that she should be allowed to remain in Belgium until her case had been reviewed (this would take up to two years). The Court of Justice held that Articles 8 and 9 did not require a Member State to allow non-nationals to remain in the country for the duration of the appeal period. What was required was that they had time to prepare an adequate defence, and that it was still possible for them to obtain a fair hearing, even though they were out of the country.

The Public Service Exemption

Article 39(4) [ex 48(4)] of the EC Treaty permits Member States to deny or restrict access to workers employed in the public service on the basis of nationality. It has been seen that the definition of workers has been an expansive one, and the Court of Justice has been concerned to widen every opportunity for persons to enjoy one of the "four freedoms" guaranteed by the Treaty. Conversely, the Court's approach to the limiting clause of Article 48(4) has been a restrictive one. It might be accepted that function of the public service is an exercise of full state sovereignty, and that Member State should have an uncluttered hand to decide the issue for themselves. Nevertheless, the Court of Justice has been insistent that it is the Court and not the Member State which decides what constitutes employment in the public service. This stance by the Court is understandable perhaps, given that there is not definition of "public service" in the Treaty, and that each Member State will have a different notion of the concept.

The issues arising out of Article 39(4) [ex 48(4)] were examined by the Court of Justice in *Sotgiu v Deutsche Bundespost* (152/73). Mr Sotgiu, an Italian national, had been employed by the German post office but was not granted the same allowances as German nationals. The Court did not define what was meant by "employment in the public sector", but set out the conditions on which Member States could use the exception. The Court said that the derogation allowed by Article 39(4) [ex 48(4)] might allow Member States to restrict admission of foreign nationals to certain activities in the public service. However, once the worker had been admitted to the public service, Article 39(4) [ex 48(4)] could not justify discriminatory measures with regard to remuneration or other conditions of employment. In other words, the exemption allowed by Article 39(4) [ex 48(4)] was to apply to entry to employment and not to conditions of service in employment. In this case, the Court also held that the definition of "public service" must be one for the Court of Justice. This was because of the varied nature of this concept in various Member States: some definitions were covered by private law and others by public law. Also "legal designations can be varied at the whim of national legislature". This judgment echoes the *Hoekstra* case, where it will be recalled, the Court ruled that the term "worker" was a Community concept.

The Commission has attempted, in a series of Article 226 [ex 169] enforcement proceedings against Member States, to obtain a strict definition of "public service". In *Commission v Belgium (Re Public Employees)* (149/79), a Belgium law reserving posts in the public service for Belgium nationals was held to be in contravention of Article 39(4) [ex 48(4)]. This was because the list of excluded jobs included nurse, plumbers and architects employed in central and local government. The Court ruled that the exception was intended to apply only to the exercise of public authority in order o safeguard the general interests of the state. The Court went on to rule that such posts normally involve "allegiance to the state". It would seem obvious that work in the police force, or the armed forces, or high ranking civil servants, or the judiciary might be covered by the exemption, but Article 39(4) [ex 48(4)] does not apply to the exercise of authority at junior level. Therefore, in *Commission v France (Re French Nurses)* (307/84), it was held to be in contravention of Article 39(4) [ex 48(4)] to reserve the appointment of nurses in public hospitals to French nationals. Likewise, in *Bleis* (C-4/91), and in *Allué* and *Coonan* (33/88) the Court of Justice held that secondary school teachers and teachers in state universities, respectively, were not covered by Article 39(4) [ex 48(4)]. This was because neither of the jobs was charged with the exercise of powers conferred by public law and is not responsible for safeguarding the interests of the state.

The Commission has also attempted to reach its own definition of the "public service". In a Notice issued in 1988 ([1988] O.J. 72/2) it has attempted to indicate those positions it thinks would rarely be covered by then public service exemption. These include public health care, teaching in state educational establishments, research non-military purposes in public establishments and public bodies responsible for the administration of commercial services.

THE RIGHT OF ESTABLISHMENT AND THE FREEDOM TO PROVIDE SERVICES

The right of establishment and the freedom to provide services envisage the pursuit of business or professional activity. Free movement for the self-employed (*i.e.* of establishment) is covered by Articles 43–48 [ex 52–58] of the EC Treaty, and the right to provide services by Articles 49–55 [ex 59–66]. The right of establishment, which is based on a recognition of qualifications, is the right of EC nationals, both natural and legal persons, to set up a business in a Member State other than their own. The right is to set up a permanent base if this is what is desired. There is some difficulty, sometimes, in distinguishing between the right of establishment and the free movement of workers, in that both concepts involve the movement from one Member State to another for permanent, or long-term, settlement.

The freedom to provide services is seen as a temporary right which does not necessarily involve residence. Here too, there is some overlap with the right to establishment. The Treaty attempts to delineate the differences by defining "services" in Article 50 [ex 60] as those:

". . . normally provided for remuneration, in so far as they are not governed by provisions relating to free movement of goods, capital and persons."

The Article also covers the activities of the professions.

The law on both establishment and services is similar, and of course, both rights are similar to the rights of workers. Article 46 [ex 56] allows for derogation on the grounds of public policy, public security and public health; the same as Article 39(4) [ex 48(4)]. The measure governing the application of these grounds, Directive 64/221, applies to both establishment and services. Directive 73/148 (which is the equivalent of Directive 68/360) allows for rights of entry and residence, and Directive 75/34 (the equivalent of Regulation 1251/70) provides for the right to remain after working on a self-employed basis, including families of the self-employed. It should be noted that there is not equivalent to Regulation 1612/68 for the self-employed. This means that they will not be eligible for the same "social and tax advantages" as nationals granted by Article 7(2).

The main thrust of Article 43 [ex 52] is to provide for the abolition of restrictions on the freedom of establishment of the nationals of a Member State in the territory of another Member State. This abolition also applies to restrictions on the setting up of agencies, branches or subsidiaries by the nationals of any Member State established in the territory of any other Member State. Article 48 [ex 58] provides that companies or firms formed, and having their registered office, central administration or principal place of business with the EC shall for the purposes of establishment, be treated in the same way as natural persons.

The Articles which cover the right of establishment can be seen to fit into three phases. The first phase is indicated by Article 43 [ex 52], which as has been shown above, provides for the abolition of any restriction on the right of establishment by the end of the transitional period. The second phase acknowledges the difficulties inherent in Articles 43 [ex 52] and 46 [ex 56]. By bringing firms and companies into the remit of the right of establishment it was realised that the law regulating companies varies from Member State to Member State. To deal with this difficulty, Article 44 [ex 54] required the Council and the Commission to draw up a general programme for the abolition of existing restrictions on freedom of establishment within the Community, and to issue directives to attain freedom for particular activities. The third phase is indicated by Article 47 [ex 57] which also requires the Council to issue directives for the mutual recognition of diplomas and other qualifications.

The first two phases relate solely to the removal of existing restrictions. Progress in these areas was quickened by two leading cases. *Reyners v Belgium* (2/74) involved an attempt by a Dutch national to gain access to the Belgium Bar. He had obtained his law degree and his doctorate in Belgium, but was refused admission to the Belgium Bar because he was not a Belgium national. The Belgium Government had argued that "the applicant could not rely on Article 43 [ex 52] because it could not be directly effective, because it was incomplete without the issue of directives required by Article 44 [ex 54]" (the second phase). The Court of Justice held that Article 43 [ex 52] was directly effective from the end of the transitional period, and that the requirement from the end of that period was on non-discrimination on the grounds of national. The issue of directives was merely to state this right easier, but the right "was not dependant on the implementation of a programme of progressive measures".

Again, in *Van Binsbergen* (33/74) the Court of Justice held Article 49 [ex 59] to be directly effective and that discrimination on the grounds of nationality is unlawful. This case concerned a Dutch national (by name Kortman) acting as a legal adviser to Van Binsbergen in a Dutch court case. During the case the legal adviser moved his residence to Belgium. He was told that he could no longer represent his client because Dutch law provided that only persons established in the Netherlands could act as legal advisers. As well as finding the Dutch law unlawful, the Court of Justice also repeated that part of its judgment in *Reyners* that the Article guaranteeing the right was not conditional on the issue of subsequent directives in respect of the specific professions.

Another case, *Thieffry* (71/76) involved a Belgium national who was qualified as an advocate in Belgium. This qualification was recognised in France as the equivalent to a French law degree and he also obtained in France, the qualifying certificate for the profession of *avacat*. Despite this his application for admission to the Paris Bar was rejected, on the grounds, that he did not hold a French law degree. The Court of Justice held that he was entitled to benefit from the right of establishment since he held a degree which was recognised as equivalent to a degree in the country of establishment, and he had fulfilled the requirements for professional training in that Member State.

It might seem that the legal professions in many of the Member States have set up protective barriers to protect their own members and to keep out competition! Another case involving a lawyer was *Vlassopoulou* (340/89). Ms Vlassopoulou was a Greek national, with a Greek law degree, who worked at the Athens Bar. However, much of her work was in the field of German law and was focused in Germany. When the she applied for admission in the German Bar her application was turned down on the ground that she did not have the necessary qualifications. The Court of Justice was asked by the German Court if it was permissible to refuse access for this reason. The Court of Justice held that national authorities must take into account the knowledge and qualifications already acquired by the person concerned in another Member State. The authorities must also make a comparison between the specialised knowledge and abilities certified by those diplomas and the knowledge and qualifications required by the national rules. If this comparison finds the qualifications equivalent, the Member State must recognise the qualification. Even if the qualification is found to be not equivalent the national authority must assess whether the knowledge and experience gained in the host Member State is sufficient to make up for the lack of qualifications.

These controversies, and the marked divergences between the legal Bars and between national governments, are a good example of the difficulties encountered by the Community in the task of setting up a system for the mutual recognition of formal qualifications. The initial aim was to pursue a "harmonisation" approach. This was taken sector by sector, or profession by profession, and was an attempt to obtain agreement by all the Member States on the minimum standards of education and training needed in order to qualify in that field. The Commission started off in the medical field, and directives were passed recognising qualifications for general practitioners, nurse and pharmacists. A directive was also passed for architects.

As might be imagined this process was long and drawn out. There was much negotiation needed to persuade each Member State to accept the qualifications of other Members States as equivalent. In fact it took seventeen years for the directive on architect's qualifications to be agreed. Clearly, it would take years to cover every sector and every profession. So, in 1989 a new approach was taken. The aim of harmonisation of qualifications was abandoned and replaced by a directive which provided for "a general system for the recognition of higher education diplomas awarded on completion of professional education and training of at least three years duration". From now on, recognition was to be based on mutual trust. As a basic principle, one Member State may not refuse entry to a regulated profession to a national of another Member State who holds the qualifications necessary for exercise of that profession in the other Member State. Furthermore, if there were major differences in the structure of a profession, or in the education or training, the Member State could insist on either an adaptation period or an aptitude test.

As with other Community rights, there are certain derogations allowed from the rights of establishment. Article 46(1) [ex 56(1)] provides for derogations providing for special treatment for foreign nationals on grounds of public policy, public security or public health. Article 45(1) [ex 55(1)] provides that the right of establishment provisions shall not apply to activities which in that state are connected, even occasionally, with the exercise of official authority. The "official authority" derogation, as it is called, was considered by the Court of Justice in *Reyners* (2/74). It will be recalled that the case concerned the application of a Dutch national for admission to the Belgium Bar which had been rejected on the ground that he was not a Belgium national. One of the justifications for this refusal was that the profession of advocate should be excepted because it was "connected organically" with the administration of justice and that an advocate was subject to strict rules and procedures.

The Court of Justice was not convinced. The Court held that the practice of a profession, taken as a whole, was different from the exercise of official authority. The Court stated:

". . . activities involving contacts, even regular and organic, with the courts, including even compulsory co-operation in their functioning, do not constitute, as such, connection with the exercise of official authority."

This is a good example of where the Court of Justice has given a narrow interpretation to one of the derogations allowed by the Treaty.

Establishment of Companies

By the terms of Article 48 [ex 58], companies or firms formed in accordance with the law of a Member State and having their registered office, central administration or principal place of business within the Community shall be treated in the same way as natural persons who are nationals of Member States. "Companies or firms" means companies or firms constituted under civil or commercial law, including co-operative societies, and other legal persons governed by public or private law, save for these which are non-profit making.

One of the difficulties in this area is that, despite a number of directives on company law, there are still major differences in the regulation and activities of companies in the 15 Member States. What is clear is that any company that meets the conditions for establishment set out in Article 43 [ex 52] will be able to do business in any other Member State. In the *German Insurance* case (205/84), the Court of Justice held that even an office managed by a third party on behalf of a company could be regarded as an establishment in that Member State.

A major move towards the establishment of companies was made in the Court of Justice judgment in *Centros Ltd v Erhvervs-og Selskabsstyrelsen* (C-212/97). Centros Ltd was properly registered as a private limited company in England and Wales. The shares were held by two Danish nationals, residing in Denmark. Although the company had been registered in England it was never the intention of the two owners that the company should do business there. The company had been registered in England because of the low capital requirements for a company to be formed. In England, company law requires no minimum share capital. The equivalent requirement to register a company in Denmark is about £17,000. As mentioned, Centros never commenced trading in the United Kingdom but requested to register a branch in Denmark. The relevant authority in Denmark refused this because in their view Centros was attempting to circumvent the Danish national rules concerning the paying up of the minimum share capital. They were, of course, correct in this assumption. The Danish Supreme Court asked the Court of Justice for a preliminary ruling on whether the refusal of the registration was contrary to the right of freedom of establishment. The Court of Justice held that the refusal to register the branch was an obstacle to exercising the freedom of establishment. The situation fell within the scope of Community law and was not purely internal to Denmark since the company had been formed in the United Kingdom. This was not considered to be an abuse of this freedom and an improper circumvention of national law. The right to form a company in accordance with the law of a Member State and to set up branches in other Member States was said to be inherent in the exercising of that freedom. The fact that a company had been set up with the sole purpose of carrying on business in another Member State was also not sufficient to amount to an abuse of those rights.

Also, according to the Court of Justice, the refusal could not be justified by the need to protect creditors or by the need to prevent fraudulent insolvency. After all, Danish creditors were exposed to risk concerning UK companies which trade in the United Kingdom and in Denmark. The creditors were aware of this risk and were protected by certain rules of Community law. The decision in *Centros* allows nationals of other Member States to circumvent their domestic company law by using a foreign company (*e.g.* a UK limited company). The judgment has been very controversial and has given rise to a large body of literature on the subject. Further discussion of the topic is beyond the scope of this book.

Nevertheless, despite the *Centros* judgment, there have been many instances of difficulties put in the way of companies attempting to establish themselves in another Member State. These to, are beyond the scope of this book. One way of circumventing the difficulties which is of increasing popularity, particularly for large companies, is to buy, or to merge with, a company already established in another Member State. This has the added advantage of an existing business culture, and there is an existing brand name on which to build.

FREE MOVEMENT OF SERVICES

Articles 49–55 [ex 59–66] cover the freedom to provide services. These provisions are broadly similar to those concerning the right of establishment. As noted above, the freedom to provide services is seen as a temporary right which does not involve residence. If residence is involved then the activities will be covered by the rules relating to the right of establishment. Article 49 [ex 59] provides that restrictions on freedom to provide services shall be progressively abolished in respect of nationals who are established in a Member State other than that for whom the services are intended. The definition of "services" is set out in Article 50 [ex 60]. This states that a service is one which is normally provided for remuneration. The Article indicates freedom to *provide* a service; it does not suggest that a person may travel from one Member State to another to receive a service. Although a number of directives attempted to protect the position of persons, who travel to another Member State to receive a service in effect, it was the Court of Justice that has extended the Treaty to include this freedom.

In *Luisi and Carbone* (286/72), two Italian residents were fined for taking too much money out of Italy when they visited another Member State on holiday. They argued that the money was to pay for services as tourists, and for medical treatment. The Court of Justice held that such action was covered by Article 49 [ex 59]. The Court said that the Article allowed persons providing the service to go to the Member State where the person for whom it is provided resides, or:

". . . the latter may go to the state in which the person providing the service is established".

The Court stated that the right to travel to receive a service was a necessary corollary to Article 50 [ex 60] (which defines services). In conclusion the Court of Justice held that it followed:

". . . that the freedom to provide services includes the freedom, for the recipient of services, to go to another Member State in order to receive a service there, without being obstructed by restrictions . . . and that tourists, persons receiving medical treatment and persons travelling for the purposes of education or business are to be regarded as recipient of services."

In a later case *Cowan* (1896/87) the Court of Justice confirmed that tourism was a service, when it held that the French government was wrong to refuse to compensate a British tourist who had been the victim of an assault in Paris.

As mentioned above, Article 50 [ex 60] gives a definition of "services". A "service" is such when it is normally provided for remuneration. This has lead to a number of "controversial" decisions by the Court of Justice in relation to the (written) constitution of Ireland. In that country, abortion is an unlawful activity; in the other 14 Member States it is a lawful, though regulated, activity. In *Grogan* (C-159/90) the question before the Court of Justice was whether abortion could constitute a "service" for the purposes of Articles 49 and 50 [ex 59 and 60]. This was a necessary question because it was also unlawful in Ireland to advertise the name and address of any abortion clinic, even that in another Member State (in this case the United Kingdom). In defiance of this law, a student union in Ireland had published the details of a UK abortion clinic. The Court of Justice had no doubt that abortion was a "service" within the meaning of Article 50 [ex 60] (it was a medical service provided for remuneration). But with regard to the dissemination of information about abortion services in another Member State, the Court of Justice managed to avoid a clash with the Irish constitution on a technicality. The students union had made the fatal "mistake" of allowing the advertisement to appear in their journal free of charge. The Court of Justice held that because there was no economic "nexus" between the distribution of the information and the supplier of the service, the Irish restriction on information was not contrary to Article 49 [ex 59].

It might seem that the rules for the provision of services are the same as those rules on the right of establishment; the difference being that the provision of services is undertaken without establishing residence (or any base) in another Member State, and establishment covers the setting up of a permanent base. However, it can be seen that Member States might view the freedom to provide services as problematic. There might be difficulties of control and discipline of undertakings outside their jurisdiction. In *van Binsbergen* (33/74) the Court of Justice held that Article 49 and 50 [ex 59 and 60] were directly effective (see Chapter 6), but nevertheless a Member State could restrict the freedom to provide services by introducing rules justified by the general good. As *van Binsbergen* concerned a lawyer, the Court gave examples including the organisation, qualification, ethics and responsibilities of the legal profession.

The position of lawyers as providers of services is interesting. Directive 77/249 provides that Member States may have special national rules for the category of lawyer who may draw up documents for transferring interests in land. The national legal authorities may also insist that lawyers from other Member States must observe the rules of conduct of the host Member State. A Member State may also stipulate that a lawyer from another Member State must work in conjunction with a lawyer who practices before the judicial authority in question.

Proposal for Reform to Free Movement Rules

The Commission has proposed a new general Directive on the free movement of Citizens (see below). (It can be found on the Commission website at *www.europa.eu/comm* as document COM (2002) 225 final). It will replace much of the secondary legislation. Originally, para.1.2 of the Preamble of the proposed Directive stated that the introduction of citizenship was "for the benefit of all citizens" and included the right of all citizens to enter and reside in the territory of another Member State. The proposals in the Directive represent a sweeping revision which would replace the present sectoral rules and specific legislative framework with a single set of rules on freedom of movement for all citizens.

Nevertheless, the proposed Directive retains some of the present requirements. Non-economic actors must still have sickness insurance and adequate resources, but only for the first four years of residence. There are still special rules for students.

It must be noted, however, that the Directive has been "watered down" as it has been debated in the various institutions. In the latest version the European Union citizen dimension has been removed.

CITIZENSHIP

The classic concept of citizenship defines citizenship as "full membership of a community." Membership of that community brings with it a "bundle" of rights, which can be classified as civic, political and social rights. Civic rights express the basic legal equality before the law. Political rights entitle the citizen to participate in the exercise of national sovereignty. Social rights are those rights that the citizen has in relation to, for example, labour, consumer and environmental law.

The concept of citizenship was spoken about from the early stages of the development of the Community. However, it was not until the Treaty on European Union 1993 (Maastricht) that the concept of citizenship was given formal recognition. The citizenship provisions are contained in Part Two of the EC Treaty in Articles 17–22 [ex Arts 8–8e]. Article 17 provides that:

"1. Citizenship of the Union is hereby established. Every person holding the nationality of a Member State shall be a citizen of the Union. Citizenship of the Union shall complement and not replace national citizenship.
2. Citizens of the Union shall enjoy the rights conferred by this Treaty and shall be subject to the duties imposed thereby."

The various rights attaching to citizenship are set out in Articles 18–21 EC. In concrete terms they confer four specific rights on all nationals of EU Member States:

(1) to move freely and reside in the territory of Member States;

(2) to vote and to stand as a candidate in local and European Parliament elections in the Member State of residence;

(3) to protection, in a non-EU country in which the citizen's own Member State is not represented, by the diplomatic or consular authorities of any other Member State; and

(4) to petition the European Parliament and to apply to the European Ombudsman and to receive a reply in the citizen's own language.

Although Article 17(2) does refer to "duties" it should be noted that no duties are set out. To many, the idea of rights without corresponding duties is a strange concept of citizenship. The usual duties of citizenship include the duty to obey the law, the duty to defend one's country, the duty to pay tax, the duty to work and the duty to vote.

The criteria set out by Article 17 for inclusion within the personal scope of the Treaty provisions on Union citizenship is the requirement of holding the nationality of one of the Member States. A Declaration attached to the TEU makes it clear that whenever a reference is made to the nationals of Member States, the question whether an individual possesses the nationality of a Member State shall be settled solely by reference to the national law of the Member State concerned. In other words, each Member State will define who are (and who are not) nationals of that Member State. This has been confirmed by the Court of Justice in *Micheletti* (369/90). The Court held that rules governing the acquisition of nationality were, according to international law, matters that fell within the competence of each Member State. The judgment is not surprising, given that competence as to nationality is jealously guarded by any country and is seen as an essential part of the exercise of their sovereignty.

The requirement for nationality of one of the Member States in order to be a Union citizen means that third-country nationals living and residing legally in the Union do not come within the scope of the citizenship provisions. This is one of the major criticisms of the citizenship provisions, for two reasons. First, it is not acceptable that up to 13 million people should be excluded from the provisions of Community law. These third-country nationals are lawfully resident in one of the Member States. Their economic activity contributes to the economic success of the Union. They pay taxes and make contributions to the social security systems of the Member States. Their cultural contributions enrich the societies of Member States.

The second criticism is that the Treaty does, in fact, give third-country nationals some of the rights of citizenship. The fact that these rights are provided for in different parts of the Treaty makes for confusion and contradictions. For example, Article 194 gives "any citizen of the Union, *and any natural or legal person residing or having its registered office in a Member State*, the right to address individually or in association with other citizens or persons a petition to the European Parliament" (emphasis added).

Article 255 grants a right of access to the European Parliament, Council and Commission "to *any citizen and any natural or legal person residing or having a registered office in a Member State*" (emphasis added).

In addition, the Treaty has created substantive rights that are not based on the concept of citizenship, but on residence criteria. For example, Article 141 provides that each Member State "shall ensure that the principle of equal pay for male and female workers . . . is applied". This right to equal pay says nothing about the nationality of the worker. The right is based solely on work done in one of the Member States of the Union. Article 153 appears to be even wider. It provides a "right of consumers to information, education and to organise themselves in order to safeguard their interests". There is no reference in this Article to citizenship or even residence.

With the above concerns and criticisms in mind, the main right of citizenship is that provided for in Article 18, which states:

> "1. Every citizen of the Union shall have the right to move and reside freely within the territory of the Member States, *subject to the limitations and conditions laid down in this Treaty and by measures adopted to give it effect*" (emphasis added).

The first and important point to be noted is that the right to move and reside is subject to such limits and conditions as are set out in the Treaty and by measures adopted to give it effect. This means that where specific legislation has been enacted, any movement or residency rights will be subject to the limitations or conditions set out in that legislation. Currently, there are three Directives which set out the rights of residence for various categories of persons. These are Directive 93/96 on students' rights to vocational training, Directive 90/265 on workers who have ceased to work but have not moved to another Member State and Directive 90/364 a "catch-all" Directive, covering those who do not have a right of residence under Community law. Each of these Directives requires Member States to grant a right of residence to those persons covered by the Directive and certain of their family members. However, all three Directives are subject to the proviso that a person has adequate resources so as not to become a burden on the social security schemes of Member States. The person also has to be covered by sickness insurance. So, although the right of residence is no longer dependent on the exercise of an economic activity, it is clearly dependent on a degree of financial self-sufficiency, so that the finances of a Member State are not called upon for support. This situation has been confirmed by the ECJ in *Grzelczyk* (C-184/99).

The question therefore arises, as to what rights can be derived from Articles 17 and 18, which do not contravene the condition that the right to move and reside is subject to the limits laid down in the Treaty. In other words, has the concept of citizenship given a new impetus to extending rights for nationals of the Member States? Or is it merely an extension of existing rights of free movement?

The first cases to come before the ECJ in which citizenship was an issue were not encouraging. The first case was *Skanavi* (C-193/94). The ECJ refused to discuss the application of Article 17 [ex 8] considering it to be of a residual character and secondary to other more specific rights. In *Uecker and Jacquet* (64 & 65/96) it was made clear by the ECJ that citizenship was not intended to extend the scope of the Treaty to cover internal situations with no link to Community law. The Court held:

"Citizenship of the Union . . . is not intended to extend the scope *ratio materiae* of the Treaty also to internal situations which have no link with Community law."

In *Boukhalfa* (C-214/94) the Advocate General in his Opinion was positive about the rights conferred by citizenship. He said:

"The recognition of European citizenship, enshrined by Articles [17–21] of the EC Treaty is of considerable symbolic value and is probably one of the advances in the construction of Europe which has received most public attention . . . it is for the Court to ensure that its full scope is attained. If all the conclusions inherent in this concept are drawn, every citizen of the Union must, whatever his (*sic*) nationality, enjoy exactly the same rights and be subject to the same obligations."

In *Boukhalfa* the ECJ was able to reach a judgment based on Article 39 [ex 48] on free movement and so did not have to consider this part of the Advocate General's Opinion.

A similar *obiter* remark was made by another Advocate General in *R v Secretary of State for the Home Dept Ex p. Shingara and Radion* (65 & 111/95). The Advocate General said:

"The creation of the citizenship of the Union . . . represents a considerable qualitative step forward in that . . . it separates this freedom [of movement] from its functional or instrumental elements (the link with an economic activity or attainment of the internal market) and raises it to the level of a genuinely independent right inherent in the political status of the citizens of the Union."

Again, the ECJ was able to resolve the issue in the case without the necessity of a discussion of citizenship.

The above cases were early cases in the jurisprudence of the ECJ on citizenship. If those early cases were not encouraging, there were at least some indications that the ECJ was willing to move to use the citizenship provisions in Articles 17 and 18 to expand the scope of Community law protection. There are now also signs that the Court regards the concept of citizenship as increasingly important.

Citizenship featured prominently in *Maria Sala v Freistaat Bayern* (C-85/96). In this case, Maria Sala was a Spanish national who had lived in Germany since 1968. Ms Sala had not worked for some years, nor was she in possession of a valid residence permit. On these facts, her application for a child-benefit allowance was refused. Ms Sala argued that this was in breach of Community law. Obviously, if it could be shown that she was a worker, then she would derive rights from Articles 6 and 39. However, it was argued that Ms Sala could derive rights from Article 18 [ex 8a] as a citizen of the Union. The Advocate General was explicit in his Opinion. He said:

"Article 8a (now 18) extracted the *kernel* from the other freedoms of movement—the freedom which we now might characterise as the right, not only to move, but also to *reside* in every Member State: a primary right, in the sense that it appears as the first of the rights ascribed to citizenship of the Union . . . It is not simply a derived right, but a right that is *inseparable* from citizenship of the Union . . . Let us say that it is the *fundamental* legal status guaranteed to every citizen of every Member State by the legal order of the . . . Union" (emphases in original).

The ECJ did not explicitly accept this argument, but nevertheless it read Article 18 on Union citizenship in conjunction with Article 12 [ex 6] on non-discrimination on the grounds of nationality and held that:

". . . a citizen of the European Union . . . lawfully resident in the territory of the host Member State, can rely on Article 6 . . . in all situations which fall within the scope *rationed materiae* of Community law . . ."

In *Sala*, it seems that the Court is prepared to "explode the link-ages" between the necessity for an economic activity and the right to reside. In *Sala*, the ECJ simply based the argument on Article 17(2) and the right granted to persons as citizens of the Union. The ECJ did not base Ms Sala's right to reside on Article 18. The Court was thus able to avoid the limiting conditions within that Article.

A similar approach was followed by the ECJ in *Bickel and Franz* (274/96). In that case, a German and an Austrian national were subject to criminal proceedings in Italy. In that part of (northern) Italy, Italian and German was spoken and a German speaking Italian national had the right to have any trial against him heard in German. This right was refused to Bickel and Franz, both of whom spoke German. The Advocate General in his Opinion took a very broad look at citizenship. He said:

". . . the notion of citizenship of the Union implies a commonality of rights and obligations uniting Union citizens by a common bond transcending Member State nationality . . . Freedom from discrimination on grounds of nationality is the most fundamental right conferred by the Treaty and must be seen as a basic ingredient of Union citizenship."

The Advocate General went on to say that refusing to allow German speaking citizens from Germany and Austria to use their mother tongue in a part of Italy where this was allowed to German speaking Italians, amounted to discrimination based on nationality. The ECJ agreed with the Advocate General. The Court held:

". . . the exercise of the right to move and reside freely in another Member State is enhanced if the citizens of the Union are able to use a given language to communicate with the administrative and judicial authorities of a state on the same footing as its nationals."

The expansion of citizenship rights was further developed in *Grzelcyzk* (C-184/99). In this case, a French national was studying in Belgium. In his third year of studies (out of four) he ran out of money and applied for a social security payment. This payment would have been given to a Belgium national in similar circumstances. However, this payment was refused to Mr Grzelcyzk as he was now without "sufficient resources", as required by the Students' Residence Directive 93/96. The ECJ held that he was entitled to the payment by virtue of his status as a Community national. The Court said:

"Union citizenship is destined to become *the fundamental status of nationals* of the Member States, enabling those who find themselves in the same position to enjoy the same treatment in law irrespective of their nationality" (emphasis added).

This reasoning by the Court is similar to that in *Sala*, but is more far-reaching. The judgment in *Grzelcyzk* begins with a finding of discrimination, and then uses the concept of citizenship to determine the personal scope of Article 12. It is because *Grzelcyzk* is a Union citizen lawfully resident in Belgium that he can avail himself of Article 12 in all situations that come within the material scope of Community law. The material scope of Community law is defined in part by the right of citizens to move and freely reside in another Member State.

In the most recent of the "citizenship" cases, the ECJ has attempted to give guidance on the application of the limitations to Article 18. It will be recalled that Article 18 provides for the right to move and reside "subject to the limitations and conditions laid down in the Treaty". In *Baumbast* (C-413/99), Mr Baumbast was a German national, who married Mrs Bombast, a Columbian national, in the United Kingdom in 1990. Mr Baumbast pursued an economic activity in the United Kingdom, initially as an employed person and then as head of his own company. However, the company failed and Mr Baumbast was unable to obtain a sufficiently well-paid job in the United Kingdom. He therefore obtained employment with a German company, working in China and Lesotho. In 1998, the UK authorities refused to grant Mr Baumbast a general right of residence, because on their view, he was neither a worker nor a person having a general right of residence under Directive 90/364. One of the questions referred to the ECJ was whether a citizen of the Union, who no longer enjoys a right of residence in the host Member State, can, as a citizen of the European Union, enjoy a right of residence by the direct application of Article 18(1)?

In his Opinion, the Advocate General described the development of free movement rules from the early days of the Community to the culmination of citizenship rules, as provided for by the Treaty on European Union (and now Articles 17–21 of the EC Treaty). He outlined how the first and earliest legislation related to the pursuit of an economic activity. The secondary legislation which was necessary to facilitate the exercise of those economic rights had not kept pace with the social, cultural and economic developments which have occurred since the 1960s. In particular, the Advocate General pointed to changes in the composition of families, with many more marriages now made up of one person who is not a national of one of the Member States.

In the Opinion of the Advocate General, the Community has developed to such an extent that Article 18 creates for citizens of the Union a right to move and to reside. In his view, the clear and unconditional wording of the first part of Article 18(1) cannot be interpreted in any other way, The activities to which that provision refers, namely to "move" and to "reside", do not require further particularisation. According to the Advocate General,

Article 18 establishes a fundamental right inn favour of citizens of the Union to move and reside freely within the Union. Nevertheless, these rights are subject to limitations and conditions laid down elsewhere in Community law. But these limitations or conditions must not be arbitrary and must not deprive the right of residence of its substantive content. Subject to the principle of proportionality, limitations may be made only if they are necessary and genuinely meet objectives of general interest recognised by the Union.

The ECJ was robust in its support for the Advocate General. It held that Article 18 was directly effective and could therefore be relied on by individuals in their national courts. The ECJ repeated its statement in *Grzelczyk* that citizenship is destined to become the fundamental status of nationals of the Member States. The Court went on to say that although there were some limitations to this fundamental right, those limitations must be applied in compliance with the limits imposed by Community law, in particular the principle of proportionality. This meant that national measures adopted must be necessary and appropriate to obtain the objective pursued. In *Baumbast* itself, the fact that Mr Baumbast or his family had never become burdens on the public finances of the United Kingdom, meant that a refusal to allow him the right of residence because his sickness insurance (with a German company) did not cover emergency treatment in the United Kingdom, would amount to a disproportionate interference with the exercise of the right to reside.

The underlying question in the above discussion has been whether the concept of citizenship is no more that the sum of existing free movement rights or whether the ECJ is moving towards a recognition of citizenship as a new autonomous source of rights? The recent case law of the ECJ and, in particular, the forceful Opinions of its Advocates General seem to show that the Court is determined to give fundamental rights status to citizenship and that the concept will lead to an independent source of rights. Nevertheless, this process is in its infancy and students should follow developments carefully.

11. FREE MOVEMENT OF GOODS

INTRODUCTION

One of the primary purposes of the European Community was the creation of a single market founded on the principles of the "four" freedoms: the free movement of goods, persons, services and capital. The free movement of goods is one of the central economic ideals of the Community. If the single market is to be achieved it is essential that goods can move freely within the boundaries of the Community. The principle of the free movement of goods has been described as one of the cornerstones of the Community. Within the Community there will no tariff or non-tariff barriers applied to imports from other Member States. Nor, once goods have arrived in the Community from countries outside the EC will there be many restriction on their movement with the "common market".

It might be helpful at this point to explain the different types of economic integration. The definition of the different types depends generally on the level of involvement of the economies that participate. At the simplest level is the free trade area. This is merely an arrangement between states in which they agree to remove all customs duties and quotas on trade passing between them. All the parties to the agreement remain free, however, to fix unilaterally the level of duty on imports coming in from countries not party to the free-trade agreement.

The next level is the customs union. This is similar to a free-trade agreement in that members agree to remove all tariffs and quotas on trade between members, but in addition the members agree to apply a common level of tariffs on goods coming in the union from outside. The next level is the common market. This is a customs union plus the free movement of persons, capital and services. This was the aim of the single market legislation in the Single European Act 1986, and which was largely attained by the end of 1992. The next stage to which the Community aspires, and the next level in economic integration, is economic union. This is the common market plus a complete unification of monetary and fiscal policy, together with a common currency. By the terms of the TEU, this was scheduled for January 1, 1999. On that date, the Member States participating in the single currency could no longer implement their own monetary policy. That role was transferred to the European System of Central Banks (ESCB), comprising the European central bank and all of the national central banks.

On January 1, 1999, 12 of the 15 Member States entered into monetary union. One Member State, Greece, failed to reach the convergence criteria needed as a condition for entry. Two other Member States, the United Kingdom and Denmark, negotiated opt-outs which allowed them to stay out of monetary union. The question as to whether or not the United Kingdom should join the other Member States is a matter of fierce debate at the present time.

The first issue of notes and coins was on January 1, 2002. Thirteen Member States (Greece had by this time met the criteria) now had a common currency. For six months, until June 30, 2002, the Euro and national currencies were used side by side. After June 30, 2002 only the Euro was accepted as legal tender. So far as the design of the coins is concerned, it was accepted that one side of the currency would have a common European Community face. However, the obverse side was to be chosen by the respective Member State. Thus, it would still be possible for "English" Euros to feature the Queen's head, if the United Kingdom decides to enter monetary union.

The Community is also a customs union, which means that the Community (and not individual Member States) fixes the external duty to be paid on goods imported from outside the Community. It also decides on a common tariff for trade with the outside world.

The purpose of the principle of the free movement of goods is to promote efficiency in production by removing all artificial barriers to trade between Member States. This is not as easy as it might appear, as Member States have a natural inclination to protect their own national producers, and their own industries. A good illustration of the difficulties faced by the Community was the need for the Single European Act 1986. Despite being one of the objectives of the original EEC Treaty, it took the SEA to set out in detail the necessary requirements for the accomplishment of the single market. This was the now-famous date of December 31, 1992.

The free movement of goods should not be seen in isolation. Together with the other three freedoms (*i.e.* persons, capital and services) it enables the "market" to operate efficiently by ensuring optional allocation of resources within the Community. The free movement of goods provisions must also be seen in the context of the rules on competition (see Chapter 12). The rules on the free movement of goods attempt to control Member State intervention in the free market, while the rules on competition attempt to control arrangements between companies (or abuses by a single dominant company) which would have a distorting effect on the single market.

TREATY PROVISIONS

There are a number of ways, some more subtle than others, by which a Member State can impede the free movement of goods. The Treaty attempts to deal with them all. The legal framework is set out in four component parts:

(1) Articles 23 and 24 [ex 9–16]. The abolition of customs duties and charges having equivalent effect.

(2) Articles 25 and 26 [ex 18–29]. The common customs tariff.

(3) Article 90 [ex 95]. The prohibition of discriminatory domestic taxation (the issue of state aids to domestic undertakings, covered by Articles 90–93 is beyond the scope of this book.

(4) Articles 28–31 [ex 30–36]. The elimination of quantitative restrictions and measures having an equivalent effect to quantitative restrictions.

CUSTOMS UNION (ARTICLES 23 AND 24 [EX 9–16])

This section of the Treaty deals with the most blatant form of protectionism. That is, when a state attempts to erect customs duties, or other charges, which make foreign goods more expensive than their domestic counterparts. By Article 23(1) [ex 9(1)], Member States are required to form a customs union:

"The Community shall be based upon a customs union which shall cover all trade in goods and which shall involve the prohibition between Member States of customs duties on imports and exports and of all charges having equivalent effect."

In addition, Article 25 [ex 12] prohibits the reintroduction of any customs duties on imports or exports of goods passing between Member States.

The provisions of Article 23 [ex 9] and 25 [ex 12] cover "all trade in goods". The term "goods" was defined in *Commission v Italy (Re Italian Art Treasures (7/68)* as "products which can be valued in money and which are capable, as such, of forming part of commercial transactions". In this case the Court of Justice said that Article 12 (now 25) would cover the effect of a duty or charge, and not its purpose. Italy had imposed a tax on the export of art treasures, and argued that the purpose of the tax was not to raise revenue but to protect the artistic heritage of the country. The Court rejected this argument and held that the rules of the common market apply to goods, subject only to exceptions expressly provided by the Treaty. Article 25 [ex 12] provides no derogation. Therefore the fact that in this case the tax was not introduced for fixed reasons, nor was much tax collected, was irrelevant. The tax had the effect of increasing the cost of the export and was covered by Article 25 [ex 12]. This "effects" doctrine can be justified. Articles 23 and 24 [ex 9–16] would be weakened if it was open to Member States to argue that a charge or duty should not be subject to the provisions of the Articles because its purpose was altruistic or non-fiscal.

The Court of Justice has always interpreted Article 25 [ex 12] strictly. In *Diamantarbeiders (2 & 3/69)*, Belgium had imposed a duty on diamonds, not for protectionist or fiscal reasons, but to raise money for Belgium diamond workers. The Court was unimpressed by the argument and held that the justification for the prohibition provided for by Article 25 [ex 12] was based on the fact that "any pecuniary charge—however small—imposed on goods by reason of the fact that they cross a frontier constitutes an obstacle to the movement of such goods".

The definition of "goods" outlined in *Italian Art Treasures* was extended in *Commission v Ireland (Re Dundalk Water Supply) (45/87)* to include the provision of products within a contract for the provision of services. In *R v Thompson (7/78)*, the term was held to include gold and silver coins, which formed part of a collection and were not in general circulation.

Charge having an Equivalent Effect (CEE)

It is relatively easy to recognise a customs duty. A more difficult concept is a charge having an equivalent effect to a duty. There is no definition of such a concept in the Treaty. As early as 1962 the Court of Justice was called on to give a definition. In *Commission v Belgium and Luxembourg (Gingerbread)* (2 & 3/62) it held that:

"a duty, whatever it is called, and whatever its mode of application, may be considered a charge having equivalent effect to a customs duty, provided that it meets the following three criteria: (a) It must be imposed unilaterally at the time of importation, or subsequently; (b) It must be imposed specifically upon a product imported from a Member State to the exclusion of a similar national product; and (c) It must result in an alteration of price and thus have the same effect as a customs duty on the free movement of products."

These charges must be interpreted in the spirit of the Treaty. In *Commission v Italy (Re Statistical Levy)* (24/68), the Italian Government had levied a charge on goods which they said would be used for compile statistical data on trade patterns. The Court held that customs duties were prohibited irrespective of the purpose for which they were imposed, and went on to say that:

". . . any pecuniary charge, however small and whatever its designation and mode of application, which is imposed unilaterally on domestic or foreign goods by reason of the fact that they cross a frontier, and which is not a customs duty in a real sense, constitute a charge . . . even if it is not imposed for the benefits of the state, is not discriminatory or protective in effect, and if the product on which the charge is imposed is not in competition with any domestic product."

The *Diamantarbeiders* case, discussed above, is a good example of such a disguised charge.

Despite the strict interpretation given by the Court of Justice, a charge may, in certain exceptional circumstances, be acceptable, and therefore outside the scope of Article 25 [ex 12]. To be permissible the charge must be within the scope of Article 90 [ex 95] (see below). Generally, to be permitted a charge must be for one of three reasons. It must be for the benefit of the importer; it must be required by Community law; or it must be part of the system of internal taxation. As might be expected the Court of Justice has refined these criteria.

One common argument put forward by Member States, is that a charge on imported goods it justified on the grounds that it is merely payment for a service which the state has rendered to the importer. It should therefore not be regarded as a CEE for the purposes of Article 25 [ex 12]. The Court of Justice has on occasion accepted this argument, but not without scrutiny. One such case was *Re. Statistical Levy* (24/68). The Italian Government had argued that the levy on goods was a charge for services rendered and should not be regarded as a CEE. The Court did not agree and said that as the statistics produced would be of a general benefit, and any advantage gained by individual importers so difficult to assess, that the extra charge could only be viewed as a CEE.

Member States commonly make charges for services rendered such as border inspections, warehouse inspections or storage charges during customs formalities. Such claims by Member States are considered carefully by the Court of Justice. In *Commission v Belgium (Re Customs Warehouses)* (132/82), a storage charge imposed by Belgium on imported goods stored for customs clearance under an EC transit scheme was held to be illegal. The charge could not be regarded as a payment for services rendered when the payment of the charge was demanded solely in connection with the completion of customs formalities. In *Bresciani* (87/75), Italy imposed a charge for the compulsory veterinary and public health inspections, which had to be carried out on imported cowhide. The Court of Justice held that Articles 23 and 24 [ex 12–16] prohibit any charge "which is intrinsically imposed on goods . . . by reason of the fact that they cross a frontier". They also held that the maintenance of a public health inspection system imposed in the general interest could not be regarded as a service rendered to an importer such as to justify the imposition of a pecuniary charge. The Court of Justice came to a similar conclusion in *Ford Espana v Spain* (170/88) where it held that a flat rate charge based on the value of goods did not correspond to the costs incurred by the customs, and there was a CEE.

If a charge is *required* by Community law it may be lawful. However, the Court of Justice has not allowed national authorities to recover charges where they are merely *permitted* by EC law. This was the thrust of the Court judgment in *Bauhuis v Netherlands* (46/76). In *Commission v Germany (Animal Inspection Fees)* (18/87) inspection fees imposed by Directive 81/389 were held to be acceptable because the conditions set out by the Court were satisfied, *i.e.*:

(a)   the fees did not exceed the actual costs of the inspections in connection with which they were charged;

(b) the inspections were obligatory and uniform for all the products concerned in the Community;

(c) the inspections were provided for by Community law in the general interest of the Community;

(d) the inspections promote the free movement of goods, in particular neutrality obstacles which could arise from unilateral measures of inspection adopted under Article 30 [ex 36] of the Treaty.

These conditions are strict. The Court of Justice in *Bakker Hillegon* (C-111/89) extended these criteria to mandatory charges made under international law.

Whether or not a charge is part of the system of internal taxation is often difficult to decide. But the difference is crucial. If a charge imposed is non-discriminatory and charged at the same rate to both domestic and imported goods then it will not be a CEE. It will not be covered by Articles 23 and 24 [ex 9–17], but will fall under Article 90 [ex 95]. This latter Article (see further below) seeks to prevent discriminatory taxation on imported goods once they are inside the territory of another Member State. The point to remember is that internal taxes must never be imposed merely because goods cross a national frontier. If a tax is imposed on imported goods it must be because domestic goods are subject to the same tax. The Court of Justice will be seeking to determine whether the charge is an internal tax, in which case Article 96 [ex 91] may apply; or whether it is a CEE, which may be covered by Articles 23 and 24 [ex 9–16]. In *Steinlike v Germany* (78/76), the Court held that:

"financial charges within a general system of internal taxation applying systematically to domestic and imported products according to the same criteria are not to be considered charges having equivalent effect."

Denkavit v France (132/78) concerned a charge on imported meat. France argued that this was a similar charge to one imposed on French domestic meat at the tine of its slaughter in the abattoir. The Court of Justice held that the charge on the imported meat was a CEE. It came to this conclusion because in order to be considered as part of the system of internal taxation the imported product must be subject to the same rate of tax as the domestic product, it must be imported at the same marketing stage and the event which gives rise to the charge must be the same for both products. Obviously, this could not be the case with imported meat.

PROHIBITION OF DISCRIMINATORY TAXATION: ARTICLE 90 [EX 95]

If it is decided that a charge or duty is a genuine tax, and not a CEE, it falls to be considered under Article 90 [ex 95]. Article 90 which was held to be directly effective in *Lütticke v Hauptsallamt Saarlouis* (57/65), states that:

"No Member State shall impose, directly or indirectly, on the products of other Member States any internal taxation of any kind in excess of that imposed directly or indirectly on similar domestic goods.

Furthermore, no Member State shall impose on the products of other Member States any internal taxation of such a nature as to afford indirect protection to other products."

A tax was defined by the Court of Justice in *Commission v France (Re Reprographic Machines)* (90/79) as a system of internal dues applied systematically to categories of products in accordance with objective criteria irrespective of the origin of the products.

The purpose of Article 90 [ex 95] is to prevent Member States discriminating against imported goods or products, or giving indirect protection to domestic products. Article 90 [ex 95] prevents the undermining of Articles 23 and 24 [ex 9–16]. Article 90(1) [ex 95(1)] does not make unlawful a Member State's adoption of fiscal measures. It merely requires that whatever system is chosen will be applied without discrimination to all goods. It should be noted that to be covered by Article 90 [ex 95] it is not necessary that the products are identical. The Article provides that products need only be "similar". Also, in *Molkerei Zentrale* (28/67), the Court of Justice held that the words "directly or indirectly" must be construed broadly to include all taxation actually and specifically imposed on the domestic products at earlier stages of the manufacturing process. The words would also cover taxes on raw materials and the assessment of tax. For example, in *Hansen* (148/77) the Court of Justice held that a German rule which gave tax relief to small businesses and co-operatives making spirits, must be extended to spirits made by similar undertakings in other Member States. In *Commission v Ireland (Re Excise Payments)* (55/79) a tax was payable on beer, wines and spirits. The tax was the same for both domestic and imported goods. However, the Court of Justice held this to be in contravention of Article 90 [ex 95] because domestic producers were given time to pay the charge, whereas importers had to pay the duty directly on importation.

In terms of goods that are "similar", a good example is the case of *Commission v United Kingdom (Re, Excise Duty on Wine)* (170/78). In the United Kingdom the duty on wine is higher than the duty on beer. Beer is drunk much more widely than wine in the United Kingdom, although the gap between them is narrowing. The United Kingdom argued that wine and beer were not "similar" because wine was largely drunk at home whereas the bulk of beer was consumed in public houses. The Court took the view that not only was it necessary to look at the current market, but allowing for changing habits and the growing popularity of wine it could be said that these two products were in direct competition with each other. What was necessary to establish a relationship of similarity was a comparison of volume consumed, price and alcoholic strength. After coming to the conclusion that wine and beer were "similar", the Court held that the higher duty on wine (mostly imported) gave indirect protection to beer (mostly domestic) and therefore contravened Article 90 [ex 95]. The Member State could use any method to remove the discrimination: it could higher the tax on domestic products, or lower the tax on imported products, or could adopt a combination of the two so long as the tax was the same for both products. And, of course, it could abolish the tax on both products!

In *John Walker* (243/84) the issue was a comparison between fruit liqueur and whisky for the purposes of Article 90(1) [ex 95(1)]. The Court of Justice held that it was not enough that both products contained alcohol. What needed to be taken into account was the respective alcoholic content, the method of manufacture and consumer's perceptions. Based on this analysis the Court decided that the products were not similar for Article 90(1) [ex 95(1)] purposes.

INDIRECT DISCRIMINATION

Once a decision has been made about whether or not goods are similar, it is relatively easy to identify direct discrimination that explicitly acts to the detriment of imported products. However, there may well be charges on duties which appear to be neutral but none the less place a heavier burden on products from other Member States. A good example of this is the case of *Humblot* (112/84). The French Government imposed road tax on a sliding scale. The criterion for the amount of tax was the horsepower (cv) of the car. The "cut-off" point was 16 cv. Below this level the tax was determined on a sliding scale up to a maximum of 1,100 FF. For cars over 16 cv there was a significant increase; to a rate of 5000 FF. Of course, this tax was applied to all cars, both French made and imported cars. In fact, however, France did not produce any cars over 16 cv. Mr Humblot imported a 36 cv Mercedes and claimed that the 5000 francs he was charged violated Article 90 [ex 95]. The Court of Justice held that such a system amounted to indirect discrimination based on nationality and was in breach of Article 90 [ex 95]. The Court said:

"The . . . additional taxation is liable to cancel out the advantages which certain cars imported from other Member States might have in consumer's eyes over comparable cars of domestic manufacture . . . In that respect the species tax reduces the amount of competition to which cars of domestic manufacture are subject and hence is contrary to principle of neutrality with which domestic taxation must comply."

After the judgments in this case the French authorities changed the rules. They introduced nine new categories under the sliding scale system. But the new categories were all over the 16 cv level. The rule was challenged again, and in *Feldain* (433/85), the Court of Justice held that the discrimination had merely been modified, but had not been removed.

A contrasting view can be seen in *Commission v Greece (Re Taxation of Motor Cars)* (C-132/88) in which a Greek tax imposed a progressively higher tax on cars, both domestic and imported, one which rose steeply for cars over 1800 cylinder capacity (cc). The cars offered were all imported since Greece produced no cars over 1600 cc. These facts would appear to be very similar to those in *Humblot*. However, the Court of Justice heard evidence that the reason for the high rates of tax for large cars was to encourage car users to move to smaller, more environmentally friendly cars. The Court held that this measure would only breach Article 90 [ex 95] if it could be shown that it discouraged Greeks from buying foreign cars. Nor did Community law prohibit the use of fiscal policy to obtain social ends, provided any such tax was based on objective criteria, and did not have a protective effect.

Another example where it was held that different taxation of "similar" products was not discriminatory is *Commission v France (French Sweet Wines)* (196/85). In this case, France taxed "traditional" sweet wine at a lower rate than ordinary wine. France justified this different treatment because they wished to provide special economic assistance to rural areas dependant on the production of this sweet wine. The Court of Justice accepted this argument, and held that there was no contravention of Community law.

Article 90 (1) [ex 95(1)] deals with the situation were products are "similar". Article 90(2) [ex 95(2)] provides that no Member State shall improve on the products of another Member State any internal taxation of such a nature as to afford indirect protection to other products. This is intended to cover products that are not similar but are nevertheless in competition with each other. So it has to be determined under which Article to bring an action. If the case is brought under Article 90(1) [ex 95(1)] *i.e.* the goods are similar, there will be prima facie no discrimination if the rates of tax are the same for both domestic and imported goods, and if the basis of assessment and the rules for collecting the tax are the same. In any event, a direct comparison can be made.

For Article 90(2) [ex 95(2)], it is not possible to make a direct comparison because the goods are different, and the criterion for assessment under Article 90(2) [ex 95(2)] is whether the tax has a protective effect. It has been seen above, that in *Commission v UK (Wine Export Duties)*, the Court of Justice has had to adjudicate on the similarity or difference between beer and wine. In the early years the Court of Justice was not troubled by whether the tax fell within Article 90(1) or 90(2). An example can be seen in *Commission v France* (168/78) where the Court did not find it necessary to distinguish between grain based spirits (*e.g.* whisky and gin), and fruit or wine based spirits (*e.g.* cognac and calvados). However, a more analytical approach is seen in later cases. In *Commission v Italy (Tax on Bananas)* (184/85) Italy imposed a tax on bananas, all of which were imported into Italy from France. There was no similar tax on apples, pears, peaches and plumbs of which Italy produced large amounts. The Court of Justice conducted an analysis of whether bananas and other fruit were similar for the purposes of Article 90(1) [ex 95(1)]. It found they were not similar, particularly as they satisfied different needs of the consumer.

QUANTITATIVE RESTRICTIONS AND MEASURES HAVING EQUIVALENT EFFECT: (ARTICLES 28–31 [EX 30–36])

The provisions of Articles 23 and 24 [ex 9–16] and Article 90 [ex 95] cover Community law on duties and similar taxes. In these areas the Community has been more or less successful in removing tariff barriers between Member States. If this was the end of the matter the free movement of goods would still not be achieved because it would be possible for Member States to restrict the free-flow of goods by imposing quotas or other forms of quantitative restrictions on the importation of goods into their territory. They could use even more subtle means, which although not in the form of a quota or other restriction, nevertheless had an equivalent effect. The prohibition of quantitative restrictions and other subtle restrictions is provided for in Articles 28–31 [ex 30–36] of the Treaty:

(a) Article 28 [ex 30], which prohibits quantitative restrictions, and all measures having equivalent effect on imports.

(b) Article 29 [ex 34] which applies a similar prohibition as Article 28 [ex 30] to exports.

(c) Article 30 [ex 36] which allows Member States to derogate from Articles 28 and 29 [ex 30–34] with regard to imports and exports, if the derogations can be justified on specific grounds.

ARTICLE 28 [EX 30]

Article 28 [ex 30] states that:

"Quantitative restrictions on imports and all measures having equivalent effect shall, without prejudice to the following provisions, be prohibited between Member States."

Although the Article covered "measures" taken by Member States the Court of Justice has interpreted the term widely to include the activities of any public or quasi-public body. This will include "measures" taken by professional bodies on whom national legislation has conferred regulatory powers. So, for example, in *R v Pharmaceutical Society of Great Britain* (266 & 267/87) the Court held "rules" adopted by the professional body, if they were capable of affecting trade between Member States, could constitute "measures" within the meaning of Article 28 [ex 30] of the EC Treaty. When the Court is called upon to decide if a particular body has sufficient authority to establish measures having the equivalent effect of a quantitative restriction, it will consider the legal status of the body, the requirements of mandatory membership, the power to enact rules of ethics, the existence of disciplinary powers, and the sanctions which the professional body may invoke if its rules are broken by one of its members.

A good illustration of the wide interpretation given by the Court of Justice is in *Commission v Ireland ("Buy Irish" Campaign)* (249/81). In this case, the Irish Government had established the Irish Goods Council, whose purpose was to encourage consumers in Ireland to buy Irish goods. The Council was funded mainly by the government, and partly by private industry, but was a private undertaking. The Court of Justice rejected the argument of the Irish government that only formally binding measures were covered by Article 28 [ex 30]: the Irish Goods Council was capable of influencing traders through its promotional activities. The Court also dismissed the argument that because the scheme had not been successful, Community law should be unconcerned with it!

Scope of Article 28 [ex 30]

The prohibition covers both quantitative restrictions and measures having equivalent effect (to quantitative restrictions). Measures having equivalent effect are often referred to as MEQRs. The concept of "quantitative restriction" was defined broadly in *Geddo* (2/73) as measures which amount to a total or partial restraint on imports, exports or goods in transit. Quantitative restrictions are usually easy to identify, and the most obvious examples are complete bans on goods, or quotas, by amount or by value, which restrict the right "to import" or export a particular product. These will clearly be in breach of Article 28 [ex 30]. There are numerous examples of such cases. In *R v Henn and Darby* (34/79) the UK Government imposed a ban on pornographic material. (This is a quantitative restriction, although it might be justified under Article 30 [ex 36]—see below.)

An MEQR is more difficult to define. Some national rules will have the effect of a quota, but the Member State will argue that the rules are neutral in that they apply equally to domestic products and imports (or that they are provided for by Article 30 [ex 36]). The Commission, in its role as "guardian of the Treaty" has given a wide interpretation to MEQRs, as has the Court of Justice. The Commission issued Directive 70/50 to guide Member States by providing a non-exhaustive list of measures equivalent to quantitative restrictions. The Directive had a limited life, being applicable only during the Community's transitional period, but it continues to be influential on the scope of MEQR, and has been the subject of many decisions of the Court of Justice.

Article 2 of Directive 70/50 defines MEQRs to include those which "make imports or the disposal at any marketing stage of imported products, subject to a condition, other than a formality, which is required in respect of imported products only". They also include any measures which subject imported products to a condition which differs from that required for domestic products and which is more difficult to satisfy. As these measures apply only to imports (or exports) as distinct from domestic goods they are called distinctly applicable measures.

Article 3 of the Directive provides that measures, which apply equally to domestic and imported goods, will contravene Article 28 [ex 30] only "where the restrictive effect of such measures on the free movement of goods exceeds the effect intrinsic to trade rules". Because the measures are neutral in that they apply to both imports and domestic goods they are called indistinctly applicable measures.

The starting point for an examination of MEQRs is the seminal case of *Procureur du Roi v Dassonville* (8/74). Belgium law provided that imported goods must have a certificate of origin, attached to them in the originating country. A company, Dassonville had imported a consignment of Scotch Whisky into Belgium from France, without the requisite certificate from the UK authorities. When Dassonville was prosecuted in Belgium they argued that the Belgium law was an MEQR. The Court of Justice agreed with the defendant. The Court said:

". . . the requirement by a Member State of a certificate of authority, which is less easily obtainable by importers of an authentic product, put into free circulation in a regular manner in another Member State, than by importers of the same product coming directly from the country of origin, constitutes a measure having equivalent effect."

However, the Court was not satisfied with this judgment linked to the facts of the case. It went further and produced its own definition of measures having equivalent effect. In what is known as the *"Dassonville* formulae" the definition declares:

"All trading rules enacted by Member States which are capable of hindering directly or indirectly, actually or potentially, intra-Community trade are to be considered as measures having an effect equivalent to quantitative restrictions."

This is an extremely broad view, and indicated that the Court of Justice will be vigilant in striking down measures which impede the free flow of goods within the Community. It should also be noted that the Court used the expression "capable of hindering . . . " Thus, the *"Dassonville* formulae" is an effects doctrine. The crucial element is the possible *effect* on trade. There is no need to show an intent to discriminate. The Court added that in the absence of a Community system guaranteeing the authenticity of the origin of a product, an individual Member State may take measures to prevent unfair practices in this connection provided that the measures were reasonable. This is subject to the further qualification that even if the measures are subject to Article 30 [ex 36] (see below) they must not constitute a means of arbitrary discrimination or a disguised restriction on trade between Member States Thus, some reasonable restraints may be permissible. This had echoes of the "rule of reason" which is discussed below.

The definition in *Dassonville* has been confirmed and applied in numerous cases. One example is the *Re Buy Irish Campaign* case, discussed above. It will be recalled that the Court of Justice held that the policy of promoting the sale of national products by means of an advertising campaign was a measure having equivalent effect. This was notwithstanding that the Irish Government had not taken any compulsory measures. The promotion or favouring of domestic products was also a feature of *Commission v UK* (207/83). This case concerned UK legislation that required certain goods to be marked with their country of origin. The United Kingdom argued that this rule applied to both domestic and imported goods, and that this information was important to consumers who used the information as an indication of quality. The Court of Justice held that the legislation was in breach of Article 28 [ex 30] as an MEQR. They said that indications of origin enable consumers to assert any prejudices they may have against foreign products.

Such prejudices are inimical to the development of a common market and the progressive approximation of the economic policies of Member States. In *Irish Souvenirs* (113/80) the Court of Justice held that Irish legislation that insisted that the word "foreign" be affixed to souvenirs not made in Ireland was an MEQR within Article 28 [ex 30]. The Court said that souvenirs were bought as a pictorial reminder of places they had visited, and this did not mean that the souvenirs had to be manufactured in the country of origin.

An interesting contrast to the *Buy Irish* case is provided in *Apple and Pear Council v Lewis* (222/82). The Council was set up by the UK Government and was financed by a levy on fruit growers in the United Kingdom. The task of the Council was to promote the consumption of apples and pears, which it did by a series of advertisements featuring typically English varieties of fruit such as Cox apples and Conference pears. They also used the slogan "polish up your English". Some of the fruit growers refused to pay the levy and argued that the scheme was in breach of Article 28 [ex 30] because it favoured domestic fruit at the expense of imported foreign fruit. The Court of Justice held that the state was sufficiently involved in the scheme for it to come within Article 28 [ex 30]. They also said that to prefer domestic goods to imported goods, solely by reasons of origin, was contrary to Article 28 [ex 30]. However, the Court then departed from its *Buy Irish* judgment. It held that it was permissible to promote a product by reference to its particular qualities. So, for example, it would be justifiable to advertise than an apple was crisp and crunchy, but not simply because it was English. A balance has to be struck between reference to quality and reference to origin, with predominance being given to the former. The underlying motive should be that competition on quality is good, whereas competition on nationality is not.

The free movement of goods can also be hindered by public procurement policies of Member States. This situation will arise when the national government, or other public authority, favours a domestic undertaking when it decides on tenders for public contracts. So, for example, the UK Government will regard favourably a tender from a British firm to construct a new motorway. (The issue of public procurement is dealt with in Chapter 14.) The Court of Justice has sought to control this tendency to favour domestic over imported products. In *Commission v Ireland (Re Dundalk Water Supply)* (45/87) the local council put out to tender a contract for water supply. One of the conditions of the tender was that the water pipes to be used had to conform to an Irish specification. A bid was put in which did not feature pipes having the Irish standard, but which did comply with international standards. The Council rejected it. They argued that it was necessary to specify an Irish standard for technical reasons, and that the only tenderer able to comply with this standard was located in Ireland. The Court of Justice accepted the Commission's argument that the Irish government should have incorporated the words "or equivalent" after the reference to the Irish standard. The Irish authorities could then verify compliance with the technical conditions without from the outset restricting the contracts to tenderers from Ireland.

Another method by which a Member State can treat imported goods less favourably than domestic goods is by price-fixing regulations. Price-fixing is a widely used means of economic regulation. The Court of Justice has been careful to ensure that the potential unlawfulness of such regulation does not impede the promotion of free trade. The problem with price-fixing is that even though it applies to domestic and imported goods alike, it may have the effect of impeding imports by preventing the import being traded at a price which will give it a competitive advantage. In *Tasca* (65/75), the defendant was charged with selling sugar above the national maximum price fixed by Italian legislation. The Court of Justice held that fixing a maximum price is not necessarily an MEQR unless it is fixed at such a level that it makes the sale of imported goods more difficult. If the maximum price is set at such a low level that an importer can trade only at a loss, then the effect of the price fixing is to discriminate against importers in breach of Article 28 [ex 30].

In *Van Tiggele* (82/77), the Court of Justice was concerned with a minimum price arrangement. The defendant was charged with selling gin below the national minimum price in the Netherlands. The Court held that if the minimum price is fixed at such a high level that the imported product is prevented from taking advantage of the fact that it is cheaper than its domestic competitor, then a breach of Article 28 [ex 30] may be established. On the facts of the case the Court held that the Dutch rule did contravene Article 28 [ex 30].

INDISTINCT MEASURES

Up to now the discussion has been mainly about rules that discriminate against imports. In this area the Court of Justice has made a positive contribution to the creation of a single market. However, an even more notable contribution has been made in the area of rules that make no distinction between domestic and imported goods, but which nevertheless have a discriminatory effect. This is the notion of indistinctly applicable measures, and which was introduced in Article 3 of Directive 70/50 (see above). An example might be helpful. Let us say that the United Kingdom has a law that requires all boxes to have rounded corners. The law applies to all boxes manufactured in the United Kingdom and to all other boxes imported for use into the United Kingdom. The law makes no reference to the country of origin of the boxes. On the face of it, the rule appears to be neutral in that it applies to all manufacturers of boxes, both domestic and foreign. In practice however it means that those manufacturers who make boxes with pointed corners cannot sell their product in the United Kingdom. A UK box manufacturer will have geared up to produce the correct box, but a foreign manufacturer will have to re-tool machinery to produce a special run of round cornered boxes. The foreign manufacturer will be at a competitive disadvantage compared with the UK counterpart, and indeed, the foreign manufacturers may not think it worthwhile to enter the market at all. Thus will be inhibited the effective competition between products from different Member States.

The possibility of indistinct measures falling within Article 28 [ex 30] is apparent from the decision in *Dassonville*. The

"*Dassonville* formula" does not require discrimination to be shown for it to be covered by Article 28 [ex 30]. However, the seeds sown in Article 3 of Directive 70/50 and in *Dassonville* came to fruition in the landmark case of *Rewe-Zentrale AG v Bundesmonopolverwaltung für Branatwein* (120/78). Luckily for students, the case is more commonly known as *Cassis de Dijon*. Cassis is a blackcurrant liqueur, usually drunk with white wine. Under German law there was a requirement for a minimum alcoholic content of 25 per cent for such spirits. Naturally, this requirement was satisfied by cassis produced in Germany. However, an importer wished to bring in cassis from France, but because French cassis was traditionally of an alcoholic content between 15 and 20 per cent, the importer could not lawfully market Cassis de Dijon in Germany. The measure was indistinctly applicable, *i.e.* it applied equally to German and French liqueurs, but its effect was to exclude French cassis from the German market. The importer argued that the German law was an MEQR. The Court of Justice rejected the German arguments relating to public health (that a high alcohol level would prevent increased consumption), the fairness of commercial transactions (that weak imported cassis would have an unfair commercial advantage over the more expensive German cassis), and protection of the consumer. The Court applied the *Dassonville* formula and held that the German law was in breach of Article 28 [ex 30], as it had a restrictive effect on trade.

However, the Court went further and established a major new principle. First it held that Member States still had some discretion:

"In the absence of common rules relating to the production and marketing of alcohol . . . it is for Member States to regulate all matters relating to the production and marketing of alcohol and alcoholic beverages on their own territory."

The Court then ruled that this independence was constrained by the influence of Community law:

"Obstacles to movement within the Community arising from disparities between national laws relating to the marketing of the production in question must be accepted in so far as those provisions may be recognised as being necessary in order to satisfy the mandatory requirements relating in particular to the effectiveness of fiscal supervision, the protection of public health, the fairness of commercial transactions and the defence of the consumer."

This means that until rules are harmonised, barriers to trade which arise out of the different laws of the Member States are capable of breaching Article 28 [ex 30]. It is however, open to Member States to justify these technical rules on the ground that they are "necessary in order to satisfy mandatory requirements." This principle whereby a restriction may be justified subject to certain conditions is known as "the rule of reason". In *Cassis de Dijon* it was up to the German authorities to demonstrate that their national rules governing the alcoholic strength of various liqueurs were justified. The German arguments have been set out above. In terms of public health they argued that if weak spirits were available, drinkers would drink more and hence build up a tolerance towards alcohol. This argument is risible and the only hint of humour in the judgment is when the Court of Justice responded by noting that most Germans drink alcoholic beverages with high alcohol content, but dilute it! The Court came to the overall conclusion that the German argument lacked coherence as an effective control of alcohol consumption. In any event, the Court added that any measure taken to protect a "mandatory requirement" must be proportionate to that end and must be the least restrictive of trade.

Although the assessment of proportionality is for the national court to decide, the Court of Justice suggested that the German authorities could achieve all their aims of protection of public health and fairness to the consumer by requiring the display of an indication of origin and of alcoholic content on the packaging of products. The measure in *Cassis* was mandatory but it failed because the Court of Justice found it was not necessary. The objectives could have been achieved by other means (labelling) less inimical to trade. So "necessary" means strictly no more then is necessary. It is this issue of proportionality that has been the means of striking down numerous "mandatory requirements".

The Court's judgment in *Cassis* was also a response to the difficulties faced by the Commission in securing agreement between Member States on the harmonisation of national measures of control. It had been expected that legislation was required to harmonise divergent national rules which created obstacles to trade between Member States. *Cassis de Dijon* is important because it assists the integration of the market through the application of Article 28 [ex 30] by judicial means. The Court of Justice held:

"There is therefore no valid reason why, provided they have been lawfully produced and marketed in one Member State, alcoholic beverages should not be introduced into any other Member State; the sale of such products may not be subject to a legal prohibition on the marketing of beverages with an alcoholic content lower than the limit set by national rules."

This is an important passage which introduces the idea of "mutual recognition". This idea is that every Member State must respect the traditions of other Member States, and that once a product has been lawfully produced and marketed in one Member State it will meet the mandatory requirements of the other Member State, unless objective evidence can show otherwise.

The Commission was not slow to take up the initiative given by the Court of Justice. In 1980 it published a Communication setting out its interpretation of *Cassis*, and in particular recognising the need for mutual recognition. The Commission stated:

"There is no valid reason why goods, which have been lawfully produced and marketed in one of the Member States shall not be introduced into any other Member State."

This communication and the principles that emerged from *Cassis* have become the cornerstone of the drive to ensure an integrated and free market for goods within the Community. The impact of the *Cassis* decision is best assessed by an examination of the abundant case law that followed.

INDISTINCTLY APPLICABLE RULES: THE MANDATORY REQUIREMENTS

It will be recalled that in *Cassis*, the Court of Justice set out the boundary of mandatory requirements. They were the effectiveness of fiscal supervision, the protection of public health, the fairness of commercial transactions and the defence of the consumers.

The rationale for mandatory requirements is not hard to find. There are many rules that regulate trade but will also restrict it, yet some of these rules may be objectively justified. It would not be appropriate to make these rules unlawful. It should also be remembered that the mandatory requirements set out in *Cassis* are not exhaustive. This is evident from *Cassis* itself where the Court of Justice stated that the mandatory requirements included *in particular* those mentioned in the judgment. That the list is non-exhaustive has been confirmed in later cases.

The mandatory requirements are also treated separately from the derogations allowed under Article 30 [ex 36] (see below). This is because the *Cassis* ruling applies only to indistinctly applicable measures. In *Gilli and Andres* (778/79) it was unlawful to sell vinegar in Italy which was not made from fermented wine. An importer had brought in apple vinegar from Germany and was prosecuted by the Italian authorities. The importer relied on an Article 28 [ex 30] defence. The Court held that the state could regulate the matter provided the regulation did not constitute an obstacle, actually or potentially, to intra-Community trade. In this case, the Court held that the measure was not necessary since the apple vinegar was not harmful to health and by fixing an appropriate label to the goods, the consumer could make a choice with regard to the purchase of the product. But the Court also stressed that the *Cassis* exceptions could only be used where rules were applied without discrimination for both national and imported products.

For measures which are distinctly applicable, *Cassis* has no relevance in terms of mandatory requirements. In such cases the state can only justify its measures under Article 30 [ex 36] as interpreted by the Court of Justice. The reason why the Court has developed the separate qualifications for indistinct measures reflects the difference between these rules and discriminatory rules. Indistinct or non-discriminatory rules are by their nature widely cast, and the court of Justice has constructed qualifications that reflect the nature of indistinctly applicable rules. This is in contrast to the narrow application of Article 30 [ex 36] to distinctly applicable rules. It should be noted however, that if a state fails to justify one of its mandatory requirements under the *Cassis* principles, it still might be able to justify it under Article 30 [ex 36].

One of the best known decisions on mandatory requirements in *Commission v Germany (Re Beer Purity Law)* (178/84). In Germany there was a law which stated that the term "bier" could only be attached to drinks made from barley, hops, yeast and water. This was the Germany beer purity law. A further law prohibits the importation of beer containing additives, unless the additives were approved. The German Government defended its rule by arguing that it was necessary to regulate the term "bier" for the sake of consumer protection. German beer drinkers were used to their beverage being made of only the four ingredients. The German Government also argued that the legislation was not protectionist in that any brewer who made beer solely with the four ingredients was free to market it in Germany. The Court of Justice was not impressed with these arguments. It said that labelling the products with a list of ingredients would equally protect consumers. That way, German beer drinkers would be able to make informed choices. Those that wished could keep to German beer but consumer choice would be expanded by the availability of beer made by different methods and with different ingredients.

German beer drinkers may even get to enjoy warm and weak English beer!

In *Walter Rau Lebensmittelwerke v De Smedt* (261/81), Belgium legislation prohibited the marketing of margarine in any container that was not cube shaped. This had a clear protective effect and was an obstacle to marketing. The Belgium Government argued that the rule was equally applicable to both domestic and foreign products of margarine, and that the measure was necessary for the protection of the consumer, who needed to be able to tell the difference between butter and margarine. The Court of Justice was unimpressed by both arguments. Although the measure was equally applicable to domestic and foreign producers Belgium produces would already be complying with the rule. A competitor, wishing to break into the Belgium market would have to have two production runs, one with their existing box shape and another with the new cube shaped box for the Belgium market. This would increase their costs and make competition more difficult. So far as the protection of the consumer was concerned, the Court held that if a Member States had a choice between various measures to obtain the same objective, it should choose the method which was the least restrictive of free trade. In this case, the Court of Justice, perhaps realising that Belgium people are quite good at reading, suggested that labelling might be the ideal solution.

Another well-known case is *Prantl* (16/83). This case concerned a German law that gave protection to a particularly shaped wine bottle, the *bocksbeutel*. Only wine from a designated area of Germany could be lawfully marketed in the bulbous *bocksbeutel*. The purpose of the rule was to prevent unfair competition by cheap imitations passing themselves off as superior wine. Mr Pantl was charged with a breach of this German law. He had imported Italian wine in a traditional Italian bottle of similar shape and design to the *bocksbeutel*. The case was referred to the Court of Justice by the German criminal court. The Court of Justice held that so long as the imported wine conformed to fair and traditional methods of production and marketing in its country of origin, its exclusion from Germany could not be justified.

The three cases discussed above illustrate the consequences of the *Cassis* approach to indistinctly applicable rules. They do not deny that a Member State has a right to control new goods that are marketed within its own territory. So for example, in the *Beer Purity* case, German brewers could produce their beers according to their ancient traditions. What was wrong with the rule was its mandatory nature; the insistence that only pure beer could be sold in Germany. The result of the rule was that foreign beer, made to other traditions, and with other ingredients, was denied access to the German market. Thus, consumer choice was denied to the German beer drinker. This is the point made by the Court of Justice in the three cases under discussion (and in many others). If the overall aims of economic integration are to be achieved it is the consumer, and not the national legislation, who will decide which goods will sell and which will not. It may well be that the consumer will stick with domestic goods. After all, old habits die hard! But if producers of goods are to retain their market share it must be because of the quality of their goods, and their ability to persuade the consumer that their goods are best: they should not be able to retain their market share by sheltering behind protectionist laws.

It has been stated earlier that the list of mandatory requirements in *Cassis* is not exhaustive. Thus, the protection of the environment has been added to the list. In *Commission v Denmark (Re Disposable Beer Cans)* (302/86), Danish law required that containers for beer and soft drinks should be returnable and able to be recycled. A national agency was set up to approve containers, and a deposit-and-return system was set up for empty containers. Although this law was discriminatory in that it made it more difficult for foreign producers, using non-approved containers, to enter the market, the Danish Government argued that the rule was justified by a mandatory requirement related to the protection of the environment. The Court of Justice held that the protection of the environment is "one of the Community's essential objectives" and may therefore justify certain limitations of the principle of the free movement of goods. This view, the Court said, had been confirmed by the Single European Act. Therefore, the protection of the environment was a mandatory requirement which may limit the application of Article 28 [ex 30]. In the present case, the Court held that the Danish rule was mostly acceptable.

In *Cinethèque SA* (60 & 61/84) the Court of Justice held that the promotion of certain art forms was capable of being a mandatory requirement. France had a rule designed to protect the cinema industry by prohibiting the distribution of video cassettes within one year of release of the film in question. The Court held that such rule was justifiable.

In *Torfaen* (145/88), a case concerning Sunday opening of shops in the United Kingdom, it was held that rules governing the opening of premises on a Sunday might be justified in that the rules reflected socio-political choices that were different between Member States. Both this case and *Cinethèque SA* might now be considered differently after *Kech* (C-267 & 268/91) (see below).

The Court of Justice has not allowed economic justification as a mandatory requirement. In *Duphar* (238/82) the Netherlands had drug regulations which involved a list of approved drugs, to be paid for out of public funds. Duphar, a drug manufacturer, was excluded from the list and challenged this exclusion in the Dutch courts. The matter was referred to the Court of Justice who said that broad economic justifications were not available to Member States. Nevertheless, the Court said that a restricted list measure might be justifiable on the grounds of the interests of the consumer, provided that the selection of drugs on the approved list did not discriminate against imports, and was drawn up using objective criteria.

The Court of Justice in *Oosthoek* (286/81) also accepted consumer protection measures as a mandatory requirement. Dutch law controlled the offer of sales promotion "free gifts" to buyers of encyclopaedia. The purpose of the rules was to protect the consumer from entering into a transaction into which they had been induced by the "free-gift". This had an effect on trade because many other Member States based their sales promotional activities on the promise of the "free-gift". Oosthoek ignored the Dutch law and when prosecuted, argued that the rule was in breach of Article 28 [ex 30] of the EC Treaty. The Court of Justice accepted the Dutch Government's argument that the rule was a legitimate means of protecting the consumer from deception and the honest trader from unfair competition.

By contrast, in *GM INNO-BM* (C-362/89), a Belgium company had distributed leaflets advertising cut-price products. This was lawful in Belgium, but the leaflets were also distributed in Luxembourg where the practice was illegal. A supermarket was prosecuted and pleaded Article 28 [ex 30] as a defence. The Court of Justice held that the ban was unlawful under Article 28 [ex 30], and was not justifiable as a consumer protection method. The ban was particularly prejudicial to small importers who were denied a very effective means of advertising.

EXPORTS: ARTICLE 29 [EX 34]

It has been seen that Article 28 [ex 30] prohibits discrimination against imports. The principles relating to Article 28 [ex 30] also apply to Article 29 [ex 34], which covers exports. For both imports and exports justification is possible under Article 30 [ex 36] (see below). However, indistinctly applicable measures will not breach Article 29 [ex 34] unless they discriminate against exports. The important point to remember about exports is that *Cassis* does not apply. The leading case is *Groenveld* (15/79).

Dutch legislation prohibited all makers of meat products from stocking horsemeat. The purpose was to safeguard the export of meat products to countries that prohibited the sale of horsemeat. Thus countries receiving Dutch meat products could be confident that the product did not contain horseflesh. The sale of horsemeat was not forbidden in the Netherlands itself. Groenveld, a Dutch firm, decided to make horsemeat sausages and to export them. When they came into conflict with Dutch law they argued that the ban on exports of horsemeat contravened in Article 29 [ex 34].

The Advocate General agreed with Groenveld, and in his Opinion stated that the Dutch rules were indistinctly applicable, but restricted trade. Therefore, the *Cassis* principle applied, and no justification for the restriction could be shown. But the Court thought differently. It held that Article 29 [ex 34] was exclusively concerned with "the establishment of a difference in treatment between the domestic trade of a Member State and its export trade". Where there was no discrimination between goods produced for the home market and those for export, Article 29 [ex 34] was inapplicable.

The Court of Justice confirmed this approach in another Dutch case, *Jongeneel Kaas* (237/82). Here, the Dutch law set out strict conditions on the content and quality of Dutch cheeses. These rules undoubtedly made export of the cheese more difficult because the Dutch cheese would come into competition with cheeses not subject to the same stringent conditions. However, the Court of Justice held that, as there was no difference, by the Netherlands, in the treatment of cheese for home market or for export, Article 29 [ex 34] did not apply. An example of when Article 29 [ex 34] will be upheld is *Bouhelier* (53/76). In this case, French law required that watches intended for export had to undergo a quality inspection in order to obtain an export licence. There was no such requirement imposed on watches for the home market. The Court of Justice held that this distinctly applicable measure was in breach of Article 29 [ex 34].

Why is Article 29 [ex 34] dependant on showing discrimination, while all that is needed for Article 28 [ex 30] is to show a restrictive effect on trade? The answer seems to be that goods due for export and goods due for the domestic market are subject to the same set of rules, at the same stage in the process of production. Whereas, goods subject to indistinctly applicable measures are subject to the "dual burden" of a set of technical rules in their state of origin, and another at the state of destination. It is this second set of technical rules which composes an extra burden on importers, and which obstructs trade. Therefore *Cassis* assists importers who challenge impediments to free trade.

DEROGATION FROM ARTICLES 28–31 [EX 30–34]: JUSTIFYING BARRIERS TO TRADE

If trade rules are discriminatory under Articles 28–31 [ex 30–34] they may however be justified under Article 30 [ex 36]. This provides that:

"The provisions of Articles 28 and 29 shall not preclude prohibitions or restriction on imports, exports or goods in transit justified on grounds of public morality, public policy or public security; the protection of health and life of humans, animals or plants; the protection of national treasures possessing artistic, historic or archaeological value; or the protection of industrial or commercial property. Such prohibitions shall not, however, constitute a means of arbitrary discrimination or a disguised restriction on trade between Members States."

As an exception to one of the basic freedoms of the common market, Article 30 [ex 36] must be interpreted strictly. And the justifications set out in Article 30 [ex 36] are exhaustive. The Court of Justice has always refused to extend the scope of justifications beyond those already in Article 30 [ex 36]. In *Re Irish Souvenirs* (113/80), the Court would not allow the Irish authorities to plead consumer protection as a legitimate measure to justify discriminatory trade barriers. In *Edward Leclerc* (229/83) the Court refused to allow the protection of cultural diversity as an Article 30 [ex 36] justification.

The key to the understanding of Article 30 [ex 36] is set out in a key passage from *Campus Oil* (72/83). The Court of Justice declared that:

"The purpose of Article 36 (now 30) . . . is not to reserve certain matters to the exclusive jurisdiction of Member States; it merely allows national legislation to derogate from the principles of the free movement of goods to the extent that this is and remains justified in order to achieve the objectives set out in the Article."

So, the scope of the justification will remain narrow, and the action taken against an import must be in proportion to the risk presented by the import, and the restriction must be the least able to achieve the end desired by the restriction. This issue of proportionality is similar to the requirements for the justification of quantitative restrictions in the *Cassis* judgment. In *Leendert van Bennekom* (227/82) the Court of Justice held that "justified" meant "necessary", and also said that the burden of demonstrating necessity rests with national authorities.

Public morality

There have been three cases, all referred to the Court of Justice by UK courts in which the public morality ground was raised. The first case, *R v Henn and Darby* (34/79) arose out of the prosecution of importers who had attempted to bring pornographic material from the Netherlands into the United Kingdom. The relevant customs legislation banned materials that were "indecent or obscene", whereas domestic legislation prohibited material only where it was likely to "corrupt or deprave". The defendants argued that the United Kingdom law was contrary to Article 28 [ex 30] because the difference between the two definitions of what was a pornographic material discriminated against imported goods since "indecency" is easier to prove than "obscenity". The Court of Justice agreed that the import ban was within Article 28 [ex 30], but that it was justified by Article 30 [ex 36]. The Court said that it was up to each Member States to determine its own standard of public morality. Once this was accepted it was necessary to consider whether the laws reflecting this standard could constitute a disguised restriction on the trade or a means of arbitrary discrimination within the terms of Article 30 [ex 36]. The Court accepted the statement by the UK Government that although pornographic material was not unlawful in the United Kingdom, there was a total ban on material of the type in the present case. Therefore, Article 30 [ex 36] could be relied on and the criminal convictions of the importers were upheld.

This margin of discretion allowed to Member States was qualified in *Connegate v H M Customs* (121/85). This notorious case concerned the importation (from Germany) of inflatable "love-dolls", which had been seized by customs on the ground that they were indecent and obscene. Once again, the importers pleaded Article 28 [ex 30] and the UK authorities argued the seizure was justified by Article 30 [ex 36], on the ground of public morality. The Court of Justice confirmed its reasoning in *Henn and Darby*, that it is for Member States to decide upon the nature of public morality for its own territory. But it added that a Member State might not rely on the ground of public morality to prohibit imports from other Member States when its legislation contained no prohibition on the manufacture or marketing of such goods in its own territory. The prohibition on imports was therefore a distinguished restriction on trade and a means of arbitrary discrimination, and as such, contrary to Article 30 [ex 36].

The difference between *Henn and Darby* and *Connegate* is that in the former the Court of Justice was convinced that there was no lawful trade at all in such goods in the United Kingdom. In *Connegate* however, there could be lawful trade in domestically produced "love-dolls" and the restriction on imports was therefore not justifiable.

The third case was *Quietlyn v Southend Borough Council* (C-23/89). Here, the Court of Justice held that Article 28 [ex 30] should be construed as meaning that national provisions prohibiting the sale of lawful sex objects from unlicensed establishments did not constitute a MEQR on imports. This was because the measure requiring licensing was to regulate the distribution of the product without discrimination against imported goods.

What seems clear from these cases is that Member States are free to decide what is the appropriate public morality for their own territory. However, they cannot place stricter burdens on imports than are placed on domestically produced goods.

Public Policy

It appears that public policy has successful on one occasion only as a derogation under Article 30 [ex 36]. In *R v Thompson* (7/78) the Court of Justice held that silver coins which were part of a collection were not legal tender, and could be regarded as "goods". A restriction on the exportation of the coins to prevent them being melted down was held to be justified on grounds of public policy.

The Court of Justice has strictly construed the public policy defence. The Court of Justice held, in *Prantl* (see above), that it may not be invoked to restrict criminal behaviour. Nor will national justification based on economic grounds be sustainable. This much was clear from the Court's judgment in *Cullet v Centre Leclerc* (231/83), a French case involving a law fixing a minimum price for petrol.

Public Security

The public security justification is often pleaded in the alternative with the public policy justification. Like the later it is strictly interpreted by the Court of Justice and is rarely successful as a defence. The leading case is *Campus Oil* (72/83), in which Irish law required a petrol importers to buy 35 per cent of their requirements from a state owned oil refinery at prices fixed by the Irish government. In defence Ireland argued for the public policy and the public security justifications within Article 30 [ex 36]. It was vital for Ireland to be able to maintain its own oil industry, particularly in times of international crisis. The Court of Justice held that the public policy argument must fail because it concerned purely economic objectives. However, the Court accepted the public security argument that it was necessary to maintain the continuity of essential oil supplies. It can be said that this case was decided on its own particular facts, and is unlikely to apply to many other situations, so that the likelihood of other successful defences under this head is remote.

Protection of Health and Life of Humans, Animals and Plants

To be successful under this heading, the measures taken to control the movement of goods must be part of a seriously considered health policy. They may not be used to justify measures intended to deal with a risk that is so remote as to be negligible.

In *Commission v Germany (Re Heat Controls on Imported Meat)* (153/78) the Court of Justice held that the purpose of Article 30 [ex 36] is to allow national legislation to derogate from the principle of free movement of goods only to the extent justified in order to achieve one of the objectives of Article 30 [ex 36], and not to act as a disguised restriction on trade. The Court of Justice has been vigilant to ensure that Member States do not abuse this derogation. A good example is *Commission v UK (French Turkeys)* (40/82). In this case, the United Kingdom banned poultry imports from other Member States, in particular imports from France. This was done, it was argued, to prevent the spread of Newcastle disease that affected poultry. The Court of Justice rejected this argument. It noted that United Kingdom poultry producers had come under increased competition from foreign producers and had lobbied the United Kingdom government to protect their position. The Court also noted that the UK Government had, without consultation, imposed the ban on the import of turkeys just before the main selling period at Christmas, and that in any event, France had in place a suitable system of control for the disease.

From these factors it was easy for the Court to conclude that the ban on imports had been imposed for commercial reasons, to block French turkeys, rather than for public health considerations. It is interesting to note that the eventual outcome of this case was an out of court payment by the United Kingdom to French turkey producers of £3.5. million.

A requirement to obtain an import licence, justified on public health grounds can be a disguised restriction on trade. In *Commission v UK (UHT Milk)* (124/81), UK law required that UHT milk could be imported only with a licence, and that all UHT milk sold in the United Kingdom must be packed in a local dairy. This had the effect that all imported UHT milk had to be unpacked, re-treated and repackaged. Thus imports of UHT milk were totally uneconomic. The Court of Justice rejected the UK Government's arguments. They declared that in fact UHT milk was made according to similar processes and rules in different Member States. Provided that proper precautions were taken at the time of the heat treatment there was no need to subject the milk to further treatment when it arrived in the United Kingdom. The licence and re-treatment requirements were no more than a disguised restriction on trade. This case also illustrates the Court's desire to recognise "equivalence" of national standards of different Member States

Of course, this is not to say that the Court of Justice will reject all purported attempts to control imports on the ground of the protection of public health. The Court must have regard for genuine fears about public health. But sometimes there is conflicting scientific evidence about whether or not a particular substance is a threat to public health. This was the issue in *Sandoz* (174/82). The Netherlands had refused to allow the sale of muesli bars that contained added vitamins on the ground that the extra vitamins were dangerous to public health. The muesli bars were legally on sale in Germany and Belgium. The scientific evidence was uncertain, and conflicting, as regards the point at which the consumption of vitamins becomes excessive. The Court of Justice took the view that a Member State is entitled to protect its public from substances, the safety of which is a matter of genuine scientific doubt. This right of a Member State is however, subject to the principle of proportionality.

Another method that a Member State may use to safeguard public health is a requirement for health inspections. If this is done at the point of entry it may make the import more difficult and may expose the import to a double burden if it has already been subject to checks in its home state. Health inspections carried out at frontiers may be an appropriate way to protect the health and life of humans (and animals and plants). However they will only be justified if they are reasonably proportionate to the end pursued, and the protection of health can not be achieved by other means. In *Commission v France (Re Italian Table Wines)* (42/82) the Court of Justice held that France had right to check Italian wine coming into the country. But in this case the excessive delays caused by waiting for customs clearance were disproportionate and discriminatory. The Court said that random checks should be sufficient to check quality, particularly as this was the method used by France to check its domestically produced wine. Some frontier checks will be justifiable. In *Rewe-Zentralfinanz*

(4/75) a health inspection on apples to control a pest, San Jose Scale, was held to be justified. The scientific evidence showed that the pest was only to be found on imported apples: domestically produced apples posed no threat.

The Court of Justice has also accepted that public confidence in a known product may justify restrictions on trade under public health measures. In *Royal Pharmaceutical Society of G.B.* (266/87) imported pharmaceutical products had commonly been supplied to patients by pharmacists in substitution for the more expensive domestic products presented by the patient's doctor. The Royal Pharmaceutical Society took steps to stop the practice, and this action obviously reduced the sales of imported pharmaceutical goods. The Court of Justice held that there was a breach of Article 28 [ex 30], but the prohibition on substitution was justifiable under Article 30 [ex 36]. The supply of a familiar named drug was a comfort to many people, which might change to anxiety if a different drug was supplied. The patient would not necessarily know the therapeutic properties of the drugs were similar, and as a consequence such measures were allowable under Article 30 [ex 36].

Protection of National Treasures

There have been no successful derogations under this heading. In *Commission v Italy (Re Export Tax on Art Treasures)* (7/68), Italy was unsuccessful in its attempt to rely on Article 30 [ex 36] to justify a special tax on art exports. There is a conflict between the free movement of goods and the protection of national treasures, and this has been recognised by the Commission. Partly because the Court of Justice has not been able to develop this area, two measures have been adopted as part of the internal market legislation. First, Regulation 3911/92 seeks to impose uniform controls at borders for protected cultural goods. Categories of protected goods are listed in an Annex to the Regulation. Then, Directive 93/7 provides that Member States retain the right to define their national treasures removed unlawfully from states.

The Protection of Industrial and Commercial Property

This heading covers those areas commonly known as intellectual property rights. It covers such items as patents, trade marks, copyright and registered designs. The issues are dealt with in Chapter 12.

CONCLUSIONS

There are a number of other derogations permitted to Member States which provide for measures to combat short-term difficulties. In the context of this book they do not merit discussion, but they are:

- Article 100 [ex 103a]: Short term and economic difficulties;

- Article 134 [ex 115]: Economic difficulty in a Member State arising out of the implementation of the common commercial policy.

The attainment of a common market in goods has been at the forefront of action taken by both the Commission and the Court of Justice. This action has been taken to further the aims of the common market and to counter the ingenuity of individual Member States in their attempts to protect their domestic markets. The battle seems mainly to have been won by the Community. This was necessary if the Community was to compete fully with the increasing harsh competition from other trading blocks and nations.

RECENT DEVELOPMENTS IN LIMITING THE SCOPE OF ARTICLE 28 [EX 30]

Article 28 [ex 30] has frequently been invoked before national courts as a defence to charges involving regulatory offences. A good example is the case of *Cinethèque* (60 & 61/84). French law banned the sale or hire of video cassettes during the first year in which the film was released. The objective of the ban was to encourage people to go to the cinema and hence encourage the cinema industry. The rule applied equally to domestic and imported videos. The law was challenged as being in breach of Article 28 [ex 30]. In his Opinion, the Advocate General thought that such a rule did not fall within Article 28 [ex 30]. Even if the rule did lead to a restriction or reduction of imports it was not specifically directed at imports, it did not discriminate against them, it did not make it more difficult for an importer to sell his products than it was for a domestic producer, and it gave no protection to domestic producers. The Court thought otherwise. It said that the restriction did fall within Article 28 [ex 30], but that it might be justified provided the objective was proportionate. This difference of approach was to be characterised by a series of cases before the Court of Justice. On the one hand, importers arguing that any restriction, for any reason, fell within the ambit of Article 28 [ex 30], and on the other, the Court of Justice suggesting that the restrictive measures were justified, or fell outside Article 28 [ex 30] altogether.

In the United Kingdom the most controversial use of Article 28 [ex 30] in recent years has been in relation to prosecutions for breaches of the law on Sunday trading, as set out in s.47 of the Shops Act 1950. (That Act has now been repealed, and the law liberalised by the Sunday Trading Act 1994.) The problem was this: the Sunday trading rules prohibited retail shops from selling goods on Sundays. Many companies flouted this law, and when the local authority prosecuted them they claimed that this particular law was an MEQR. They argued that if they could not open on a Sunday their trade would decline by 10 per cent, and this would include imported goods. In this respect though, imported goods were in no worse a position than domestic goods: the reduction in total sales would effect all goods equally. The issue came before the Court of Justice in *Torfaen BC v B & Q* (145/88).

The Court of Justice adopted the same reasoning as it had in *Cinethèque*. The rule was caught by Article 28 [ex 30] but could still be justified if it reflected a legitimate part of national socio-cultural characteristics and provided that the prohibition did not exceed the effects intrinsic to trade rules (*i.e.* the measure was proportionate). In other words, a Member State may issue rules concerning Sunday trading provided the measures comply with the principle of proportionality. The problem was that it was up to the national court to decide the issue of proportionality. Unfortunately, in the Sunday trading cases, different UK courts came to different conclusions.

It could be said that the Court of Justice had become concerned at the number of "Article 28 [ex 30] defences" that came to it on references from national courts. In two French cases, *Conforama* and *Marchandise* (C-312 & 332/89), concerning the legality of national rules that restricted the employment of staff on Sundays, the Court of Justice reiterated its judgment in *Torfaen*, but held that the rules were not so restrictive as to be disproportionate to their objectives. A measure of the growing reluctance of the Court of Justice to decide these types of cases came in the final Sunday trading case, *Stoke-on-Trent BC v B & Q* (C-306/88). Despite all its earlier rulings, the issue of Sunday trading had not been settled in the United Kingdom. Here the Court repeated again its *Torfaen* judgment; but instead of leaving the issue of proportionality to the national court, the Court of Justice held that the Sunday trading rules were lawful and were proportionate.

The plethora of "Article 28 [ex 30] defence" cases and the difficulties experienced by national courts in deciding the issue of proportionality must have persuaded the Court of Justice that a new approach was required. The Court adopted an approach similar to the Opinion of the advocate general in *Cinethèque* which held that some restrictive rules fall entirely outside Article 28 [ex 30]. In *Keck and Mithouard* (C-267 & 268/91) the Court signalled its intention to determine the limits of Article 28 [ex 30]. Kech and Mithouard, two supermarket owners sold goods at a loss, which was contrary to French law. When they were prosecuted, they argued that the law was contrary to Article 28 [ex 30] as it restricted the volume of imported goods. The Court of Justice said that it considered it "necessary to re-examine and clarify its case law on this matter". It said it was doing so in view of the increasing tendency of traders to invoke Article 28 [ex 30] to challenge rules which limited their commercial freedom, even though the rules were not aimed at products from other Member States.

The Court drew a sharp distinction between obstacles to the free movement of goods arising from rules laying down the requirements to be met by goods, such as designation, form, size, weight, composition, presentation, labelling and packaging on the one hand, and rules relating to methods of sale on the other hand. Restrictive rules applying to the requirements to be met by the goods continue to be governed by *Cassis de Dijon*. By contrast, national rules restricting or prohibiting certain selling arrangements will not be treated as hindering intra-state trade provided they apply to all affected traders operating within the Member State concerned, and also provided that they "*effect in the same manner, in law and in fact*" the marketing of domestic goods and imports from other Member States.

There can be little doubt that the Court of Justice intended *Keck* to make a departure from its previous case law whereby any prohibition that decreased the volume of sales, and thus of imports from other Member States, amounted to an obstacle to the free movement of goods. The Court confirmed this itself when it declared ". . . contrary to what has been previously decided". Unfortunately, it did not say which of its previous decisions was being overturned. What *Keck* appears to be saying, is that if rules (in this case, selling arrangements) laid down by a Member State were not by nature such as to prevent their access to the market or to impede access any more that it impeded the access of domestic products, then such rules fell outside Article 28 [ex 30] entirely. Thus, it can now be argued that the Court of Justice distinguishes between rules that relate to the characteristics of the goods (still covered by *Cassis*), and those rules concerning selling arrangements for the goods (now outside Article 28 [ex 30]).

The importance of *Keck* cannot be overstated. This can be seen from the fact that the Court took so long to reach its decision. The case was also the subject of two Opinions by the Advocate General. After his first Opinion, the case was transferred from the Second Chamber to the Full Court.

It would seem to be obvious that the Court of Justice in *Keck* had clear intentions. The Court was dismayed by the increasing number of cases coming before it that relied on the "Euro" defence. The Court of Justice also wished to give guidance to national courts so that they could dismiss fanciful attempts to equate Community internal market rules with purely local affairs. The Court of Justice wanted to create an effective test that would be easily understood and applied in the national courts.

The key to this test was the division between rules relating to the characteristics of the product and selling arrangements (as stated above). If the issue related to the former, the matter fell within the scope of Article 28 [ex 30] and would be unlawful, unless it could be justified. If the issue was a selling arrangement, the matter fell outside Article 28 [ex 30] altogether. In other words, there was no Community aspect to the dispute.

The judgment in *Keck* was mostly welcomed, although there has been some criticism, notably from an Advocate General. Nevertheless, the principle to come out of *Keck* has been followed in subsequent cases. In *Clinique* (C-315/92), legislation that prohibited the use of misleading names on cosmetics was held to be within Article 28 [ex 30]. The Court of Justice said that this was because the measure required imported products to change the appearance of their packaging. This amounted to a product bound measure and was not a selling arrangement. A similar decision was found in the *Mars* case (C-470/93). In *Tankstation* (C-401 & 402/92) the Court held that national rules which provided for the compulsory closing of shops, in this case petrol stations, were outside the scope of Article 29 [ex 30]. The Court reached the same conclusion with regard to the Sunday opening of shops in Spain in *Punto Casa* (C-69 & 258/93). In *Hünermund* (C-292/92), the Court of Justice, repeating *Keck* almost verbatim, held that a rule which prohibited pharmacists from advertising medical products which they were allowed to sell was not caught by Article 28 [ex 30]. The Court said that the rule was not directed towards intra-Community trade; that the rule applied evenly as between all traders; and that though it might have some impact on the overall volume of sales this was not enough to render it an MEQR for the purposes of Article 28 [ex 30]. This case is significant in that it established that advertising fell within selling arrangements.

This was emphasised in the later case of *Leclerc-Siplec* (C-412/93), where Advocate General Jacobs said "where it not for the judgment in *Hünermund* it would perhaps not have been clear that the phrase 'national provisions restricting or prohibiting certain selling arrangements' in *Keck* covered rules on advertising". This brought advertising into the category of selling arrangements.

This category of "selling arrangements" is the most serious difficulty to emerge from the *Keck* judgment. The difficulty lies in the fact that selling arrangements are stressed as the important factor at the expense of market access. This was the major criticism of Advocate General Jacobs in his Opinion in *Leclerc-Siplec*. The case concerned a French law, which prohibited distributors (including Leclerc-Siplec) from advertising unleaded petrol imported by them and sold in their supermarkets. Advocate General Jacobs believed that a non-discriminatory selling arrangement could still obstruct market access. He said, "a rule permitting certain products to be sold in only a handful of small shops in a Member State would be almost as restrictive as an outright ban on importation and marketing". The Advocate General said that the threat was especially significant in advertising. Advertising can have a huge effect on market access, "it is difficult to contend that . . . a total ban on advertising a particular product which can lawfully be sold could fall outside Article 30 (now 28)". The restriction in *Hünermund* was not significant, but it is possible for a more severe restriction to be placed on advertising such that it greatly impedes market access. To prevent a non-national manufacturer from advertising his products in another Member State, and therefore making that product known to consumers in that Member State, would be as restrictive as prohibiting the manufacturer from selling the product at all. As Advocate General Jacobs pointed out:

"If a German brewer is prevented from advertising on television, he will find it difficult to penetrate the French market, which will continue to be dominated by the well-established domestic brands".

The Advocate General also gave as an example the situation of a business that wished to advertise its goods on television that can be purchased by telephone in any Member State. This form of advertising is obviously a selling arrangement. But if this selling arrangement was prohibited in one Member State then it would serve as an outright ban. Advocate General Jacobs also disagreed that a discrimination test would be useful. He said that:

". . . from the point of view of the Treaty's concern to establish a single market, discrimination is not a helpful criterion . . . the fact that a Member State imposes similar restrictions on the marketing of domestic goods is simply irrelevant."

The answer, according to Advocate General Jacobs is that "all undertakings which engage in a legitimate economic activity in a Member State should have unfettered access to the whole of the Community market, unless there is a valid reason for denying them full access to part of that market". The test for securing this should be "whether there is a substantial restriction on that access". He therefore proposed adding to the *Keck* rule a requirement that there be no substantial restriction or barrier to market access. If there was, then it would be caught by Article 28 [ex 30].

The Court of Justice in its judgment in *Leclerc-Siplec* held that the ban on advertising was concerned with selling arrangements and therefore outside Article 28 [ex 30]. The Court avoided the market access approach suggested by the Advocate General. Nevertheless, in a subsequent case, *Familiapress* (C-368/95), the Court did take into account that selling arrangements could have a direct bearing on the product. The case concerned an Austrian law, which prohibited publishers from including prize competitions in their papers. A German publisher who published a paper with a prize crossword was prevented from selling the paper in Austria. The Austrian argument was that the national law related to a method of sales promotion and was therefore, according to *Keck*, outside Article 28 [ex 30]. The Court of Justice was not convinced:

". . . even though the relevant national legislation is directed against a method of sales promotion, in this case it bears on the actual content of the products, in so far as the competitions in question form an integral part of the magazine in which they appear. As a result, the national legislation in question . . . is not concerned with a selling arrangement within the meaning of the judgment in *Keck* . . ."

Moreover, since it requires traders established in other Member States to alter the contents of the periodical, the prohibition at issue impairs access of the products concerned to the market of the Member State of importation and consequently hinders free movement of goods. It therefore constitutes in principle a measure having equivalent effect within the meaning of Article 30 [now 28] of the Treaty."

Although the rationale of *Keck* has infiltrated many subsequent judgments by the Court of Justice, the reasoning of the Court, and the fact that the Court has seemingly ignored the Opinion of its Advocate General, has come in for much academic criticism. The limits of Article 28 [ex 30] have yet to be firmly set and developments in this area should be followed with great care.

12. COMPETITION LAW

INTRODUCTION

The origins of Community competition law lie in Articles 81 [ex 85] and 82 [ex 86] of the Treaty of Rome. The Articles are similar to and were based on, the American legislation the Sherman Act of 1890, which was set up to control the large trusts in the United States. Hence, the term "anti-trust" law is synonymous with competition law.

The concept of free competition is a fundamental element in the Treaty of Rome, which embraces the premise that any restriction on free competition is intrinsically reprehensible. But in order to control fair competition in a common market, some form of state intervention is necessary. This necessitates a tricky balancing act. On the one hand, the Community has to intervene to prevent abuses of industry that would act to the detriment of the market and consumers. On the other hand, the Community must be careful to avoid intervention that hinders growth and which results in inefficient business practices. It is the attempt to achieve this balance that is the basis of competition law. There is the need to regulate the anti-competitive dealings of firms contrasted with the need to allow the consumer the full benefits of perfect competition. The traditional economic view is that without regulation, market power would tend towards a concentration of power in the form of oligopoly or monopoly. That would mean that the oligopoly or monopoly would benefit at the expense of the consumer, because the consumer would have a restricted choice. So, according to the traditional view, perfect competition was not possible, and state intervention was necessary to ensure that balance between the opportunities for businesses to maximise their profits and a wide consumer choice. This was the underlying approach adopted in Europe after the Second World War, particularly in Germany, where it was seen as a means of avoiding dominance by large producers.

A more recent influence is the theory put forward by a giving of economics, loosely called the "Chicago School" that perfect competition is possible and that state intervention is unnecessary and indeed, harmful. On this basis only minimal control by the state is required. Competition law in the Community reflects the influence of these two contrasting economic theories. So, one can detect the balancing act throughout the workings of competition law.

THE PURPOSE OF COMPETITION LAW

The task of the Community law is set out in Article 2 of the Treaty. Article 2 refers to the promotion of the harmonious development of economic activities by the creation of a common market and the progressive approximation of the economic policies of the Member States. The main objectives of European competition policy can be summarised as follows:

(a) to create and maintain a single market for the benefit of producers and consumers. This concept of market interaction is the primary objective of competition policy;

(b) equality of competition and the prevention of market power—the "level playing field" concept;

(c) the promotion of efficiency to ensure firms rationalise their production and distribution and keep up to date with technical progress.

The legal framework for competition law in the Community is set out in Article 3(g) which requires the institution of a system ensuring that competition in the common market is not distorted. The competition rules are seen as being complementary to the provisions on the free movement of goods in Articles 28 [ex 30] to 30 [ex 36]. Competition law is directed towards three kinds of economic activity:

(i) Article 81 [ex 85] restricts trading agreements between otherwise independent business undertakings which may effect trade between Member States and which distort competition within the common market.

(ii) Article 82 [ex 86] restricts the abuse of a dominant market position by large undertakings.

(iii) Regulation 4064/89 attempts to control mergers of undertakings which may result in the abuse of a dominant position.

The main piece of secondary legislation is Regulation 17/62. It is important, at this point, to know that it is the Commission which has the task of ensuring that competition in the Community is not distorted by companies making their own agreements which might be obstacles to trade. The Commission is the "police force" of competition law, and their role is discussed later in this Chapter under "Enforcement of Competition Law". It should also be explained that as part of its task the Commission will issue decisions requiring undertakings to bring any infringements to an end. Any infringement that the Commission cannot resolve by means of a decision will be brought before the Court of First Instance (CFI). From a decision by the CFI an appeal lies to the Court of Justice. Students should be aware of the nomenclature adopted by the Community to differentiate the different actions in competition law. A Commission decision is always published in the Official Journal (OJ), so the year and number and page of the OJ follow the name of the decision. A case before the CFI is prefixed with the letter T (tribunal) and an appeal to the Court of Justice is suffixed with the letter P (*pourvoi* or appeal).

The application of the rules by the Commission, and the interpretation of the rules by the Court of Justice, has not been done by looking at the wording of the provisions alone. The rules are enforced in the light of the general objectives of the Treaty. In *ICI Commercial Solvents v Commission* (6 & 7/73), the Court of Justice held:

"The prohibitions in Articles 85 (now 81) and 86 (now 82) must be interpreted and applied in the light of Article 3(f) of the Treaty which provides that the activities of the Community shall include the institution of a system ensuring that competition is not distorted, and Article 2 of the Treaty which gives the Community the task of promoting 'throughout the Community harmonious development of economic activities'."

ARTICLE 81 [EX 85]

Article 81(1) [ex 85(1)] prohibits all agreements between undertakings, decisions by associations of undertakings and concerted practices which may affect trade between Member States, and which have as their object or effect the prevention, restriction or distortion of competition within the common market. Article 81(2) [ex 85(2)] provides that any agreements or decisions prohibited pursuant to Article 81 [ex 85] shall automatically be void. Article 81(3) [ex 85(3)] enables the Commission to "exempt" agreements which fulfil certain conditions.

Article 81(1) [ex 85(1)]

All of the terms of this Article have been the subject of judicial interpretation by the Court of Justice. They can be considered under the following headings: agreement; undertakings; decisions by associations of undertakings; concerned parties; effect on trade between Member State, prevention, restriction or distortion of competition; object or effect; and, within the EC.

Agreements

The term "agreements" is not defined in the Treaty but has been interpreted widely by the Court of Justice, and by the Commission. In *Cartel in Quinine* ([1969] O.J. L192/5) the Commission insisted it included even non legally binding agreements such as a "gentleman's agreement". In *BMW v Commission* (32/78) an attempt was made by BMW's Belgium subsidiary to prevent car dealers there from selling the cars to other Member States. The Belgian dealers were asked to sign a form of assent, and it was made clear that the form was not a contractual document. Nevertheless the Court held that this was an "agreement" under Article 81(1) [ex 85(1)].

Undertakings

The Treaty has not defined the term "undertakings" but like "agreement", it has been subject to liberal and wide interpretation by the Court of Justice. It includes any legal or neutral person engaged in economic or commercial activity involving the provision of goods or services. In *Re UNITEL* ([1978] O.J. LI57/39) the Commission decided that an opera singer was capable of being an undertaking. The important point is that the body or association must have been established to make a profit. Thus, in *SAT v*

Eurocontrol (C-364/92) the Court of Justice held that Eurocontrol was not an "undertaking". It had been set up to collect fees payable by airlines for traffic control services, and undertook these tasks in the public interest with a view to improving air transport. There was not a sufficient economic element in their work.

Decisions by associations of undertakings

The most usual type of "association" covered by Article 81(1) [ex 85(1)] is the trade association. In *Vereringing van Cementhandelmen v Commission* (8/72) the Court of Justice held that a non-binding recommendation made by a trade association may amount to a decision. If compliance with the recommendation by the undertaking to which it is addressed has an appreciable influence in the market then that recommendation will amount to a decision. In *AROW v BNIC* ([1982] O.J. L379/1) the Bureau National Interprofessional de Cognac had fixed a minimum distribution price for cognac, arguing that this was necessary to guarantee quality. The Commission decided that this argument could not be sustained, as there were other quality control measures in the cognac industry.

Concerted Practices

Once again, this term has been widely interpreted. The term means some kind of co-ordinated action which, although it may fall short of an agreement, knowingly substitutes practical co-operation for competition. In *ICI v Commission (Dyestuffs)* (48/69), ICI was the first of a number of businesses to raise the price of aniline dye in Italy. Other producers of this product, accounting for 85 per cent of the market quickly followed this rise. A similar pattern of price increases had occurred previously. The companies argued that the price co-ordination was simply a reflection of parallel behaviour in an oligopolistic market, where each producer followed the leader. When the matter came before the Court of Justice the Commission was able to demonstrate collusion. Four of the parent companies had sent telex messages indicating price rises to their subsidiaries within an hour of each other, and each message was similarly worded. This had happened on more than one occasion. The Court of Justice held that this behaviour amounted to a "concerted practice" arising out of co-ordination. This was apparent from the behaviour of the parties and was designed to replace the risk of competition and the hazards of competitors' spontaneous reactions. The Court did say that parallel pricing would not necessarily amount to a concerted practice under Article 81(1) [ex 85(1)] unless it leads to competition which did not accord to normal conditions of the market.

In *Suiker Umie v Commission* (40–48/73) a major sugar producer had distributed sugar in the Netherlands only with the consent of the producers in that country. This weakened the competitive pressures on sugar production in the Netherlands. The producers argued that they had not agreed to any plan to that effect and that there was no concerted practice. The Court of Justice held that there was no need for an actual plan. A concerted practice included:

"Any direct or indirect contact between such operators, the object or effect of which is either to influence the conduct on the market of an actual or potential competitor or to disclose to such a competitor the course of conduct which they themselves have decided to adopt or contemplate adopting on the market."

However, the Commission does recognise the distinction between genuine, independent price rises and concerted practices, particularly if the agreement is to the benefit of the consumer. In *Eurocheque* ([1992] O.J. L95/50) the Commission approved uniform bank charges under the Eurocheque scheme because of the clear advantage to tourists and travellers.

Effect on trade between Member States

The agreement, decision or concerted practice must affect trade *between* Member States. So, any agreement that confines itself to trade within one Member State, or with exports outside the Community, will not come under Article 81(1) [ex 85(1)]. (Although it may be covered by the domestic law of the Member State). The test for deciding whether an agreement is within Article 81(1) [ex 85(1)] is set out in *Société Technique Minière (STM) v Maschinenbau* (56/65):

"It must be possible to foster with a sufficient degree of probability on the basis of a set of objective factors of law or of fact that the agreement in question may have an influence, director or indirect, actual or potential, on the patterns of trade between Member States."

This test has been applied on a number of occasions. In *Pronuptia* (161/84) there was an attempt to partition the market on national lines in that an agreement between Pronuptia, the franchiser and its franchisee, limiting the latter to a defined territory, was found by the Court of Justice to contravene Article 81(1) [ex 85(1)]. This was so, even though the franchisee had no intention of operating outside the area of restriction. It was the potential effect on trade that was enough to bring it under Article 81(1) [ex 85(1)].

Prevention, restriction or distortion of competition

The major point of European law is to prevent an altering or distortion of the competitive balance between undertakings. This distinction of competition is most clearly seen in horizontal agreements, that is an agreement between undertakings on the same level. For example two producers or two distributors who agree the same price rise or agree to give each other exclusive rights in specific natural territories. It is relatively easy to see that these agreements partition what should be a single market. It is also easy to see that trade is affected and consumers are denied the benefit of competitive producers from other Member States. However, a vertical agreement, that is one between a manufacturer and a distributor may be more difficult to determine as inimical to competition. Indeed, some vertical agreements can work to a consumer's advantage.

This issue of vertical agreements was examined by the Court of Justice in the important case of *Consten and Grundig v Commission* (56/64). The German manufacturer of electronic goods, Grundig, entered into an exclusive dealing agreement with Consten, a French distributor. By the agreement, Consten had the sole right to distribute Grundig products in France, and also had the exclusive rights to use Grundig's trademark (GINT) in France. In return, Consten agreed not to re-export Grundig products to any other Member State, effectively banning parallel imports and exports. However, another French distributor, UNEF, bought Grundig products in Germany, and sold them in France, at a lower price than Consten. Because of this, Consten brought an action against UNEF in the French court for infringement of the trademark. However, UNEF applied to the Commission who held that the Grundig/Consten agreement contravened Article 81(1) [ex 85(1)]. The argument found its way to the Court of Justice. The Court found that the agreement did contravene Article 81(1) [ex 85(1)]:

". . . the contract between Grundig and Consten, on the one hand by preventing undertakings other than Consten from importing Grundig products into France, and on the other hand by prohibiting Consten from re-exporting those products to other countries of the common market, indisputably affects trade between Member States."

The Court went on to say that "there is no need to take into account the concrete effects of an agreement once it appears that is has as its object the prevention, restriction or distortion of competition. Thus, *Consten and Grundig* decided that Article 81 [ex 85] applies for vertical agreement. This has been criticised because it has been argued that vertical agreements are often beneficial to consumers since they lead to improvements in the promotion and distribution of products. But it is clear that such agreements are equally capable of partitioning the market, as was the case in *Consten and Grundig*. Vertical supply agreements can be covered by Article 81 [ex 85], as affecting trade between Member States even if they are not in any way concerned to affect trade outside one Member State. But such an agreement could have an effect on trade coming into the state.

A good example is *Brasserie de Haecht v Wilkin (No.1) (23/67)*. This case concerned a Belgium café, which in return for a loan, entered into an exclusive agreement to obtain supplies from a brewery. The café owner, Wilkin, later challenged the legality of the agreement. The café was a small business and the agreement when viewed in isolation did not seem prejudicial to the common market in any way. However, the Court of Justice found that there were a large number of similar agreements in existence. It held therefore that the agreement could affect trade as a result of the combined operation of all the similar agreements in the Member State. The agreement, when viewed in the light of a combination of the objective, factual or legal circumstances, was capable of having some influence, direct or indirect, on trade between Member States.

Object or Effect

The question that arises here is how is it decided that the "object or effect" of an agreement is actually to distort competition? In *Consten and Grundig* the Court of Justice held that it was not necessary to conduct a full market analysis if it was clear than an agreement was to restrict competition. This was confirmed in *STM* (56/65). A German firm agreed to give STM the exclusive right to sell its earth moving equipment in France, on condition that STM did not sell competing machinery. STM wished to get out of the agreement (they could not make any money on sales) and argued that the agreement breached Article 81(1) [ex 85(1)].

The Commission agreed with STM, but the Court of Justice did not. The Court said that there was a two-stage process in order to determine an infringement of Article 81 [ex 85]. The first stage was to look at the purpose or intention of the agreement, by looking at the clauses of the agreement itself. If an *intention* to restrict competition was evident from that examination, the fact that the involvement of one of the participants had a negligible effect on competition was irrelevant. The agreement would breach Article 81 [ex 85].

If, however, the agreement did not indicate an intention, the second stage was to consider the consequence of the agreement. The Court set out the issues for consideration. They would include the nature of quantity of the products covered by the agreement, the position and size of the parties in the market of the producer and exclusive dealer. Whether the agreement is isolated or part of a network, the severity of the restrictions and the opportunities allowed or parallel import and export of the products. In *STM*, the Court held that the agreement did not contravene Article 81 [ex 85].

Within the EC

It would seem to be logical to suggest that Community law had no jurisdiction outside the boundaries of the Member States of the Community. However, this is not the case with European competition law. Competition law is founded on an *effects doctrine*, and if the effects of an agreement, wherever made, are felt within the Community then the agreements are within the scope of Article 81 [ex 85]. In the *Aniline Dye* case (see above) four of the parties were established outside the Community. As the effects of their concerted practices were felt within the Community the Court of Justice found them liable for infringements of Article 81(1) [ex 85(1)].

This issue was decided definitively in *Ahlstrom v Commission (Wood Pulp)* (89, 104, 114, 116, 117, 125–129/85). None of the wood pulp producers in this case was established in a Member State of the Community. Nevertheless, they supplied two-thirds of the wood pulp in the common market. The Court of Justice held that the undertakings had been in breach of Article 81(1) [ex 85(1)]. The key factor, according to the Court, was the place where the agreement or concerted practice was *implemented*.

The list of Agreements Likely to Breach Article 81(1) [ex 85(1)]

Article 81(1) [ex 85(1)] contains a list, paras (a)–(e) of the kinds of agreement which will be prohibited. This list is not exhaustive and provides no more than a guide to the sort of agreements that will fall foul of the prohibition. The examples include the following:

- price fixing;
- control of production markets or technical developments;
- exclusive distribution agreements;
- franchise agreements.

If they are found to be in breach of Article 81(1) [ex 85(1)] they are, by virtue of Article 81(2) [ex 85(2)], automatically void. This means that they cannot be enforced in law, or used as a defence before a national court. It should be remembered though, that even if an agreement is in breach of Article 81(1) [ex 85(1)] it may be granted exemption by the Commission under Article 81(3) [ex 85(3)].

Exemptions from Article 81(1) [ex 85(1)]

The main exemptions are set out in Article 81(3) [ex 85(3)] which provides that Article 81(1) [ex 85(1)] does not apply to any agreement or category of agreement between undertakings, or any decision or category of decisions by associations of undertakings which contribute to improving the production or distribution of goods or to promoting technical or economic progress, while allowing consumers a fair share of the resulting benefits, provided the agreement does not:

(a) impose on the undertaking concerned restrictions which are not indispensable to the attainment of these objectives;

(b) afford such undertakings the possibility of eliminating competition in respect of a substantial part of the products in question.

To obtain an individual exemption the party must apply to the Commission. The procedure is set out in Regulation 17/62L. Article 4(1) of the Regulation provides that full notification of the agreement must be given to the Commission. This is the only method by which exemption can be granted. By Article 19(1) of the Regulation, all parties to the agreement have the right to be heard, and any third party also has such a right if they can establish "sufficient interest". This could mean that a competitor, who might be affected by an agreement, could put their case to the Commission. The decision to grant exemption must be published in the Official Journal.

A careful reading of Article 81(3) [ex 85(3)] will indicate that there are four conditions to be satisfied before an exemption may be granted under Article 81(3) [ex 85(3)]; two of them are positive, two are negative. The two positive conditions are that an agreement must contribute to improving the production or distribution of goods or to promoting technical or economic progress and the agreement must allow consumers a fair share of the resulting benefit. The negative conditions are that there must be no unnecessary restrictions, and there must be no elimination of competition.

The conditions are linked and in each case, all must be satisfied, though in practice the first positive condition is regarded as the most important. If an exemption is granted it is for a specific period, conditions may be improved, and the Commission reserves the right to revoke the agreement.

The process of obtaining an individual exemption is necessarily a long one, given that the Commission must fully investigate and then give a fully reasoned decision. A time-scale of two–three years is not uncommon. To alleviate the problems this can cause the Commission has adopted two measures, one informal, the other formal.

The Commission has attempted to reserve formal individual decision for what it considers to be important cases, and has encouraged undertakings to consult them informally about agreements. In these informal dealings the Commission will meet with the parties to an agreement, and if satisfied, the Commission will issue a "comfort letter". This will state that in the opinion of the Commission, the agreement does not infringe Article 81(1) [ex 85(1)], or is of a type which falls within the exempt category. The file is then closed, although if circumstances change it may be reopened.

The "problem" with a comfort letter is that it does not have the legal status of a full decision issued after following the formal procedure. In *Lancome v ETOS (Perfume)* (99/79), the Court of Justice held that comfort letters are administrative letters outside of the framework of the Treaty, and do not bind national courts. Nor can they be invoked before the Court of Justice in an annulment procedure under Article 230 [ex 173] of the EC Treaty.

In attempting to grant exemptions, or to issue comfort letters, the Commission, in addition to the four conditions discussed above, will examine the application for exemption in the light of policy objectives in relation to agreements between undertakings. The Commission is more likely to grant exemptions, or issue comfort letters, to agreements that encourage the use of new technology, which results in economies of scale and better faster production methods. An examination of the case law of the Court of First Instance and the Court of Justice, and of Commission decisions, will show that price-fixing agreements, agreements limiting production or controlling markets, or which attempt to retain dominance in a national market, will be highly unlikely to secure exemption.

The formal process by which the Commission has avoided the necessity of a long involved investigation before issuing an individual exemption is the practice of issuing a "block exemption". This process came about because of the burden placed on the Commission by the large number of applications for individual exemptions. The delays caused obvious difficulties for business and the Commission has increasingly relied on its powers to issue block exemptions. A series of regulations has been issued in areas where agreements are generally beneficial rather than anti-competitive. The advantage of the block exemption process is that the undertakings can make their own assessment as to whether or not their agreement falls within a particular block exemption. Indeed, they can tailor the terms of their agreement so that their agreement matches the terms set out in the block exemption. If an agreement marches the terms of the block exemption there is no need for the agreement to be notified to the Commission. Block exemptions have been issued in the following categories:

(a) exclusive distribution;

(b) exclusive purchasing;

(c) specialisation;

(d) research and development;

(e) motor vehicle distribution;

(f) franchising.

Each block exemption contains its own individual rules, which must be satisfied in every respect. Each of the exemptions contains "white" clauses. These are clauses that are specifically permitted. There are also "black" clauses. These are clauses that are expressly forbidden because they would restrict or distort competition. Any agreement which contained a "black" clause would be outside the scope of a block agreement.

The whole area of block exemptions is under review by the Commission with a view to making the procedures more easily understood and more "user friendly".

ARTICLE 82 [EX 86]: A DOMINANT POSITION

Article 81 [ex 85], as has been seen, seeks to control the activities of independent undertakings which collude. Article 82 [ex 86] regulates the activities of undertakings in a dominant position and who seek to use that dominant position in an anti-competitive manner. The Article does not apply only to these organisations which have a monopoly position, but extends to undertakings which share an oligopolistic market with a small number of other companies.

Article 82 [ex 86] provides that:

"Any abuse by one or more undertaking of a dominant position within the common market or a substantial part of it shall be prohibited as incompatible with the common market in so far as it may affect trade between Member States."

This prohibition is followed by an illustrative list of abusive practices. There are three elements in Article 82 [ex 86]. They are:

    (i)   a dominant position;

   (ii)   an abuse of that position; and

  (iii)   the abuse must affect trade between Member States.

A Dominant Position

The dominant position must be within the common market or a substantial part of it. The classic definition of dominance was given by the Court of Justice in *United Brands v Commission* (27/76) as:

". . . a position of economic strength enjoyed by an undertaking which enables it to hinder the maintenance of effective competition on the relevant market by allowing it to behave to an appreciable extent independently of its competitors and customers and ultimately of consumers."

This definition has been repeated in a number of cases, and it was extended in *Hoffman La Roche* (85/76) as follows:

"Such a position does not preclude some competition . . . but enables the undertaking which profits by it, if not to determine, at least to have an appreciable effect on the conditions under which the competition will develop, and in any case to act largely in disregard of it so long as such conduct does not operate to its detriment."

In order to prove dominance it is necessary to examine the "relevant product market". On the one hand, the undertaking under investigation will want to define the market as widely as possible as this will reduce the opportunity for dominance. On the other hand, the Commission (who will prosecute the undertaking for an alleged abuse of a dominant position), will want to define the market as narrowly as possible, as this will make it easier to prove dominance.

This argument is well illustrated by the famous case of *United Brands v Commission* (22/76). United Brands were producers of bananas, which they marketed as "Chiquita" bananas. They held 40 per cent of the EC market in bananas. The Commission alleged that they had infringed Article 82 [ex 86] in a number of ways. United Brands argued that the proper comparison was not with other banana producers, but with the whole of the fresh soft-fruit trade. They argued that bananas competed with other fresh fruits in the shops, at prices which consumers would compare with other fruit before making a decision to buy, and that bananas were only one of a number of fruits chosen as a desert. The Commission argued that there was a particular demand for bananas that could not be met by other fruits. In particular, the banana had a special dietary role in the lives of the very young, the sick and the very old. It was the specific qualities of the banana that induced customer preference and these particular qualities could not be found in other fruits. The Court of Justice agreed with the Commission. It held that the relevant product market was bananas and not fruit generally. The Court said that the key test was "substitutability". The relevant product market turned on whether the banana could be:

"singled out by such special features distinguishing it from other fruits that is only to a limited extent interchangeable with them and is only exposed to their competition in a way that is hardly perceptible."

In *United Brands*, the Commission had carried out a great deal of research into the various markets, and was able to convince the Court of Justice. It had learnt its lesson in the first case it brought before the Court of Justice on Article 82 [ex 86]. In *Continental Can* (6/12) the Commission argued that the companies involved had a dominant position in the market for cans for meat, cans for fish and metal tops. It did not explain why these markets were separate from each other, or from the general market in cans and containers. In its judgment, the Court of Justice stressed the importance of defining the relevant product market. It was necessary to identify "the characteristics of the product in question by virtue of which they are particularly apt to satisfy an inelastic need and are only to a limited extent interchangeable with other products". The Court held that the Commission had failed to define the product market properly and the Commission's decision was quashed.

In *Continental Can* and *United Brands*, the Court focused on the importance of substitutability. The Court also indicated two types of substitutability. The first is demand-led substitutability, that is, the extent to which the consumer can obtain similar goods or acceptable substitutes. The second type is supply-side substitutability, that is, the ease with which other undertakings can supply goods or acceptable substitutes.

Demand-led substitutability tests are those in which products compete with each other from the point of view of the customer. This test is well illustrated in *United Brands*. But it can also apply in very narrow markets. In *Hugin Kassaregister* (22/78) the Commission held Hugin in breach of Article 82 [ex 86] for its refusal to supply spare parts to Liptons, a company which repaired Hugin cash registers. The Commission defined the relevant product market as consisting of spare parts for Hugin machines required by independent repairers. Hugin insisted that the relevant product market was the whole of the cash register market. The Court of Justice found that the spare parts were not interchangeable and held that the Commission's decision was the correct one.

In the more recent case of *RTE & ITP v Commission* (C-241/91 and C-242/91 P) the Court accepted that there was dominance in the narrow market of information on the content of BBC and Irish television programmes.

Supply-side substitutability is concerned about how easy or otherwise it is for a manufacturer to switch production from the product of another. If it is easy for one manufacturer to switch into the same product market as one of its competitors, then dominance in that product will be difficult to sustain. This was the issue in *Continental Can v Commission* (6/72) where the argument was about packaging containers and the scope of the market. In this case the Court of Justice stressed the crucial importance of defining the relevant product. The Commission had argued that the companies had a dominant position in the market for cans for meat and fish, and metal tops. It was unable to explain why these markets were separate from each other, or from the general market in cans and containers. Because of this, the Court quashed the decision of the Commission. The Court said that it was necessary to identify the "characteristics of the products in question by virtue of which they are particularly apt to satisfy an idealistic need and are only to a limited extent interchangeable with other products".

The Geographical Market

In addition to proving dominance in the relevant product market, it is necessary also to prove dominance in the relevant geographical market. This means more than showing a dominant position in a substantial part of the common market. What must also be taken into account is the economic importance of the area as defined together with such factors as the pattern and volume of production, and the habits of consumers in that area.

In *United Brands* (22/76) the Court of Justice held that consideration was required for the opportunities for competition "with reference to a clearly defined geographical area in which the products marketed and where the conditions are sufficiently homogenous for the effect of the economic power of the undertaking concerned to be able to be evaluated". In *United Brands,* the Court of Justice held that three of the (then nine) Member States could be excluded from the definition of the relevant geographical market. This was because those states, France, Italy and the United Kingdom, had special rules for the import and sale of bananas. The remaining six states had a free market in bananas and thus, could be defined as the relevant geographical market. The Court said that the six states formed "an area which is sufficiently homogenous to be considered in its entirety".

It has to be borne in mind that the geographical market is not necessarily identical to the physical size of the market. In *Suiker Unie* (40/73) the Court of Justice held that dominance of the sugar market in Belgium and Luxembourg was dominance of a substantial part of the commercial market.

Dominance in Fact

It is often difficult to assess dominance. To prove such a state, the Commission will need to produce a detailed economic analysis. There are a number of features to this analysis. The key factor will be the actual market share of the undertaking under interpretation. In *Hoffman-La Roche,* the market there held by Roche was more than 80 per cent and in *Continental Can,* the share of the German market was between 70 and 80 per cent. The Court regarded these high levels of market share as proof of dominance. But it is not only majority market share that will be indicative of dominance. In the *United Brands* case a relatively low market share of 40 per cent was held to be a dominant position. This was because of the fragmentation of the market by other competitors, the next biggest having only 15 per cent of the market.

The economic analysis conducted by the Commission will also take into account the financial and technical resources of the undertaking. In *Continental Can,* the Court was influenced by the ready access to international capital markets. A further important factor is the ability of the undertaking to control production and distribution. This was a significant factor in *United Brands,* where the undertaking owned the plantations, had its own shipping fleet and conducted its own marketing.

ABUSE OF DOMINANT POSITION

It should be noted that Article 82 [ex 86] does not prohibit dominance, but the abuse of that dominant position. Article 82 [ex 86] itself gives four specific examples of such abuse. They are:

(a) directly or indirectly imposing unfair purchase or selling prices or other unfair trading conditions;

(b) limiting production, markets or technical development to the prejudice of consumers;

(c) applying dissimilar conditions to equivalent transactions with other trading parties, thereby placing them at a competitive disadvantage;

(d) making the conclusion of contracts subject to acceptance by the other parties of supplementary obligations which, by their nature, or according to commercial usage, have no connection with the subject of such contracts.

The instances of abusive behaviour set out in Article 82 [ex 86] are only examples—they are not exhaustive. The Commission and the Court will attempt to prohibit any abuse that is either exploitative or anti-competitive. An exploitative abuse is one where the dominant undertaking takes advantage of its position by imposing unfair or harsh trading conditions. An anti-competitive abuse is one which seeks to reduce or eliminate the competition, or to prevent new competition entering the market. In *Continental Can*, the Court of Justice held that a takeover or a merger could amount to the abuse of a dominant position. The Court stated that "abuse may occur if an undertaking in a dominant position strengthens such a position . . . that the degree of dominance reached subsequently fetters competition".

Examples of Abuse

Unfair or discriminatory prices

An unfair price is one that bears no reasonable relationship to the economic value of the product. It is usual that such prices are excessively high as the result of pressure from a dominant supplier. Nevertheless, unfair low pricing can constitute an abuse. This type of predatory pricing by an undertaking seeks to increase its existing market position by squeezing potential competitors out of the market. The dominant firm lowers its prices (often below the base cost level) and the smaller firm, unable to follow, has to retreat from the market. As soon as this happens the dominant firm is now free to raise its prices to any level it wishes. Such a practice obviously restricts competition and is prohibited by Article 82 [ex 86]. The leading cost in this area is *AKZO Chemie* (C-62/86). Here, the Court held that to fix prices lower than average variable costs was unlawful if it was part of a scheme to undermine a competitor's position on the market.

Discriminatory pricing arises where different customers are charged different prices without objective justification. This might seem surprising, as local market conditions often lead to different prices for the same goods. This indeed, was the argument put forward by United Brands. The Court of Justice rejected this argument. It held that United Brands was not sufficiently connected to the local markets and that, in any event, it had also acted abusively by imposing restrictions on resale to its customers and had deliberately undersupplied other customers to prevent sales beyond the customer's own markets. This was regarded as a serious breach of Article 82 [ex 85].

Refusal to Supply

In *Commercial Solvents v Commission* (6–7/73), Commercial Solvents have been supplying a chemical to another firm, Zoja, who used the chemical to produce the drug ethambutol. Zoja was one of only three producers of ethambutol in the Community. Commercial

Solvents decided to manufacture ethambutol itself and refused to supply Zoja, who made a complaint to the Commission. The Court upheld the Commission's decision that Commercial Solvents had abused its dominant position. Another example of abuse arising out of the refusal to supply is the *Magill* case (C-241 & 242/911). Three television companies had printed their own separate guides to forthcoming programmes and used copyright protection to prevent third parties (such as Magill) entering the market. The Court of Justice held that the companies must make their listings available to any third party who requested them. A reasonable fee could be charged for this. The Court was influenced by what it saw as consumer demand for such a product.

Articles 81 and 82 [ex 85 and 86]: Enforcement and procedure

The powers and procedures of the Commission in enforcing competition law are set out in Council Regulation 17/62. The Regulation empowers the Commission to ensure that the Treaty is observed, to address to undertakings decisions and recommendations for the purposes of eliminating infringements of Articles 81 and 82 [ex 85 and 86], and if necessary, to levy fines. [It should be noted that Mergers are now covered by a separate Regulation, 4064/89—see below]. The important parts of the Regulation are as follows:

- Articles 2–8 deal with the issue of exemptions and negative clearance. Undertakings may notify the Commission of an action they propose to take and apply for negative clearance. Or, agreements between undertakings may be notified to the Commission (on Form A/B) in order to achieve individual exemption under Act 81(3) [ex 85(3)]. If the Commission agrees to an exemption, the parties to the agreement will not be subject to fines if the Court of Justice later holds that the agreement is unlawful. By virtue of Article 3, the Commission can, on its own initiative, or on a complaint by a Member State or an individual, investigate and take decisions requiring the undertakings concerned to bring the matter to an end.

- To relieve the heavy workload in this area the Commission has developed the semi-informal method of the block-exemption. Agreements covered by a block exemption need not be notified to the Commission provided no unnecessary terms are included. The issue of comfort letters by the Commission also saves time, although these are not legally binding.

- To balance the powers given to the Commission, Article 19(1) of the Regulation provides that, before taking a decision adverse to an undertaking, the Commission must allow the undertaking the right to be heard on matters to which the Commission has objected. By Article 19(2) other interested parties (*e.g.* a competitor) also have the right to be heard. By Article 19(3) the Commission must publish a summary of the application of the undertaking, and invite interested parties to submit comments.

Powers of the Commission to Investigate

Regulation 17/62 gives the Commission extensive powers of investigation and detection necessary for its enforcement duties. By Article 11 the Commission is able to make an informal request for information. If this informal request is unsuccessful the Commission may invoke the formal procedure provided for in Article 11. This imposes a duty on governments and competent authorities of Members States to co-operate with the Commission in investigations and to comply with requests for information. (The Commission must state the purpose for which the information is needed and the possible fines for non-compliance.)

The powers of investigations available to the Commission are set out in Article 14. The Commission can examine the books and records of an undertaking, and take copies of such books and records. They can ask for "on the spot" explanations and can enter the land, premises and vehicles of undertakings. Prior warning of an investigation must be given to Member States, but this is not necessary for individual undertakings. Indeed, any prior notification might prejudice the success of the Commission in conducting its investigation. In *National Panasonic* (136/79) the Commission gave no advance warning of a "dawn raid", but the Court rejected Panasonic's claim that prior notice should have been given and held that the Commission was entitled to carry out such investigations as are necessary to discover any breaches of Articles 81 or 82 [ex 85 or 86].

In another dawn raid, in *Hoechst v Commission* (46/87–227/88) the chemical firm Hoechst refused to allow Commission officials onto their premises on the grounds that the officials did not have a valid German search-warrant. The Court of Justice held that a decision by the Commission under Article 14 was sufficient on its own for the Commission to gain access. A refusal to admit Commission officials has two consequences. The first is that the national authorities can be called on the assist; they are under a duty to do so. The second consequence is that a refusal to allow in officials will give rise to financial penalties. In *Hoechst*, Commission officials had waited for fifty-five days before it eventually achieved access. Hoechst was fined 1,000 ECU (the forerunner to the Euro) for each of those days. In *Hoechst*, the Court of Justice held that the right to enter premises related only to premises of the undertaking and not to the premises of individuals.

When the Commission starts its investigation, they must give the undertaking concerned an opportunity of being heard on the matters raised in the Commission complaint. This right to be heard must also be extended to third parties, provided they can establish a sufficient interest. In *Hoffman La Roche* (85/76) the Court of Justice ruled that undertakings must be given "the opportunity during the administrative procedure to make known their views on the truth and relevance of the facts and circumstances alleged and on the documents used by the Commission to support its claim that there has been an infringement".

In the investigation of alleged infringements of competition law the Commission is, from time to time, bound to come across information which is considered to be confidential or to be a business secret. By Article 19 of Regulation 17/62 the Commission and Court is obliged to have regard to the "legitimate interests of undertakings in the protection of their business secrets". In *AKZO*, the Court held it was up to the Commission, subject to review by the Court to decide whether a document contains business secrets. If it did contain such secrets, its contents must not be divulged. Undertakings may also seek to prevent the Commission examining documents on the grounds that they are privileged as between a client and lawyers. In cases such as this the Court has to balance conflicting needs; effective enforcement against the rights of the defence. The right of access to documents is now set out in Article 255 of the Treaty. The right of access is not absolute. It is subject to "general principles and limits on grounds of public or private interest".

In *AM & S v Commission* (155/79) the Court held that professional privilege was a partial right. It did extend to documents relating to rights of defence that had been submitted by independent lawyers. It is hard to see now the Court of Justice could have come to a different conclusion, as this right of legal privilege exists in all the Member States. However, it further held that this right did not extend to in-house legal advice.

An interesting case is *Adams v Commission* (145/83). Mr Adams was employed by Hoffman-La Roche in Switzerland. He secretly passed company documents to the Commission, which showed that the company was breaching Article 82 [ex 86]. Mr Adams had requested confidentiality from the Commission. He then left Hoffman-La Roche and set up a business in Italy. However, when the Commission has finished with the documents they returned them to Hoffman-La Roche, who were then able to identify Mr Adams as the whistle-blower. When Mr Adams next visited Italy he was arrested and charged with industrial espionage, his wife committed suicide, he was convicted and he lost his business in Italy because of a loss in his credit rating. He was successful in an action for damages under Article 288 [ex 215] against the Commission, but his award was reduced by half because of his contributory negligence. He had not told the Commission that he could be identified from the documents, and he had returned to Switzerland from the safety of Italy.

Penalties

By virtue of Article 15 of Regulation 17/62 the Commission may impose fines for infringement of Articles 81 and 82 [ex 85 and 86] which are intentional or due to negligence, ranging from 1,000 ECU to 1,000,000 ECU, or 10 per cent of an undertaking's turnover, whichever is the greater. A number of factors will be taken into account in deciding the level of the fine. These include the duration and gravity of the infringement, the economic importance of the parties (and their behaviour) and the short of the relevant product market, whether the infringement is deliberate and the amount of profit from the illegal activities. All fines imposed by the Commission are subject to appeal to the Court of First Instance and ultimately to the Court of Justice.

The Commission has imposed heavy fines on undertakings for clear breaches of the competition rules. The Commission can impose a fine on one undertaking so that it will act as a deterrent to others. It did this in *Musique Diffusion Française v Commission* (100–103/80), although in this case the Court of Justice reduced the fine because the Commission had not been completely accurate in some of its assessments. The largest fine on a single firm is the 75 million ECU imposed on Tetra Pak for a range of abusive practices prohibited by Article 82 [ex 86]. When Tetra Pak appealed to the Court of First Instance in *Tetra Pak v Commission* (T-83/91) the Court pointed out that the fine only amounted to 2.2 per cent of the firm's total turnover. The highest aggregate fine imposed on a group of undertakings is 248 million ECU. This was levied on over thirty cement manufacturers.

The Relationship between Articles 81 and 82 [ex 85 and 86]—Mergers

Originally, the Commission was of the opinion that Article 81 [ex 85] would not apply to mergers or acquisitions; or concentrations as they are called in the Community. So, if competition was distorted by a merger or concentration of companies, it was Article 82 [ex 86] that would be appropriate measure to deal with it. The issue arose in *Continental Can* (6/72) where the Commission was faced with a series of take-overs and mergers in European companies by Continental Can. The Commission invoked Article 82 [ex 86] on the grounds that Continental Can had abused its dominant position. The Court of Justice found against the Commission, but on the grounds that it had failed to conduct a sufficiently thorough analysis of the relevant product market. However, the Court also said that the Commission had restricted itself by refusing to consider Article 81 [ex 85]. In the view of the Court, Articles 81 and 82 [ex 85 and 86] sought to achieve the same aim although on different levels and therefore the two Articles cannot be interpreted in such a way that they contradict each other.

The Court of Justice held that Article 81 [ex 85] could apply to concentrations in *BAT and Reynolds v Commission* (142 & 156/84). This case concerned a complex series of share cross-holding between various tobacco companies. The Commission had decided that the arrangements did not infringe either Article 81 or 82 [ex 85 or 86], but two competitor companies objected to the decision. The Court considered Article 81 [ex 85] and agreed that this Article could apply if the investing company could obtain legal or *de facto* control of the commercial conduct of the other company. When it considered Article 82 [ex 86] it agreed with the Commission that no anti-competitive object or effect had been established, and therefore Article 82 [ex 86] did not apply either.

This complicated state of affairs was unsatisfactory. Neither Article 81 nor 82 [ex 85 or 86] had been passed with mergers or concentrations in mind, and it was obvious that special legislation was required to address the special problems in this area. Indeed, the Commission had held this view for some time and shortly after the *Continental Can* case they had put forward a proposal for a Regulation on merger control. However, it took 16 years for the Council to adopt Regulation 4064/89 on the control of concentrations between undertakings. This came into force on September 21, 1990 and now provides the legal foundations for Community policy in this area.

The Regulations acknowledge the principle of subsidiarity in that above certain levels the Commission will investigate mergers (or concentrations), and if the merger is below the levels as set out in the Regulations the merger will remain a matter for national competition authorities. There is some tension between the Commission who wish to lower the limits and so extend its competence, and national authorities who do not wish to see the principle of subsidiarity eroded further.

The levels set by the Regulation which require notification to the Commission are as follows:

(a) the undertakings concerned have a combined world-wide turnover exceeding 5,000 million ECU;

(b) at least two of the undertakings have an EC-wide turnover of at least 250 million ECU; provided that each of the parties does not derive two-thirds of its business in the EC in a single Member State.

As soon as a proposed merger has been notified to the Commission the undertakings concerned must suspend activity for three weeks. During this time the Commission will investigate the proposal and will either declare it compatible with the aims of the Community, or will initiate proceedings to prevent the merger. The Commission then has four months in which to issue a decision. The Commission has to judge whether a merger would significantly impede effective competition in the common market as a whole or in a substantial part of it. In making this appraisal the Commission will take into account the structure of the markets concerned, the market position of the parties, actual and potential competition (both inside and outside the EC), freedom of choice for third parties, barriers to entry, the interests of consumers, and technical and economic progress.

The Commission has allowed all but one of the proposed mergers. It did not agree with the proposed merger between Aerospatiale (a French firm), and de Haviland (a UK firm), both aircraft manufacturers. The reason given by the Commission for the prohibition was that because both companies had substantial market share, there was a distinct possibility that a combined company would use its economic strength to dominate the market. This is a situation the Commission seeks to avoid, but there is no doubt that the Commission must tread carefully, as this is one particular area where politics and the perceived economic needs of companies are often in conflict.

Most of the Member States have their own domestic law to control mergers. It would be counter productive, and time consuming, if both domestic authorities and the Commission were to investigate a proposed merger. In order to avoid this, the Regulation introduced the concept of "one-stop control". This means that if the proposed merger comes within the terms that make it necessary to report it to the Commission, then the Commission alone will carry out the investigation. The national authorities will not be involved.

But there are safeguards in both directions. Article 22(3) of Regulation 4064 provides that a Member State can ask the Commission to investigate a merger below the threshold. Alternatively, by Article 9, the Commission can refer a proposed merger to a Member State. This might happen if a Member State notifies the Commission that a proposed merger threatens to create or strengthen a dominant position, which would impede competition in that Member State. However, the Commission does not seem to favour this approach, as it has only made two referrals to national authorities. One of these was the proposed merger between two brick manufacturers, Tarmac and Streetly. The merger would have a considerable impact on the UK market, but little impact on the rest of the Community. In these circumstances it was appropriate for the United Kingdom authorities to investigate the matter. In the event, the UK authorities decided that an investigation was not necessary.

Reform of Competition Law

There is little doubt that the heavily centralised authorisation system administered by the Commission was necessary and has proved to be very effective for the establishment of a "culture of competition" in Europe. In the early years of the Community, competition policy was not widely known in many of the Member States. When one of the main purposes of the Community was the integration of national markets, centralised enforcement of Community competition rules by the Commission was the only appropriate system. It enabled the Commission to establish the uniform application of Articles 81 and 82 [ex 85 and 86] throughout the Community and it created a body of rules, which are now accepted by the Member States and by industry.

The Commission now believes that this system, which has worked so well, is no longer appropriate for a Community with 15 (soon to be 25) Member States. In 1999 the Commission proposed reforms to the system in a White Paper on Modernisation of the Rules Implementing Articles 85 and 86 (now 81 and 82) of the Treaty.

Because national competition authorities (NCAs) and national courts had no power to apply Article 81(3) [ex 85(3)] all requests for exemptions had to go to the Commission. Efforts to promote decentralised application of Community competition laws have suffered because of the need to obtain Commission clearance. As a result of the huge amount of work heaped on the Commission the rigorous enforcement of competition law has suffered.

In the White Paper, the Commission noted that it must devote its attention to the most important cases where it can operate more efficiently than national bodies. To this end it has already adopted various measures such as the *de minimis* Notice for Agreements of Minor Importance and block exemption regulations. The Commission has come to the conclusion that it must adapt the present system so as to relieve companies from unnecessary bureaucracy, to allow the Commission to become more active in pursuit of serious competition infringements and to increase and stimulate enforcement at national level.

The proposed reform involves the abolition of the notification and exemption system and its replacement by a Council regulation, which would render the exemption rule of Article 81(3) [ex 85(3)] directly applicable without the prior decision of the Commission. Therefore, Article 81 can be applied by the Commission or by NCAs or by national courts. This will have the effect of paving the way for a decentralised application of Community competition laws by NCAs and courts. This will eliminate unnecessary bureaucracy and compliance costs for industry and would stimulate the application of Community competition rules by national authorities.

When the reforms go ahead (in 2004) there will be a concurrent jurisdiction of the Commission, NCAs and national courts. The Commission will retain the function of ensuring the coherent application of the rules throughout the Community. The Commission will reserve the power to remove a case from the jurisdiction of the NCAs and to deal with the case itself if there was a risk of divergent policy. There is also a clear obligation for national courts to avoid conflicts with Commission decision and with judgments of the Court of First Instance and the Court of Justice.

These are far-reaching proposals and developments as they unfold should be followed carefully.

13. SOCIAL POLICY

INTRODUCTION

The Treaty of Rome was essentially an economic treaty. It would be a mistake to believe that the few statements on social policy had been placed in the Treaty for altruistic reasons. What few provisions there where on social policy had been incorporated into the Treaty, mainly on the insistence of France, who already had comprehensive national social policy provisions, and did not wish to be at a competitive disadvantage against the other Member States. The statements on social policy are set out in the Preamble to the Treaty:

"*Resolved* to ensure the economic and social progress of their countries by common action . . .

Affirming as the essential objective of their efforts the constant improvement of the living and working conditions of their peoples."

Article 2 of the EC Treaty stated that one of the objectives of the Community was to include an "accelerated standard of living." This has now been amended to read "the raising of the standard of living and the quality of life." But essentially the Treaty was conceived in economic terms.

To look at social policy in particular, one should start with what is known as the harmonisation provision. This is covered by Article 94 [ex 100] which provides for the approximation of measures as directly affect the establishment or functioning of the common market. Measures based on Article 94 [ex 100] require unanimity in the Council for adoption. It is not surprising therefore that not much progress was made in this area. Progress was achieved by the addition of Article 95 [ex 100a], which required a qualified majority vote in the Council. Article 308 [ex 235] can also be used to "attain . . . one of the objectives of the Community". This is a "fail-safe" provision in that it allows action to be taken if the Treaty has not provided the necessary powers in other Articles. Unanimity in the Council is required.

Although not strictly social policy provisions, the student should be aware of the social ramifications arising out of the provisions for the free movement of workers (Articles 39–42 [ex 48–51]), freedom of establishment (Articles 43–48 [ex 52–58]), and freedom to provide services (Articles 49–55 [ex 59–66]). These are discussed in the relevant chapters.

The third and major area relates to actual social policy. This is covered by Articles 136–145 [ex 117–122] and Article 158 [ex 130a]. Article 136 [ex 117] states that:

"The Community and the Member States . . . shall have as their objectives the promotion of employment, improved living and working conditions, so as to make possible their harmonisation."

Article 140 [ex 118] states:

". . . the Commission shall encourage cooperation between the Member States and facilitate the coordination of their action in all social policy fields particularly in matters relating to (*inter alia*) employment and working conditions."

For both Article 136 [ex 117] and Article 137 [ex118] it is envisaged that the Commission shall make studies, deliver opinions and consult with Member States There is no provision for legislation. Under Article 137 [ex 118] Member States are required to pay particular attention to encouraging improvements in the "working environment", in the health and safety of workers, and to attempt to harmonise conditions in these areas. There are powers to legislate in this area by means of qualified majority voting. Article 139 [ex 118b] requires the Commission to endeavour to develop the dialogue between management and labour at European level.

The most important of the social policy provisions is Article 141 [ex 141 [ex 119]] (see below). This provides that Member

States shall maintain the application of the principle that men and women should receive equal pay for equal work.

Article 158 [ex 130a], which sets out provisions for economic and social cohesion, underwent considerable amendment in both the SEA and TEU. The relevant provisions are now set out in Articles 158–176 [ex 130a–t] (Article 157 [ex 130] itself covers competitiveness in industry). The main features of these Articles are the promotion of harmonious development and the reduction of economic and social disparities in the regions. Article 174 [ex 130r] is of interest because it provides that action on the environment is now a Community objective. Such action shall aim to preserve, protect and improve the quality of the environment, contribute towards protecting human health and ensure a prudent and rational utilisation of natural resources.

The early years in the life of the Community saw most of the efforts in the economic sphere. This is understandable, but the economic emphasis of the Community has also coloured its approach to social policy. In Community terms "social policy" is largely directed to the employment sphere, the relationship between management and worker. "Social policy" does not have, in Community terms, the wide remit that might be expected by a UK reader. It does not, for example, cover housing policy; nor, until recently, did it cover state social security systems. This narrowness of the remit of Community social policy should become evident throughout the remainder of this chapter.

It was not until the early 1970s that real thought was given to social policy beyond its economic parameters. The first Social Action Programme was published in 1974. The objectives of the programme were ambitious; full and better employment, and the improvement of living and working conditions. The reality was more limited! The measures passed under the programme included the Collective Redundancies Directive 75/120 and the Transfer of Undertakings Directive 77/187, which, although giving rights in a few specific areas, came nowhere near the objective as set out in the programme for "full and better employment". In terms of worker participation, the programme yielded only limited rights of information and consultation. The programme was also responsible for some health and safety measures.

The recessions of the mid-1970s and early-1980s dampened any enthusiasm Member States may have had for achieving agreement on social policy. During this period there was a movement towards a more deregulated labour market, particularly in the United Kingdom. This often led to conflict between the Council who now favoured "flexibility" in labour relations, and the Commission, who persisted in proposing measures that would regulate the conduct of the market particularly with regard to workers in "weak" positions.

A change of direction was signalled by the Single European Act 1986 (SEA). Much credit is due to Jacques Delors, then President of the Commission, who advocated a link between the completion of the internal market and the development of social policy. The SEA itself provided some new provisions in social policy (see below), but it was the signing of a new Action Programme that provided the most impetus. This Action Programme was mainly Council inspired, so it did not propose much to disturb the new flexibility of the market. It did however lead to the European Parliament and the Commission producing their own reports. This in turn led to a Commission paper entitled "The Social Dimension of the Internal Market" and out of this came the Community Charter on the Fundamental Rights of Workers, which was adopted in December 1979. It is commonly known as the Social Charter. The final draft of the Charter, even though it had been watered down significantly from the initial draft, was not acceptable to the United Kingdom, and the United Kingdom refused to adopt the declarations. The Social Charter was therefore signed by eleven of the (then) Member States.

The Social Charter itself was only persuasive and was not subject to the jurisdiction of the Court of Justice. However, the implementing directives are binding and have been adopted under a number of different Treaty provisions. These will be discussed below. The Social Charter sets out 12 themes, or rights. They are:

(1) free movement of workers based on the principle of equal treatment in access to employment;

(2) employment and remuneration based on the principle of fairness;

(3) improvement of living and working conditions;

(4) social protection based on the law and practices proper to each Member State;

(5) freedom of association and collective bargaining;

(6) vocational training;

(7) equal treatment of men and women;

(8) information, consultation and participation of workers;

(9) protection of health and safety at the workplace;

(10) protection of children and adolescents;

(11) protection of elderly persons;

(12) protection of the disabled.

Shortly after the Social Charter, the Commission published the Action Programme to implement the Social Charter. The Action Programme reviewed actions already undertaken, and then proposed 47 new proposals, some of them for implementation at national level (on the subsidiary principle), and about 28 that required action at Community level. To date progress has been limited, with progress confined to those familiar areas of Community activity. One measure was a Directive (92/56) which amended the Collective Redundancies Directive 75/129. This amendment reflects the experience of the earlier Directive, and attempts to address the transnational nature of modern companies.

A further measure, which was the subject of controversy in the United Kingdom, was the Working Time Directive (93/104). This Directive provides for a maximum period of a 48-hour week, 11 consecutive hours of work out of 24 hours, a minimum of four weeks paid holidays and the maximum of 8 hours employment for higher workers. This directive was the subject of much controversy in the United Kingdom because the legal base of the directive is Article 137 [ex 118], which allows for health and safety measures to be implemented by qualified majority. The United Kingdom argued that the Directive was a measure harmonising employment conditions, which should have been implemented under Article 94 [ex 100] or Article 308 [ex 235], both of which require unanimity. In *UK v Council* (C-84/94), the United Kingdom unsuccessfully challenged this legal base.

A third measure was the Pregnancy and Maternity Directive (92/85). This Directive provides for a uniform level of social protection for pregnant and breast feeding workers. It provides for minimum levels of maternity leave and for the elimination of health risks at work. Under Article 10 of the Directive, a pregnant worker, either full or part-time, may not be dismissed.

This change of direction towards a more coherent social policy was continued in the Treaty on European Union (Maastricht). The draft treaty contained a social chapter which extended, or introduced, rights for workers. It also proposed changes in the voting procedures in the Council. However, in the treaty negotiations the United Kingdom was totally opposed to the increase in powers to the Community in this area. It was particularly opposed to the extension of qualified majority voting to the measure of harmonisation, as this would remove the effective veto that the United Kingdom had. As no progress was possible in the negotiations because of United Kingdom intransigence in this area, a compromise was reached. The social chapter was removed from the TEU, but was contained in a Social Policy Protocol to the Treaty signed by (the then) eleven Member States but excluding the United Kingdom. This is commonly known as the Social Chapter. The Protocol notes the agreement between the 11 Member States to build on the *acquis communautaire* in social policy and authorises the 11 Member States to use the Community institutions for this purpose. Also attached to the protocol is an agreement between the 11 Member States to "implement the 1969 Social Charter".

When any measures were proposed under the Social Chapter, the United Kingdom would take no part in the discussions, nor would it vote. Any measures taken under the Social Chapter would not have effect in the United Kingdom.

The new social policy Articles set out a series of objectives. There are:

(i)   improved living and working conditions;

(ii) improved living and working conditions;

(iii) proper social protection;

(iv) dialogue between management and labour;

(v)   the development of human resources with a view to lasting high employment;

(v)   the combating of social exclusion.

Although the Social Chapter provided for legislation to have effect in the eleven of the (then) 12 Member States, it was used only sparingly. This was because many social policy measures could be adopted under the EC Treaty and this was preferred whenever possible as the United Kingdom would be included. The use of Treaty provisions to adopt social policy measures was an attempt to prevent a "two-speed" Europe and the prospect of social dumping. If, under the Social Chapter, the United Kingdom was not affected by some new employment measure, the United Kingdom would be more attractive to employers, who could relocate to the United Kingdom with its low labour costs and regulations, but with the benefit of being part of the internal market.

In fact, only two Directives were adopted under the arrangements of the Social Chapter. They were the European Works Council Directive (94/45) and the Parental Leave Directive (96/34). The aim of the former is to necessitate the establishment of works councils so as to improve information and consultation procedures for employees in respect of decisions made by management. The Parental Leave Directive allows parents to take three months unpaid leave for child-care purposes. This entitlement is for any time between birth up to the age of eight. Employees cannot be dismissed for exercising this right and they are entitled to return to the same or equivalent job at the end of the parental leave.

This is now of academic interest. In May 1997, the United Kingdom officially confirmed that it intended to end its opt-out of the Social Protocol and Social Chapter. The Social Chapter has now been incorporated into the main body of the Treaty and is set out in Articles 136–145 [ex 117–120].

Social policy under the Treaty of Amsterdam

The Treaty of Amsterdam, among other aims, took the opportunity to amend the Treaty of Rome and the Treaty on European Union. Although many parties were frustrated that the new treaty did not go far enough in its review of the EC, there were some important developments in the area of social policy. In an attempt to summarise the above discussion and to point the way forward, these developments are mow sketched out.

The main areas of reform in social policy are as follows:

(a) the introduction into the Treaty of a specific chapter on employment;

(b) the introduction of a new non-discrimination clause; and

(c) the incorporation of the Social Chapter into the main body of the Treaty (discussed above).

The higher profile now being given to social rights is evidenced by the addition of a new paragraph to the preamble to the Treaty on European Union. This paragraph confirms that the Member States will confirm their attachment to the "fundamental social rights as defined in the European Social Charter . . . and in the 1989 Community Charter of Fundamental Social Rights of Workers". This means that the respect for social rights is accepted as one of the general principles underlying the Community.

The new non-discrimination clause is now Article 13 [ex 6a], which states that Member States will take action to "combat discrimination based on sex, racial or ethnic origin, religion or belief, disability, age or sexual orientation". This is obviously more sweeping than the original non-discrimination provisions of the Treaty, which merely prohibit discrimination on the grounds of nationality. Although the new Article is to be welcomed, any action under the Article will be limited given that any initiative based on this Article would be subject to unanimity in the Council.

Also, Article 2 EC, which sets out explicit aims of the Community, has the addition of the promotion of "equality between men and women".

The most important innovation in social policy is the insertion into the Treaty of a new Chapter specifically relating to employment. First there is an amendment to Article 2 [ex B] of the TEU which now stated that one of the objectives of the Union is "a high level of employment". In addition, Article 3(i) of the Treaty states that an aim of the Community is "the promotion of co-ordination between employment policies of the Member States with a view to enhancing their effectiveness by developing a co-ordinated strategy for employment".

The new Chapter (or Title) on Employment is found in Title VIII [ex VIa] of the Treaty. This Title covers Articles 125–130. The student is recommended to read the individual aims of these relevant Articles. The new employment chapter follows the wishes of the Commission to ensure better co-ordination of employment strategies between Member States. Nevertheless it remains something of a compromise between the differing views of the Member States and the need to remove the fear that the Community would be given real power to make employment policy.

EQUAL PAY

Under Article 141 [ex 141 [ex 119]] of the Treaty each Member State is required to maintain the principle that men and women should receive equal pay for equal work. The Article states:

"Each Member State shall ensure that the principle of equal pay for male and female workers for equal work or work of equal value is applied. For the purposes of this Article, 'pay' means the ordinary basic or minimum wage or salary or any other consideration whether in cash or in kind which the worker receives, directly or indirectly, in respect of his employment from his employer."

Equal pay without discrimination based on sex means:

(a) that pay for some work at piece rates shall be calculated on the basis of the same unit of measurement;

(b) that pay for the same work at time rates shall be the same for the same job.

It should not be thought that this noble social ambition was entirely altruistic. Certainly, there was a social objective in the improvement of living and working conditions of Community workers. Also, equal pay had long been recognised as an international labour law standard. However, the major influence for the insertion of Article 141 [ex 119] in the Treaty was an economic one. The reason was to avoid a competitive disadvantage to those states that already had equal pay legislation. The main actor was France who insisted on Community involvement because it already had equal pay legislation, particularly in the textile industry. By inserting Article 141 [ex 119] into the Treaty, France could be sure that labour costs in the Member States would be subject to the same factors. Article 141 [ex 119] did not produce a rush by Member States to adhere to their obligations to equalise pay between men and women. Neither did the Commission do much to take any enforcement action against the Member States. It took the action of a determined woman who, by reason of Article 234 [ex 177] references took three cases to the Court of Justice in an attempt to establish the right to equality.

Ms Gabrielle Defrenne was an air hostess with the Belgium airline SABENA. Her contact required her to retire at 40 (after that age her looks would deteriorate!), whereas male cabin crew could continue working to normal retirement age. She also discovered that she was paid less than her male colleagues were and that she would receive a smaller state pension than men did. It was over the state scheme that she brought her first action. In *Defrenne v Belgium (No.1) (80/70)*, the Belgium court addressed three questions to the Court of Justice.

(1)   Does the retirement pension granted under the terms of the social security scheme financed by contributions from workers, employers and the state subsidy, constitute a consideration which the workers receives indirectly in respect of his employment from his employer?

(2)   Can the rules establish a different age limit for men and women crew members in civil aviation?

(3)   Do air hostesses and stewards in civil aviation do the same work?

The Court of Justice was able to ignore the second and third questions since it adopted a restrictive approach in its answer to the first question. It said:

"A retirement pension established within the framework of a social security scheme laid down by legislation does not constitute consideration which the worker receives indirectly in respect of his employment from his employer within the meaning of the second paragraph of Article 141 [ex 119] (now 141) of the EEC Treaty."

In other words, state social security schemes, including the state pension scheme, were outside the scope of Article 141[ex 119] and discriminatory treatment was lawful. This judgment caused problems on issues relating to the relationship between contractual and social security benefits, particularly in the United Kingdom (see below).

Ms Defrenne was not deterred by this setback, and in the second case, she brought an action against her employer. In *Defrenne v SABENA (Defrenne No.2)* (43/75), she claimed equal pay with her male colleagues. This time the Court of Justice responded in an ambitious way. First, it said that:

"Article 119 (now 141) also forms part of the social objectives of the Community, which is not merely an economic union, but is at the same time intended, by common action, to ensure social progress and seek the constant improvement of the living and working conditions of their peoples, as is emphasised by the Preamble to the Treaty . . . This double aim, which is at once economic and social, shows that the principle of equal pay forms part of the foundations of the community".

The Court also ruled that the provisions of Article 141 [ex 119] were sufficiently clear and precise to have direct effect, and this would be both vertical and horizontal. In bowing to the submissions of the United Kingdom and Ireland that back dating equal pay claims would cause financial hardship, the Court of Justice held that Article 141 [ex 119] could not be ruled on to support retrospective claims before the date of the judgment, *i.e.* May 8, 1976.

In *Defrenne v SABENA (Defrenne No.3)* (147/77), Ms Defrenne, as in her first case, was again unsuccessful. On this occasion she sought to challenge the different retirement age for male and female employees in the aviation industry. The issue was whether a "working conditions" relating to retirement fell within the direct effect of Article 141 [ex 119]. The Court of Justice held that it did not and this matter was left to national and not Community competence. (The Equal Treatment Directive 76/207 now deals with the issue of retirement ages.) However, in *Defrenne No.3*, the Court repeated its view that:

". . . respect for fundamental personal rights is one of the general principles of Community law, the observance of which it has a duty to ensure. There can be no doubt that the elimination of discrimination based on sex forms part of those fundamental human rights."

Although Article 141 [ex 119] is the only specific mention of equal treatment in the Treaty, it has become increasingly important as a principle going far beyond equal pay, and is now the fundamental social principle of the Treaty. The initial reasons for the place of Article 141 [ex 119] in the Treaty may have been economic, but it has developed as a powerful tool in the hands of the Commission who have issued directives in this area. More particularly, it has been used by the Court of Justice who, in a series of wide ranging judgments has extended the scope and influence of Article 141 [ex 119] far beyond anything the founders of the Treaty could have envisaged. The fact that Article 141 [ex 119] is directly effective has meant that individuals have been able to pursue claims before their national courts. They have done so with vigour.

In addition to Article 141 [ex 119], the following directives have been adopted:

    (a)   Directive 75/117, Equal Pay Directive;

    (b)   Directive 76/207, Equal Treatment Directive;

    (c)   Directive 79/7, Social Security Directive;

    (d)   Directive 86/378, Equal Treatment in Occupational Social Security;

    (e)   Directive 86/613, Equal Treatment of the Self-Employed.

These Directives will be examined in their context below.

The Meaning of Pay

As was seen at the start of this Chapter, Article 141 [ex 119] provides that pay is much more than a mere wage or salary. The Court of Justice has adopted a liberal interpretation to the question of what constitutes pay. One reason for this is to put as much as possible within Article 141 [ex 119] so that the equal pay provisions can be used against private employers on the basis of horizontal direct effect. Another reason is that if the Court only included basic salary, it would be possible for unscrupulous employers to circumvent the Article by providing non-cash perks, such as company cars. As the following discussion shows the Court has found most employment based benefits to be pay.

Supplementary Payments

In *Worringham v Lloyds Bank* (69/80), the bank operated two pension schemes: one for male employees which required a contribution of 5 per cent from employees; and one for female employees which was non-contributory. In order not to infringe the Equal Pay Act 1970 male employees were paid a supplement of 5 per cent of their gross pay. The employee did not receive this money; it was deducted directly from the salary and paid directly into the pension fund. On a complaint from female workers, the Court of Justice held that the supplementary payments were pay. They came to this conclusion for two reasons. First, if a male employee left the scheme before pension age he would be entitled to a reimbursement of those sums; and second, the contribution was included in gross salary for the purposes of calculating certain benefits and social advantages such as redundancy payments and unemployment benefits. Thus the supplements were a payment received directly as a result of the employment and the discriminatory consequences brought them within the ambit of Article 141 [ex 119].

Sick Pay

In *Rinner-Kuhn* (171/88), a part-time cleaner challenged German legislation permitting employers to exclude from sick pay those working less than 10 hours a week. Most of the part-time workers were female. The Court of Justice held that national legislation which permitted employers to differentiate between two groups of workers, one of which was mainly female, infringed Article 141 [ex 119].

Non-Pay Benefits

In *Garland v BREL* (12/81), the Court of Justice rejected the idea that Article 141 [ex 119] only applied to contractual benefits. The case concerned the entitlement to free fail travel given to employees of British Rail, and their families. When the employee retired, the families of female employees lost these concessions, while families of male employees continued to enjoy the concessions. The Court of Justice held that such benefits, available even after the end of employment, were still caught by Article 141 [ex 119]. This was because they had been granted as a result of the employment relationship.

The Problem of Pensions

It is clear from *Defrenne No.1* (80/70) that contributions paid into a statutory social security scheme are not pay within the meaning of Article 141 [ex 119]. This was confirmed by the Court of Justice in *Barber v GRE* (262/88), a case of great importance in the area of occupational pension schemes. However, before considering *Barber*, the case of *Bilka Kaufhaus v Weber Von Hartz* (170/84) must be discussed. This case concerned the relationship of the state pension scheme to private pensions, particularly those private pension schemes which were supplementary to, or in replacement of the state scheme. Although this case has German, it was of great significance to the United Kingdom, where private occupational pension schemes can be used to replace, or contract-out of the State Earnings Related Pension Scheme (SERPS). The facts of the case involved a pension scheme set up in accordance with German law, but originating in a collective agreement and incorporated into the contract of employment. The occupational pension *supplemented* the state pensions scheme and was financed solely by employer contributions. The Court of Justice held that the scheme fell within Article 141 [ex 119]. The Court stressed that the supplementary nature of the scheme and its relationship to the employment in question was more important than social policy. The Court said:

"The contractual, and not the statutory, origin of the disputed scheme is confirmed by the fact that the scheme and its rules are considered to form an integral part of the contracts of employment between Bilka and its employees."

The Court of Justice returned to the question of pensions in *Barber*. Mr Douglas Henry Barber was a member of a pension scheme set up by the Guardian Royal Exchange (GRE). The Scheme was non-contributory and "contracted-out" of SERPS. Under the scheme, the normal pensionable age for women was 57, and for men, 62 years. The terms of the scheme provided for an immediate pension to be payable if an employee retired in the 10 years before normal pensionable age. Mr Barber was made redundant at the age of 52 and the terms of his contract of employment provided that in the event of redundancy, a male member of the pension fund was entitled to an immediate pension at age 55 and women at age 50. Mr Barber was thus entitled to an immediate redundancy payment, but he argued that a woman in a similar position would be entitled to an immediate pension: he had therefore been discriminated against.

At the Court of Justice the UK Government argued that *Bilka-Kaufhaus* covered only supplementary schemes and that contracted-out pensions, which replace the state pension rather than supplement it, did not come within Article 141 [ex 119] (but were social security and covered by Article 137 [ex 118]).

The Court of Justice did not agree. It ruled that:

(a) The benefits paid by an employer to a worker in connection with compulsory redundancy fell within the scope of Article 141 [ex 119], whether they were paid under a contract of employment, by virtue of legislative provisions or on a voluntary basis.

(b) A pension paid under a contracted-out private occupational pensions scheme fell within Article 141 [ex 119].

(c) It was a breach of Article 141 [ex 119] to improve an age condition based on different pensionable ages in the national statutory social security scheme. The application of the principle of equal pay must be ensured in respect of each element of remuneration in order to ensure the transparency of the pay system. Therefore, in terms of retirement ages, and entitlement to redundancy payments, men and women must be treated equally.

In *Barber*, the Court of Justice imposed a temporal limitation. The ruling only applies to a claim for entitlement to an equal pension form the date of the judgment, May 17, 1990. This is an exception to the normal rule that judgments are retrospective. The ruling was justified on the grounds that in the light of the Social Security Directive (79/7) and the Occupational Social Security Directive (86/378), Member States were entitled to consider that Article 141 [ex 119] did not apply to pensions paid under contracted-out schemes and that it was still possible to discriminate in this area. Nor did the Court of Justice wish to "upset retroactively the financial balance of many contracted-out pension schemes".

Such was the controversy over the retroactive nature of the *Barber* judgment that it was later incorporated into the TEU by means of the "Barber Protocol". It should be noted that the temporal limitation of *Barber* applies to *benefits* under a pension scheme. In a later case, *Vroege* (C-57/93), the Court of Justice held that there was no limitation on access to a pension scheme. The right to access should have been clear since the judgment in *Bilka-Kaufhaus*.

The ruling of *Barber* also makes redundant much of the Occupational Social Security Directive (86/378). The Commission introduced Directive 96/97 to amend Directive 86/378 to reflect the ruling.

Despite being of such importance, the *Barber* case asked more questions that it answered. The new questions were addressed by a series of ten cases that came before the Court of Justice. A discussion of the cases is beyond the scope of this book, and the interested reader is referred to a specialist work on sex discrimination in pension schemes.

EQUAL WORK: DIRECTIVE 75/117

In an equal pay claim it is fairly easy to compare the situation where a man and a woman are doing the same job for the same employer in the same establishment. This was the situation in *Defrenne*. However, there are a number of situations where the situation is not so clear. It may be that the man and woman do the same work, but at different times; or they may work for the same employer, but at different establishments; or in a particular group of workers there are only women. There is also the situation where a job requires skills and qualifications that are not needed in another job, but the latter is paid more.

Directive 75/117 was introduced to implement and define the scope of Article 141 [ex 119]. Hence, the limitation of direct effect of directives (*i.e.* vertical effect only) will not apply here, as complaining employees will be able to rely on the Article, against an employer in the public or the private sector.

Article 1 of the Directive introduces the principle of equal pay for work of equal value. It was soon decided that Article 141 [ex 119] could not be restricted by a requirement by Member States that the person whose work was being compared be employed at the same time. In *Macarthys Ltd v Smith* (129/79) a woman brought a claim alleging a breach of Article 141 [ex 119] because she was paid £10 less per week than the man who had previously held her current position. The Court of Justice held that the test of comparability should be:

". . . entirely qualitative in character in that is it exclusively concerned with the nature of the service in question."

The Court said that comparisons should be confined to concrete situations where it was possible to make appraisals based on the facts of the case. They would not entertain hypothetical comparisons. To do so would require comparative studies of entire industries, which would bring the matter outside the scope of Article 141 [ex 119]. Article 141 [ex 119] could only apply to actual comparisons where work was actually performed by a man and a woman within the same establishment or service. However, the work being compared need not necessarily be identical work. It could include jobs displaying a high degree of similarity.

An interesting case is *Murphy v An Board Telecom Eireann* (157/86). This case was brought by a woman who performed work of greater value than her male comparator but she received less pay than the man. The Court of Justice held that the woman was entitled to equal pay with the male comparator: but it would go no further than that. It did not say that there should be precise proportionately between services and pay, nor did it say that a woman performing work of higher value than a man should be paid more than the man. The case is also illustrative of the sophistry some employers will engage in to defeat equal pay claims. In *Murphy*, the applicants were telephone maintenance workers who were paid less than a man who was a store labourer. The Irish authority found that the applicants' work was of higher value and, therefore, not "like work" (*i.e.* work of equal value). Even though she was paid less than the man!

Direct and Indirect Discrimination

Direct discrimination occurs when one sex is treated differently to another to its detriment. Article 141 [ex 119] covers such situations as it prohibits wage discrimination "based on sex". Direct discrimination is relatively easy to identify. A clear case of direct discrimination can be seen in *Dekker* (C-177/88) in which a pregnant woman was refused a teaching job. The Court of Justice held that since only a woman could be refused employment on the ground of pregnancy, such a refusal constituted direct discrimination based on sex. Not even the financial loss suffered by the employer could justify direct discrimination.

Indirect discrimination occurs when an apparently neutral condition has a disproportionate and adverse impact on one sex. This type of discrimination is more difficult to determine. Article 141 [ex 119] covers indirect discrimination. In addition, Directive 75/117 states that the principle of equal pay refers to "the elimination of all discrimination on grounds of sex with regard to all aspect and conditions of remuneration". In *Macarthys Ltd v Smith* (129/79), the Court of Justice held that differences in pay could be based on objective factors such as age, skill, seniority and qualifications, provided that such factors were no a form of indirect or disguised discrimination. It would be for the national court to decide on the facts of the case whether the factor was discriminatory.

The first recognition by the Court of Justice of direct and indirect discrimination came in *Defrenne No.2*, although in a rather confusing way. The Court referred to two types of discrimination, which they called overt discrimination (direct) and disguised discrimination (indirect). This distinction does not help in understanding the difference between direct and indirect discrimination. Direct discrimination is rarely overt: if it was it would be easy to eliminate. Usually direct discrimination is hidden from the public eye. Conversely, indirect discrimination is usually open for all to see; this is because the practices do not purport to discriminate. Indeed, there will often be no intention to discriminate, the practice being the traditional way of doing things.

The first case to come before the Court of Justice on the issue of direct/indirect discrimination was *Jenkins v Kingsgate (Clothing Productions) Ltd* (96/80). This case is also one of several cases concerned about the difference in pay between full-time and part-time workers. In *Jenkins*, the employer paid full-time employees 10 per cent more than part-time workers doing the same job. All but one of the part-time workers were women. The employer argued that the reason for the difference in pay was to discourage absenteeism and to encourage more efficient use of the machinery by full-time workers. The question to the Court of Justice was whether it was contrary to Article 141 [ex 119] to pay part-time workers less than full-time workers when the part-time group is exclusively or predominantly female. The Court of Justice ruled that a difference in pay between full-time and part-time did not amount to a form of sex discrimination *per se* against female workers unless it could be shown:

"it was in reality merely an indirect way of reducing the pay of part-time workers on the ground that the group of workers was composed exclusively or predominantly of women."

The ruling was ambiguous in that it did not resolve the question as to whether it was sufficient for the employer to show that there was no intention to discriminate, or whether the employer must show an objective justification for the pay policy.

The ambiguity was addressed in *Bilka-Kaufhaus v Weber von Hartz* (170/84), which was discussed earlier in relation to occupational pension schemes (see above). The facts of the case were that Bilka, a department store, had established a pension scheme for their employees. Part-time employees could join the scheme only if they had worked full-time for at least 15 years over a total period of 20 years. Ms Weber, who did not meet these qualifications, claimed that the scheme infringed Article 141 [ex 119]. This was because the discrimination was suffered disproportionately by women, since most of the part-time workers were female. (In *Bilka*, 98 per cent of part-time workers were female.) Bilka argued that the exclusion of part-time workers, from the scheme was intended solely to discourage part-time work, since part-time workers refused to work late or on Saturdays. In order to ensure the presence of an adequate workforce during those periods it was necessary to make full-time work more attractive than part-time work, by making the pension scheme open only to full-time workers.

Objective Justification

The Court of Justice upheld its decision in *Jenkins* and held that, if a considerably smaller proportion of women than men worked full-time, and if the difference in treatment could only be based on sex, the exclusion of part-time workers from the pension scheme would infringe Article 141 [ex 119]. However, the Court said, such difference in treatment would be permissible if it could be objectively justified. The Court then supplied a three-stage test for national courts to apply. There is objective justification if:

". . . the means chosen for achieving that objective correspond to a real need on the part of the undertaking, are appropriate with a view to achieving the objective in question and are necessary to that end."

It is up to national courts to make findings of fact as to what extent the employer has objectively justified the differences in the pay policy. If the only defence is "objectively justified factors unrelated to any discrimination on the grounds of sex", then it must be that unintentional acts of indirect discrimination are prohibited by Article 141 [ex 119]. The presence or absence of intention is irrelevant. Even if an employer is operating with a benign motive, to favour one particular group, they may have still indirectly discriminated against another group. In *Rinner-Kühn* (171/88), part-time workers were excluded from a sick pay scheme established under German legislation. The Court of Justice held that the German government's arguments were "only generalisations about certain categories of workers, (and) do not enable criteria which are both objective and unrelated to any discrimination on grounds of sex to be identified".

An instance of indirect discrimination arising out of a provision in a collective-bargaining agreement arose in *Kowalska* (33/89).

Here, the complainant was refused a severance grant on her retirement. Under the terms of a collective-agreement only full-time employees were entitled to such a severance grant. It was accepted that the part-time workers were predominantly female. The Court of Justice held that the prohibition of discrimination contained in Article 141 [ex 119] was mandatory and applied not only to the actions of public authorities, but to all agreements which were intended to regulate paid labour collectively. In the instant case, as the collective agreement lead to discrimination against female workers it must be regarded as infringing Article 141 [ex 119].

It cannot always be said that a difference in pay between two workers occupying the same post will be discriminatory. It may be possible to explain the difference and to show that it can be put down to factors unconnected with the sex of the worker. It could be argued that this would not be a defence at all, but merely proving that there was no discriminatory practice in the first place.

Job Evaluation Schemes

Article 1(2) of Directive 75/117 provides that where a job classification system is used for determining pay, it must be based on the same criteria for both men and women and exclude any discrimination on grounds of sex. By Article 2 of the Directive, Member States are required to introduce into national legal systems the necessary measures to enable all employees who consider themselves wronged by the failure to apply the principles of equal pay to part-time their claims by judicial process after recourse to other competent authorities. Under Article 6 of the Directive, Member States must take the necessary measures to ensure that the principle of equal pay is applied and that effective means are available to take care that this principle is observed. This does not necessarily mean that this must be done by means of a job-evaluation scheme.

Nevertheless in *Commission v UK (Re Equal Pay for Equal Work)* (61/81) the United Kingdom was found to have breached the Equal Pay Directive by failing to implement a job classification system which would assist in determining whether work was "of equal value" with other work. At that time in the United Kingdom, a job classification scheme could only be introduced with the consent of the employer, and the legislation did not provide for any other way of determining pay for work to which equal value had been attributed. The Court of Justice held that a Member State must give power to some authority to decide whether work had the same value as other work, after obtaining such information as may be needed. The defects in the domestic legislation, Equal Pay

Act 1970, were remedied by Equal Pay (Equal Value Amendment) Regulations 1983.

If a job evaluation scheme is set up by an employer it must not be discriminatory. The system must take into account the attributes of both sexes. *Rummler v Dato-Druck* (237/85) gave the Court of Justice the opportunity to review a job description scheme set up by an employer. The complainant was a woman who challenged the criteria of the job evaluation. As she found it physically difficult to lift 20kg parcels she had been placed in a lower paid category of worker. She argued that for her this was heavy physical work that should have qualified her for a higher grade. The employer argued that the job only made light physical demands. The issue before the Court of Justice was whether the job evaluation scheme was indirectly discriminatory, but nevertheless could be objectively justified by the employer. The judgment of the Court of Justice is not easy to follow, but in essence it held that a job evaluation scheme which was based on muscular effort, fatigue and physical hardship was not in breach of Article 141 [ex 119] so long as it took into account, in so far as the nature of the tasks carried out permitted, criteria for which workers of each sex showed particular aptitude. The Court said that it was the scheme as a whole that must be examined to see whether it amounted to discrimination. Criteria based exclusively on the values of one sex contained a "risk of discrimination".

In some cases, an employer might establish a job evaluation scheme but the employee may find it difficult to bring an equal pay claim because the criteria of the scheme are difficult to determine. This was the scenario in *Danfoss* (109/88). As part of a job classification scheme, an employer used criteria that included flexibility and seniority. Using these (neutral) criteria the employer paid individual supplements in addition to the basic wage, but the worker did not know what criteria were applied to them and how they were applied. The Court of Justice held that where neutral criteria were applied, resulting in systematic discrimination against female workers, they must have been applied in an abusive manner, since it was inconceivable that the work carried out by female workers would b generally of a lower quality. The Court characterised the scheme as lacking "transparency". In such a case the proof of justification rests with the employer. In *Danfoss*, the Court held that for supplements paid to reward adaptability to variable work schedules, or the place of work, the employer could justify the increments in accordance with the *Bilka* test. In respect of the criteria of seniority the Court fudged the issue. It recognised that payment for seniority had an adverse impact on women but held that since seniority nearly always had an effect upon the way a worker carried out their duties there was no need to justify the seniority criterion.

In *Danfoss*, the Court of Justice refused to rule on whether separate collective bargaining agreements were a valid defence to an equal pay claim. But this issue, and the "market forces" defence, came before them in *Enderby v Frenchay Health Authority* (127/92). Ms Enderby was a speech therapist, a profession which was mainly female. She argued that she was less well paid than clinical psychologists, and pharmacists, professions that were predominantly male. It was agreed that all three jobs were of equal value. The Health Authority that employed Ms Enderby advanced two arguments. First, the rates of pay for the different professions had been decided by separate regular collective bargaining processes in which there was no evidence of discrimination as regards any of the profession. The second argument of the Health Authority was that of market forces. That is, it was difficult to appoint clinical psychologists and that to attract them to work for the NHS it was necessary to pay a higher rate. The Court of Justice rejected the first argument, but was sympathetic towards the second. With regard to the separate collective agreement the Court said:

". . . if the pay of speech therapists is significantly low than that of pharmacists and if the former are almost exclusively women while the latter are predominantly men, there is a *prima facie* case of sex discrimination, at least where the two jobs in question are of equal value and the statistics describing that situation are valid."

It was up to national courts to assess whether it should take into account those statistics, whether they cover enough individuals, whether they illustrate purely fortuitous or short-term phenomena, and whether, in general, they appear to be significant. The onus will be on the employer to show justification, but the employer will not be able to rely on collective bargaining as objective justification. If it was possible so to rely the employer could "easily circumvent the principle of equal pay by using separate bargaining processes".

When it came to the market forces defence the Court of Justice ruled that the needs of the market might constitute adequate justification, depending on whether the proposition of the increase in pay was in fact attributable to the need to attract suitable candidates to the less popular job. However, an employer would have to show that the whole of the increase in pay was necessary to attract new employees.

Finally, on indirect discrimination, the case of *R v Secretary of State for Employment Ex p. Equal Opportunities Commission* is interesting. A UK statute, the Employment Protection (Consolidation) Act 1978, set out threshold conditions for employment rights. A full-time worker was eligible for these rights after two years' continuous service; a part-time worker (someone who worked between 8 and 16 hours a week) had to have 5 years' continuous service for the same rights and those working less than 8 hours a week could never qualify for the employment rights. The Equal Opportunities Commission was able to show that the delayed rights for part-time workers and the total exclusion of workers employed for less than 8 hours affected women to a greater extent than men. The Secretary of State had argued that the whole purpose of the thresholds excluding part-time workers was to bring about an increase in the availability of part-time work and, therefore, any indirect discrimination was "objectively justified". Although this argument had found favour with the Divisional Court and the Court of Appeal, the House of Lords found that this indirect discrimination was not objectively justified. This was because no evidence had been produced to support this assertion, and there was evidence to show that in France the lack of any exclusion on hours worked had not led to difficulties in providing part-time jobs.

EQUAL TREATMENT

Article 141 [ex 119] clearly establishes the principle of equal pay for equal work. However this equality is expressed only in terms of pay: the principle of equal treatment of men and women in areas apart from pay is not expressly referred to. This reflects the early economic nature of the Treaty, and the requirement to equalise conditions of competition among Member States, by ensuring that female labour costs were the same as male labour costs. Nevertheless, Article 141 [ex 119] had a social aim, as well as an economic objective, and this social aim was to be expressed in a commitment to achieve equality in the treatment of men and women, although this equality was confined to the workplace. As was shown earlier, *Defrenne No.3* established that "the elimination of discrimination based on sex forms part of those fundamental human rights" guaranteed by Community law. At about the same time as the *Defrenne No.3* judgment, the Council had adopted Directive 78/207 on equal treatment in conditions of employment.

Directive 76/207

The aim of the Directive (which was based on Article 308 [ex 235]) is set out in Article 1, which provides for the principle of equal treatment as regards access to employment, including promotion, and to vocational training and as regards working conditions. Article 1(2) excluded matters of social security, but the Directive provided that the Council was to adopt future legislation in this area. This was done by Directives 79/7 and 86/378, both discussed below.

The principle of equal treatment is defined in Article 2 as prohibiting all discrimination on the grounds of sex either directly or indirectly by reference in particular to marital or family status. Many of the provisions of this Directive are similar to the Equal Pay Directive, 75/117. However, it is different from the Equal Pay Directive in that it permits several exceptions to the equal treatment provisions. These exceptions, or derogation, are set out in Article 2.

The first derogation, in Article 2(2) relates to exemption from the equal treatment principle for activities for which the sex of the worker constitutes a determining factor. An obvious example of this might be work as an actor, when it could be legitimately expected that a female would play a female role. The case of *Commission v UK (Equal Treatment for Men and Women)* (165/82) concerned an exemption to the Sex Discrimination Act 1975 which allowed discriminatory treatment in private households, and in firms employing fewer than six staff. The Court of Justice held that while individual exemptions might be appropriate, blanket exemptions were not. The Court went on to find that a ban on men to the profession of midwife was justified in view of the fact that "personal sensitivities" could play an important role in the relationship between midwife and patient. However, when these was an exemption for certain occupations the reasons for the exemption must be re-assessed periodically, in order to decide, in the light of social developments, whether there is justification for maintaining the exclusions concerned. By, Article 9(2) of the Directive, the Member States must notify the Commission of the results of this assessment.

In *Johnston v Chief Constable of the RUC* (222/84), a female member of the Royal Ulster Constabulary challenged the decision of the RUC to refuse to renew her contract of employment. The RUC had decided as a matter of policy not to employ any women as full-time members of the RUC Reserve, as women were not trained in the use of firearms. The Court of Justice held that the exemption allowed by Article 2(2) might apply to some activities carried out by police officers, but not to police activities in general. However, the Court accepted that the carrying of firearms might create additional risks of assassination without hearing any evidence to support the implication that women could not be trained to use firearms just as safely and effectively as men. The actual decision on the facts of the case was left for the national court, taking into account the principle of proportionality.

PREGNANCY AND MATERNITY

The second derogation to the principle of equal treatment is set out in Article 2(3) and provides that the Directive shall be without prejudice to provisions concerning the protection of women, particularly as regards pregnancy and maternity. The Directive recognises that it is legitimate to protect women's needs in respect of their biological condition during pregnancy and thereafter until physiological and mental functions have returned to normal and, to protect the special relationship between mother and child in the immediate period after childbirth. Although pregnancy was not an issue in *Johnston*, the Court of Justice held in that case that Article 2(3) did not apply to allow women to be excluded from a certain type of employment on the ground that public opinion demanded that women be given greater protection than men against risks which affected men and women in the same way.

The Court of Justice also questioned whether the refusal to renew Mrs Johnston's contract could not be avoided by allocating to women duties which, without jeopardising the aims pursued, can be performed without firearms. The first challenge to the pregnancy derogation was an unusual one. In *Hoffman v Barmer Ersatzkasse* (184/83), a father claimed six months paternity leave following the birth of his child, while the mother went back to work. His argument was that the Equal Treatment Directive went beyond the protection of women both before and after childbirth, and that its purpose was to allow for the case of the child on a long term basis. On this interpretation, the Directive should be open on an equal basis to men and women who wished to take care of children over a long period. The father claimed that the refusal to grant the paternity leave was contrary to Directive 76/207. The Court of Justice dismissed his argument. They said that the Directive was not designed to settle questions concerned with the organisation of the family, or to alter the division of responsibility between parents, and that parental leave may legitimately be reserved to the mother. The Court also said that Member States have a reasonable margin of discretion as regards with the nature of the protective measures and the detailed arrangements for their implementation. This case can be seen to be entrenching the role of the mother as primary carer. By protecting the "special relationship between a woman and her child" it deprives the father of the opportunity to develop such a relationship by refusing to give the parents the choice has to who would take the leave.

There was no doubt that the Directive permitted Member States to maintain protective provisions that discriminated in favour of women in relation to pregnancy and maternity. What was not so clear was whether it prohibited measures that discriminated against women on grounds of pregnancy. For example, was a dismissal of a woman from employment because she was pregnant a breach of the principle of equal treatment? Or was it impossible to compare a pregnant woman with a man in order to decide that they had been treated unequally? This was to cause particular problems in the United Kingdom, but the first case to come before the Court of Justice was a Dutch case, *Dekker v Stichting Vormingscentrum voor jong Volwassenen* (C-177/88). Ms Dekker applied for a job as an instructor. At the time of her application she was three months pregnant. Although she was the most suitable candidate for the job she was not appointed, because the employer would not have been able to obtain reimbursement from his insurers of the maternity benefits the employer was obliged to pay during the maternity leave. The employer would therefore not be financially able to employ a replacement during the absence and would be short-staffed.

The Court of Justice was unequivocal. It said that only women can be refused employment on grounds of pregnancy and such a refusal therefore constitutes direct discrimination on the grounds of sex. A refusal to employ on account of the financial consequences of absence due to pregnancy must be regarded as based essentially in the fact of pregnancy. Such discrimination could not be justified.

If the judgment in *Dekker* seemed far-reaching, it was quickly to be reined in by the Court of Justice. In *Hertz v Aldi* (C-179/88), Ms Hertz was away from work on maternity leave. However, her pregnancy was complicated and she was ill for the maternity leave period. This illness continued beyond the period of the maternity leave and she was still unable to return to work. After a further period of absence because of the sickness she was dismissed. The employer argued that it was normal practice to dismiss employees who were ill for so long.

The Court of Justice held that although pregnancy related discrimination was a form of direct discrimination, the Directive did not apply to dismissal due to illness-related absence outside of the maternity leave time granted. It was necessary to look at national legislation to consider whether there was any direct or indirect discrimination in the grounds of dismissal. The Court went on to say that in the case of an illness manifesting itself after the maternity leave period, there is no reason to distinguish an illness attributable to pregnancy or confinement from any other illness. Of course, both male and female workers are equally exposed to illness, and if in an employment situation a male worker who is sick would have been dismissed, there can be no direct discrimination if a female in similar circumstances is also dismissed.

This judgment has been criticised for two reasons. First, it makes the extent of protection against dismissed for pregnant women dependant on whether Member States grant maternity leave by means of national legislation. Thus, Directive 76/207 would not apply uniformly in the different Member States but would vary according to the length of maternity leave provided in each. The second criticism is that the case is an example of the limitations of the equality model adopted generally by the Community. This requires women to be compared with men, for the purposes of treating them in the same way, except for some exceptional cases (*i.e.* pregnancy). In these exceptional circumstances they are entitled to "special" treatment which recognises their difference from men. It is argued that what is really needed is a recognition that discrimination law should be used as a way to remedy the disadvantage faced by pregnant women in the labour market, in order to ensure that they enjoy substantive equality.

In *Habermann-Beltermann* (C-421/92), the Court of Justice was asked whether it was compatible with Directive 76/207 for an employee who had chosen to work at night, to be dismissed on becoming pregnant, because of national legislation which prohibited pregnant women from night working. The Court of Justice held that such a prohibition is, by virtue of Article 2(3), perfectly compatible with the Equal Treatment Directive. However, the Court noted that the contract of employment in question was an open-ended contract and held that to terminate a woman's contract of employment on account of the prohibition would be contrary to the objective of protecting such persons, and would deprive the Directive of its effectiveness.

In *Habermann-Beltermann*, the Court specifically limited its ruling to the case of a woman working without a fixed term contract. This issue was also of importance in *Webb v EMO Air Cargo* (C-32/93).

In 1987, a Mrs Stewart, an employee of EMO, discovered she was pregnant. Her baby was due in February 1988 and, as was her right, she notified her employer that she would take maternity leave and then return to work. In July 1987, EMO employed Mrs Webb as a replacement for Mrs Stewart for when she went on maternity leave. Initially, Mrs Stewart and Mrs Webb were to work together so that one could train the other. At the initial interview for the job, Mrs Webb had been told that she was being recruited specifically to cover for the period of maternity leave, although it was indicated that she might be kept on permanently after Mrs Stewart returned to work. Mrs Webb was given an open-ended contract.

Within two weeks of starting work Mrs Webb discovered that she too was pregnant. When they were informed of this EMO sacked her. Mrs Webb complained to an industrial tribunal (now called an employment tribunal) that her dismissal was indirect discrimination, but her claim was rejected by the tribunal and by a special Employment Appeals Tribunal. The appeal to the Court of Appeal was also rejected, on the ground that as a man who had been off sick would have been sacked; Mrs Webb had been treated no differently from a man. There was therefore been no discrimination. This ignored the fact that pregnancy is not an illness!

When the case finally wound its way to the House of Lords, that Court was persuaded to make an Article 234 [ex 177] reference to the Court of Justice. The Court of Justice was unequivocal. It rejected the arguments put forward by the United Kingdom and held that the dismissal of a pregnant women, *who had been recruited for an indefinite period*, could not be justified on grounds relating to her inability to fulfil a fundamental condition of her employment contract (emphasis added).

It should be noted that an area of uncertainty had been created, when the Court of Justice took particular care to emphasise the open-ended or indefinite duration of Mrs Webb's contract. The Court of Justice was following its previous decision in *Habermann-Beltermann*, but it is difficult to see how a difference in the type of contract will have much significance in law. If it is discriminatory to dismiss a woman on the grounds of pregnancy, it can make no difference whether the contract is open-ended or for a fixed period. It seemed obvious that this issue would require further litigation. The uncertain state of affairs did not last long. In June 1998, the Court of Justice heard the case of *Brown v Rentokil Ltd* (C-394/96). Mrs Brown worked for Rentokil, which had a clause in its contract of employment that any employee absent for more than 26 weeks continuously would be dismissed. Mrs Brown became pregnant in August 1990, and later in the same month she developed a pregnancy-related illness and took sick leave. She never returned to work. A week before the end of the 26-week period, Mrs Brown received a letter from the company terminating her employment. She had her baby two weeks after the termination of her employment. As she did not have the then requisite two years' service she was not entitled to maternity leave.

When Mrs Brown brought a case alleging sex discrimination before an industrial tribunal, it was rejected. The tribunal said that "it is plain that . . . an absence through illness related to . . . pregnancy but beginning long before the applicability of the statutory maternity provisions does not fall . . . into the automatic category of being discriminatory because the dismissal was due to pregnancy". The EAT dismissed Mrs Brown's appeal because it considered itself bound by the decision of the Court of Appeal in *Webb*. The Court of Session held that there was no discrimination within the meaning of the Sex Discrimination Act. It added that, since in *Hertz*, the Court of Justice had established a clear distinction between pregnancy and illness attributable to pregnancy, a claim based on absence due to pregnancy could not succeed.

On a further appeal to the House of Lords, the case was referred to the Court of Justice. The case was noticeable, particularly for the very wide-ranging view of the issues taken by the Advocate General in his Opinion. The Advocate General set out what he considered to be the principles established by the previous case law. According to the Advocate General, the main principle was that once a female worker had exhausted her entitlement to maternity leave, periods of absence for reasons of sickness, even if those reasons could be traced back to pregnancy, could not be attributed to the normal risks of pregnancy but must be viewed in the same light as the absence of any other worker. The Advocate General proposed that the dismissal of a woman while pregnant, by taking into consideration a situation that only women can experience, should constitute direct discrimination contrary to Article 5(1) of the Equal Treatment Directive. In his view, this was the "only possible interpretation". The Advocate General pointed out that in 13 of the Member States, a woman would also be protected against dismissal while she was pregnant but before she took maternity leave. It was only in the United Kingdom and Ireland that such legislation was not in place (though it is now, in the United Kingdom, in the Employment Rights Act 1996).

The judgment of the Court of Justice was a welcome clarification of the law. The Court dismissed the "sick man" defence. The Court said:

"Those disorders and complications which may cause incapacity for work, form part of the risks inherent in the condition of pregnancy and are thus a specific feature of that condition."

The Court further said:

". . . dismissal of a female worker during pregnancy for absences due to incapacity for work resulting from her pregnancy is limited to the occurrence of risks inherent in pregnancy and must therefore be regarded as essentially based on the fact of pregnancy. Such a dismissal can affect only women and therefore constitutes direct discrimination on grounds of sex."

This last statement is unequivocal. It does not matter whether the dismissal is for pregnancy, or the consequence of pregnancy, such as the inability to perform a job because of absence. Nor does it matter that the dismissal is in accordance with an absence policy that is applied to all employees.

The judgment in *Brown*, was also exceptional in that it was a rare occasion in which the Court of Justice specifically overruled one of its previous decisions. The Court said that its judgment in *Brown* was "contrary to the Court's previous ruling in *Larsson*" (C-400/95). So where a woman is absent because of illness resulting from pregnancy and that illness arose during pregnancy and persisted during maternity leave, none of the absence may be taken into account for computation of the period justifying her dismissal under national law. Thus, the entire period from the beginning of pregnancy to the end of maternity leave is a protected period.

Now that the provisions of the Pregnant Workers Directive have been implemented into English law it might be thought that *Brown* is an outdated case. Indeed, if a female was to be dismissed now, in similar circumstances to Mrs Brown, that female could rely on the provisions of the Employment Rights Act 1996 and would not need to plead European law. However, Article 5 of the Equal Treatment Directive and the case law of the Court of Justice interpreting it, will continue to be essential in order to clarify the question whether the periods for which a pregnant woman has been prevented from working because of her pregnancy may be added to the periods preceding her pregnancy and following her maternity leave, for the purposes of calculating absences from work such as to justify dismissal.

It could be argued that in granting a "protected period" in which a woman is protected against dismissal for pregnancy, the Court of Justice has shown a logical inconsistency. If a woman is protected for any given period from dismissal for pregnancy related illness and that illness extends beyond the protected period, a dismissal at that stage is still based on pregnancy and a woman is dismissed because she is a woman. However, the *Brown* decision can be seen as a pragmatic attempt by the Court of Justice to balance the right to equal treatment with the need to distribute the "costs" of motherhood. One can assume that the Court of Justice was influenced by its Advocate General in *Hertz* that "if complications resulting from confinement are severe, a female worker may be unable to work for several years, without an employer being able to dismiss her". There is also the view held by the Court that to extend an open-ended protection to a few women affected by severe post-natal problems, in statistical terms fortunately a minute percentage of cases, may jeopardise the chances of all women wishing to enter the labour market.

Thus, it could be argued that the Pregnant Workers Directive does not provide women with the protection it seemed to initially herald. True, it makes it unlawful to dismiss a woman during her pregnancy, it provides the right to maternity leave and it sets out a framework of health and safety provisions. But it takes the maternity leave period outside the protection of sex discrimination rules. Indeed, a double-edged sword for women!

This timidity on the part of the Court of Justice can best be explained in political terms. It was well known that certain Member States, including the United Kingdom, objected to the promulgation of the Pregnant Workers Directive. No doubt, the Court of Justice was sensitive to the possibility of a fierce reaction from a Member State to a judgment that required full pay to women on maternity leave, for very long periods of time.

It is significant that *Brown* may now close the chapter on sex discrimination in pregnancy.

The third derogation to the principle of formal equality is in Article 2(4) of the Directive. This Article permits measures giving "a special advantage to women with a view to improving their ability to compete on the labour market and to pursue a career on an equal footing with men". This was the decision of the Court of Justice in *Kalanke v Frei Hausestadt Bremen* (C-450/93). However, in *Kalanke* the Court held that positive discrimination in favour of women, in the form of a quota of women in particular jobs, was contrary to the Equal Treatment Directive.

Scope of the Protection

Directive 76/207 requires the abolition of all relevant laws, regulations and administrative provisions contrary to the principle of equal treatment. It also requires provision to be made to declare null and void or to amend any provisions in collective agreement or individual contracts of employment which are contrary to the principle of equal treatment.

Article 3(1) provides that there shall be no discrimination whatsoever on the grounds of sex in the conditions, including selection criteria, for access to all jobs or posts, whatever the sector or branch or activity and to all levels if the occupational hierarchy. Discrimination in selection criteria is seen in the already discussed case of *Dekker*. Even though national rules forced the refusal to employ a pregnant woman, the Court of Justice held that the employers were in direct contravention of Articles 2(1) and 3(1) of the Directive.

What sometimes causes confusion is the distinction between equal pay and equal treatment in conditions of work. Article 5 of the Directive covers conditions governing dismissal, and has been the subject of much judicial interpretation by the Court of Justice. In *Burton v British Railways Board* (19/81), the applicant applied for voluntary redundancy when he was aged 58. His claim was rejected since it was below the minimum age of 60, which had been set for male employees. Since the minimum age for females was 55, Mr Burton complained of sex discrimination. The Court of Justice was asked whether the different age conditions in access to voluntary redundancy was contrary to Directive 76/207. It ruled that they were not. In the view of the Court, the reason for the different age conditions was not to discriminate on the grounds of sex, but because the redundancy scheme was mirroring the state statutory retirement scheme and this exception for different pension ages was allowed by Article 7 of Directive 79/7. (This aspect of the case is now overruled by the decision of the Court of Justice in *Barber* where it was held that the calculation of pensionable age for the purpose of redundancy is now governed by Article 141 [ex 119]). As Article 7 of Directive 79/7 allows for exceptions from equal treatment, the Court of Justice has attempted to define it narrowly. This is illustrated in *Roberts v Tate and Lyle* (151/84). In this case the applicant challenged the compulsory early retirement scheme operated by her employer, which provided that men could receive an immediate pension ten years before their normal retirement date, whereas women could only receive on five years before. The Court of Justice held that access to a redundancy scheme was covered by Article 5 of Directive 76/207, and not excluded by Article 7 of Directive 79/7. This was because it was not linked to the state social security system. In those circumstances the grant of a pension to persons of the same age who are made redundant amounts merely to a collective measure adopted irrespective of the sex of those persons in order to guarantee them all the same rights. Thus there was no discrimination on the grounds of sex.

This is a narrow interpretation because Article 7 of Directive 79/7 allows Member States to exclude from the scope of the equal treatment principle "the determination of pensionable age for the purposes of granting old-age and retirement pensions *and the possible consequences thereof for other benefits*" (emphasis added). It would have been easy to accept the argument that a redundancy benefit could be affected by different statutory pension ages for men and women.

Burton was again distinguished in *Marshall v South West Area Health Authority* (152/84). In this case, Mrs Marshall challenged the policy of the Health Authority which required her to retire at age 60, whereas men could continue to work to age 65. The Court of Justice held that her compulsory retirement was a dismissal falling within the scope of the Equal Treatment Directive, rather than as a consequence of the different statutory pensionable ages falling within the scope of the exception in Article 7 of Directive 79/7.

It now appears that the complications concerning the relationships between social security and pay have become clear. The cumulative effect of the ruling in *Bilka*, *Barber* and *Moroni* is that only state social security schemes can benefit from the exception in Article 7 of Directive 79/7. All other payments are now "pay" and therefore covered by Article 141 [ex 119].

Equal Treatment in Matters of Social Security—Directive 79/7

Directive 79/7 implements in matters of social security the principle in Directive 76/207 of equal treatment for men and women. The Directive was adopted on the basis of Article 308 [ex 235] of the EC Treaty and Article 1 states as its purpose "the progressive implementation . . . of the principle of equal treatment for men and women in the field of social security". The word "progressive" is important. As has been seen above, the Directive provides for various exceptions to the equal treatment principle. This is unlike the Equal Pay Directive 75/117, which allows no derogations.

Article 2 states that the Directive applies to the "working population" which it defines as "self-employed persons, workers and self-employed persons whose activity is interrupted by illness, accident or involuntary unemployment and persons seeking employment", and to "retired or invalided workers and self-employed persons". It should be noted that the provisions of this Directive cover only employment related social security benefits.

But not all social security benefits. Article 3(1) sets out the benefits covered by the Directive. They are:

(a)   statutory schemes which provide protection against sickness, invalidity, old age, accidents at work or occupational diseases and unemployment; and

(b)   social assistance, in so far as it is intended to supplement or replace those statutory schemes.

The personal scope of the Directive has been interpreted widely by the Court of Justice. In *Drake v Chief Adjudication Officer* (150/85), the Court applied the Directive according to the function of the benefit. In the case, a woman had given up work in order to look after her disabled mother. She was refused an invalid are allowance on the ground that such an allowance was not payable to a married woman who was living with her husband; though it would be paid to a married man living with his wife. The Court of Justice held that the Directive must be interpreted as including any benefit which in a broad sense forms one of the statutory schemes referred to, or a social assistance scheme designed to supplement or replace such a scheme. The fact that the benefit which forms part of a statutory invalidity scheme is paid to a third party and to the disabled person, does not place it outside the scope of the Directive. This is a sensible judgment. Although Ms Drake had not become an invalid herself, she had given up work in order o care for someone else who was an invalid. The Court of Justice took the view that the allowance paid to carers was simply the way chosen by the national law to allocate social security benefits consequent on invalidity.

As noted above, the Directive covers only employment related situations. In *Achterberg* (48, 106 & 107/88) the Court of Justice held that the Directive does not cover those who have never worked. The same case also ruled that persons who give up work for a reason other than the five mentioned in Article 3(1), *e.g.* to look after children, fall outside the scope of the Directive.

The material scope of the Directive has been interpreted less widely than the personal scope, particularly in more recent cases. This may be that the Court of Justice is aware of the controversy of upsetting the social security regulations of Member States and may be part of the period of consolidation the Court is going through at the moment. In this area the Court insists that there must be a strong link between one of the risks listed in Article 3(1) and the benefit paid. In *R v Secretary of State for Social Security Ex p. Smithson* (243/90) the Court of Justice held that to be covered by the Directive the benefit "must be directly and effectively linked to the protection provided against one of the risks specified in Article 3(1) of the Directive". So, a claim for housing benefit, which had been denied by British social security rules, was not within the scope of the Directive. The Directive applied only to statutory schemes providing protection against the five risks set out in Article 3(1) and not to any need for finance to enable a person to meet housing costs.

The Court of Justice was equally restrictive in *Jackson and Cresswell* (C-63 & 64/91). It held that a general benefit, in this case a supplementary allowance intended as a replacement for a wage, was not covered. The Court said that as the national scheme exempted claimants from the obligation to be available for work, the benefits could not be regarded as being directly and effectively linked to protection against the risk of unemployment.

The Meaning of the Equal Treatment Principle

Article 4 of the Directive defines the principle of equal treatment as meaning that there shall be no discrimination whatsoever on grounds of sex either directly or indirectly by reference to marital or family status, in particular concerning:

(a) the scope of schemes and conditions of access thereto;

(b) the obligation to contribute and the calculation of contribution;

(c) the calculation of benefits including increases due in respect of a spouse and for dependants;

(d) the conditions governing the duration and retention of entitlement to benefits.

It will be noted there that the wording of Article 4 expressly prohibits direct and indirect discrimination; it has not been left to interpretation by the Court of Justice as was the context of pay in Article 141 [ex 119]. In *Drake* the Court of Justice held that the refusal to pay an invalidity allowance to a married woman where it was payable to a married man infringed Article 4. It took much the same line in *Integrity v Rouvroy* (C-373/89) which concerned exemptions from social security not allowed the same exemption. This was held to be contrary to Article 4.

In the equal pay litigation many of the cases concerned part-time workers, who are mainly female. There are similar cases in this area, particularly cases of indirect discrimination. One such case is *Teuling* (30/85). Under Dutch law, all incapacitated workers were entitled to a benefit equal to 70 per cent of the statutory minimum wage. It was also possible to increase the benefit to 100 per cent, but this depended on having dependant spouse and children. Ms Teuling claimed this system was indirectly discriminatory against women. The Court of Justice agreed that if a considerably smaller proportion of women than of men were entitled to such supplements, this would be contrary to Article 4 unless the benefit could be justified by factors unrelated to sex. Although the decision as to whether the benefit was objectively justified was left to the national court, the Court of Justice appeared to accept the justification of the social policy arguments which were put forward.

In *Ruzius-Wilbrink* (102/88), a Dutch law granted disability allowance to persons who were incapable of working. The benefit was based on past earnings, which discriminated against those being paid less than the minimum weekly wage, particularly part-time workers. The plaintiff was a female part-time worker who claimed that as most part-time workers were female, the criteria on which the benefits were based were discriminatory. The Court of Justice held that there was effective indirect discrimination in breach of Article 4 of the Directive. However, it was up to the national court to decide whether or not this could be objectively justified. The Court of Justice did not accept that it would be objective justification if a person could receive more in benefits than they had received in wages.

Derogation from the Principle of Equal Treatment

This is provided for by Article 7 of the Directive and has been briefly mentioned in the discussion on Directive 76/207. Article 7 permits Member States to exclude various matters from the principle of equal treatment. The most important of the exclusions are the determination of pensionable ages for the purposes of granting old age and retirement pensions, and the possible consequences thereafter for other benefits, and the granting of old age or invalidity benefits deriving from a wife's entitlements.

As has already been indicated, the approach of the Court of Justice to the exceptions in Article 7 has been to restrict it to old age pensions and retirement pensions and consequences arising therefrom. The Court has not allowed the restriction to cover dismissal from employment. This has been seen in cases discussed earlier, such as *Burton*, *Roberts* and *Marshall*. In *R v Secretary of State for Social Security Ex p. EOC* (C-9/91) the Court of Justice held that Article 7 may justify a difference in the member of national insurance contributions required for a full pension between men and women. The Court said that the different periods of contribution was acceptable because it was necessarily linked to the different pensionable ages allowed by Article 7.

Equal Treatment in Occupational Pension Schemes

Directive 86/378, which was based on Articles 94 and 308 [ex 100 and 235] was anticipated by Article 4(3) of Directive 79/7 and was intended to extend the principle of equal treatment in state social security schemes to private or occupational pension schemes. However, much of the significance of Directive 86/378 has been lost as a result of the *Barber* judgment which held that pensions paid under an occupational pension scheme was "pay", and therefore covered by Article 141 [ex 119]. This has the advantage that questions relating to different retirement ages or pension entitlement are covered by Article 141 [ex 119], and this avoids the problems of the direct effect of directives. The *Barber* case made much of the Directive redundant and the Commission has introduced legislation to bring it in line with the decision in *Barber* and other subsequent cases.

Equal Treatment for the Self-Employed: Directive 86/613

Directive 86/613 was adopted under Articles 94 and 308 [ex 100 and 235] and is complementary to Directives 76/207 and 79/7. Article 1 applies the principle of equal treatment to men and women engaged in an activity in a self-employed capacity or contributory to the pursuit of such an activity, in relation to those aspects not covered by other directives. The scope of the Directive is set out in Article 2 to include the self-employed including farmers and members of the liberal professions, and their spouses who are of employees or partners but who participate in the same activities.

Remedies

Each of the Directives has a provision that a Member State must introduce into their legal systems such measures as are necessary to enable all persons who consider themselves wronged to pursue their claim by judicial process. Remedies are discussed in detail in Chapter 4, but it is worthwhile noting that many of the cases on remedies have been sex discrimination cases. The Court of Justice has also consistently stated that, although the remedy available is a matter for the national courts, any remedy available for a breach of Community law must be no less favourable than for a breach of an internal law. Also, the procedure to be adopted for claiming a remedy for a breach of Community law must in no case render it impossible in practice to exercise the right to such a remedy.

In *Von Colson* (14/83), an applicant for a job was refused employment because of her sex. Under German law the only compensation available was a refund of expenses, which in the case amounted to a small amount of money for bus fares to the job interview! The Court of Justice ruled that full implementation of the directives required that any sanction must be such as to guarantee real and effective judicial protection, and must also have a deterrent effect on the employer. If a Member State chooses to penalise sex discrimination by an award of compensation (damages) that compensation must be adequate in relation to the damage sustained and must amount to more than purely nominal compensation.

In *Marshall No.2* (C-271/91) the Court of Justice confirmed the principle of effective compensation in Von Colson. The Court also held that the fixing of an upper limit on compensation, and the refusal to award interest, were both in breach of Community law as either or both of them could avoid the payment of full compensation. In *Emmott* (C-208/90), the Court held that limitation periods under national law do not begin to run until the full implementation of the relevant directive. However, in *Steenhorst-Neerings* (C-338/91) the Court limited its ruling in *Emmott* by allowing a limit on the retroactivity of claims. In *Steenhorst-Neerings* Dutch legislation provided that back-claim for invalidity benefit could not be for more than one year before the date from which they were claimed. The Court of Justice found that the limiting provision was justified. This could mean that "full and effective" compensation was impossible to obtain and the judgment seems at odds with *Emmott*. Nevertheless, *Steenhorst-Neerings* has been confirmed by the Court of Justice in *Johnson No.2* (C-410/92).

Conclusion

A glance at any of the plethora of statistics on the subject will show that women do not, generally speaking, have equal pay with men. The statistics will show that women take up most of the jobs at the low paid end of the market, particularly among part-time workers. Nor do women enjoy the same equality of opportunity with men. Men fill most of the "top" jobs in the city, in industry and commerce, in politics and the judiciary. So the law had only limited success in eliminating the disadvantages faced by women in the labour market.

Many reasons can be advanced for this, but a full discussion is beyond the scope of this work. However, two factors seem to have a major impact. First, is the very notion of equality. Community law has adopted a very formal notion of equality, based on a male norm of working, and which fails to take into account women's role in family life and their position as the major carers in society. The second factor to be recognised is that law itself is not capable of eliminating sex discrimination. There needs to be a re-focusing on the whole series of structural disadvantages faced by women, and of their causes.

14. OTHER ISSUES

COMPANY LAW

If there is to be freedom of establishment, and the free movement of capital, throughout the Community then it seems sensible that undertakings operating in the Community should not be subject to vastly different rules depending on which Member State the undertaking is situated. An undertaking that operates in a Member State which has heavy supervision and complex regulation is at a competitive disadvantage against an undertaking in a less regulated regime. Thus within a common market there is a need to smooth out the differences in Member State regulations and supervision so that undertaking act on a "level playing field". This is the rationale behind the Community company law programme.

The constitutional basis for this programme for company law harmonisation is founded upon the Right of Establishment, and Article 44(g) [ex 54(2)] of the Treaty of Rome. The relevant part of this Article states:

". . . co-ordinating to the necessary extent the safeguards which, for the protection of the interests of members and others, are required by Member States of companies or firms . . . with a view to making such safeguards equivalent throughout the Community."

The result of activity in the Community has been a plethora of directives, in the company law sphere, and the capital market sphere, many of them of a complex and technical nature, beyond the scope of this book. These will be mentioned in passing and the main discussion given up to those Directives that have an important influence on the fundamentals of company law. It will be seen that all the directives aim for "harmonisation", or "approximation", or "co-ordination". There is no attempt to require Member States to introduce a uniform law.

Capital Markets

There are a number of directives in force concerned with the capital markets and securities legislation. These include a directive concerning the admission of securities to Stock Exchange listing (Directive 80/390) which has been implemented in the United Kingdom by Part IV of the Financial Services Act 1986. The Insider Dealing Directive (89/592) has been implemented by Part V of the Criminal Justice Act 1993. This changes the laws previously set out in the Insider Dealing Act 1985. The Investment Services Directive (93/22) and the related Capital Adequacy Directive (93/6) are intended to remove barriers to the single market in financial services between Member States. The basic idea is known as "home licence" authorisation, *i.e.* an investment firm should receive authorisation from its home state, and this will, subject to certain safeguards, allow it to do business on a cross border basis, or by setting up a branch in another Member State.

The Company Law Harmonisation Programme

Many of the directives which have received the approval of the Council of Ministers have, on the whole, been beneficial, and the changes and reforms implemented by them have been consistent with the direction in which internal law reform was moving. However, the difference in drafting styles between the Community and the United Kingdom legislature has led to some difficulties in implementation. In some areas directives have been held up because of UK opposition.

The First Company Law Directive (Directive 68/151) was passed in 1968. Thus when the United Kingdom joined the (then) European Economic Community in 1973, s.9 of the European Communities Act 1972 (ECA) attempted to implement the provision of the Directive relating to the *ultra vires* acts of a company. At the time of the UK accession, the strictness of the UK *ultra vires* doctrine was incompatible with Community law. Section 9 of European Communities Act 1972 was consolidated as s.35 of the Companies Act 1985. The wording of s.35 proved to be unsatisfactory and with effect from February 1991 it was replaced by ss 35, 35A, 35B and 322A of the Companies Act 1985 as amended by the Companies Act 1989. The development of this area of company law is now a fruitful source of examination topics for company law students!

Until the Second Company Law Directive (77/91) much of the United Kingdom law on the allotment and maintenance of share capital was governed by the common law. As a result of the Directive the law is now set out in ss 80 and 89 of the Companies Act 1985.

The Fourth Company Law Directive (78/660) had a major impact on the presentation of United Kingdom company accounts. This Directive was initially implemented by the Companies Act 1981 and was then consolidated in the Companies Act 1985. The new rules represented a major departure from previous UK practice. For the first time the basic rules for the presentation and accounting measurement of income and expenditure, assets and liabilities, were laid down by law. Up until then, the United Kingdom had been more concerned with the provision of accounting information than with precise methods of presentation. In the same area of accounting standards, the Seventh Company Law Directive (83/349) and the Eighth Company Law Directive (84/253) brought about major amendments to the Companies Act 1985.

The Twelfth Company Law Directive (89/667) is of interest. Before this Directive was implemented in the United Kingdom it was a UK requirement that every registered company, of whatever size, must have at least two members (the owners of a company). The Directive provided that it was now possible to have (in some circumstances) a single member company. There are now a number of such companies registered in the United Kingdom.

A controversial piece of legislation is the Fifth Draft Company Law Directive. This Directive has provision for the structure and functioning of companies in areas such as general meetings, boards of directors and their powers, and shareholders rights. These are not controversial. However, the Directive also contains provisions on the "difficult" subject of employee participation in management. In the original draft the employee was to be given the right to participate in the management of a company on the basis of a "dual board" structure; there was to be a supervisory board and a board of management. (The employees would make up one-third of the supervisory board.) This was based on the long established practice of German company law. This proposal met with much opposition, particularly from the United Kingdom and the provisions of the Directive had to be "watered down". The new provisions allow for a variety of alternative methods of employee participation, which could be combined with either a single board structure or a dual board structure. However, as the United Kingdom has indicated that it is opposed to any compulsory form of employee participation it is unlikely that this Draft Directive will make much progress.

Both the Draft Ninth Company Law Directive and the Draft Tenth Directive, on groups of companies and cross-border mergers of companies respectively, have met with little progress. In part this is due to the opposition of the UK Government to the provisions of employee participation they contain.

Apart from Directives aimed at the harmonisation of company law, the Community has been active in other directions. By Article 293 [ex 220] the Member States are required to enter into negotiations to secure for the benefit of their nationals the mutual recognition of companies and firms. This led to the Convention on Mutual Recognition of Companies in 1968. The Convention requires Member States to recognise companies formed in other Member States. The basic rule is that recognition is to be accorded to any company that has its statutory registered office in any of the Member States.

An innovative and imaginative proposal is the draft regulation for a "European Company". This would allow a new type of company whose existence would transcend the national boundaries of Member States. The company would be registered in a Member State but would be subject to a Community set of rules.

Conclusion

This brief look at Community influences is intended to convince the reader of the reach of the Community into this area. Although it is not always apparent, even to the company law student, much, if not most, of the changes in the UK company law are brought about by our membership of the Community, and the requirement to implement Community legislation, especially Directives. As the single market is consolidated we can expect more moves to harmonisation. The process is a continuing one and is bound to broaden and accelerate.

PUBLIC PROCUREMENT

Often the largest contracts are those awarded by the state, or local authorities or other bodies governed by public law, such as the police or utility authorities. These bodies are often spending public monies, and are contracting for large amounts of money. Some obvious examples are the building of a new motorway, or a new hospital. Every year the Community's public authorities and privatised utilities spend €720 billion buying goods and services. In 1994 this represented 11.5 per cent of the Member States' Gross Domestic Product, nearly €2,000 per citizen of the European Union. The Commission has calculated that ninety-eight per cent of contracts awarded by various public bodies are awarded to contractors of the home state. There are, of course, many reasons for this. Public authorities have a natural inclination to "keep the money at home". This way they are supporting home industries and enhancing local economies. The award of a contract to build, for example, a new motorway, will have a positive impact on local employment, and might increase the national esteem of the contractor.

In the past there have been many suggestions that the awarding of contracts in the public sector has not been fair and open so far as overseas tenders are concerned. Indeed, there is ample evidence to suggest that foreign contractors are "frozen out" of the tendering process. This could be done in a number of ways. The contract could be advertised locally so it would be difficult for an overseas company to be aware of the possibilities of tendering for the contract. Or the contract itself could require national specifications which an overseas contractor would find difficult to meet. This was the substance of the case in *Commission v Ireland (Re Dundalk Water Supply)* (45/87). The contract specification for the town's new water supply system included a stipulation that certain pipes used in the project should conform to a special Irish standard. It was made clear to an interested firm that a tender based on the use of Spanish made pipes would not be acceptable to the awarding authority. This was in the face of the assertion that the Spanish pipes were perfectly compatible with the overall requirements of the Irish standard, and that they were suitable for the particular project. The Commission brought an action under Article 226 [ex 169] (see chapter 5) against Ireland. The Court of Justice held that Ireland was in breach of its Community obligations.

In the 1970s the Commission came to the conclusion that the process of awarding contracts in the field of public procurement needed to be placed on a basis of open and fair competition. It did this by a series of directives that regulate the procedures under which governments, other public bodies and utilities award contracts.

The public procurement regime is established by a series of directives which apply throughout the Community. It aims, in general, to ensure that public sector and related contracts are only awarded following a fair and competitive tendering process— open to contractors beyond national boundaries—on the basis of the lowest price or the most economically advantageous offer.

The Scope of the Public Procurement Regime

In outline, there are six procurement Directives:

(i) The Public Works Directive 93/37

This applies to contracts in writing for building or civil engineering works by state, regional, or local authorities or similar bodies and to certain works contracts which are more than 50 per cent funded by public bodies. So, for example, this Directive applied to the contract for the construction of the Channel Tunnel.

(ii) The Public Supplies Directive 93/36

This applies to contracts in writing for the purchase or hire of products by state, regional or local authorities and certain other non-commercial bodies, such as health and education authorities.

(iii) The Public Services Directive 92/50

This applies to contracts (not already covered by the Works or Supplies Directives) which provide for services to be provided to public bodies.

(iv) The Utilities Directives 93/38

This is a very detailed Directive, and applies to contracts, whether for the purchase of products, works or services, with entities operating in the water, energy, transport and telecommunications sectors.

Ensuring compliance with the legislation by public procurement agencies in the Member States is a very varied and difficult problem. There are many types of action that can lead, deliberately or unwittingly, to the breaching of the rules. This can include the splitting of contracts so that each separate contract falls below the minimum covered by the Directives (see below); the failure to provide full information to companies considering tendering, and the use of discriminatory terms in contracts. Aggrieved companies may be reluctant to complain in case they jeopardise future contracts and as noted above, procurement agencies are often subject to local political and economic pressures. For these reasons it was necessary to develop two "Remedies" Directives designed to ensure the correct application of the Directives shown above. These Directives were:

(v) The Compliance Directive 89/665

This sets out remedies available for breach of the Works, Supplies and Services Directives.

(vi) The Remedies Directive 92/13

This provides similar remedies for the breach of the Utilities Directive.

Coverage of Directives

It would not be possible to apply the Directives to every single contract, and so thresholds have been applied. Only contracts of a minimum estimated value are subject to the regime. So, for example, public sector supplies and services contracts are covered by the appropriate Directive if they are over 200,000 Euros (approximately £155,000).

If the body awarding the contract wishes to lay down technical specifications they must be set out in the contract documents. The contract must use specifications that are in common use in Europe. The documents must not specify any particular brand name, trademark or origin, or if such reference is made, they must be followed by the words "or equivalent".

One of the ways of restricting the award of a contract, noted above, is by limiting the advertisement of the contract to the localised press. To counter this, all the Directives provide that procurement contracts are advertised in the Official Journal of the European Communities (OJ). In addition, the Directives set out model forms of tender notice.

When it come to selecting the contractor there a number of methods that can be used. They are called the "Open", the "Restricted", and the "Negotiated" procedures. For the Open procedure any interested party may tender for the contract. The contract document must be sent to any contractor within six days of the request. For the Restricted procedure only suppliers selected by the utility or public body may submit tenders for the contract. This procedure is used when the awarding body wishes to be certain that all those tendering have the ability to complete the contract. There must be at least five tenderers invited to tender and invitations to tender must be sent simultaneously to all suppliers or contractors. The Negotiated procedure occurs when the contracting authority negotiates the terms of the contract with the person(s) selected by it. At least three bodies must be invited to negotiate, and objective selection criteria must be used.

The general rule is that the contracting authority must award the contract to the offer, which is either at the lowest price, or is the most economically advantageous to the contracting authority. If the award is made on the latter basis, it must indicate the objective criteria on which it intends to base its decision. An offer that appears exceptionally low can only be rejected after the contracting authority has sought an explanation for the low price, and the reply has not been convincing.

Once a contract is awarded notice is placed in the Official Journal, which details the reasons for awarding the contract. A rejected candidate is entitled to be told the reasons for the rejection.

Remedies

The Compliance and Remedies Directives set out minimum remedies for the breach of the public procurement rules. If a body feels they have been unfairly discriminated against they may bring legal proceedings. The national court has a number of choices if it finds for the complainant. It can grant an interim order to suspend the procedure leading to the award of a contract; it can order the setting aside of a decision; or it can award damages to a supplier who has suffered loss or damage as a consequence of the breach.

Alternatively, a complainant may approach the Commission, which is entitled to take action to enforce the provisions of a Directive.

Conclusion

It has never been easy for a contractor from another country to win public sector contracts. The public procurement rules are designed to make it easier for them to do. The rules have been sketched out above (the precise rules are detailed and complicated and beyond the scope of this book). The basic Community legal framework needed in order to meet the objectives of open and fair public procurement has been established as described above. It is designed to strike a balance between legal certainty and operational flexibility. The results already achieved on the transparency front are highly encouraging. As far as the economic impact of the rules is concerned however, the data available is less favourable.

The most visible effect of the Directives has undoubtedly been a major increase in the transparency of contract award procedures. The number of contracts advertised in the Official Journal has steadily increased. The total of procurement notices rose from 12,000 in 1987 to nearly 105,000 in 2002, and further increases are projected.

The major problem however, is non-compliance. Some Member States have not incorporated the Directives into national law. Only three Member States have fully implemented all texts. It also seems that in a number of sectors, contracting entities are not seeing the benefits that justify the efforts necessary to fulfil the obligations imposed by the Directives. Another problem is that the share of imports for public procurement contracts remains modest. It has been estimated that direct cross-frontier business has risen from 1.4 per cent in 1987 to only 3 per cent in 1995.

The Community public procurement policy and legislation is now in place. What is now needed is the political will to make the free market in public contracting a reality.

INDEX